Victorian Literature and the Victorian State

THE JOHNS HOPKINS UNIVERSITY PRESS

Victorian Literature and the Victorian State

Character and Governance in a Liberal Society

Lauren M. E. Goodlad

The Johns Hopkins University Press
Baltimore and London

© 2003 The Johns Hopkins University Press
All rights reserved. Published 2003
Printed in the United States of America on acid-free paper
9 8 7 6 5 4 3 2 1

The Johns Hopkins University Press
2715 North Charles Street
Baltimore, Maryland 21218-4363
www.press.jhu.edu

Library of Congress Cataloging-in-Publication Data

Goodlad, Lauren M. E.
  Victorian literature and the Victorian state : character and
governance in a liberal society / Lauren M.E. Goodlad.
      p. cm.
Includes bibliographical references (p.) and index.
  ISBN 0-8018-6963-3 (hardcover : alk. paper)
   1. English literature—19th century—History and criticism.
2. Politics and literature—Great Britain—History—19th century.
3. Literature and society—Great Britain—History—19th century.
4. Literature and state—Great Britain—History—19th century.
5. Liberalism—Great Britain—History—19th century.   6. Great
Britain—Politics and government—1837–1901.   7. Social problems
in literature.   8. State, The, in literature.   9. Liberalism in literature.
I. Title.
  PR468.P57 G66 2003
   820.9′358—dc21   2002154081

A catalog record for this book is available from the British Library.

Contents

Preface

> The fact is, that a good government, like a good coat, is that which fits the body for which it is designed. A man who, upon abstract principles, pronounces a constitution to be good, without an exact knowledge of the people who are to be governed by it, judges as absurdly as a tailor who should measure the Belvidere Apollo for the clothes of all his customers.
> — THOMAS BABINGTON MACAULAY,
> "ON MITFORD'S HISTORY OF GREECE"

Why do John Stuart Mill, Harriet Martineau, and Dr. James Phillips Kay, all of whom are cast loosely as "Benthamites," differ so widely both from Jeremy Bentham and often from one another? Why is it that novels written to critique the New Poor Law are more invested in charity than in a kinder, gentler vision of the welfare state? Charles Dickens took an avid interest in a wide variety of philanthropies, and directly oversaw Urania Cottage, a rehabilitative home for fallen women. Why is it, then, that *Bleak House*, his great midcentury novel, is as derisive of charitable ladies as it is of the lawyers, politicians, and policemen who staff Britain's principal public institutions? Why, for that matter, do H. G. Wells's utopian romances tell so strongly against the Fabian socialism he openly supported?

The answers to these and many similar questions are complicated and potentially far-reaching. From one particular point of view, however—that of a scholar engaged in cross-disciplinary Victorian studies, trailing, as it were, on the long coattails of the new historicism[1]—there is a concise answer that I would like to suggest from the start. Victorian Britain was a *liberal* society: "liberal" first and foremost in the sense that, throughout the century, centralized institutions and statist interventions were curbed to preserve the "self-governing" liberties of individuals and local communities.

To be sure, *liberalism* is "a notoriously elusive" term (Bellamy, "Introduction" 1); "a nonsystematic and porous doctrine subject to historical change and local variation" (W. Brown 142). Since the nineteenth century it has been variously employed to denote diverse political agendas, a set of capitalist economic ideologies, and a broad cultural investment in promoting freedom. In Victorian Britain, liberalism most persistently asserted itself as antipathy toward statist interference—a discourse that anticipates the ardent neoliberalism or "paleo-liberalism" of our own day.[2] But there is another and broader liberal tradition— "a large tendency," as Lionel Trilling once defined it (6)—which is equally important to understanding the Victorian culture described in this book. If the first discourse seems naively to exalt the "free" economic and voluntary activities of discrete individuals, the broader tradition marked by Trilling is more demanding in its conception of citizenship and, at the same time, more likely to view the state as a potential aid to individual and social welfare. Although in hindsight Victorian liberalism is, therefore, best characterized by its pervasive tensions and paradoxes, it is also important to stress the remarkably durable liberal mythology—the ideals, vocabulary, and assumptions—to which contemporaries consciously and unconsciously subscribed. Although many Victorians did not regard themselves as political liberals, most were responsive to the overall projects of liberating individuals from illegitimate authority while simultaneously ensuring their moral and spiritual growth.

Of course, such potentially ambivalent goals could not but engender contradiction and debate. For, in liberal thought, freedom paradoxically signifies "the antonym, the limit *and* the objective" of governance (Barry et al. 2). There was—and remains—a tension within liberal thinking between *negative* liberty (the lodestar of a free society for many radicals, free traders, and eulogists of England's national character) and *positive* liberty (an idea that slowly took hold among social reformers, even those who began by clamoring for laissez faire). Samuel Smiles's best-selling *Self-Help* (1859) opens by affirming a sacred tenet of British liberalism. The "function of Government," he declares, "is negative and restrictive": to protect property rather than to promote virtue among citizens (2). Yet the positive impulse to build character and promote social betterment by collective means of some kind permeates the diverse liberal thought of Thomas Chalmers, John Stuart Mill, Thomas Babington Macaulay, T. H.

Green, Octavia Hill, Beatrice Webb, and Winston Churchill—just as it does the later works of Michel Foucault.[3]

It is common in recent critical discourse to define *liberalism* more narrowly, invoking the term to describe bourgeois economic ideologies from John Locke's legacy to the neoliberalism of the present day. Thus, according to John Frow, the liberal social imaginary "draws upon a more or less coherent set of philosophical presuppositions" including negative liberty, methodological individualism, antistatism, and free market capitalism (424–25).[4] Yet to define liberalism in such a constrictive fashion, and to strip it of its internal contradictions, is to forget that "through the nineteenth and twentieth centuries there has grown up a long tradition of attacking" bourgeois self-interest—a humanist tradition that runs deep in liberal culture and extends through Marx and beyond (Pocock, *Virtue* 60; cf. 103–4). My purpose in thus promoting a more rigorous and expansive understanding of liberalism is neither to dissent from a critique of neoliberalism such as Frow's nor to urge a return to a liberal politics such as Trilling's. Rather, I believe that diminished conceptions of Victorian culture impair historicist critique and, in so doing, reduce critics' power to illuminate present-day concerns.

A more complete understanding of Victorian liberalism should include such insistently (if also imperfectly) antibourgeois discourses as the civic republicanism carried over from the seventeenth century, the romantic-influenced "modern" liberalism of the post–French Revolutionary era, and the religious-inflected liberalism of many nineteenth-century Evangelicals and dissenters.[5] In such discourses the recurrent term *character* stands for an antimaterialist concept of the individual which was deeply at odds with *homo economicus*, the hedonistic subject of capitalist ideology. To build "character" in the nineteenth century was, therefore, to resist atomization and embourgeoisement: whether by fortifying the republican's virtuous citizen qualities, by developing the romantic's individuality and diversity, by strengthening the Christian's moral obligations to God and community, or—as often as not—by diverse appeals to all of these ends. Hence, for the purposes of this book, laissez-faire economic theory is understood as an influential (but not uniformly dominant) ideology, the application of which disrupted the antimaterialist underpinnings of liberalism from within. Although politico-economic tenets were often cast as moral prescriptions, their ultimate tendency was to advance the depersonalized and materialistic view of the individual against which the language of character—civic, romantic, and Christian—

was persistently pitted. In the following chapters I demonstrate how deep-seated conflicts of this kind expressed themselves in the idiosyncratic development of British governance and, at the same time, how Victorian literature repeatedly sought the means by which to transcend this divided legacy: to build character without imposing on Britain's hallowed self-governing ideal.

Exploring these questions has necessarily involved my working with an expanding body of scholarship on nineteenth-century discipline, much of which is indebted to Michel Foucault's seminal analyses of modern power. As I discuss at length in chapter 1, critics have long recognized various problems intrinsic to Foucault's genealogical method. Yet Foucault's influence has continued to prompt critics interested in Victorian governance to think more about Bentham than about those who rejected him; more about panopticism than about why it was that nineteenth-century Britons declined to build any Panopticons.[6] Although the last decade has seen a remarkable efflorescence of nuanced post-Foucauldian Victorian studies—a critical legacy to which my own work is indebted—I maintain that we have yet fully to document the differences between the disciplinary subject of Foucault's Franco-oriented and presentist genealogy, and the modes of character idealized by and produced in Britain's self-consciously liberal society over the course of the nineteenth century.

Victorian Literature and the Victorian State does not, of course, single-handedly take on the whole of this potentially vast critical project—for no single volume could. It is neither an exhaustive account of Victorian liberalism, nor of character, nor of governance (a subject I approach through the later-Foucauldian idea of "pastorship"). My humbler aim has been to provide a critical and historiographic account of specific works of Victorian literature as they converged with major developments in the idiosyncratic expansion and modernization of the British state. In so doing, I have sought to mine literature's rich relation to the large-scale rationalizing developments that have long occupied social historians: poor law, sanitary, educational, and civil service reforms, as well as the century-long attempt to substitute organized charity for the state.[7]

If my turn toward social history thus facilitates a distancing from genealogical presentism, my focus on literary texts represents something else still. In the chapters that follow, I read Victorian novels in the company of social scientific treatises, journalistic essays, propagandistic tales, and official reports. As socially embedded writings, nonliterary texts—from Sir James Kay-Shuttleworth's early-Victorian work on public health, to Winston Churchill's turn-of-the-century speeches on national insurance—offer ample critical opportunities to mine ideological contradictions, locate myths, and explore underlying worldviews. Yet the novels of Charles Dickens, Frances Trollope, Anthony Trollope, George Gissing, and H. G. Wells provide something more. Victorian novels, as Andrew Miller has written, provide "the most graphic and enduring images" of the impact of modernization on individual and social experience (7). Such works are extraordinary precisely because they were products of a middle-class engagement with the social world. Their richness is owing to historical conditions that yoked Victorian fiction to the bourgeois process, even as they constituted it as "a major affirmative response"—a protest against capitalist instrumentalization—in the name of human creativity (R. Williams, *Marxism* 50). Novelists were compelled, therefore, "to negotiate between their moral condemnation and their implication in what they opposed" (A. Miller 7).[8]

Hence, for my purposes the most important feature of Victorian novels is their intense grappling with contemporary worldviews, particularly as liberal notions of character and community clashed with the inevitable recourse to modern "pastorship"—that is, to governing innovations inside and out of the expanding state. Here is the duel that, in one form or another, I trace in Frances Trollope's imaginative encounter with the New Poor Law; Dickens's vexed relation to sanitary reform, organized charity, and education; and Anthony Trollope's picture of the model public servant. This kind of historicist enterprise has necessarily involved much emphasis on the synchronic rather than the diachronic: on elaborating deep-seated conflict, variation, and unevenness, rather than on charting unequivocal and hegemonic change. What is offered, therefore, is both a detailed account of the relation between select works of Victorian literature and specific historical debates about character and governance; and, potentially, a useful post-Foucauldian critical frame for studying the Victorian past.[9]

In a late essay on the study of modern society, Foucault asserted that the "word *rationalization* is dangerous. What we have to do is analyze specific rationalities rather than always invoking the progress of rationalization in general" ("Subject" 210). Although the chapters that follow do not conform to any specific Foucauldian method of analysis, they do strive to achieve this level of commitment to critical and historical specificity. In the introductory chapter, "Beyond the Panopticon," I set up a number of theoretical and historiographic premises for the book as a whole, while pursuing one argument to its full: Foucault's genealogical works on discipline are less useful to the Victorianist than are his later essays on governmentality, pastorship, and liberalism. Here, and throughout the book, I emphasize the Victorians' fierce allegiance to a multifarious liberal thought with origins in classical philosophy, Anglo-Saxon mythology, Puritan dissent, Enlightenment theology, Scottish moral philosophy, and German-Romanticism. Although it was the first nation to industrialize, Britain was (as Max Weber repeatedly observed) the last to adopt the centralized bureaucratic structures of the Continent. Throughout the century Britons tenaciously imagined themselves through character, an antimaterialist concept of the individual. Yet character and the moral worldview on which it was predicated were threatened precisely by the materialist underpinnings of a modern state: by depersonalizing bureaucracy, social scientific knowledge, and, more generally, by processes of commodification, embourgeoisement, and the development of a mass culture. Self-consciously progressive authors such as J. S. Mill, Harriet Martineau, Charles Dickens, George Gissing, and H. G. Wells thus faced a terrible quandary. Their paradoxical task was to imagine a modern governing agency that would be rational, all-embracing, and efficient, but also antibureaucratic, personalized, and liberatory.

The remaining chapters are devoted to developing these themes through key conjunctures between Victorian literature and the Victorian state. In "Charity, the Novel and the New Poor Law" I ask what was at stake for Britain's self-consciously moral governing classes when poor law practices were altered to suit a rationalized politico-economic conception of the individual in society. From the ambitious philanthropy of Thomas Chalmers and Dr. James Phillips Kay to the works of Harriet Martineau (*Poor Laws and Paupers Illustrated* [1836]), Charles Dickens (*Oliver Twist* [1837]), and Frances Trollope (*Jessie Phillips: A Tale of the New Poor Law* [1843]), the story I tell refutes the common assumption that the 1834 Poor Law Amendment Act precipitated an era of centralized bureaucracy. Yet, although the act by and large conformed to liberal predilections, its tacit privileging of *homo economicus*—a materialist challenge to character—menaced the hallowed moral vision of a Christian and civic economy, woven through with personalized charitable bonds between rich and poor.

Chapter 3, "Is There a Pastor in the *House?*," is an in-depth analysis of *Bleak House* (1852–53) from the point of view of midcentury politics, sanitary reform, philanthropy, and policing. As A. O. J. Cockshut quipped long ago, Dickens's response to the crucial political issue of state intervention is a "loud-mouthed evasiveness" (59). For Dickens modern Britain is a shepherdless nation of diminished individuals, from the hapless Jo to the clueless Mr. Snagsby. But Chadwickian technocracy, personified by the terrifying master-agency of Mr. Tulkinghorn, presents a bleaker prospect still. Although he earnestly searches for modern alternatives to laissez faire, the author of *Bleak House* falls back defensively on the home and the gendered moral worldview on which domesticity and the rhetoric of the personal depend. Even organized philanthropy—the precursor to modern social work, and the Victorians' favorite alternative to state intervention—is renounced through Dickens's satire on Mrs. Pardiggle.

Dickens's portrayal of midcentury deadlocks anticipates still graver crises: in particular, the Crimean debacle and the middle-class revolt against government by an upper tier of "Barnacles." In chapter 4, "An Officer and a Gentleman," I describe the resolution of this crisis in the context of civil service reform. The Northcote-Trevelyan *Report* drew on Coleridgean philosophy, Anglicist colonial policy, and university reform to promulgate a new ideal of gentlemanly character and a myth of disinterested governance by well-bred men. Anthony Trollope, a post office official, was a resolute critic of recruitment by competitive examination. *The Three Clerks* (1858), a brooding novel in the style of Dickens, criticized the *Report*, which Trollope misleadingly tied to the clamorous cult of the businessman. Ironically, however, Trollope's Barsetshire novels precisely articulate the civil service character ideal: a perfect synthesis between ambitious self-making and staid gentlemanliness.

Although the idea of born-and-bred gentility thus provided a basis for mid-Victorian constitutional consensus, it was far less amenable to Charles Dickens. The author's lifelong support for working-class education bespoke a commitment to democratic character-building ideals, but one that was persistently confuted in the novels. In chapter 5, "A Riddle without an Answer," I examine the relation between *Our Mutual Friend* (1864–65) and nineteenth-century educational reforms: from Sir James Kay-Shuttleworth's early-Victorian statist agenda to the mid-Victorian return of laissez faire in working-class education, and the contemporaneous focus on educating a governing-class elite. Bradley Headstone, a product of Kay-Shuttleworth's ambitious teacher training efforts, is locked in a fatal contest with Eugene Wrayburn, a public school man. Dickens's inability to imagine either educational ideal as a foundation for character building speaks to the corrosive embourgeoisement first articulated in *Oliver Twist*, and extended in his satire on the Veneerings.

"Dueling Pastors, Dueling Worldviews," the concluding chapter, offers a comparative analysis of two visions of national pastorship, each undergirded by a distinctive philosophy of character. As participants in the 1905–9 Royal Commission on the Poor Laws, leaders of the prominent Charity Organization Society, or COS (1869–1913), clashed with their Fabian socialist opponents, including Beatrice and Sidney Webb. The contest between the COS's idealist emphasis on "mind and will" and the Fabians' on expert social engineering spoke directly to late-Victorian anxieties over the nation's declining world power while typifying the idiosyncratic development of British sociology. Contemporaneous literature adds a telling proviso to this debate since it is, I argue, more pessimistic than either side. George Gissing's 1889 novel *The Nether World* harshly examines middle-class philanthropic ideologies even while reaffirming the moral worldview from which they derive. In H. G. Wells's turn-of-the-century scientific romances, and E. M. Forster's dystopic fable "The Machine Stops" (1909) a discernible split between Edwardian real and liberal ideal implies the impossibility of revitalizing the nation's mythic character. I conclude with a discussion of the political middle course developed in the New Liberal politics of David Lloyd George and Winston Churchill. Unlike either Fabian technocracy or organized charity, the New Liberal agenda adopted a classically liberal approach to national pastorship, shoring up old mythologies through Whig-like legislation and inventing a new mass tradition in the notion of "national insurance." Here, as elsewhere, Foucault's suggestive essays on governmentality, as applied to Britain's idiosyncratic institutional, cultural, and literary history, help to elucidate the century-long paradox of securing pastoral care for the building of character in a nation of allegedly self-reliant individuals and communities.

In writing this book, I have accrued more debts than I can faithfully acknowledge. But I will try. Steven Marcus and David Cannadine directed my dissertation at Columbia University. At the University of Washington this germ developed into a book under the mentorship of two wonderful senior colleagues, Kathleen Blake and Marshall Brown. I received travel support from the Royalty Research Grant, and leave time as a fellow of the Walter Chapin Simpson Humanities Center and recipient of the President's Junior Faculty Development award. For the latter especially, I am grateful for the encouragement of my former chair, Shawn Wong.

George Behlmer introduced me to the Victorian idea of "character building." John Toews, another colleague in history, provided much-needed insight into German-Romanticism. Former colleagues who read parts of the manuscript and offered many helpful comments include Srinivas Aravamudan, Gary Handwerk, Mona Modiano, Ross Posnock, and Henry Staten. Many students, but especially David Hennessee, Tabitha Sparks, and Lauren Stasiak, contributed to the creative process. Outside of Seattle I owe thanks to Amanda Anderson, Eleni

Coundouriotis, Richard Dellamora, Frances Ferguson, Robbie Goh, Elaine Hadley, Ann Humpherys, John Maynard, Andrew Miller, Adrienne Munich, Bruce Robbins, Jeffrey Spear, and three new colleagues, Jed Esty, Adam Sutcliffe, and Joe Valente. At the University of Illinois, where I currently teach, Peter Garrett and Julia Saville carefully read the manuscript in its entirety. Johns Hopkins's reader—whomever that sage person may be—offered many valuable suggestions.

Some of the chapters in this book contain material previously published in journals. I thank Indiana University Press for permission to reproduce sections of "'Making the Working Man Like Me': Charity, Pastorship and Middle-Class Identity in Nineteenth-Century Britain; Thomas Chalmers and Dr. James Phillips Kay," which appeared in the summer 2001 issue of *Victorian Studies*, a revised version of which is now part of chapter 2. I thank the Modern Language Association of America for permission to reproduce parts of "Beyond the Panopticon: Victorian Britain and the Critical Imagination," a version of chapter 1 which appeared in the May 2003 issue of *PMLA*. Finally, I thank Cambridge University Press for permission to reproduce, "Is There a Doctor in the *House?* Sanitary Reform, Philanthropy, and Professionalism in Dickens's Mid-Century Fiction," which appeared in the September 2003 issue of *Victorian Literature and Culture*, and is an abridged version of chapter 3.

Cindy and Jerry Eisenberg, my parents, have provided through all these years a bedrock of support. My son, Alex, has grown up alongside this book; I can only hope that it is half as unique as he is. It is becoming hard to remember a time when Tim Dean was not my very good friend. Michael Miller helped me through the roughest of spots. And Mark Sammons, whom I was fated to meet while working on a different project, has seemed to make all things possible.

Victorian Literature and the Victorian State

CHAPTER ONE

Beyond the Panopticon

The Critical Challenge of a Liberal Society

> [The] philosophical problem of our day is not to try to liberate the individual from the state, and from the state's institutions, but to liberate us both from the state and from the type of individualization which is linked to the state. We have to promote new forms of subjectivity through the refusal of this kind of individuality which has been imposed on us for several centuries.
>
> — MICHEL FOUCAULT, "THE SUBJECT AND POWER"

As characterized more than a decade ago by Catherine Gallagher, new historicism proposed a more sophisticated approach to the study of literary texts. Rather than show either literature's passive affirmation of ideology, or its subversive unmasking of it, new historicism would offer "a third alternative in which the very antagonism between literature and ideology becomes, in specific historical environments, a powerful and socially functional mode of constructing subjectivity." To a critical practice eager to submit subjectivities to a "hermeneutics of suspicion," Foucault's genealogical methods present important benefits ("Marxism" 43–44).[1] As genealogists of discipline, searching locally for the effects of power as it is applied on human bodies, critics look beyond illusory notions of the self, and, as a result, beyond deceptive oppositions between freedom and constraint. Rigorously anti-essentialist, the genealogist attempts to historicize a multifaceted power, productive as well as repressive, concentrated neither in potent individuals, hegemonic classes, dominant ideologies, nor institutional apparatuses. By "dissolving all claims to subjective fixity," genealogy invokes a new scholarly engagement, a "strategic intervention" in which critics unearth the determinants of truth making (Harootunian 123).

Since the 1980s Victorianist scholars have creatively applied this critical mandate to the study of nineteenth-century Britain. Feminist scholars have demonstrated the profundity with which constructions of gender and sexuality are implicated within histories of the political, resulting in a far-reaching transformation of what the political and its history are understood to include. Since the advent of postcolonial theory and criticism, studies of racial, national, and ethnic ideologies have also been integrated within and alongside models of subjectivity based on class, gender, and sexuality. The importance of such groundbreaking study cannot be overstated.

Yet, insofar as such scholarship has been predicated on genealogical assumptions, new historicism's ascent has not been free of certain ironies. Foucault's influence on critical thinking about the past has continued unabated, even as scholars have abundantly described problems in the genealogical framework. Indeed, more than twenty years after the publication of *Discipline and Punish*, it is something of a commonplace that what purports to be an anti-essentialist account of modernity tends toward a totalizing paradigm in which human subjectivity is reduced to the effect of an inescapable mode of domination—"panopticism."[2] I myself have argued that new historicism is burdened by methodological inconsistency: in particular, by failures to address incompatibilities between genealogy's emphasis on power relations and materialist emphases on cultural analysis. Indeed, "culture," a concept developed by such Marxist theorists as Antonio Gramsci and Raymond Williams, has neither an integral place nor an adequate correlative in Foucault's method of analysis (Goodlad, "Middle Class").[3]

In the following chapter I aim to stimulate thinking about the application of Foucault's legacy to Victorian studies while, at the same time, providing a theoretical and historical foundation for analyzing nineteenth-century literature and governance. Foucault's genealogical method, with its special reliance on panoptical institutions, presents numerous problems for the scholar of Victorian Britain. His late works on governmentality, which were written in response to the resurgence of liberal economic ideologies in the last decades of the twentieth century, provide a better model for studying Victorian Britain's idiosyncratic modernization. To make this theoretical analysis more clear, I first turn to a brief overview of the relevant historical contexts.

The Victorian State: A Historical View

The most curious fact about the nineteenth-century state is that it never existed. . . . It eludes [scholars] between the oligarchic administration and interfering paternalism of the eighteenth century, on the one hand, and the social service democracy on the other. For the former was not dead before the latter had been born — H . R . G . G R E A V E S , *The Civil Service in the Changing State*

This tendency [towards centralization] is most dangerous. We have hitherto been for the most part locally governed. Responsibility had been very much distributed. . . . This is . . . the black cloud on the horizon, that we are gradually approaching the state of Continental countries where the government is responsible for everything, for whatever goes wrong the government is blamed. . . . I am against doing anything to forward this tendency. If country gentlemen are not to have some power and responsibility, they will not act.

— SIR CHARLES WOOD

Sir, the Devil was expelled from heaven because he objected to centralisation, and all those who object to centralisation oppose it on devilish grounds.

— EDWIN CHADWICK

It is a commonplace of many social histories that British governance differed from that of most Continental countries. Britain's centralized state was smaller, less intrusive, and more reliant on local and voluntary supports, but—for all that—highly effective in maintaining social stability at home, and exploiting colonial interests abroad.[4] By the early nineteenth century, the dense and overlapping web of parish, borough, and county institutions which had evolved under this minimally centralized system of governance extended the circle of political interest to the middle ranks of society. Hence, the government of early-nineteenth-century towns, as Boz's satire on "Our Parish" suggests, had as much to do with the obscure self-importance of beadles, vestry clerks, and aldermen as it did with the paternalistic rule of the upper classes (Dickens, *Sketches* 1–24). This governing structure was seen by the Victorians as the hallmark of an exceptional liberal heritage including the myth of pre-Norman Anglo-Saxon liberty, the civic republican tradition, Puritan dissent, Lockean individualism, laissez-faire political economy, and, in the nineteenth century, aspects of the romantic movement, including German philosophical influences. Invoking this manifold legacy, Victorian Britons imagined themselves as citizens of a self-governing nation and heirs to ancient constitutional liberties. By custom, by nature, by established tradition—even by divine will—Britons were, it was believed, a vanguard people, able to contrast their freedoms to the noxious state interference endured by Continental and Oriental peoples.[5]

It is, therefore, also a commonplace that the Victorian state expanded in response to the urgent social pressures of urbanization and industrialization—its piecemeal and unsystematic development unaided by popular consensus or a consistent philosophical agenda. Centralized measures such as the 1834 New Poor Law and the 1848 Public Health Act were widely disliked. Edwin Chadwick, the Benthamite disciple who crafted them, was likened to the Catholic pope and accused of imprisoning the queen in a workhouse (Fraser 71; Finer 176). The majority of Britons were like Sir Charles Wood, an upper-class Whig, deeply allied to local control, civic voluntarism, personalized philanthropy, and individual self-help (see epigraph). Direct government interference "was something [they] hardly knew and did not like the idea of" (Best 251). Self-government (as contemporaries liked to style their preference for local, voluntary, and ad hoc practices) was held to be "a quintessential feature of British national character" (Harris, *Private* 18). Hence, as chapter 3 details, Chadwick's technocratic "Sanitary Idea" so antagonized mainstream opinion that it precipitated a lasting backlash. Not until the fin-de-siècle socialism of the Fabians did Bentham's legacy enjoy a significant resurgence.

In *Constitutional Bureaucracy* (1969) Henry Parris attributes a much greater role to Bentham, arguing that his influence, rather than the pressure of circumstances alone, triggered the so-called nineteenth-century revolution in government. On the whole, however, Parris's thesis has had less sway among historians than Oliver MacDonagh's "pragmatic" model. For MacDonagh the gradual centralization, rationalization, and expansion of the Victorian state began as a response to urgent social crisis, and continued as a result of the self-generated momentum of administrators themselves.[6] With the midcentury decline of Benthamite reform, Chartism, and other radical challenges to the status quo, liberal ideas flourished in the fabled equipoise of the mid-Victorian constitutional consensus. The ideal of "disinterested" governance, first articulated by civic republican–minded Whigs, effloresced in the vintage liberalism of the Gladstone era. An all-embracing moral philosophy as well as a political agenda, mid-Victorian liberalism trumpeted the progressive benefits of free trade and low taxation, individual and community self-reliance, parliamentary representation for the propertied, and a civil service staffed by well-bred gentlemen. Liberal governance in this distinctive British form withstood many pressures, holding its ground until the unprecedented exigencies of World War I.

There is, to be sure, much evidence to support Mary Poovey's claim that the Benthamite-influenced reforms of the 1830s constituted the epistemological foundations for "the professionalized, bureaucratized apparatuses of inspection, regulation, and enforcement that we call the modern state" (*Making* 115–16). Yet, as I argue in chapter 2, even the cornerstone of those reforms—the landmark 1834 New Poor Law—was, for all its centralizing features, an attempt to strengthen local government, abolish the largesse of the Old Poor Law, and institute laissez faire. According to the Royal Commission's report, the act was "intended to produce rather negative than positive effects": to deter pauperism rather than to treat it (qtd. in Loch, "Controverted" 238–39). In the 1890s, as Britain's global preeminence began visibly to decline, a vocal minority demanded a shift from "laissez faire" to "savoir faire" (Searle 97). Reforming the poor laws became the primary object of the Fabians, who sought to improve national efficiency and build national character by establishing a multipronged state that would both prevent and cure. H. G. Wells, whose Fabianesque utopias are described in chapter 6, lamented the ignorant "distrust" that prevented the Victorians from permitting "the State" to govern "in a business-like way" (*Machiavelli* 17). From such a view late-Victorian and Edwardian Britain profoundly lacked the modern rationality described in Poovey's account.

Victorian liberals were also zealous enthusiasts of parliamentary commissions of inquiry. Such putatively objective fact-gathering bodies were invaluable to a government that promised firm but constitutional responses to a wide range of modern problems. Yet, while Blue Books and the legislative redress that sometimes followed them exemplified a recognizably bureaucratic approach to governing the new social domain, it is important to distinguish between these British developments and the intrusive state apparatuses described by Foucault in *Discipline and Punish*. Statutory innovations such as the introduction of policing were, throughout the century, ridden by "delay, compromise and half measure" (Gatrell 257). Centralized inspection was hampered—as in the case of the New Poor Law—by the insufficiency of resources, and the lack of meaningful coercive power. Diminutive staffs (between ten and twenty officials to inspect the nation's multifarious workhouses) necessarily meant that much was left to "local discretion" as well as to "the personality of the individual inspector" (Fraser 53; cf. Wood 79–83). Enterprising officials such as Sir James Kay-Shuttleworth, a pioneer in working-class education, had "limited freedom of action" with which to implement their grand designs (Paz, "Limits" 168–69).[7] These and many similar accounts too numerous to detail support Derek Fraser's claim that any history of the nineteenth century "which does not emphasise the practical, pragmatic, unplanned, *ad hoc* response of the state is in a major respect deficient" (117).

It is also important to recognize that many Victorian administrators were themselves staunch liberals who used their official position to forward laissez-faire social policies. The elite members of the Newcastle commission of 1858–61 demonstrated the decidedly anti-interventionist cast of their ideas when they sought to delimit working-class education in the interests of self-help and economy. There was, in their own words, "a material difference . . . between the political and social circumstances of [Britain] . . . and those of countries where the central administration wields great power over a people . . . habituated to the control of a searching police, and subjected to the direct action of the government" (qtd. in Best 251). To preserve that "material difference" Robert Lowe, vice president of the Education Department, sought to reverse the gains of reformers such as Kay-Shuttleworth. In 1842 Samuel Laing, a middle-class radical and travel writer, had argued that the Continental man was an "educated slave," "his personal bodily and mental actions . . . fitted on him by his master, the state, like clothing on a convict" (496, 495). It is surely significant that almost twenty years later the genteel and conservative-leaning liberals on the Newcastle commission invoked similar rhetoric to justify a policy of retrenchment. The adoption of market forces, Lowe believed, would ensure that such schooling as was provided at government expense would be, if not necessarily efficient, then at least "cheap" (qtd. in Fraser 85). As so-called disinterested government was less loath to punish crime than to foster education, "it was . . . in its policeman guise rather than in its paternalistic guise that the Victorian state" first demonstrated "its power and purposes" (Gatrell 259).

With such attitudes coming both from within and outside of the Victorian state, it will come as no surprise that the size of nineteenth-century government was, by Continental standards, "absurdly small." In 1832 the entire British civil service numbered 21,300, while in 1846 its French counterpart numbered just under a million (Roberts, *Victorian* 12–13). Even in 1914, by which point the British nation was—to the mind of one die-hard liberal—"in danger of being governed to death," the civil service had only grown about tenfold, numbering some 280,000 ("Encroaching" 51; Schultz 297). The high-minded aim of the 1853 Northcote-Trevelyan *Report* on civil service reform was to create a Coleridgean clerisy to disseminate enlightenment in a liberal society. Yet more than twenty years later, one insider wistfully remarked on the "effluence of . . . supreme power" enjoyed by Continental officials. The English service, he declared, conferred "neither status nor consideration" on its appointees (Scoones 349).

The other side of the limited scope of the Victorian state was the formidable voluntarism of the Victorians themselves. Throughout the century and beyond, "most of the functions performed by government in other societies were . . . performed by coteries of citizens governing themselves." The multiplicity of charities and self-help organizations created a "dense network of self-governing social institutions that encircled the citizen at every level." As late as 1911, the receipts of registered philanthropies exceeded the state's poor law expenditures (Harris, "Society" 68), while nineteenth-century charitable organizations employed twice as many paid workers as did the poor law authorities (Prochaska 384–85). In 1889 the Church of England recorded the voluntary activities of more than forty-seven thousand home "visitors," a number that would almost double by 1910 (Behlmer, *Friends* 34). The Charity Organization Society (1869–1913), whose founding members included John Ruskin, Octavia Hill, and Sir Charles Trevelyan, sought to annex the state's negative functions to a permanent corps of organized volunteers. In so doing, it pioneered modern social work. Dickens's Mrs. Pardiggle, portrayed as a self-important busybody, was in actuality a harbinger of the future, representative of an increasingly authoritative and professionalized social practice (see chaps. 3 and 6).

Scholars have also stressed the profound and long-lingering influence of the ancien régime. The system of patronage which cemented eighteenth-century British society in the absence of modern bureaucracy was not eradicated overnight (Dandeker 48); nor, for that matter, was a conservative liberal like Anthony Trollope, himself a civil servant, entirely convinced that it should be (see chap. 4). It took decades to subdue the "Old Corruption"—the customary use of places and other emoluments to "bribe, reward, or buy" political supporters (Rubinstein 55). According to David Cannadine, local aristocrats continued to dominate county affairs until the 1880s and were not entirely replaced by modern bureaucrats until the local government reforms of the 1930s (141, 165–66).

These wide-ranging aspects of Britain's idiosyncratic modernization have been noticed by critics as diverse as Alexis de Tocqueville, Karl Marx, Max Weber, G. M. Young, Antonio Gramsci, Charles Taylor, and, as we shall see, Michel Foucault.[8] Weber, in particular, referred continually to the interesting sociological fact that England, the first nation to develop modern capitalism, was also "the slowest of all countries to succumb to bureaucratization." Indeed, England was still, to Weber's mind (ca. 1914), "only partly in the process of doing so" (*From Max Weber* 228). For all of these reasons Foucault's *Discipline and Punish*, written from a presentist perspective with French contexts foremost in mind, is a distorting lens through which to peer at the modernization of

Britain's idiosyncratic, self-consciously liberal, decentralized, and "self-governing" society. It is the aim of this chapter to demonstrate where those distortions have been most significant, and, in so doing, to prepare the ground for a more suitable historiographic frame.

Whose Panopticon?

To reject [Bentham's] half of the truth because he overlooked the other half, would be to fall into his error without having his excuse. For our own part, we have a large tolerance for one-eyed men, provided their one eye is a penetrating one.— JOHN STUART MILL, "BENTHAM"

According to *Discipline and Punish*, Jeremy Bentham "laid down the principle that power should be visible and unverifiable." It is the particular genius of Bentham's design that power can be both of these things at once, for the inmate of the Panopticon "must never know whether he is being looked at at any one moment; but . . . must be sure that he may always be so." In this way the Panopticon "automatizes and disindividualizes" power (201–2): panoptical power inheres in the machine, regardless of who operates it.

The implication is that, having once imagined the perfect machinery for power's exercise, Bentham sought to invest power wholly in machinery. Who would run the Panopticon? Foucault rightly emphasizes that the question is irrelevant to the technical functioning of Bentham's machine, but he misleadingly suggests that the question is also irrelevant to Bentham. Whereas Foucault imagines the Panopticon as a model of society *as a whole*, Bentham defined it as a "principle of construction"—integral but subordinate to society at large. Indeed, society's most critical function was to superintend those to whom it delegates panoptical power: for Bentham recognized in his invention not only "a new mode of obtaining power of mind over mind, in a quantity hitherto without example," but also one that must be *"equally* . . . secured . . . against abuse"* (*Works* 40; emph. added; cf. Blake 3–4).

Thus, from Bentham's utilitarian perspective—unlike Foucault's genealogical perspective—the exercise of power was itself secondary to the substantive individual and social aims on behalf of which power was exercised. Crucial to Bentham's political economy, for example, was that the machine be remunerative as well as disciplinary. Indeed, Bentham envisioned the Panopticon as a privately run enterprise, not a public institution: "I would farm out the profits, the no-profits, or if you please the losses, to him who, being in other respects unex-ceptionable, offered the best terms" (47; cf. Himmelfarb, "Haunted" 41–42). Be-cause the genealogist is indifferent to such contexts, he risks overlooking the ef-fects they impose on the inspection principle. Thus, Foucault amply notices Bentham's stipulation that "the persons to be inspected should always feel them-selves as if under inspection," but virtually ignores its supplement: "What is also of importance is, that for the greatest proportion of time possible, each man should actually *be* under inspection . . . [so that] the inspector may have the sat-isfaction of knowing, that the discipline actually has the effect which it is de-signed to have. . . . [and so that he can supervise] such transient and incidental directions as will require to be given and enforced, at the commencement at least of every course of industry" (44). Clearly, such "designs" and "directions" as are necessary to running a profitable business mitigate the automatization and disin-dividualization of disciplinary power—neither of which was itself a priority for Bentham. Tellingly, Bentham envisioned *himself* as the governor of the first panoptical prison (Himmelfarb, "Haunted" 58–63). Throughout his text he stressed the need to exercise caution in the vesting of power. To prospective pro-prietors of panoptical schools, he urged, "be sure of the master; for the boy's body is not more the child of his father's, than his mind will be of the master's mind" (64). Such admonitions cast doubt on the depersonalization so central to Foucault's genealogical analysis. Indeed, Bentham was not entirely remote here from Thomas Chalmers, who stressed the personal element in charity (see chap. 2), or Sir James Kay-Shuttleworth, who stressed the personal element in teaching (see chap. 5).

Bentham's plan also included considerable machinery to protect the panop-tical institution against the "abuse" of the governor: special superintendents whose monitoring functions would themselves be both abetted *and* superin-tended by the public—"the great *open committee* of the tribunal of the world" (46). Foucault acknowledges that the Panopticon is thus itself "subjected to . . . inspections," and "democratically controlled"; that it is, in effect, a "transparent building in which the exercise of power may be supervised by society as a whole" (207). Inexplicably, however, Foucault notices these important stipulations only to conflate the subject position of the unseen observer with that of the sightless observed. The prototype of Foucault's "disciplinary individual" is always the in-mate—the object of panopticism's "faceless gaze"—never the observer in the central tower (227, 214). Following Julius, the nineteenth-century penologist who provided the "birth certificate" for modern French discipline—Foucault argues that the Panopticon replaces ancient spectacle with modern surveillance (216–17). It would, perhaps, be more accurate to say that Bentham's inspection house sought to open surveillance to the spectatorship of the bourgeois world.

For Bentham, then, at least two subject positions characterized a post-Panopticon society: the inmate in the cell, and, crucially, the vigilant citizen-observer in the tower. Such preconceived asymmetries are difficult to historicize in the absence of materialist concepts (e.g., class) which help to explain why certain populations appear destined to take their place as citizens and others, delinquents. Indeed, from this perspective the Panopticon is the epitome of class society in the making, rather than a suitable structure for an anti-essentialist analysis of power. As Jenny Sharpe has argued, the notion of "an omnifunctional, free-floating power breaks down any distinction between relations of domination and subordination" (9). If the invention of the profit-making Panopticon teaches us anything, it is that power, however ubiquitous, does not circulate equally.

Bentham's late-eighteenth-century architectural idea was but a prelude to a far more ambitious design: the massive *Constitutional Code* (1830). In this little-remembered opus Bentham produced the blueprint for a totalizing raison d'état. What Bentham called the "Pannomion" was a complete code of directive laws to be enacted and overseen by a supreme and "omnicompetent" legislature whose members, in turn, were the elected representatives of a sovereign people. John Stuart Mill saw the genius of the *Code* in its "devising means for preventing rulers from escaping from the control of the majority" ("Bentham" 165). For Mill, whose distinctive liberal instinct was to hallow individuality, the majority was itself the most likely abuser of disciplinary power in a modern society. This crucial insight was utterly alien to Bentham's rigorously formalist mentality.

Still, it is worth clarifying that the thrust of Bentham's dream was not, as readers of Foucault might imagine, to subject society to the faceless surveillance of the state. Like his Fabian heirs, Bentham endowed government with a strong positive function; a "tutelary" purpose harking back to the Hobbesian idea that human interests must be artificially harmonized. Yet Bentham envisioned the *Code* as an open-ended system through which simultaneously to secure the deployment, legitimization, *and* oversight of disciplinary power.[9] In Bentham's scheme the citizen, however implausibly, was empowered both to enact and inspect the instruments of his own tutelage. Isolated subjection, like that of the incarcerated inmate of the Panopticon, was reserved for a small minority of incurable delinquents.

In spirit, then, Bentham's was not precisely the dream of a bureaucratic utopia presided over by benevolent administrative experts—not the dream, in other words, of Edwin Chadwick and, decades later, the Fabians. Bentham's dream, a reaction to the abuses of the ancien régime, is best understood as a call for accountability: for Bentham was profoundly skeptical about the human capacity to exercise power without abusing it. "Jealousy, not confidence," he wrote, with the potential mismanagement of the Panopticon in mind, "is the characteristic of wise laws" (qtd. in Himmelfarb, "Haunted" 42). Hence, the "visibility" of power was crucial to Bentham's philosophy of government, but its "unverifiability" related only to one subordinate component of the master machine (Foucault, *Discipline* 201). Foucault's genealogy misleads us by recognizing Bentham's invention as a mechanism of power, while setting aside the substantive aims on behalf of which that power was, in theory, to be mobilized.[10]

In one of the most famous passages from *Discipline and Punish* Foucault describes the plague-stricken city of seventeenth-century France: an "enclosed, segmented space, observed at every point, in which . . . power is exercised without division" (197–98). Clearly, Foucault saw Bentham's Panopticon as the "generalizable model" of this hitherto "exceptional" mobilization of power; a "formula" for the efficient and continuous deployment of discipline (205, 209). Crucial to his anti-essentialist premise, however, is the move away from the *Panopticon*—the material prison—and toward *panopticism*, a "movement" wherein disciplinary technologies exceed their institutional boundaries and "stretch" to "an indefinitely generalizable mechanism" (216; cf. 209). Indeed, without this generalizing motion, Foucault's account of the Panopticon becomes, in effect, precisely the kind of flawed Marxist analysis he sought to avoid: an Althusserian-like theory in which reified "Ideological State Apparatuses" (such as the Panopticon) directly dominate through subject constitution.[11] Thus, the shift from "exceptional discipline" to "generalized surveillance" enables Foucault to specify that discipline should *not* be identified with institutions, but understood, instead, as "a type of power," and "a modality for [power's] exercise" (209, 215).

For the post-Foucauldian critic at least one searching question arises: how can the genealogist account for "a historical transformation" of this kind when his analysis focuses on the effects of already existing power relations (209)? By excluding substantive and linguistic concepts such as culture, ideology, values, and norms, Foucault renders himself unable to explain how (much less why) certain struggles and their outcomes become consolidated and institutionalized (cf. Habermas, *Philosophical* 287). He defuses this problem only by invoking the material details of French history. Early-modern France saw the "swarming" both of exceptional institutions *and* their generalized offshoots, while the "*state-control of the mechanisms of discipline*" increased under successive absolutist, revolutionary and Napoleonic regimes (211, 213). With the special exception of the Panopticon, Foucault draws largely on these Continental developments. He is far less interested in Britain, where a self-consciously liberal and vehemently Protestant national culture helped to ensure that the growth of centralized, modern institutions remained subject to deep-seated popular hostility.

That is not, of course, to deny the formidable achievements of administrative pioneers such as Edwin Chadwick and Dr. James Phillips Kay (later Sir James Kay-Shuttleworth)—whose voluntary efforts to prepare Manchester for cholera in 1832 did indeed resemble Foucault's plague-stricken city (see Kay, *Moral* 19–20). Nor is it to deny the effects of bureaucratic experimentation in the colonies, which, as I argue in chapter 4, influenced British civil service reform. Nor is it to overlook the simple fact that over the course of the nineteenth century (and especially after 1870) the rationalization, centralization, and expansion of Victorian government proceeded apace. It is, however, to suggest that, inasmuch as so astute a civil servant as Matthew Arnold was prompted to declare in 1869, and not without justice, that the British people "have not the notion, so familiar on the Continent . . . of *the State*" (*Culture* 83–84), the application of Foucault's presentist genealogy to Victorian Britain would appear to entail at least one logical problem. Can a model in which panopticism is both "generalized" *from* and concentrated *in* exemplary modern institutions be applied successfully to study a society in which such institutions were only beginning to evolve? Clearly, Victorianist scholars seeking to account for the generalization of panopticism must either modify Foucault's analysis accordingly, or willingly conflate Britain's material history with that of France.

Governmentality

If the state is what it is today, this is so precisely thanks to this governmentality, which is at once internal and external to the state, since it is the tactics of government which make possible the continual definition and redefinition of what is within the competence of the state and what is not, the public versus the private, and so on; thus the state can only be understood in its survival and its limits on the basis of the general tactics of governmentality.

— MICHEL FOUCAULT, "GOVERNMENTALITY"

In effect, what defines a relationship of power is that it is a mode of action which does not act directly and immediately on others. Instead it acts upon their actions: an action upon an action, on existing actions or on those which may arise.

— MICHEL FOUCAULT, "THE SUBJECT AND POWER"

All that the best laws and the best government can accomplish is assuring to exertion its true reward, by providing for the security of person and property, by promoting education, and by diffusing religious instruction to encourage the formation of those habits of industry and virtue which alone can be the sources of the welfare and the prosperity either of individuals or communities

— HENRY HOWICK

Fortunately, Foucault himself provides additional resources for the former enterprise. His late thinking on governmentality, still in progress at the time of his death, is less a coherent paradigm than a set of revisions pertinent to the post-genealogical study of modern societies. Foucault's writings from this period clearly aim to provide alternatives to the objectivizing domination and statist emphases of *Discipline and Punish*, thereby illuminating the study of discipline in a self-consciously liberal society.[12]

First, Foucault dramatically improves upon genealogy's impoverished model of human subjectivity. In contrast to the dominated bodies of genealogy, governmentality presumes active subjects who are both conscious and "free."[13] By excepting relations of physical force (which are inapplicable to his theory), Foucault defines power as that which is exercised over agents for whom choice is possible: "subjects who are faced with a field of possibilities in which several ways of behaving . . . may be realized" ("Subject" 221). By thus introducing human agency, Foucault articulates a position that is theoretically compatible with materialist concepts such as "culture" and "ideology." Foucault's revised subject can, for example, be likened to Pierre Bourdieu's notion of the "habitus." For Bourdieu subject constitution entails the profound acculturation of mind and body, a process through which conscious individuals become unconsciously complicit in perpetuating cultural norms. Normativization works through the deployment of "symbolic power"—a power that, like Foucault's, is distinct from physical force. Symbolic power thus describes the multifarious ways in which individuals learn to recognize the legitimacy or naturalness of certain actions and beliefs (Bourdieu 51–52, 81–89, 163–70). While the notion of subjectivities habituated through the circulation of symbolic power is hardly liberatory, it does, like Foucault's revised position, endow individuals with the capacity to resist rather than comply with norms.

According to Foucault's later essays, power operates *indirectly*—through the mediation of human actors engaged in diverse relations with one another. Power relations thus consist in modes of action upon the actions of others. Freedom and power agonistically provoke each other, each representing the precondition of the other's possibility. To be free is not—as in crude liberal thought—to escape to some autonomous realm outside of power, but, rather, to exercise one's own power to influence and be influenced by others. Foucault's revisions thus constitute a relational theory of power, predicated on enduring contest and the possibility of change. Just as Bourdieu's "habitus" provides a suitable analogy for subjectivities as formed by indirect relations of power, so Gramsci's notion of a dynamic, always contested "hegemony" provides a useful equivalence for Foucault's revised view of the underpinnings of truth (see Gramsci 365–76).

Foucault's revisions further demand a reevaluation of the state. Whereas *Discipline and Punish* persistently returned—despite its own anti-essentialist intentions—to the importance of state apparatuses, the essay on "Governmentality" asks us to reconsider precisely this tendency. The state, Foucault argues, is but "a mythicized abstraction" of power and, consequently, less central "than many of us think." Rather than reify state domination, scholars must study the "'governmentalization' of the state": the extent to which the state itself depends on external relations of power (103). In thus locating power largely outside of the state's aegis, governmentality anticipates Foucault's vivid articulation of liberalism as a critique of raison d'état: as the "moment it became apparent that if one governed too much, one did not govern at all" ("Space" 242; cf. Gordon, "Governmental" 15).

It would be hard to overstate the relevance of such thinking to nineteenth-century Britain. Throughout the century Britain's ruling classes strove to govern *indirectly:* to implement parliamentary power in ways that encouraged self-help, philanthropy, voluntarism, and local government. In the 1830s the British electorate cautiously affirmed the state's mandate to maintain social stability. The parliamentary reforms of this era authorized the state to promote brutally deterrent poor laws and efficient policing, but not to administer or, indeed, to compel such measures. In this process the purpose of the nation's legendarily "free" constitution was redefined: emphasis shifted away from the historic protection of "natural" rights (i.e., the rights of the landed elite to curb the state's potential tyranny), and toward the protection of property (for which end the state might play a useful role).[14]

Here was a foundational moment in what Max Weber has described as the intimate relation between capitalism, and the rationalization of the social order (*Law* 350; *Economy* 2:1465 n. 14). Nevertheless, in securing the stability on which capitalist development depended, Britain's leaders—as Weber recognized—resisted or curtailed unpopular statist measures. Their goal was not "regular bureaucratic intervention," but, rather, the liberal ideal of a "moralistic but pluralistic self-governing order" (Parry 127). As a mentality of rule, explains Nikolas Rose, liberalism abandoned the "megalomaniac and obsessive fantasy of a totally administered society," situating itself in relation to the putatively self-regulating domains of economy and civil society (43). Whig arts of government perfectly illustrate liberal governance in this form: their aim was precisely to regulate "the general conduct of individuals . . . without the need for intervention" (Foucault, "Space" 241).

Indeed, according to Whig-Liberal ideology, intervention was invariably counterproductive. As George Cornewall Lewis, a leading Whig, asserted in 1832, "All the praiseworthy endeavours of rulers to make men good by law have utterly failed" (qtd. in Mandler, "Tories" 90). Addressing Parliament in 1840, Henry Howick, in actuality one of the most "dirigiste" of Whigs, epitomized their philosophy of governance. In addition to protecting person and property, he argued, government may "promote," "diffuse," and "encourage" the "virtue" of citizens. But it cannot attempt to enforce or, as in Bentham, mechanically to generate such virtue (qtd. in Parry 114). Harriet Martineau, the celebrated popularizer of political economy, articulated the same idea in her 1837 study of *Society in America*. "Laws and customs cannot be creative of virtue: they may encourage and help to preserve it; but they cannot originate it." Laws, in other words, may operate negatively (by punishing crime), and indirectly (by "encouraging" virtue). But positive social improvement ultimately derives from the personal efforts of individuals: by "each one being as good as he can make himself" (2:244). Victorian Whigs and their allies thus assumed that government "could play only a small part in changing human behaviour" (Parry 114). As civic republican and theistic moralists, they explicitly rejected the felicific calculus, Bentham's mechanistic and hedonistic model of the human subject. In so doing, they envisioned themselves as the disinterested guardians of a progressive social order, the engine of which was the self-reliant character of individuals, families, and communities.

Foucault's late works help us to analyze liberalism in this form by calling attention to the covert positive effects of a laissez-faire ideology that proclaimed its own inactivity. Historians of the period have emphasized the ostensible neutrality, passivity, even apoliticism, of Victorian government—the popular perception of a "disinterested" state "standing above and apart from" society's "open-ended evolution" (Parry 178; Harris, *Private* 183; cf. Best 251; Freeden 179). But, like Marx and Engels before him, Foucault alerts us to the tension between government's purposely unobtrusive form, and its potentially powerful effects.[15] Although Whigs such as Howick insisted that individual virtue "alone" creates prosperity, they called on the state to protect property, "assuring to exertion its true reward." In so doing, the state undertook to steady Adam Smith's invisible hand. Whig-Liberal governance was thus demonstrably unlike the disciplinary society of Foucault's genealogy. Nonetheless, the power to exercise force curtailed dissidence, warranting the ostensible consensus on which self-consciously liberal societies depend.[16]

Yet what interested Foucault more than the state's negative power to repress, were the more subtle, diffuse and positive processes of "governmentalization." There he evoked an intricate play of indirect power relations, both inside and out of the state, which "incite," "seduce," "make easier or more difficult"; a power that, unlike statist repression, is "a way of acting upon . . . acting subjects by virtue of their acting or being capable of action" ("Subject" 220). Foucault's notion of empowered actors provoking one another through a dense web of indirect relations provides a fitting model for what the Victorians themselves saw as a dynamic civil society. Indeed, Walter Bagehot's 1856 contrast between the simple domination required to rule a "rough despotic community" and the challenge of governing liberal Britain perfectly anticipates Foucault's paradigm. A "free intellectual community," wrote Bagehot, "is a complicated network of ramified relations, interlacing and passing hither and thither, old and new. . . . You are never sure what effect any force or any change may produce on a framework so exquisite and so involved." For Bagehot the relation between civil society and the state is, like Foucault's relation between freedom and power, agonistic rather than antithetical, with each constituting the conditions of the other's possibility. Thus, even though the liberal state is proportionately small, "the scale of operations is so much enlarged by the continual exercise of civil liberty, that the real work is ultimately . . . immense" (*Works* 10:254–57). Bagehot thus articulated a characteristically mid-Victorian equipoise between the energy of "free" individuals and the duty of statesmen to provide rationalizing influence.

From Disciplinary Individualism to Pastorship

The hardest lesson for Government or urchin to learn is, what it ought not do. It is perhaps the highest attainment of a constitutional Government, to *confide in the People.* . . . [I]t is not the province of the Government to train the mind of the people. [Government should protect person and property, but it] is not the duty of Government to feed the people, to clothe them, to build houses for them, to direct their industry or their commerce, to superintend their families, to cultivate their minds, to shape their opinions, or to supply them with religious teachers, physicians, schoolmasters, books, or newspapers.

— EDWARD BAINES, *Letters to Lord John Russell on State Education*

I could shape for you other plans, for art-galleries, and for natural history galleries, and for many precious, many, it seems to me, needful things. . . . [O]ur British constitution . . . has fallen dropsical of late, and has an evil thirst, and evil hunger, and wants healthier feeding. You have got its corn laws repealed for it; try if you cannot get corn laws established for it, dealing in a better bread;— bread made of that old enchanted Arabian grain, the Sesame, which opens doors;—doors, not of robbers', but of Kings' Treasuries.

— JOHN RUSKIN, "OF KINGS' TREASURIES"

In *Discipline and Punish* "disciplinary individualism" described the central paradox of the modern condition. Individuality—that is, what counts for individuality in modern societies—entirely depends on the effects of discipline. What particularly fascinated Foucault was how the state's introduction of "formalizing" technologies in the eighteenth century (e.g., examinations) paradoxically *individualized.* The more one was monitored and assessed, the stronger one's individuality became. This "reversal"—from an individuality born of "noble deeds" to one born of "secret singularities"—was momentous, not least because it marked the historical emergence of the human sciences (192, 193). The same fascination led to the elaboration of "biopower" in the first volume of *The History of Sexuality.*

The chief problem with this important concept was its inability to distinguish between the dominatory power of "state apparatuses" and the normativizing tendencies of civilization in and of itself—the kind of everyday socializing processes emphasized in Bourdieu's habitus. As Edward Said has argued, Foucault confused "the power of institutions to subjugate individuals" with the

simple fact "that individual behaviour in society is frequently a matter of following rules and conventions" ("Foucault" 151). Theorized in this way, the disciplinary individual "lacks any kind of autonomous identity" and, therefore, any
capacity to treat of "substantive ethical or socio-political questions" (Norris 54,
60). Critics influenced by Foucault's analysis of power are thus unable to historicize self-reflective or critically detached subjectivities (A. Anderson, "Temptations"). Genealogy privileges discursive "manipulation" "at the expense of psy-
chic understanding" (Lane 4).

As though in reply, Foucault's essays on governmentality reformulate the paradox of disciplinary individualism by introducing human agency, and, in theory,
de-emphasizing the state. Foucault now identifies the power to individualize
with *pastorship*, the ancient Christian concept of the shepherd's intensive care for
his flock. In *Discipline and Punish* Foucault had made clear that the Panopticon's
object was "to strengthen the social forces": developing the economy, spreading
education, and "rais[ing] the level of public morality" (208). Reconceptualized
as pastorship, these crucial productive processes are now detached from panopticism's specific institutional features, from its implicit raison d'état, and from
the dominatory analysis of power. From the seventeenth century on, Foucault
explains, secularized forms of pastorship sought to strengthen society by maxi-
mizing the productive potential of individuals ("Politics" 60, 82). Paradoxically,
however, the same processes through which modern societies promote well-
being—although now conceived in the form of indirect influence, rather than
direct institutional domination—entangle the individual in a normativizing web.
The "relations between the growth of capabilities and the growth of autonomy
are not as simple" as early-modern thinkers "may have believed" ("Enlightenment" 48). A continuing manifestation of this paradox is the modern social security system, which, while beneficial to individual welfare, has the "perverse effect" of encouraging dependence on a rigid and rule-bound system ("Social" 160).

Pastorship so defined lends itself to an analysis of various British developments. At the turn of the century Britain's New Liberal politicians attempted to
elude the paradox of state welfare by introducing national insurance financed
through workers' contributions (see chap. 6). But for most of the Victorian era
a more apt British articulation of the paradox was the self-reliant individual "encircled . . . at every level" by an elaborate network of voluntary social practices
(Harris, "Society" 68; cf. Gunn 32–33). At the same time, the most prominent
social critics were convinced that Britain's most serious problem was the *lack* of
pastorship. Pastorship thus provides a powerful tool for conceptualizing Victo-

rian governance: sufficiently flexible to describe the aims and achievements both of voluntarists and statists, philanthropists and bureaucrats, staunch individualists such as Edward Baines and humanitarian critics such as John Ruskin (see epigraphs).

That said, Foucault's specific elaboration of pastorship significantly diverges from British contexts. His focus on the Continent leads him back to the multifarious activities of Continental states in the seventeenth and eighteenth centuries. As Christianity's notion of exhaustive and individualizing pastoral guidance became secularized in postfeudal Europe, it developed through a broad notion of "police": "a governmental technology peculiar to the state; domains, techniques, targets where the state intervenes" ("Politics" 77). This raison d'état, moreover, was continuous with an epistemological shift of sorts: a shift from the model of the family (seen as a microcosm of feudal rule) to the model of population (a mass abstraction reified through statistical analyses).[17]

These aspects of Foucault's study of governmentality arguably compromise his determination to avoid overemphasizing the state. Nevertheless, that is of far less consequence to the Victorianist. Foucault was well aware that the governmentalization of Catholic, absolutist France substantially differed from that of Protestant, liberal Britain, with its wide variety of voluntary, local, and ad hoc practices.[18] According to Weber, the efforts of the Stuart monarchy to "impose a coherent system of 'Christian welfare policies'" were thwarted by the resistance of the local gentry—the very same group that successfully delayed the development of modern bureaucracy well into the twentieth century (*Economy* 2:1062; cf. 2:971). As Nancy Armstrong has argued, Puritan treatises "represented the family as a self-enclosed social unit in whose affairs the state could not intervene" (18). Hence, while Parliament was, in many respects, a formidable site of centralized power, the development of pastorship in early-modern Britain was unlike the "rather typically French effort of policing" ("Space" 241).

In the nineteenth century, through the groundbreaking efforts of self-appointed middle-class statisticians such as Nassau Senior and James Phillips Kay, a modern notion of population—in Mary Poovey's term, a "social body"—impressed itself indelibly on the Victorian imagination. The mid-nineteenth century saw a proliferation of Royal Commissions of Inquiry and a zealous "faith in information" and social statistics (O. Anderson, "Administrative" 283). But the idea of an abstract population, along with the objectifying materialist stance on which it depends, was also subject to relentless challenge by powerful rivals for epistemological authority. Kay himself embodied both sides of these divided allegiances:

a statistician and proto-bureaucrat, but also a disciple of the power of person-alized bonds to revivify a Christian and civic community. For these and many other reasons a critical practice that aims to discover the path of governmental-ization in nineteenth-century Britain must distance itself from Foucault's work on France, and focus on the "specific rationalities" common to the Victorians.[19]

In early-modern France, Foucault alleges, the family "disappear[ed] as the model of government, *except for a certain number of residual themes of a religious or moral nature*" ("Governmentality" 99; emph. added). These "themes," as read-ers of Martineau, Gaskell, Carlyle, Dickens, Ruskin, and a host of others will readily recognize, were—so far from "residual"—the source of Victorian liter-ature's characteristic *frisson*. Dickens's midcentury idealization of the doctor-as-hero (see chap. 3), and Ruskin's call for "healthier feeding" are, therefore, but two examples of a literature virtually teeming with demands for committed pas-torship in a nation of allegedly self-reliant individuals and communities. Such demands took precisely the form of moral and religious imperatives. These were not calls for a more efficient population (although such calls existed and would reach a crescendo at the turn of the century), but pleas on behalf of the shep-herdless poor for the reinvigoration of community and character-building bonds between upper and lower ranks. Describing the persistence of religious belief in nineteenth-century Britain, Charles Taylor has pointed to the "radical diver-gence" between French and Anglo-Saxon societies. It "would be a mistake," he argues, to regard Britain's liberal reforms "as part of a smooth, continuing, uni-directional move towards 'secularization,'" since the "initial impulse underlying reform was a deeply religious one" (*Sources* 399, 401). Thus, British govern-mentalization differed from French for at least two reasons: first, because of the persistence in Britain of a moral, religious, and familial way of conceptualizing pastorship; and, second, because, from the view of many influential contempo-raries, British pastorship—left to the discretion of voluntary and local efforts—was woefully insufficient.

What seems clear, then, is that for Victorian and Edwardian Britons, pas-torship was not a legacy of early-modern history, but a vexing contemporary issue: a source of breast-beating moral angst, political controversy, and con-flicted social desire. Novels such as *Bleak House* (1852–53) and George Gissing's *The Nether World* (1889), both of which portray a pastorless nation, thus point to the centrality of a distinctively British modern paradox. This is not the Fou-cauldian paradox of the individual's dependence on external and normalizing forms of authority (a point to which I will return), but the uniquely British paradox of the middle- and upper-class Victorians who demanded effective governance only to be confounded by their own ingrained liberal predilections. Dickens was representative in his desire for a catachrestic pastoral authority: one that would be rational but unbureaucratic, omnipresent but personal, authoritative but liberatory, efficient but English. To illuminate this paradox further and, at the same time, to develop certain themes that recur in the following chapters, it will be helpful to introduce two concepts necessary to describing the specific rationalities of nineteenth-century liberalism.

Worldview and Character in a Liberal Society

The nature of modern civilization . . . requires . . . [the] "calculability" of consequences. Fully developed bureaucracy operates in a special sense "sine ira ac studio" ["without bias or favor"]. Its peculiar character and with it its appropriateness for capitalism is the more fully actualized the more bureaucracy "depersonalizes" itself, i.e., the more completely it succeeds in achieving that condition which is acclaimed as its peculiar virtue, viz., the exclusion of love, hatred, and every purely personal, especially irrational and incalculable, feeling from the execution of official tasks. In the place of the old-type ruler who is moved by sympathy, favor, grace, and gratitude, modern culture requires for its sustaining external apparatus the emotionally detached, and hence rigorously "professional," expert; and the more complicated and the more specialized it is, the more it needs him.

— MAX WEBER, *Max Weber on Law*

Go into the quiet cornfields of heavy Wiltshire, and talk awhile with the clod pulling rustic. . . . Nothing hitherto has been done towards civilizing him . . .

No Government, no Cabinet, no Minister can produce the change that is needful in this matter. No Houses of Parliament can pass a law that shall be efficient to make labour respected and respectable. Laws they may pass by dozens with their assumed omnipotence, but they will be wholly inoperative. . . . Every aristocrat may do much in his own sphere; be he an aristocrat over thousands of acres, or an aristocrat over hundreds of factory children, or simply the humblest of aristocrats guiding some score of men in a founder's yard.

— ANTHONY TROLLOPE, *The New Zealander*

Nineteenth-century British liberalism was not a monolithic discourse or political rationality but a cacophony of diverse, though mainly optimistic, viewpoints on culture and society. Broadly construed, liberalism included, but was not limited to, the high-minded cooperation sought by John Stuart Mill, Thomas Chalmers's Christian and civic community, Harriet Martineau's vision of a society fueled by individual self-improvement, Walter Bagehot's staid confidence in the dynamism of civil society, Samuel Smiles's populist assertion of individual will, Matthew Arnold's conviction in the enlightening potential of a cultured elite, and Bernard Bosanquet's fin-de-siècle citizen ethic. What united these and still other identifiably liberal positions was their common adherence, though typically pressured and often contradictory, to an antimaterialist and moral worldview.

In the chapters that follow I describe Victorian literature and society in relation to two antithetical, or "dueling," worldviews: one moral and idealist and the other materialist. By *worldviews* I refer to sets of beliefs that, for all their preponderance, were fluctuating and contested (rather than statically dominant), and more palpable and plain than underlying epistemological questions (however inextricable from them). The concept of "worldview" neither precedes nor supersedes the idea of governmentalization as inhering in indirect relations of power both inside and out of the state. Rather, like "culture," it is a concept that permits the heterogeneous manifestations of governmentalization to be described as a coherent construction, however provisionally. Worldview thus describes the habits and assumptions that Victorians brought to bear as they played the part of conscious actors within "the network of ramified relations" evoked by Bagehot. Such assumptions, moreover, often took the form of nationalist or class-based myths (e.g., the Anglo-Saxon myth, the middle-class myth of the self-made man, and the upper- and upper-middle-class myth of disinterested governance).[20]

In highlighting the pervasive effects of dueling worldviews over the course of the century, my intention is not to delineate two discrete belief systems, and to align specific Victorians with one or the other. Rather, all Victorians were, to some extent, syncretic thinkers drawing from two alternative worldviews, each of which made powerful claims to modern authenticity. In the following chapters I describe the contours of this duel in philosophical terms (as a contest between idealism and materialism), in sociological terms (as the priority of moral character vs. that of environmental or physical condition), in rhetorical terms (as the subjective language of personal relations vs. the objective language of law or social science), in political and pastoral terms (as voluntarism vs. centralized bureaucracy), and in intellectual terms (as, e.g., Coleridge's legacy vs. Bentham's).

In so doing, however, I demonstrate much blurring both within and between each set of oppositions. John Stuart Mill's influential blend of Coleridge and Bentham in philosophy, politics, and social science suggests that syncretic liberal thinking was itself more prominent than its purely moral or materialist counterparts.[21] Throughout this book I indicate the ease with which ardent moralists, devoted to character building and steeped in the language of the personal, were also avid record keepers, statisticians, and ambitious organizers. At the same time, Mill's powerful critiques suggest that the increasingly mass scale of Victorian society, and the commodifying effects of capitalism, presented serious threats to the moral worldview, independently of bureaucratic or social scientific interventions. Modern civilization itself, including such everyday practices as window-shopping in the nation's capital, came to stand for "the increasing pretensions, impersonality and mobility of social and commercial life" (A. Miller 5). Throughout the century, then, liberals of many stripes trumpeted their moral allegiances even as they tolerated and, at times, sanctioned processes of rationalization and embourgeoisement.

It is possible, of course, to describe such a state in transitional terms, as a long-evolving shift from traditional to modern worldviews. For the most part I deliberately avoid this construction because my point is to emphasize the degree to which arguably traditional concepts such as "character" retained enormous authority to pronounce upon and shape modern life. Hence, Max Weber's distinction between traditional and modern modes of authority provides a helpful analytical tool, since it is organized around substantive definitions rather than historical shifts: by questions of "what" rather than "when."[22] For Weber modernity is characterized by an instrumentalist rationality that is epitomized by bureaucratic rule, but not reducible to the latter's effect. Hence, "bureaucratic *authority* has not always appeared concurrently with *bureaucratization*." Indeed, Britain is Weber's cardinal example of a country where a "calculable" rationality was achieved by nonbureaucratic means (*Law* 350; emph. added).

Significantly, Weber represents bureaucratic rationality as an assault on the foundations of the moral worldview: it is a depersonalization of the personal; a suppression of an entire realm of relational affect (love, hatred, sympathy, favor); an attempt to transform the liberal ideal of mutual relations between autonomous actors into atomized and objectifying relations of institutionally mediated power. In all of these ways Weber helps us to see, on the one hand, that bureaucracy was antithetical to cherished liberal convictions and, on the other, that as a self-consciously liberal society, resistant to bureaucratization but bent on progress, industrial age Britain had inevitably to discover suitable rational-izing alternatives. Exploring Britain's distinctly liberal path to modern govern-ance, especially as it developed in and through literature, is thus a principal aim of this book.

Inseparable from Victorian antimaterialism was a particular concept of indi-viduality, signified by (selective usages) of the term *character*. In its liberal mean-ings character was the antithesis of Foucault's disciplinary individual. For J. S. Mill it consisted in a confirmed "habit of willing" wrested away from the de-termining power of hedonistic conditioning (*System* 120–21). T. H. Green, the influential Oxford philosopher, drew on Mill as well as German-Romanticism when he argued that the capacity for self-developing character was "the mark of a truly free person" (Bellamy, "Green" 134). At the turn of the century—as though to contest the very idea of an impersonal population—Green's disciple, Bernard Bosanquet, asserted a "view which treats men not as economic ab-stractions, but as living selves with a history and ideas and a character of their own" ("Character" 105).

According to Stefan Collini, "the ideal of character . . . enjoyed a prominence in the political thought of the Victorian period that it had apparently not known before and that it has, arguably, not experienced since" (*Public* 94).[23] In the chap-ters that follow I situate that ideal at the very nub of dueling worldviews, shap-ing the contours of Britain's idiosyncratic modernization. As a concept in which human subjectivity is cast in moral terms, character played many distinct parts. One of its most visible manifestations was a popular nationalist form. Through-out the century the stalwart self-reliance of Anglo-Saxon Protestants was ob-sessively pitted against the alleged servility of Catholic rivals and Oriental sub-jects. Thomas Arnold epitomized such contrasts: a "thorough English gentleman—Christian, manly and enlightened," he insisted, "is more . . . than Guizot or Sismondi could comprehend," and "a finer specimen of human na-ture than any other country . . . could furnish" (qtd. in Strachey 232). Samuel Smiles produced a more democratic version of the same nationalist myth when he described character as a "self-originating force," latent in every individual, but cultivated especially in Britons (*Character* 27).

In the high-minded social thought of J. S. Mill, the organized charity of Thomas Chalmers, and the Anglicist colonial policy of Charles Trevelyan, char-acter assumed a recognizably *prescriptive* form. This early-nineteenth-century view of the human telos—drawing on classical, romantic, and Evangelical philosophies of self-development—implied the limitless improvability of all human beings, regardless of class, race, and, to a certain extent, sex/gender. That said, the idealized pastoral relations through which character building on this scale was seen to take place depended on intrinsically unequal relations between rich and poor, educated and uneducated, colonizer and colonized. Liberal governance (both domestic and colonial) was thus structured around a hallowed but contradictory concept of the social bond. Pastorship was conceived as a reciprocal relation between morally equal actors, even as vast inequalities of wealth and power were tolerated and, indeed, stabilized.[24]

Nevertheless, for all its tolerance of inequality, the prescriptive idea of character generated thoughts of boundless transformation and universal improvement. Such dynamic rhetoric thus gestured toward a level of political and social change which, in the wake of middle-class enfranchisement, working-class political agitation, and colonial rebellion, became increasingly undesirable to the propertied classes. This conservative trend was the political underside of the mid-Victorian drift toward a *descriptive* language of character. Such notions—whether based on class, race, environmental conditioning, or any other material determinant—implied a comparatively limited view of individual improvement and, thus, a naturalization of relatively fixed sociopolitical hierarchies.

Of course, one of the most powerful tools for describing character was the new human sciences: the burgeoning knowledge bases of medicine, psychology, sexology, ethnology, and criminology, to name just a few. Through such discourses character could be stripped of its romantic and religious claims to transcendence, and reduced to an objectified set of criteria. In 1862 Mary Elizabeth Braddon paused from her tale of adultery and murder to dispute phrenology's authority to read the secrets of the human heart: "Heaven keep us," she expostulated, if character is held to depend on "bulbous projections," to "be measured by the compass or weighed in the scale" (*Aurora Floyd* 369). In the chapters that follow I explore the materialist incursion on character in the depersonalizing effects of the New Poor Law, the sanitary ambitions of Edwin Chadwick, and the Fabians' turn-of-the-century call for bureaucratic utopia. Nevertheless, I also focus on specific ways in which such social scientific authority was detoured by powerful liberal resistance.

My readings thus make clear that social scientific knowledge was not the only (or even primary) path to producing relatively stable descriptions of character. The inimitable qualities attributed to the mid-Victorian gentleman, for example, represented a different descriptive notion, based on the symbolic power of class. Such a power was less empirical than social scientific knowledge, but, for that very reason, more amenable to liberal sensibilities.[25] The gentleman's aura was predicated on quasi-feudal appeals to social hierarchy. In the mid-Victorian period these traditional credentials were deliberately modernized, rationalized, and improved through, for example, civil service, public school and university reform. What described the gentleman was therefore both rationalized and empirical (the predictable outcome of an elite education), and thoroughly mystified (an indefinable tone ambiguously derived from blood, breeding, or both). In this fashion the character of the British gentleman became a powerful descriptive basis for a myth of disinterested governance by an Oxbridge elite, a crucial means by which upper-class and aristocratic power was maintained.

This mode of descriptive character flourished in a period of relative political quiescence; but it was hardly invulnerable. Indeed, its most serious challenge derived from within capitalist development itself: in the increasing leveling and materialism to which character might be subject in a mass bourgeois culture. The depersonalizing logic of the New Poor Law suggested that economic independence was the single most important mark of social status: outweighing such old-fashioned notions as character (see chap. 2). Such a logic was as threatening to the born-and-bred gentleman, who might find his authority outstripped by the wealthy *parvenu*, as it was to the proverbial working-class worthy fallen on hard times despite his or her reputable character. Anti–New Poor Law novels such as *Oliver Twist* and *Jessie Phillips* responded to this materialistic assault on character by depicting the disastrous consequences of embourgeoisement. Divested of its transcendent moral content, and subject to impersonal economic criteria, character would devolve into a mere facade: a superficial display of vulgar accouterments and "respectable" pretensions. In the 1850s and 1860s Anthony Trollope's Barsetshire novels masterfully naturalized the transcendent moral authority of the gentleman's character (see chap. 4). By contrast, Dickens's contemporaneous *Our Mutual Friend* brooded over the tension between the limitless self-improvement once promised by prescriptive character, and the born-and-bred gentlemanliness privileged by descriptive character (see chap. 5). At the end of the century Gissing's novels paradoxically subscribed to the old prescriptive ideal while, at the same time, representing individuals who were all but powerless to defy the impersonal dominion of large-scale economic forces (see chap. 6).

In the chapters that follow I locate these and other questions of character and worldview as they emerged in the literary and social contexts surrounding historically specific debates over governance, including poor law, sanitary, educational, and civil service reform. As my approach is deliberately synchronic, I do not foreground any single narrative of epistemological change over the course of the century. Nevertheless, in a general and preliminary way my readings suggest that it was the depersonalizing effects of an increasingly mass bourgeois society, rather than social scientific knowledge (whether generated inside or out of the state), which posed the most immediate threat to nineteenth-century liberal ideals. The importance of massification becomes especially evident in J. S. Mill's prescient critique of modern civilization. As Mill's insights into liberalism also figure in several later chapters, I conclude by describing the fascinating overlap between Mill's Victorian legacy and Foucault's late works on governmentality.

John Stuart Mill, Michel Foucault, and Power in a Liberal Society

It [is] now perceived that such phrases as "self-government," and "the power of the people over themselves," do not express the true state of the case. . . . [T]he "self-government" spoken of is not the government of each by himself, but of each by all the rest. . . . [W]hen society is itself the tyrant—society collectively, over the separate individuals who compose it—its means of tyrannizing are not restricted to the acts which it may do by the hands of its political functionaries. Society can and does execute its own mandates . . . it [can practice] a social tyranny more formidable than many kinds of political oppression, since . . . it leaves fewer means of escape, penetrating much more deeply into the details of life, and enslaves the soul itself.   — JOHN STUART MILL, *On Liberty*

It is here that the question of liberalism comes up. It seems to me that at that very moment it became apparent that if one governed too much, one did not govern at all. . . . From the moment one is to manipulate a society, one cannot consider it completely penetrable by police.

— MICHEL FOUCAULT, "SPACE, KNOWLEDGE, AND POWER"

No less than Michel Foucault, John Stuart Mill devoted his life's work to the problem of individuality in modern societies. Although he was raised by James Mill to be Bentham's scion, Mill's careful reading of romantic thinkers such as Tocqueville, Coleridge, and Wilhelm von Humboldt persuaded him that human individuality—the diversification and strengthening of character—was the highest social good. Mill became the arch-exponent of a principled liberal middle ground. Just as he sought a synthesis between Bentham's and Coleridge's philosophies, so he attempted to cultivate an "art of government" which would simultaneously centralize and diffuse knowledge, thus producing "the greatest dissemination of power consistent with efficiency" (*Liberty* 164; cf. *Autobiography* 116). That said, Mill was as loath as Foucault to believe that liberty could be guaranteed by "laws and institutions." His lifelong exhortation to civic participation anticipated Foucault's insight that "liberty is what must be *exercised*" ("Space" 245). Mill's prescient critique of mass society helps to explain how a calculable modern rationality developed from within a culture that was, to a very large extent, politically, intellectually, and philosophically opposed to that end.

The thesis of Mill's remarkable 1836 essay on "Civilization" is that material progress deteriorates character and diminishes individual power. Mill begins by stipulating that modern society is civilized "in the narrow sense": its achievements chiefly material rather than broadly human. Indeed, in point of "cultivation" (a Coleridgean concept) modern civilization is arguably "stationary" or "retrograde" (119). The reason is simple. Because civilization consists in rudimentary forms of cooperation—division of labor, protection of property, and other forms of dependence on "general arrangements"—individuals need no longer exert their strength, wit, or courage to survive (129). Thus, in a civilized society character atrophies as "power passes from individuals to masses," and "the weight and importance" of individuals "sinks into greater and greater insignificance" (126).

Mill's thesis not only belies the ubiquitous myth of Britain's stalwart national character; it also derails the searching political, philosophical, and constitutional debates of the day. Mill himself persistently urged a liberal balance between civil and state authority and between local and centralized government. He also supported a progressive social agenda including popular education, administrative, and democratic reform.[26] Yet, as Mill tells it, none of these liberalizing measures in themselves provides a safeguard against the further decline of individuality. Rather, civilization advances through a self-perpetuating dynamic: as the scale and complexity of the "general arrangements" on which individuals depend become ever greater, power increasingly passes from individuals to masses. Political forms—for example, local as opposed to centralized government—reverse the alienation of power only insofar as they are successful in fortifying individuality.[27]

For Mill the moral and intellectual consequences of individual disempowerment are devastating. It is in this respect that Mill's thought, for all its gradualism, most closely approximates that of his revolutionary contemporary Karl Marx.[28] With so few "inducements to call forth energy of character," Mill writes, the majority of people are motivated by nothing but the desire for wealth (129). Such embourgeoisement is vastly amplified by the influence of mass culture. Urban anonymity reduces the significance, even the possibility, of individual repute. Tradesmen resort to exaggerated advertisements to attract would-be patrons. Newspapers speak "in the same voice at once," disseminating ideas with the speed of a telegraph, and facilitating an all but "irresistible" popular will (125). Reading matter is produced at so prodigious a pace that the "world . . . gorges itself with intellectual food, and in order to swallow the more, *bolts* it" (134 n). Representation begins visibly to dominate reality: success "depends not upon what a person is, but what he seems" (133). Depersonalization advances— regardless of entrenched resistance to bureaucratic forms—as a function of the sheer scale, pace, and multiplicity of civilized social relations. For Mill, as for Marx and Engels, modern civilization thus entails a systematic "suppression of individuality" (*German* 464).

Whereas eighteenth-century thinkers such as Bentham had touted the virtues of public opinion, Mill shows that opinion itself has become both the product and the agent of specious value: "The individual becomes so lost in the crowd, that though he depends more and more upon opinion, he is apt to depend less and less on well-grounded opinion" (132). Mill is but a step away from the homogenized masses he drew in *On Liberty* (1859) more than twenty years later: ruled by the "despotism of Custom," tyrannized by popular norms, leveled by conformity in education, politics, commerce, and the arts. For Mill civilization thus foments "so great a mass of influences hostile to Individuality, that it is not easy to see how it can stand its ground" (117, 121).

Mill's ideas for combating these trends illustrate his drift from the Benthamite stance of his father. In a general (and important) sense Mill articulates the germ of *positive* liberty: the anti-laissez-faire-ist notion that progress will be retarded so long as societies "slumber, and leave things to themselves" ("Civilization" 136). Significantly, however, in "Civilization" Mill's main vision of positive action is to strengthen "the influence of superior minds over the multitude" (135). Mill's Coleridgean interest in producing a tier of intellectual pastors thus anticipates Gladstone's mid-Victorian civil service agenda, and Matthew Arnold's idea of "Culture": in each of these cases the elevation of the many is seen to depend on authorizing and diffusing the cultivation of the few. Such explicit appeals to social hierarchy have earned Mill the reputation of an "aristocratic liberal" (see Kahan).[29]

Seen from this perspective, Mill occupies the vanguard role he enjoys in Raymond Williams's account of English social thought (*Culture* 49). Mill's critique, which was itself indebted to Tocqueville, reappears as the darker side of Trollope's midcentury writing.[30] Decades later, in the wake of national education and adult male enfranchisement, Gissing decried a generation of youth sufficiently educated to read, but "incapable of sustained attention" (*New Grub Street* 496). Williams has rightly emphasized the danger of such reflexive recoil from the popular: "There are in fact no masses," he urges, "only ways of seeing people as masses" (*Culture* 300). From this view Mill's stirring critique is at the forefront of an earnest but elitist line of liberal thinking, the counterproductive effect of which is to reify the classed, gendered, and racialized boundaries between high culture and low.

But, as the parallels with Foucault suggest, Mill's legacy is not reducible to that elitist tendency. Rather, in "Civilization" Mill articulated what is, in effect, one of the first postmodernist analyses of modern society. As Regenia Gagnier has argued, the 1890s, which saw the burgeoning of a mass consumer culture, "initiated an ideology of choice dependent on the proliferation of images" (*Idylls* 54).[31] Mill's "postmodernist" move was not only to foresee the reign of representation in a commodity culture, but also to articulate its impact on the individual as a "mass of influences." As in Foucault's late works, Mill describes a society in which individuals are free to choose the terms of their own subjugating dependence. It is because power is, for Mill as for Foucault, conceived as a mode of action on the action of others that societies retain a glimmering potential for liberation. Both thinkers visualize this as the potential for diversifying individuality and enhancing the exercise of individual power. Yet for both Mill and Foucault this emancipatory project—the project of promoting "new forms of subjectivity"—is, paradoxically, a veritable minefield of potentially "perverse effects" (Foucault, "Subject" 216; "Social" 160). Indeed, in his final reflection on the Enlightenment project, Foucault asked, "How can the growth of capabilities be disconnected from the intensification of power relations?" ("Enlightenment" 48). For Mill, as for Foucault, pastorship—the means by which to build individuality without homogenizing individuals—is the central problematic of a modern liberal society.

Hence, Mill can in many respects illuminate the study of Victorian governmentalization as much as Foucault himself. Although Mill's works demonstrate that nineteenth-century Britain was, for all its liberal allegiances, subject to perverse effects, Britain's history remains significantly distinct from the Continental examples studied by Foucault. Mill's contemporaries, I have demonstrated, jealously withheld ruling power from the state. The state they built was imagined as the guarantor of private property and, to a certain extent, as a neutral seat from which the civilized character of enlightened gentlemen might be gradually diffused. It was not until after World War I that the state was viewed as a bureaucratic structure through which to implement the policies of professional experts. To the contrary, Mill's contemporaries fought zealously to reserve that function for themselves; to safeguard the personalized quality of pastoral power, or— from another view—to neglect pastorship altogether.

Hence, in the British context the study of governmentalization becomes, in Mill's terms, the question of how so-called self-government failed to be the government of "each by himself," and became instead the government "of each by all the rest" (*Liberty* 46). Or, to put the same problem in Gagnier's terms, governmentalization is the question of how the individual's power to choose devolved into "an ideology of choice"—as powerless to emancipate individuals as is an uninformed public opinion to warrant the integrity of a representative democracy. Such a view of governmentalization demands a critical practice sensitive to the distinctive textures of Britain's liberal past: to its material history, to the kinds of social relations facilitated by that history, to the philosophical frame that gave those relations subjective meaning, and to the literary texts through which that frame was represented. It is to the further development of such a critical practice that the remaining chapters aim to contribute.

CHAPTER TWO

Making the Working Man Like Me

Charity, the Novel and the New Poor Law

> It will be observed that the measures which we have suggested are in-
> tended to produce rather negative than positive effects; rather to remove
> the debasing influences to which a large portion of the labouring popula-
> tion is now subject, than to afford new means of prosperity and virtue. We
> are perfectly aware, that for the general diffusion of right principles and
> habits we are to look, not so much to any economic arrangements and
> regulation as to the influence of a moral and religious education. . . . But
> one great advantage of any measure which shall remove or diminish the
> evils of the [Old Poor Law] is, that it will in the same degree remove the
> obstacles which now impede the progress of instruction, and interrupt its
> results; and will afford a free scope to the operation of every instrument
> which may be employed for elevating the intellectual and moral condition
> of the poorer classes.
>
> —*Report . . . for Inquiring into the Administration and*
> *Practical Operation of the Poor Laws*

Britain's early-nineteenth-century middle classes coalesced from within a pressured moral worldview. Despite the advance of materialist thinking, liberal discourses of various kinds testified to the profoundly moral bearing of character
and community. In this chapter I focus on the impact of charity and the poor
laws. The 1834 Poor Law Amendment Act (the "New Poor Law") was discernibly influenced by a certain kind of Benthamite thinking. But to recognize
this influence is neither to equate the post-1834 workhouse with Bentham's
Panopticon, nor to argue that the panopticism Foucault describes in *Discipline
and Punish* was, through poor law reform, generalized by analogous means.[1] Although Edwin Chadwick influenced the administrative shape of the act, the notion of deterrent poor laws had in fact originated among the landowning gentry. It was their (economically desirable) shift from paternalism to a view in
which Providence sanctioned individual responsibility which paved the way for

reform. Such religious and, on the whole, conservative applications of political economy were more influential during this period than the Benthamites' radical, secular, and pro-bureaucratic variations on the theme.[2]

Hence, in the view of its Whig and liberal Tory supporters, the New Poor Law was a "negative" (laissez-faire) measure, intended to promote individual self-reliance, and to empower local ratepayers. In theory the law would reduce pauperism by implementing the "workhouse test": limiting all relief to the deterrent confines of the workhouse. This policy would, in turn, facilitate "less eligibility," ensuring that the situation of the dependent inmate "not be made really or apparently so eligible as the situation of the independent labourer of the lowest class" (Chadwick, "New" 499). Theory and practice widely diverged, however, because the Poor Law Commission was not empowered to enforce the workhouse test. In addition, even cooperative parishes were often unable to reduce "eligibility" in the manner prescribed, since the condition of the lowliest independent laborer was typically beneath bare subsistence. In general, however, the act's political supporters were banking on the salutary effects of rationalized local government, not centralized intervention. By replacing antiquated parish methods with elected boards of thrifty ratepayers, the Whigs hoped to promote efficiency-minded management by liberal or "self-governing" means (Parry 125–26).

Modifying popular behavior was, of course, central to that end, but government's contribution, the reformers argued, would consist primarily in removing the "debasing influences" of the past. The Old Poor Law had interfered with the natural order, as it was now conceived, by encouraging laborers to ask what the parish was "bound to do for [them]," not what they were bound to do for themselves (Loch, "Pauperism" 130). Hence, the 1834 act's remedy was a policy that, by making poor relief a punitive last resort, annulled laborers' traditional rights to parish support. So far from a carceral regime, the new law made paupers feel like "unwelcome guest[s]" (S. and B. Webb, *English* 269; cf. K. Williams 88). As represented in New Poor Law propaganda, such as Harriet Martineau's *Poor Laws and Paupers Illustrated* (1833–34), a "less eligible" workhouse policy worked almost magically, transforming paupers into industrious aspirants to middle-class status within a matter of days.

To be sure, Edwin Chadwick, the Benthamite disciple who became zealous secretary to the Poor Law Commission, had a more far-reaching vision in mind. Ever the ambitious technocrat, Chadwick saw the reform of the Old Poor Law as a prelude to centralized education and policing. But, in aiming to implement pastoral measures by centralized legislative means, Chadwick ran counter to the sentiments of most of his contemporaries, including the elite Whigs on whose favor he was professionally dependent (see Finer 147–53; Donajgrodzki, "Social Police"). The middle- and upper-class Britons who supported the New Poor Law were fearful of unchecked pauperism and deeply preoccupied with working-class morality. These anxieties helped to justify the law's most controversial (and Benthamite) feature: the formation of a centralized commission to gather information and oversee local reforms. Yet to appoint a body to provide "general directions" for the benefit of "local self-government" was not, Lord John Russell made clear, to install a Continental-style pastoral bureaucracy (qtd. in Fraser 53). "We are perfectly aware," wrote the Royal commissioners, that legislative "arrangements and regulation" are not the appropriate means through which to seek the "general diffusion of right principles" (qtd. in Loch, "Controverted" 238–39). Implicit in this statement was the core belief that, as one leading Whig asserted in 1832, all efforts "to make men good by law" are doomed to fail (Lewis qtd. in Mandler, "Tories" 90). Hence, here, as so often in Victorian discourse, the privileging of the personal and moral over the bureaucratic and legal asserted itself even in a document that is widely regarded as the forerunner to modern bureaucracy in Britain.

The 1834 act can be regarded as a Benthamite measure for at least three reasons: its tacit behavior-modifying appeal to individual self-interest (the crux of "less eligibility"), its introduction of centralized administrative oversight, and its attempt to displace a personalized "character" test with an impersonal test of economic need. Chadwick's influence notwithstanding, there is much evidence to suggest that the latter feature was adopted reluctantly. The framers, that is, recognized the claims of good character to an exemption from punitive poor relief. But in large towns especially they foresaw the difficulty of adjudicating on such delicate matters. The Old Poor Law had presumed a society of stable communities and face-to-face relationships; a social order in which "the profligacy or industry of each individual [would] be known."[3] Under modern conditions, the commissioners reasoned, local officials would be unable completely to dispel the "impression" of unjust decision making and might, therefore, resort either to "indiscriminately granting or indiscriminately refusing relief." Hence, the advisability, however alien to the prevailing mind-set, of replacing personalized assessments of character with "fixed rules and tests that can be depended upon" (qtd. in Loch, "Controverted" 250). Here, then, in the Royal Commission's ambivalent (and largely unsuccessful) attempt to implement the impersonal workhouse test, irrespective of character, was the act's most ambitious imposition of bureaucratic uniformity on a resistant culture.

The New Poor Law should not, therefore, be regarded as the moment in which bureaucratic authority became the dominant mode in Victorian governance. Rather, as local authorities clashed with Somerset House, and practice diverged from theory, the New Poor Law worked unevenly to meet the standards of "calculability" which, as Max Weber has shown, are necessary to capitalist development. In analyzing Britain's idiosyncratic modernization, Weber distinguished between a modern (calculable and depersonalized) rationality and bureaucracy, a structure through which that rationality might be implemented. In this chapter, as elsewhere, I follow Weber in arguing that Victorian Britain adopted certain forms of bureaucratic rationality (however variably and reluctantly) but, by and large, implemented that rationality through distinctively British structures and social relations, in contrast to the state bureaucracies of the Continent.

Hence, to view the New Poor Law from within the culture that produced it, it is crucial to recognize the contiguity of philanthropy and other voluntary practices, especially as they shaped the moral self-perceptions of the increasingly powerful middle classes. For these newly enfranchised citizens were, as Jerome Christensen writes, committed to forwarding "the Enlightenment project of homogenizing mankind in the guise of the bourgeoisie" (28). In so doing, middle-class moral reformers tended to disdain statist solutions, aiming instead to reconstitute a "common morality" by restoring personal contact between rich and poor (Storch 156; cf. 147).

In *Discipline and Punish* Foucault contrasts France's centralized state to the "private religious groups that," in Britain, had "for a long time" executed "the functions of social discipline" (213; cf. "Space" 241, 247). For the most part new historicist critics have left this distinction unexplored. Their inclination to do so is, perhaps, connected to historians' practical tendency to treat charity and the poor laws as two specialized and, therefore, discrete fields of inquiry. What historians have provided is a kind of split-screen approach to documenting nineteenth-century attitudes and responses to social welfare. Immersed in sifting between the theory and the practice of the New Poor Law, one is hardly aware of the degree to which these statist developments were overshadowed by voluntary and philanthropic endeavors. Reviewing the history of charity, it is not always clear how ardent middle-class volunteers saw their civilizing mission in relation to the gradual expansion and modernization of the state.

In the readings that follow I attempt to bridge this critical gap by focusing on the tensions between the world as structured by charitable relations and that by the 1834 act's underlying modern rationality. These tensions, I must emphasize, are not reducible to a battle between old-fashioned religious authority and its modern secular antagonists. Political economy was often understood in decidedly Christian and Evangelical terms: as the workings of Providence. Britain's civic-minded philanthropists were at the vanguard of the rising interest in statistics and social science, even as they resisted "un-English" centralization. Hence, those who were the most invested in the liberal ideal of self-reliant individuals and communities often spearheaded innovations that later became associated with the bureaucratic state.

In the following chapter I look at a diverse range of social texts, asking what was at stake for a self-consciously moral and newly enfranchised middle class when the conditions under which support was provided for the impoverished were altered to suit rationalized and legalized politico-economic conceptions of the individual and society. To what extent did the act's tacit privileging of *homo economicus* subvert the antibourgeois ideal of *homo civicus*, reversing what Thomas Chalmers had upheld as "the ascendancy of the moral over the material part of our constitution" (3:288)? My focus, therefore, is not the impact on working-class lives, but on the worldview of the governing classes.

In answering these questions, it is also necessary to distinguish between two modes of modern representation. On the one hand, I describe an increasingly bourgeois tendency to judge individuals in terms of economic and other materialistic criteria. On the other, I describe a social scientific rationality in which individuals were evaluated in terms of the objectifying knowledge of the new human sciences. It was by and large the former, I suggest, which posed the most immediate and perceptible threat to moral ideals as the post–New Poor Law stress on material prosperity fomented competitive individualism and bourgeois pretense. But charitable movements—even as they attempted to cure bourgeois ills, cultivate personalized bonds, and keep legislative alternatives at bay—were, at the same time, pioneering many of the social scientific methods that, in the twentieth century, became the province of the welfare state.

I begin with a discussion of charity, arguing that the idea of a civilizing mission, predicated on personalized pastoral relationships between rich and poor, was central to establishing the moral authority of the urban middle class. Then I move to the New Poor Law, focusing on Harriet Martineau's propagandistic *Poor Laws* series. The next two sections discuss two popular novels that negotiated the divide between charitable ideals and post–New Poor Law embour-geoisement: Charles Dickens's *Oliver Twist* (1837–38) and Frances Trollope's *Jessie Phillips* (1842–43). I conclude the chapter by placing these questions of character and worldview within a wider historiographic frame, integrating my analyses of New Poor Law literature with the work of recent poor law historians.

Making the Working Man like Me

For many middle-class Britons the new preoccupation with working-class morality was part of the quest to translate economic gains into cultural and political power. Campaigning in 1868, J. A. Roebuck, the prominent radical member of Parliament, claimed that his lifelong object had been "to make the working man as . . . civilized a creature as I could make him"; "*I wanted to make the working man like me*" (qtd. in R. Johnson, "Educating" 90). In so doing, Roebuck articulated a civilizing mission that had become a defining focus for many Victorians, inside and out of radical circles. The project of "mak[ing] the working man like me" entailed an idealized vision of Christian and civic community based on charitable bonds and their pastoral effects.

Historians have begun to emphasize the profoundly relational aspects of Victorian philanthropy, and its role in constituting middle-class power. The church and the urban mission, writes Simon Gunn, were "key institutions in the social organization of urban property holders and a natural focus for collective action" (35). Howard M. Wach has described a bourgeois sphere of emotional intimacy founded on religious institutions, domestic life, and literary self-consciousness. According to such a Habermasian paradigm, religion and the home became the source of "transcendent values" that were politically energized in the public sphere. Through a range of improving activities—lectures and statistical societies as well as charity—middle-class Britons constructed the moral identity upon which their class agency depended. The civic culture they built in provincial cities such as Manchester imposed order on a growing urban mass, quite apart from the aegis of the nineteenth-century state (Wach, "Civil Society" 285–87; "Unitarian" 541–42; Habermas, *Structural* 43–51).

Britain's middle classes thus enhanced their individual and collective agency by partaking in self-consciously moral and moralizing activities. Although they took place in the public sphere, as moral activities (rather than business or politics), they were commensurate with the aims of the middle-class family. "It is from" the secret fountains of "domestic life," Sarah Ellis gushed in a representative panegyric on the middle-class home, "that those streams of affection are supplied, from which we have to draw, in our intercourse with society, and with the world" (83). Ellis's conduct manuals testify to the perceived desirability of a Habermasian link between domestic affections and the public sphere. Through such rhetoric it was possible to imagine civic life as an extension of one's own homely realm—in other words, as personal. Troubling differences between private sanctuary and public marketplace, between domestic cooperation and capitalist rivalry, between feminine self-sacrifice and masculine competition were, at least provisionally, superseded by a notion of civil society in which private and public mores were intimately linked and seamlessly bound.

This perceived crossover between private and public life was both practically and symbolically reinforced by charity. Charity's ostensibly familial bonds provided a means of maintaining social discipline while simultaneously intensifying the moral mission at the heart of middle-class identity. Drawing on gift theory to explain this process, Alan J. Kidd points out that middle-class charity presumed to alleviate poverty—to make the working man like me—without challenging the entrenched social inequalities between donors and recipients. Kidd thus reasons that the Victorian "obsession" with character, including the determination to withhold charity from the "undeserving" poor, was a means to simulating mutual exchange between unequal actors. Impoverished recipients of charity "reciprocated" by exhibiting moral probity and, in so doing, enhanced the status of their benefactors (183, 186–87).

Kidd's anthropological analysis of Victorian charity illuminates the intersubjective ideal at the core of the middle classes' character-building project. Belief in the intersubjective potential of certain social relations, like the putative quid pro quo between middle-class benevolence and laboring-class moral improvement, helped to reconcile otherwise glaring contradictions between hierarchy and equality in Britain's self-consciously liberal society.[4] Charitable pastorship purported to provide a common investment in character building: a basis on which to unite individuals and to bridge private and public lives. Just as important, character itself—whether construed in humanist or Christian fashion—provided a conceptual basis for the potential equality that intersubjectivity described. Because it was measured in moral terms, equality of character might be seen as a basis for social cohesion and collective purpose regardless of economic or political differences between classes or, for that matter, sexes.

In the following discussions I emphasize the importance of this ideal of mutuality between *moral* equals, an ideal founded rhetorically in the language of

the personal. Personality, by which I mean the attributes of intimacy and famil-
iarity which symbolically authenticate certain social relations, enlivened the
dream of intersubjectivity. Personal bonds between aspiring moral equals promised to fill what Chalmers had decried as the "mighty unfilled space between the
high and the low" (1:27). Such rhetorical emphases provided a crucial symbolic
space in which provisionally to transcend competitive relations, class divisions,
and political and sexual inequalities.[5] Thus, in the dynamic decades prior to and
just after male middle-class enfranchisement in 1832, Britain's socially ascendant commercial and professional classes constructed a self-authorizing vision
of a moral, liberatory civic culture overseen by middle-class pastorship. Charitable
giving, whether or not it included the committed pastorship of the "home ministry," was thus a defining middle-class experience (see Behlmer, *Friends* 31–73).

Thomas Chalmers and the Christian and Civic Community

It is not enough that you give money, you must give it with judgment. You must
give your time and attention. You must descend to the trouble of examination:
for instance, will charity corrupt him into slothfulness? What is his particular
necessity? Is it the want of health or the want of employment? Is it the pressure
of a numerous family? You must go to the poor man's sick-bed. You must lend
your hand to the work of assistance. You must examine his accounts. You must
try to recover those wages which are detained by the injustice or the rapacity of
the master. You must employ your mediation with his superiors, and represent
to them the necessities of the situation.

— THOMAS CHALMERS, *On Charity*

Charity once extended an invisible chain of sympathy between the higher and
lower ranks of society, which has been destroyed by the luckless pseudo-
philanthropy of the [Old Poor Law]. Few aged or decrepid [sic] pensioners now
gratefully receive the visits of the higher classes—few of the poor seek the counsel, the admonitions, and assistance of the rich in the period of the inevitable
accidents of life. The bar of the overseer is however crowded with the sturdy
applicants for a legalized relief, who regard the distributor of this bounty as their
stern and merciless oppressor, instructed by the compassionless rich to reduce to
the lowest possible amount the alms which the law wrings from their reluctant
hands. This disruption of the natural ties has created a wide gulph [sic] between

the higher and lower orders of the community, across which, the scowl of hatred
banishes the smile of charity and love

— DR. JAMES PHILLIPS KAY, *The Moral and Physical*
Condition of the Working Classes . . . in Manchester

Significantly, social inequality posed no philosophical dilemma for Thomas
Chalmers, the early-nineteenth-century Scottish evangelical whose model of organized charity became an important foundation for nearly all subsequent endeavors of this kind. Although "pauperism" was a modern nemesis requiring immediate redress, "poverty," Chalmers believed, was God's way of ensuring that
communities be formed over mutual obligations of benevolence and need
(Brown 119–20). As a Christian political economist, Chalmers contended that
"a right moral is essential to a right economic condition" ("Dr. Thomas
Chalmers" 375). In this respect Chalmers both unwittingly served bourgeois interests, and anticipated the antibourgeois critiques of John Ruskin and William
Morris, as well as the municipal socialism of the fin de siècle.[6]

In *The Christian and Civic Economy of Large Towns* (1821–26) Chalmers combined the providential worldview of the enlightened moralist with charitable visiting methods eventually adopted by professional social workers. The latter aspect of his legacy has prompted Mary Poovey to stress the likeness between
Chalmers's philanthropic network and Edwin Chadwick's poor law design. But
to view Chalmers as a bureaucratic prototype—or, for that matter, an aristocratic
throwback—is to risk missing what is most distinctive in a figure capable of
evoking both characterizations. Crucial to understanding Chalmers is recognizing the intersubjective moral assumptions underlying his idealized vision of
the pastoral relation and the rhetoric of personality which helped to sustain it.

Chalmers's pastoral community was offered as an alternative to the pernicious
interference of the Old Poor Law. Abolishing the law, he argued, "would . . .
do much to bring out those otherwise checked and superseded sympathies, that,
in the flow of their kindly and spontaneous exercise, are more fitted to bind the
community . . . than all the legalised charities of our land" (1:57). Charity,
Chalmers wrote, was the "spontaneous" "free-will offering" of individuals. Poor
relief, by contrast, transformed "a matter of love, into a matter of angry litiga-
tion" (qtd. in Hilton 101). In 1817, fifteen years before the Royal Commission
that brought Chadwick to the fore, Chalmers unveiled a plan to abolish poor
laws entirely. Local clergymen, teachers, and responsible parishioners must unite
to minister to the needy *personally*.[7]

Chalmers's chief aim in combating pauperism was moral, not economic. Like the proponents of the New Poor Law, he sought to inculcate laborers' self-reliance; but, whereas the former purposed to rely almost entirely on negative deterrence, Chalmers urged positive pastoral intervention. The "disciples of political science," he warned, must look to "men who are fitted to expatiate among the people"—in other words, to pastors—in order to elevate that "element of character" without which "the country will never attain a healthful condition" (1:10–11). Chadwick touted the financial savings of the New Poor Law, and only later campaigned for educational "prevention" (see Finer 147–48). By contrast, Chalmers sought to devote ratepayers' savings to the further proliferation of local pastoral institutions: to churches and schools. The ideal laboring-class community would sustain itself through individual self-help aided by kinship and community support. Neither poor laws nor the indiscriminate help of the rich, Chalmers insisted, ought to "arrest a process so beautiful" as "the Help of the Poor for Each Other" (qtd. in Young and Ashton 76). Nevertheless, underlying this ideal of the self-sufficient laboring-class neighborhood was Chalmers's tacitly hierarchical notion of charity.

Chalmers saw charity as an active Christian principle—integral to the path of achieving "Christian freedom"—not a passive obligation like the rates paid to maintain a poor law. Like Francis Hutcheson and Adam Smith, he held that moral propensities were innate; but, he insisted, the self-discipline of true Christians surpassed mere human instinct. The Christian's duty was to extend the realm of positive principle, transforming society into "a godly commonwealth of Christian communities" (Brown 111–12). Charity thus consisted not only in a monetary exchange but also (and more primarily) in a pastoral exchange involving the "judgment," "examination," and "time and attention" of donors. For Chalmers, in other words, charity described a deeply interpersonal relation: "that benevolence which moved the giver to sift each case, even at the cost of self-sacrifice in time and energy, so that the relief forthcoming was the most likely to promote the moral character and the sturdy independence that was [its] chief aim" (Young and Ashton 75). For the same reason, philanthropic work must remain a local endeavor with each pastor "concentrat[ing] the full influence of his character and office, on his own distinct and separate" precinct (1:96).

To implement an experimental ministry of this kind, Chalmers eventually persuaded Glasgow's town council to create a new parish, St. Johns (see Brown 124–51; Young and Ashton 70–72). Devising methods that would later be adopted by professional social workers, he divided St. Johns into twenty-five "proportions," each overseen by a trained deacon. Chalmers's deacons—volunteers chosen from among his most devoted and well-off parishioners—were instructed to visit each home on a regular basis and encourage individual and community self-reliance. When that failed, they were to assist in finding suitable employment for a destitute applicant or, if necessary, to make small donations of their own. Only after exhausting these methods and after securing the agreement of another deacon was any applicant to be granted a regular stipend from parish funds.

Chalmers thus advised a combination of tireless vigilance and Christian benevolence. Deacons should carefully investigate and monitor the character of each inhabitant while attempting to win the "confidence and regard" even of the most disreputable (qtd. in Brown 132–33). This "ardent zeal" for "household visitations," combined with Chalmers's well-known reputation for electrifying sermons, helped to create a legendary public persona. The *Encyclopedia Britannica*'s late-century description of St. Johns evokes an almost supernatural pastoral agency. Dr. Chalmers, it claims, presided over "the whole of this complicated parochial apparatus," "watching" and "controlling every movement" while providing more than "mere superintendence" (375; cf. Brown 102).

In her comparison of Chalmers and Chadwick, Poovey is as interested in these "charismatic" aspects of Chalmers's influence as she is in the formal similarities between Chalmers's voluntary organization and Chadwick's legislative mechanisms. "The point of juxtaposing Chalmers's [charismatic] preaching with the New Poor Law," Poovey explains, is "to argue that both the incitement of the former and the coercion of the latter installed *disciplinary individualism* as the normative model of agency for most British subjects for most of the nineteenth century" (*Making* 112; emph. added). For Poovey disciplinary individualism, a Foucauldian concept, describes a paradigmatic paradox: the individual's "voluntary" compliance with a rationalized order (99). As she first describes this effect in relation to Chalmers's public speaking and then details the course of his pastoral organization, Poovey makes several important observations. Despite profound ideological and political differences, Chalmers's voluntary network and the New Poor Law were formally similar: both "combined local implementation with central oversight" (105).[8] Urging self-imposed restraint over working-class sexuality and middle-class commerce, Chalmers preached an "abandonment of self to the social." Poovey therefore concludes by likening the disciplinary outcomes of charisma and bureaucracy: both result in "a universal and voluntary surrender of self to the larger whole" (104, 106).

Poovey's description of the nineteenth-century subject thus reduces volition to the paradoxical effect of a disciplinary process—whether that process involves charismatic incitement or bureaucratic coercion, and whether its target is upstanding ratepayers or destitute laborers. In so doing, she bypasses a pervasive tension between free will and social determinism which, as Catherine Gallagher and Amanda Anderson have shown, exercised many contemporaries.[9] In book 6 of *A System of Logic* (1843) John Stuart Mill rejected the equivalence, central to Poovey's analysis, between incited and coerced action. Indeed, for Mill the desire to emulate those we admire—to respond to a "strong feeling of admiration or aspiration"—illustrates the human capacity for autonomy at work. Although not all individuals will attain it, self-direction of this kind imbues the individual with an empowering consciousness of "moral freedom." "A person feels morally free," Mill writes, "who feels that his habits or his temptations are not his masters but he theirs" (*System* 840–41; cf. A. Anderson, *Tainted* 23–40). Hence, the difference between what Poovey describes (disciplinary individualism), and what Mill seeks to assert (the potential for individual autonomy), is the difference between the mastered self of a disciplinary regime, and the self-mastery of a free moral agent. Moreover, the theistic counterpart to Mill's secular concept is Chalmers's "Christian freedom." Through adherence to Christian principles, Chalmers held, individuals liberate themselves from the limitations of merely instinctual motives.

To be sure, some may doubt whether there is any meaningful difference between the self-mastery Mill and Chalmers describe, and what Poovey defines as voluntary compliance to a rationalized order. The difference can be captured by considering the goals of a society based on each. Whether from Chalmers's Christian and Scottish philosophical standpoint, or Mill's secular and utilitarian alternative, understanding individuals as autonomous moral agents allows for a conception of society as composed by intersubjective relations—a goal to which no dominatory regime could aspire. Recognizing the importance of this aim is crucial to understanding the conflict between the mode of modern selfhood inscribed by self-authorizing charity, and that by the depersonalizing bureaucratic rationality of the New Poor Law.

That Poovey does not acknowledge the centrality of an intersubjective ideal in the nineteenth-century British worldview is suggested by her analysis of Chalmers's charismatic public speaking, the immediate effect of which, she asserts, was "a scene of discipline." With Foucault's equation between human subjectivities and the effects of power on docile bodies clearly in mind, Poovey details how "the bodies of more than 1400 people" were "disciplined . . . into a single body." But the ultimate disciplinary effect of the preaching, she explains, was "emulation" (*Making* 102, 105). In so saying, Poovey makes no distinction between the total "surrender of self" entailed in the merger of fourteen hundred bodies and the arguably different self-surrender—a form of deliberate moral self-making like that described by Mill—of the parishioner who consciously emulates Chalmers by partaking in pastoral work and, potentially, "inciting" his or her own charismatic effects. Chalmers's preaching, she writes, "created a single social body from the competitive individualism that supposedly guaranteed and signified freedom and autonomy in a market society" (102). Here Poovey invokes a narrowly bourgeois economic creed, laissez faire, to describe a notion of freedom and autonomous individuality which, in Chalmers's view, depended on man's latent moral instinct and his capacity for Christian transcendence. Secular political economists erred, according to Chalmers, precisely because they trusted all to a negative premise: the "unfettered principles of nature." In actuality, he insisted, the liberalization of society depended on a positive pastoral imperative to "pervade" a man's being, "raising the whole tone of his mind" and "infusing . . . along with the elements of passion and interest, the elements of duty, and of wisdom, and of self-estimation" (1:10). For Chalmers competitive individualism no more described freedom than the model of *homo economicus* defined the true Christian. Rather, freedom was immanent in the positive duty to build a godly commonwealth of Christian communities. Both individual autonomy and the intersubjective ideal might, in other words, be achieved through untiring personal efforts to improve working-class morality.

Poovey thus overlooks the intersubjective utopianism at the heart of prominent strains of liberal thinking. But there are other aspects of her critique which warrant the closest regard. Poovey's point—that bureaucracies profess to provide the institutional means through which to generalize charismatic individuality (105)—is crucial.[10] In the case of Chalmers the historical record testifies to the depersonalizing and repressive consequences of bureaucratization. According to Stewart Brown, "most St. John's deacons, although zealous about decreasing pauperism, neglected the other, more demanding responsibility Chalmers had assigned to them—that of serving as friend and adviser to the community." In a way that unquestionably lessens the difference between Chalmers's positive pastoral ethic and the New Poor Law's negative deterrence, Brown concludes that Chalmers failed sufficiently "to emphasize [the deacons'] communal responsibilities," allowing them "to evolve into an impersonal and perhaps callous group of poor-relief managers" (135).

Yet we still must distinguish between the contradictory practice that empirical research may reveal, and the rhetorical claims and philosophical assumptions that are the critic's special concern. Poovey stresses that Chalmers delegated supervisory responsibility to the deacons because "the parish was too large for one man to cover" (102). But Chalmers's professed goal was also to multiply, not monopolize, the pastoral role. Indeed, the perceived reciprocity between the charity of the rich and the moral improvement of the poor was, for Chalmers, the mainspring of a liberal social order. Superimposing the Enlightenment's progressive teleology on a sacrosanct notion of social hierarchy, he insisted that philanthropy's unequal social relation culminated in the enhanced moral autonomy of the recipient. In so doing, he helped to invent a modern liberal and middle-class (rather than aristocratic) version of paternalism, predicated on the theoretical perfectibility of human character. "We certainly invite . . . [the committed philanthropist] to assume a locality to himself, and head an enterprise for schools, in behalf of its heretofore neglected population," Chalmers wrote. But far better, he insisted, was to guide the poor in becoming "the most effective instruments of their own amelioration" (qtd. in McCaffrey 59).

The institutional embodiment of this process through which guidance from above culminated in self-reliance below was the parish school. Because it encouraged "frequent intercourse between the higher and lower orders of life," schooling facilitated the symbolic balance between social hierarchy and moral equality (Chalmers, qtd. in McCaffrey 47). Parochial education might, in the words of John McCaffrey, "close the divisions of urban society through a mutual early experience in the republic of letters" (47). As a professor of moral philosophy, Chalmers replaced impersonal lectures with viva voce examinations in order to enter "into [the] closest . . . and most stimulating contact with his pupils" ("Dr. Thomas Chalmers" 376). At the popular level Chalmers supported the innovative pedagogy of David Stow, one of his Glasgow parishioners. Stow's stress on "convincing the judgment and impressing the conscience" of pupils (Brown 136), regardless of their class and gender, helped to persuade early-Victorian Britain's chief educational official, Sir James Kay-Shuttleworth, to advocate popular education based on "love" rather than the "fear of punishment" or the "hope of reward" ("Pauper" 31; cf. Brown 106, Selleck 134–38).

Through the parish school, wrote Chalmers, "that very influence which binds the teacher to the families, does, though by a looser and feebler tie, bind the families to each other. One great desideratum in large towns is acquaintance-ship among the contiguous families. And to promote this, every arrangement it-self right, should be promoted which brings out the indwellers of one vicinity to one common place of repair, and brings upon them one common ministra-tion" (1:59). Like the church's deacons, parish schoolteachers occupied the so-cially superior place in an exchange between pastoral benefactors and benefici-aries. To neutralize the potentially disruptive effects of social inequality, Chalmers described the pastoral relation between teachers and the community as an extension of family ties. The teacher's vertical "influence" over the com-munity was likened to the ("looser and feebler") horizontal relations between "contiguous families." Like the sincerest proto-Habermasian, Chalmers thus urged "acquaintanceship" among neighbors. But, rather than stress the com-municative consensus that might unite a civil society so conceived, Chalmers fo-cused, instead, on the unifying force of the pastoral hierarchy. He left no doubt that, in invoking collective public space ("one common place of repair"), his ul-timate object was to enforce a pastoral authority from above ("one common ministration"). The institutions Chalmers had in mind were the parochial churches and schools that he encouraged throughout his life. But the model he sketched might easily include the secular complements (e.g., libraries, lecture halls, and Mechanics' Institutes) increasingly favored by his Victorian succes-sors. Chalmers's vision thus epitomized the ways in which fundamentally au-thoritarian and hierarchical social relations might be rhetorically constructed so as persuasively to evoke a liberal and intersubjective ideal.

Chalmers's early Scottish precedent exerted considerable influence on later Victorian and Edwardian charity movements. But Chalmers was not unique in promulgating a voluntary philosophy in which socially integrated civic institu-tions, underpinned by the vertical bonds of personalized pastorship, were seen to promote ideal communities. Prosperous British and U.S. Unitarians in grow-ing commercial cities such as Boston, Manchester, Liverpool, and London ad-vanced a comparable civic order. Beginning in the 1820s, writes Wach, middle-class "voluntary societies channeled a portion of elite-based wealth into a new urban culture" in which not only charities, churches, and schools, but also lec-ture halls, libraries, and useful-knowledge societies were instituted to impose order on "an incipient mass urban society" ("Unitarian" 541–42). Unitarian the-ology was particularly suited to a civilizing mission of this kind: promoting ab-stract spiritual equality while exhorting the tireless improvement of self and society (McCalman 327–28; cf. R. K. Webb, "Gaskells" and "Emergence"). Inspired by Chalmers's Glasgow example, Joseph Tuckerman, a Boston clergyman admired by many British Unitarians, urged the founding of Domestic Missions on both sides of the Atlantic, to provide "personal contact, counsel, and judiciously distributed material aid" for the downtrodden. In so doing, Tuckerman, like Chalmers, employed bureaucratic means, such as "meticulous records of pastoral visits," to undertake intimate character-building ends (Wach, "Unitarian" 540, 543).

Tuckerman's pastoral ministry was predicated on an idealist philosophical premise like Chalmers's: just as Chalmers asserted the "ascendancy of the moral over the material part of our constitution," so Tuckerman sought to elevate "the character, the mind, the soul" (qtd. in Wach, "Unitarian" 544). Unitarian Domestic Missions thus sought to transcend socioeconomic boundaries by forging bonds that one British disciple described as "heart acting on heart, conscience on conscience, soul on soul, man on man (qtd. in R. K. Webb, "Gaskells" 147). These high-minded intersubjective goals were further promoted by William Ellery Channing, another renowned Boston Unitarian, whose controversial preaching influenced Tuckerman, Ralph Waldo Emerson, Harriet and James Martineau, and Elizabeth Gaskell, to name a few. In works such as "Self-Culture" (1838) Channing urged spiritual rather than materialistic progress, insisting that "degradation of mind" was the most devastating consequence of poverty. A self-described "leveller," Channing sought to "raise the low . . . from a degrading and brutal indigence" (qtd. in Wach, "Unitarian" 545, 546). These influences remained perceptible in Gaskell's *North and South* (1854–55), a novel in which "equality of friendship" is offered as a solution to "unchristian" industrial class conflict (122; cf. Uglow 130). Gaskell's rough-edged mill owner grows from a man with "no general benevolence—no universal philanthropy" to an ardent supporter of voluntary institutions that "attach class to class" through "actual personal contact" (211, 421).[11] Decades later, a similar goal was articulated by Octavia Hill, the daughter of a prominent Unitarian family and a principal figure in the Charity Organization Society (COS). From the 1870s until World War I, Hill and her COS allies resisted the rise of statist welfare polices, urging organized charitable visiting as a means of bringing "the rich and the poor, the educated and uneducated, more and more into communication" (Nord, *Apprenticeship* 121). Chalmers's Glasgow precedent, Unitarian civic culture, and the Charity Organization Society's later efforts to organize charity (as we shall see in chap. 6) thus shared a common vision. In each case organized voluntary practices, with significant governing effects, were justified by, and understood through, the perceived progressive outcome of a personalized approach to "making the working man like me."

Dr. James Phillips Kay and the Manchester Civic Ideal

[The] errors [of the working classes] are not more their fault than their misfortune, and they, who would rescue them from their condition, must depend not alone on elevating them physically, but must seek to produce a strong and permanent moral impression.

— DR. JAMES PHILLIPS KAY, *The Moral and Physical
Condition of the Working Classes . . . in Manchester*

One of the most influential figures to emerge during this period was Dr. James Phillips Kay. A devoted disciple of Chalmers, Kay later became a pioneering civil servant. As an Edinburgh medical student, Kay had befriended Chalmers. In Manchester, where he set out to launch his career, Kay, whose mother was a Unitarian, mingled in prominent Unitarian circles. Indeed, Kay was a veritable paragon of the middle-class civic identity, joining the prestigious Manchester Literary and Philosophical Society, volunteering his professional services to the local medical dispensary, and supporting the Mechanics' Institute and the District Provident Society. As a committed member of the latter society, Kay engaged in Chalmers-like pastoral guidance, visiting the homes of the poor to offer counsel and encourage thrift. In his ongoing correspondence with Chalmers, Kay described such activities as the "best cause," regretting his inability to devote even more time to "directly aiding" the poor through his "own personal exertions" (qtd. in Selleck 79; cf. 51, 80). Chalmers's influence was also evident in Kay's eventual criticism of the medical dispensary. Unlike the character-building philanthropy urged by Chalmers—and like the Old Poor Law—the dispensary, Kay came to believe, thwarted "noble self-reliance" while failing to cultivate personal bonds between patrons and recipients (qtd. in Selleck 81).

The Moral and Physical Condition of the Working Classes . . . in Manchester (1832), Kay's well-known account of his voluntary efforts to prepare a teeming industrial city for the arrival of cholera, set out to articulate a Chalmers-like call to restore a natural social hierarchy. "Charity," he claimed, "once extended an invisible chain of sympathy between the higher and lower ranks of society, which has been destroyed by the luckless pseudo-philanthropy of the [Old Poor] law" (48–49). In order to prevent "explosive violence," the governing classes must restore this bond by winning "confidence" and "promot[ing] domestic comfort, virtue, and knowledge" (112). This pastoral agenda might have been penned by Chalmers himself. Indeed, in a prefatory letter to Chalmers, a distinguishing feature of the second edition, Kay publicly assured his mentor that "the physical and moral elevation of the poor" depended on the "minute personal interference of the higher ranks" (11).[12]

Yet there are other elements in Kay's philosophy which conflict with the personal pastoral ethos and intersubjective ideals he inherited from Chalmers. Kay's text stressed the importance of "statistical investigations"—a practice he later promoted (with the help of prominent Unitarians) through the founding of one of the nation's first statistical societies (Selleck 82–85). Of course, in many ways the Gradgrindian facts thus sought by Manchester's self-appointed social scientists reinforced the aims of the town's self-appointed pastors. Kay was not unique in attempting to fill both roles: simultaneously viewing the poor as objects of middle-class knowledge, and subjects in a reciprocal (if necessarily unequal) pastoral relationship. At Kay's invitation Chalmers became a corresponding member of the statistical society (F. Smith 27). As we have seen, Chalmers employed bureaucratic methods to achieve character-building ends.

Nevertheless, Kay's particular focus on statistics points to important underlying differences. Chalmers envisioned society as an extended family—seamlessly coherent so long as voluntary pastoral relations were dutifully maintained. In Kay's rather different construction, society was a "general mass" that, unlike a living organism, required artificial means to identify dangers within its constituent parts. That is why statistics were so crucial: able to fulfill a social need for which "there is no natural faculty." Statistical inquiries of the kind Continental governments had long conducted were thus necessary to stabilizing the "mutual dependance" that, as Chalmers saw it, itself provided the requisite foundations for collective social life (Kay, *Manchester* 18). Kay thus consciously allied himself not only with charity and Christianized political economy, but also with the emerging human sciences. The result was a profound split. In *Manchester* the social scientist's materialist, environmentalist, and statist tendencies jarred against Chalmers's voluntarist legacy—challenging the primacy of an overarching providence, and the self-authorizing acts of individuals and communities.

Kay thus urged a very different kind of pastorship from Chalmers's. Not only "individual exertion," but also "general enactment" was necessary to ensuring social well-being (13). Britons must arm themselves with "minutely accurate" facts about working-class conditions (19). To stave off physical dangers, Kay urged his readers to authorize "organized centres of medical police," "directed by scientific men" such as Kay himself (13). It was this environmentalist agenda that attracted Chadwick when his interests shifted from the cost-saving intentions of the New Poor Law to the broader social aims of public health. What Chadwick found in *Manchester* were the rudiments of a logic wherein the working-class's *moral* condition followed from its *physical* condition and might, therefore, be regulated by legislative and bureaucratic devices.[13]

It is, nevertheless, easy to understand why, with no benefit of hindsight, Kay was unaware of the split in his thinking. An ardent volunteer who later became a civil servant, the young Kay drew no clear boundaries between citizen action, local government, and centralized oversight. Written prior to the debates surrounding the New Poor Law's controversial centralizing features, *Manchester* bore none of the anxieties that exercised the vehement opponents of "un-English" legislation. With the deliberate exception of the Old Poor Law—one of the main villains of the text—Kay evoked an unfettered civil society in which dynamic cities such as Manchester were free to determine their moral destinies. Like Harriet Martineau, Chalmers, and many others influenced by the rationalist theology of the period, Kay believed in a world intrinsically ordered by "a presiding Providence"; by "the perpetual influence of a mighty source of moral causation" (5). For Kay that meant that "individual exertion" and "general enactment" might be mutually reinforcing endeavors. Kay did not foresee that, from a Benthamite perspective, individuals were subject to selfishness, ignorance, and prejudice and might, for any of these reasons, impede legislative goals. Nor did he foresee that from a Millite perspective legislation might be seen to threaten individual exertion on the grounds that "what is done for the people benefits them only when it assists them in what they do for themselves" (Mill, qtd. in MacDonagh, *Early* 68).

Just as Kay did not foresee the conflict between voluntary and legislative action, so he did not anticipate the ways in which environmentalist emphases might trench upon the philanthropist's most cherished ideals. Kay's demand for "minutely accurate" knowledge about the moral and physical condition of the working classes threatened to transform a putatively intersubjective pastoral exchange into an objectifying relation of power. In effect, Kay called attention to and amplified the empiricist ambitions already latent in the charitable mission—in, for example, Tuckerman's maintenance of detailed records to document the

moral effects of his pastoral activities. In so doing, Kay unwittingly exposed the
conflict between idealist and materialist renderings of the modern individual in
society.[14]

Chadwick's 1842 sanitary *Report* demonstrates the unintended consequences
of Kay's important precedent. Directly influenced by *Manchester*, Chadwick's
groundbreaking *Report* showcased the kind of regulatory devices and statistical
investigations that Kay had recommended. Although Chadwick attempted to
placate his adversaries by balancing centralized oversight with local execution,
he made no significant overtures toward the rhetoric of the personal. Rather,
working-class morality became wholly subject to environment. Although the
Sanitary Idea thus marked Chadwick's shift from a negative politico-economic
philosophy to a positive social program, entirely absent was the direct pastorship
that Kay had described as the "best cause." As the implicitly idealist language
of character was superseded by the explicitly materialist and increasingly technical language of "conditions," the idea of pastorship as a reciprocal, mutually
humanizing, and potentially intersubjective social relation faded from view.

Kay's 1835 switch from private doctor and citizen activist to zealous Assistant
Poor Law commissioner further demonstrates the potential affinities between
Chalmers's legacy and the New Poor Law.[15] Kay had argued that "the evils suffered by the poor" often "flow[ed] from their own ignorance or moral errors"—
a premise as complementary to the new regime as to Chalmers's philosophy
(*Manchester* 5). Yet Kay had sketched a vision of poor law reform in which pastorship, not deterrence, dominated. Kay advocated the recruitment of local administrators (with no centralized oversight) to undertake comprehensive pastoral duties. The Old Poor Law regime was manifestly incompetent to
"discriminate" individual character. But, he maintained, a "superior" body of officials could achieve the ends of personalized charity (49, 50). If "men of some
education," "of high moral character," and "possessing great natural gentleness"
were employed to visit the homes of the poor, a character-building pastoral bond
might be forged (50). As laboring-class self-reliance gradually improved, poor
law expenditure "might at length" be reduced until only the most friendless and
incapable required it. Like Chalmers, Kay thus looked forward to stimulating
charity from within the laboring community, urging the formation of *"mutual
relief"* societies for that purpose (51).

Hence, Kay's poor law strategy featured neither deterrent legislation nor a
prominent role for the workhouse. Rather, his attempt to instate personalized
pastorship as a public function anticipated the eventual rise of professional so-

cial work. That said, as an assistant commissioner, Kay managed to persuade himself, at least for a time, that the pastoral aims he had long supported might be achieved by means of the 1834 act. Kay became a model commissioner, organizing unions, building workhouses, resisting opposition from high and low, exposing fraud, and, above all, reducing expenditures (Selleck 128–29). In so doing, he helped to defend and to implement a system fundamentally unlike his own Chalmers-inspired ideal. Under the principles of 1834 the crucial task of "discriminating" character was displaced by the impersonal workhouse test, pastoral visitation played no part, and outdoor relief of the kind Kay had described in *Manchester* was officially proscribed. In spite of these glaring disparities, Kay saw fit ebulliently to affirm his "high moral and intellectual enjoyment in effecting and witnessing [the] mighty change" of this "almost magical" legislation (qtd. in Selleck 116).[16]

Unsurprisingly, as Kay's zeal for laissez-faire policies cooled, he gravitated toward the 1834 act's one potentially pastoral provision. Kay became an enthusiast of pauper education, in support of which he argued against the "less eligibility" principle at the heart of the law's politico-economic rationality. In the words of his biographer, Kay abandoned Manchester school conventions to become "an apostle spreading a message of salvation through education" (Selleck 131). The extent to which this shift marked a resurgence of Chalmers's influence became evident in the *Training of Pauper Children* (1839), a report in which Kay praised the innovative theories of the Swiss reformer Johann Heinrich Pestalozzi. Like David Stow, whose Glasgow model Kay later supported in his post as secretary to the Educational Committee of the Privy Council, Pestalozzi envisioned teaching as a potentially intersubjective relation—a magnetic and mutual attraction between teachers' charisma and pupils' "natural craving after truth" (*Training* 31). Hence, Kay's far-reaching educational philosophy, like Chalmers's and Tuckerman's pastoral precedents, balanced abstract spiritual equality against socioeconomic difference: working-class students were posited as autonomous moral and intellectual agents, even as they were located in the lower echelons of an allegedly natural hierarchy. Pauper education in this form, explicitly predicated on the tutelary impact of "love" (31), offered Kay a means through which to visualize a simultaneously personal and institutional approach to "making the working man like me."

The moral identity of many middle-class Britons, I have argued, was first constituted through ardent civic participation. The writings and voluntary activities of Thomas Chalmers, Tuckerman's Unitarian disciples, and James

Phillips Kay thus illustrate the prominence of middle-class voluntarism in the years leading up to the passage of the New Poor Law. Britain's prosperous urbanites cultivated a dutiful citizen self: bound by symbolic family ties to the wider community and, consequently, obligated to provide elevating guidance to the lower orders. Through the rhetoric of the personal, this civilizing mission was imagined as a reciprocal and potentially intersubjective pastoral relation. Chalmers and his cohorts believed that a transcendent moral equality neutralized the divisions of class while the liberatory aim of building character justified the pastor's interventions. The individual they envisioned was the author of self-determined acts that could be shaped, but never wholly determined, either by environmental conditions or legislative devices.

In his seminal text on *Manchester* James Phillips Kay set out to reaffirm this worldview, calling on the *"united exertions of the individual members of society"* to *"procure a moral and physical change in the community"* (12). Nevertheless, determined to improve the poor by every means possible, and focused on the multifarious effects of the new urban and industrial environment, Kay sought to supplement this pastoral mandate with modern innovations. In effect, Kay's call for statistical inquiries stipulated what Chalmers's rhetoric had tended to obfuscate and naturalize: the need for the upstanding citizens of a "free" society to undertake disciplinary functions that, in "despotic" nations, were managed by the state.[17] Nevertheless, to submit the working-class condition to the objectifying gaze of the social scientist was not only to jeopardize charity's intersubjective ideal, but also, as a result, to undermine the autonomous moral faculties on which one's own middle-class identity was predicated.[18] Consciously or not, Kay's shift from poor law administration to education enabled him to mute these contradictions as he renewed his commitment to reciprocal pastoral relations. Kay's professional trajectory thus foreshadows the potentially destabilizing effects of the New Poor Law on middle-class identity and the underlying moral worldview.

"Important Trifles": Harriet Martineau and the Culture of Respectability

Looking back on his childhood, Kay's son recalled a visit with his father to Ambleside, the home of the noted author Harriet Martineau (Lord Shuttleworth 334). Like Kay, Martineau embraced the ideal of a Christian and civic community overseen by diligent middle-class exemplars. By the time she moved to

Ambleside, Martineau was the head of her own household as well as a celebrated woman of letters. In that capacity she delivered weekly lectures to promote the moral improvement of her servants and working-class neighbors.[19]

Martineau was the author of several important works, including *Society in America* (1837), written after her transformative experience with the U.S. abolitionist movement. But Martineau's early writing on political economy and the New Poor Law were of a different caliber. These blatantly propagandistic texts, as Deirdre David observes, transform "complex problems into happy fables" (*Intellectual* 43; cf. Freedgood, "Banishing"). Nevertheless, precisely because they are didactic—proclaiming middle-class truths for the benefit of a working-class or youth readership—Martineau's early works reveal much about the truth-teller's assumptions. In Kay's *Manchester* the social scientific quest to objectify working-class morality clashed with the ideal of character as an autonomous moral force and of charity as a reciprocal bond between rich and poor. Martineau's *Poor Laws and Paupers Illustrated* (1833–34) presents yet another contradiction. Written at the behest of leading Whigs (Longmate 53–54), the tales imply that the New Poor Law will almost magically cure pauperism, obviating the need for charity. Whereas Chalmers had presented the parish school as the institutional embodiment of a community of moral equals, Martineau places a very different establishment—the deterrent workhouse—at the center of an atomized society driven by a fervid desire for respectable status. Tales such as "The Hamlets" thus anticipate the striking difference between a Christian and civic community and the post–New Poor Law era's increasing tendency to privilege material prosperity and its signs.

In Martineau's fictional fishing hamlet the Old Poor Law has encouraged pauperism by providing generous indoor and outdoor relief. Laboring-class demoralization has become critical, with paupers rioting in local shops and middle-class people sinking under the "pressure" of ever-increasing rates ("Hamlets" 16). As the tale opens, the exasperated guardians decide to give newcomer Mr. Barry a chance to experiment with his "fancy" notions (17). Although Barry is a voluntary activist, his proposals resemble the Royal Commission's recommendations. Most important, Barry aims to deter workers' undesirable behavior, not, like Chalmers or Kay, to guide their moral development through pastoral care. His plan thus sets aside the high-minded end of personalized character building in favor of a speedy scheme of manipulating self-interest. To reduce the desirability of parish support, Barry cuts off outdoor relief and converts the workhouse from a refugial to a "less eligible" and deterrent institution.

Barry's workhouse inmates (unlike Dickens's in *Oliver Twist*) are neither starved nor physically abused. Following the Royal Commission's rationale, treatment of able-bodied inmates is strictly uniform: executed without respect to nuances of character, whether damning or exonerative. Barry's first act is to replace the wooden railing with a solid brick wall, and close up the peephole "so that the gaieties of the road could no longer be seen" (21). The symbolic purport of these changes is unmistakable. The Old Poor Law workhouse was—like the parish school with which Chalmers sought to replace it—an organic part of the community. Residents such as Goody Gidney, who has called the workhouse home for seventy years, were full and free participants in the community culture. The new deterrent workhouse measures up to higher standards of cleanliness and functionality than many Old Poor Law structures. But, unlike them, it is marked off and excluded from the social body.

Martineau's tale thus illustrates a symbolic strategy reiterated by many practices of the new regime: for example, the ultra-durable but uncomfortable workhouse uniform; the sufficient but unappealing bread and water diet; the hygienic but humiliating compulsory bath; and the task of work—physically laborious, but materially unproductive and financially unremunerative (see Crowther, *Workhouse* 42, 195). In each case a formally rational institutional practice achieves a doubly deterrent effect, mortifying pauper bodies in a way that symbolizes their social negation. According to the new social order, paupers are neither subjects in a reciprocal character-building relation nor objects of prolonged sociological investigation or carceral reform. They are, instead, what Steven Marcus has described as "the first unperson[s] in modern history" (*Engels* 236).

Unlike the penitentiaries imagined by eighteenth-century reformers such as Bentham, the new-model workhouse is only crudely rehabilitative. As Martineau tells it, deterrence is so effective, and pauperism so much the artificial product of bad laws, that the workhouse's ultimate object is to eliminate its own constituency. It takes less than a day for Martineau's paupers to grasp the message inscribed in the Royal Commission's plan—that, in the words of one man, "I would rather have half a meal, and eat it where I please, than a whole one in a prison" (48). When the governor reminds him that he is not in a prison because he is there by choice, the meaning of "less eligibility" crystallizes. The very next morning inmates of both sexes "rush through the portals," in a symbolic remerging with the social body, "with ideas about pauperism very different from what they had had . . . twenty-four hours before" (51).

Martineau's glimpse inside the workhouse thus portrays the commission's recommendations as a radical but speedy cure for epidemic pauperism. Never-theless, like many fictional representations of the New Poor Law, "The Hamlets" concerns itself more with events outside the workhouse than in it. This pattern is important because it entails a move from the isolated tutelary effects of less eligibility to the more far-reaching and less calculated impact on the culture at large. In this way Martineau's tale points to a momentous change in nineteenth-century consciousness: the unintended consequence of reducing grave moral questions to rationalized materialistic criteria.

As we have seen, the reforms that Martineau was promoting in her *Poor Laws* series were the culmination of a thirty-year-long assault on laborers' custom-ary entitlement to parish support—a movement to affirm individual responsi-bility by abrogating spurious "rights." The deterrent workhouse would achieve this end by dehumanizing the dependent poor, ritually excluding them from the wider society. Such a process could be justified on moral grounds: if financial distress was the sign of moral turpitude, then to reward such error through the Old Poor Law was to interfere with the workings of providence. But, the ques-tion remained, was morality reducible to economic success? Could individual character—those inner, spiritual qualities that throve under pastoral guidance—be judged by the legal directives of an un-English centralized body? By at-tempting to substitute a test of need for a personalized evaluation of character, the law seemed further to sunder "the natural ties" that Kay and Chalmers had seen as the foundation of a Christian and civic economy. It subverted Chalmers's call to affirm "the ascendancy of the moral over the material part of our consti-tution" (3:288). Indeed, the New Poor Law privileged a bourgeois-materialist register of value which, so far, had been deemed inferior to the moral qualifica-tions on which middle-class identity had itself been predicated. In the name of *homo civicus*, a hallowed Whig-Liberal and middle-class ideal, it reified *homo eco-nomicus*, the subject of bourgeois self-interest and bureaucratic tutelage.

That was especially true insofar as the law became associated with the secu-lar Benthamite worldview of Edwin Chadwick, secretary to the Poor Law Com-mission. Moralists such as Kay might teach themselves to regard the law as but the negative side of a liberalizing process that would be positively driven by ed-ucational and charitable pastorship.[20] But for Chadwick and his ilk the law pre-sented an opportunity to solidify a materialist worldview in which atomized in-dividuals pursued self-interest in mechanically predictable ways. Chadwick unambivalently defined morality in objective terms—as a variable that could be quantified and measured through, for example, the reduction of poor rates. For

Chadwick deterrent poor laws were but the first wedge in a full-scale bureaucratic approach to "making the working man like me."

As the celebrated popularizer of politico-economic shibboleths, Martineau readily incorporated hedonistic assumptions into her poor law fiction. Her intent was clearly to present deterrence as a means by which working-class habits might be almost instantaneously transformed. Yet, as though to anticipate her eventual rejection of materialist simplifications, Martineau's tale went further. As her narration shifted from the workhouse to the larger community, Martineau moved beyond the shallow logic of less eligibility. Beneath hedonistic contrivance she depicted a world in which material assets and the accompanying bourgeois semiotic practices increasingly determined one's lived social reality. Although Martineau herself did not attach a name to this reign of bourgeois representation, the practices she described are recognizable as the Victorian era's obsession with respectable appearances.

Hence, the main protagonist of "The Hamlets" is not Mr. Barry, but an orphan girl, interestingly named Harriet. Instead of the workhouse, Harriet and her brother Ben have been placed in the service of a fisherman, Monks, and his wife. Mr. Monks is the archetypal debauchee of the Old Poor Law. Mrs. Monks, however, is proud and resourceful: concerned to maintain her family's independent status. Yet, while the reader is expected to admire her skillful self-reliance, she is, significantly, neither good-humored nor affectionate. In this and other respects Martineau's tale stands in marked contrast to the middle-class ideal of the home as an intimate space in which to cultivate a transcendent citizen ethic (a variation of which Martineau herself promoted in later works such as *Deerbrook* [1839] and *Household Education* [1848]). In "The Hamlets" the home functions primarily as a privatized breeding ground for bourgeois respectability.

In the course of the tale Harriet and Ben develop from indigent pauper children into upstanding ratepayers—worldly achievements that occur without reference to spiritual and communitarian ends. The workhouse school teaches children like Harriet to aspire to economic independence. It does not—like the Glasgow model that so impressed Kay—aim to build humanizing bonds between teachers and pupils. As a result, "The Hamlets" is less a tale of character building than an ironic anticipation of Mill's 1836 essay on "Civilization." As we saw in the last chapter, Mill offered a prescient critique of a mass bourgeois society: a world in which success "depend[ed] not upon what a person is, but what he seems" (133).

In a chapter called "Important Trifles" this process of embourgeoisement is

enhanced by the two Miss Barrys, to whom Harriet has come in the role of informant, revealing a plot she has overheard to undermine their father's reforms.
As a reward for saving the workhouse, Harriet is given some tips on frugal
housekeeping. This exchange is made more than emblematic by Miss Emily's
subsequent account of middle-class self-help. "If my sister and I didn't take
[such] care," she tells Harriet, "my father would be just as likely to go into the
workhouse . . . as to help other people to keep out of it." Only the saving of
"shillings and pence" prevents such a family from "sink[ing] down into poor
people" (80). Harriet responds by pondering one of the most searching questions of the nineteenth century: "What made the difference between a poor person and a gentleman"? (81–82). As though to answer her query, the conversa-
tion shifts to the self-defeating habits of laborers who deliberately minimize
their style of living in order to qualify for pauper relief. The result is a subject-
constituting moment in which Harriet is seen at last to penetrate the secrets of
middle-class existence, recognizing its pure negation in pauperism, and its positive materialization in bourgeois respectability. As Harriet skips home "mer-
rily" from the scene of her class betrayal, she contrasts the pleasures of middle-
class domesticity to the perils of "that dismal-looking workhouse" (86).

Harriet's conversion is but the beginning. Throughout the hamlet the culture of demoralized dependence is utterly transformed into a driving will-to-
material-improvement. Long-standing charity organizations now apply their
funds toward further reducing the rates, for local laborers no longer wish to be
associated with the poor for the sake of paltry gains. The new working-class culture is marked by the relentless desire to increase the social space between one's
own respectability and the ignominious workhouse by appropriating and dis-
playing ever more domestic "comforts." Thus, the narrator expresses not a trace
of ambivalence when Harriet and Ben nearly drown while earning extra pence
toward the purchase of a bench for Miss Emily to sit on when she visits the
Monks's cottage.

The complete triumph of deterrence is celebrated in a series of emblematic
moments, each involving the workhouse. When (thanks to Harriet's and Ben's
tireless labor) Mr. Monks's status shifts from profligate rate absorber to respectable ratepayer, his character—or, rather, what signifies character in the new
materialist culture—is instantly transformed. He is next seen shunning his old
friend, workhouse inmate Goody Gidney, and complaining to Mr. Barry about
the tremendous costs of relieving the "idle." Since the major adult recipients of
relief are now the aged and the sick—that is, those theoretically exempt from

deterrence—Monks's repudiation of the aged pauper has no rational tutelary aim.[21] In this way "The Hamlets" provides insights into a culture in which social legitimacy fundamentally depends upon precarious material assets. In such a culture, the tale suggests, the pretense to *symbolic* assets—those respectable airs cultivated to amplify the distance between haves and have-nots—tends toward irrational excess.

The same tendency is further illustrated by Goody Gidney's pauper burial, a kind of figurative excommunication of a once cheerful member of the community (cf. Laqueur, "Pauper" 109–31). In an ironic reversal Goody's death is described as a "relief" to the parish. When too few workhouse inmates remain to serve as Goody's mourners, no laborer is "good-natured enough to offer to appear to be a pauper even for a single hour" (174). This communal renunciation of the pauper body paves the way for the ceremonious locking-up of the empty workhouse, its deterrent function now an internalized feature of the reigning bourgeois culture. The tale closes with Mr. Barry, the middle-class savior of middle-class living, at last enjoying his retirement, "for once, heedless of the time" (181).

In representing the new-model workhouse as an effective means to solving the problem of pauperism, Martineau thus implies a number of far-reaching consequences. Chalmers's ideal community was unified by a common investment in character building. Laboring-class parishioners would demonstrate their moral fiber through communal as well as individual self-reliance: helping, when necessary, to relieve the misfortunes of their poorest neighbors. In Martineau's tale the absence of "good-natured" confraternity and the anxious unwillingness even "to appear to be a pauper" marks the rise of a bourgeois-individualist identity (based on acquired assets and pretentious display) and the corresponding decline of a moral identity (based on stable and fully knowable relations within the community).

Martineau's tale thus stands out as a prescient fable of poor law reform, an ironic complement to Mill's essay on "Civilization." Bourgeois individualism was not, of course, invented by the 1834 act. Chalmers lamented bourgeois influences throughout his works, and Carlyle had announced the arrival of a materialistic age in "Signs of the Times" (1829). Implementation of the new policies was controversial and extremely uneven, particularly in industrial areas where the workhouse test offered an impracticable remedy for cyclical unemployment. The New Poor Law did not, therefore, instantly neutralize the countervailing priorities of moralists, nor induct a materialist worldview overnight.

Nevertheless, as a fictional glimpse of a social order in which atomized bour-geois individualism supplants the Christian and civic ideal, Martineau's tale is an important precursor to the novels of the post–New Poor Law era.

"What Makes the Difference between a Poor Person and a Gentleman?" Charles Dickens's Parish Boy's Progress

Oliver gradually throve and prospered under the united care of Mrs. Maylie, Rose, and the kind-hearted Mr. Losberne. If fervent prayers, gushing from hearts overcharged with gratitude, be heard in heaven—and if they be not, what prayers are!—the blessings which the orphan child called down upon them, sunk into their souls, diffusing peace and happiness.

— CHARLES DICKENS, *Oliver Twist*

About midway through *Oliver Twist: The Parish Boy's Progress* (1837–38) Dick-ens pictures an ideal rural community much like that of Thomas Chalmers.[22] Rescued from the criminal underworld by the benevolent Maylies, Oliver at-tends services at the village church. There a "neat and clean" laboring popula-tion kneels "reverently in prayer." As exemplary community volunteers, the Maylies pay "many calls at the clean houses" of their working-class neighbors and execute regular "commission[s] of charity" (216). Of course, Dickens was not a Chalmers disciple, and, in novels such as *Bleak House*, he satirized the pre-tensions of organized philanthropy (see chap. 3). Nevertheless, *Oliver Twist* is an impassioned critique of the New Poor Law's disdain for precisely those com-munal values stressed in *The Christian and Civic Economy of Large Towns*.[23] As an idealized portrait of charitable reciprocity at work, the bond between the Maylies and Oliver entails "the purest and most amiable generosity on one side; and the truest, warmest, soul-felt gratitude on the other" (216).

Yet to say that *Oliver Twist* is a Chalmersian text, envisioning personalized charity as the cornerstone of a just communal order, is but to scratch the surface of Dickens's complicated fictional response to the New Poor Law. Less opti-mistic than Chalmers, the young novelist was acutely sensitive to the bourgeois individualism described in Harriet Martineau's tale and Mill's essay on "Civi-lization." His aim was unquestionably to restore charitable bonds between rich and poor. Yet the novel, by and large, implies that British society has already, with few exceptions, forsaken charitable ideals in favor of materialistic and self-ish ideologies. In *Oliver Twist* this narrative split—between sentimental ideal and realist critique—is complicated by fundamental questions of character and pastorship which haunted Dickens throughout his career.[24]

When Martineau's young protagonist asked, "What makes the difference between a poor person and a gentleman?" she was advised, in effect, to acquire domestic comforts and to cultivate respectable airs. Dickens subjects this view of social progress to a two-pronged assault. He produces a trenchant satire on bourgeois respectability, and, further, pits that aberration against an exalted picture of authentic middle-class virtue. Yet Dickens's idealization of middle-class character contradicts his social critique, and, in so doing, distances him from the organized character-building ambitions of Chalmers and Kay. For, while Dickens is at pains to document the demoralizing effects of the bourgeois environment, he is even more determined to extol Oliver's *innate* immunity to such damage. The result is a novel in which not only character but also knowledge itself—the means by which truth is ascertained and asserted—becomes the object of narrative contest.

Although *Oliver Twist* made an indelible contribution to the iconography of the New Poor Law, Dickens's critique of the new regime is, in fact, imprecise. Despite the numerous aspersions cast on "philosophers," "Boards," and the principles of 1834, the Twistian workhouse is, in many respects, indistinguishable from an Old Poor Law establishment (House 98).[25] Significantly, Dickens's workhouse never assumes the post-1834 symbolic position of a place especially marked for social exclusion. Although it is undeniably a low and deterrent place—only the helpless would suffer such demeaning subsistence—these are not, as in Martineau's tale, strategic conditions, specific to the place. They are, on the contrary, representative features of Victorian poverty, both inside and out of the workhouse. Unquestionably, as Sowerberry's apprentice, the workhouse bastard is at the very bottom of the household hierarchy—beneath even Noah Claypole, who, as a Charity School boy, is himself an object of scorn. Nevertheless, Dickens's point is less to emphasize the particular stigma of Oliver's lowly status than to demonstrate the extent to which a stigmatizing degradation characterizes the moral condition of the poor as a whole. Thus, the Twistian workhouse is a symptom, not a cause, and Dickens's interest in it is subordinate to a full-scale social critique.

At the fore of that critique are the early-Victorian governing classes who, as Dickens depicts them, have almost entirely abandoned their pastoral obligations. Oliver is first misjudged by the workhouse board, threatened with jail for begging, and, under suspicion of thievery, driven out of villages by vicious dogs.

Later he is brought before Mr. Fang, a police magistrate who takes pleasure in incarcerating the destitute (26, 61, 94). Thus bereft of pastorship, Dickens's laboring masses exhibit a predatory selfishness that is both analogous and ultimately traceable to the bourgeois self-interest of the governing classes. Working-class life is pervaded by a crude competitive instinct, variously expressed in Noah's petty tyranny, Fagin's greed, Bumble's self-importance, and Mrs. Sowerberry's jealousy. Although Dickens repudiates "the beautiful axiom that self-preservation is the first law of nature" (73), he portrays it as the self-fulfilling prophesy of a prevalent ruling-class ideology. Materialistic self-interest has so completely saturated British social life that the cant of "well-fed philosophers" is indistinguishable from the maxim of thieves: "a regard for number one holds us all together" (41, 289). Hence, so far from improving the working-class moral condition, as in Martineau's tale, bourgeois individualism has all but destroyed it.

Dickens thus gleefully ridicules the tutelary scheme trumpeted by Martineau: the idea that, by manipulating self-interest and encouraging materialistic competition, would-be paupers are miraculously transformed into respectable aspirants to middle-class status. When Oliver expresses a disinclination to steal, the Dodger taunts him with his lack of "pride," and willingness to "be dependent" on the labor of others (128). Similarly, Noah's ambition "to be a gentleman" leads him to Fagin's gang. His eventual career as a shady informant is facilitated by "respectable attire" (283, 358). And, when Nancy is sent out to kidnap Oliver, she is given a basket and door key because such "respectable" accouterments look (according to Bill Sikes) "real and genivine like" (93). Dickens thus employs comic satire to insert a stabilizing boundary between the presumably authentic virtues underlying Mr. Brownlow's "very respectable-looking personage," and the transparent depravity of bourgeois sham (73).

In this way the novel stages an imagined return from the disturbing materialistic flux represented by Martineau to the stable hierarchy of a Christian and civic community. As Dickens tells it, Mrs. Sowerberry, the wife of a solvent tradesman (of the kind likely to have been enfranchised by the Reform Act of 1832), is as boorish as her servant, Charlotte. A local official, enamored of his own importance, Mr. Bumble might easily claim middle-class status in the world of "The Hamlets." But Dickens will not have it so. Whereas Oliver, as Steven Marcus has remarked, speaks "the language of angels" (*Dickens* 80)—and even Nancy, the denizen of "noisome" "stews," rises to magniloquence (Dickens, *Oliver* 266)—no feats of verbal transcendence are possible for Mr. Bumble. On the contrary, the beadle's coarse speech and manners reflect his debasing bourgeois cultural inheritance and, as a result, predetermine the farcical outcome of his attempt to cultivate middle-class domesticity.

An even more telling indictment of false bourgeois coin is Dickens's sustained contrast between the widow Corney and Rose Maylie. Comfortably nestled within her official workhouse lodgings, Corney's warm hearth, silver tea service, and cozy pets are the very material antitheses of pauperdom. Yet, whereas Rose's "cheerful, happy smile" was "made for Home," Mrs. Corney's counterfeit domesticity conceals a grasping avarice as sharp as Fagin's and a manful determination to rule the roost. "If ever angels be for God's good purposes enthroned in mortal forms," the narrator warbles, Rose is such an angel (194). "Oh, Mrs. Corney, what a Angel you are!" effuses Mr. Bumble, in a satiric variation on this theme, when he learns that his beloved receives free coals and candles with her rent-free lodgings (183). While Harry Maylie proves his nobility by sacrificing worldly advantage in order to marry Rose, Bumble eventually realizes that he has "sold [him]self . . . for six teaspoons, a pair of sugar-tongs, and a milk-pot; with a small quantity of second-hand furniture" (240).

Ironically, Bumble has sold himself into the workhouse in exchange for the kind of bourgeois domesticity Martineau's cottagers cultivate by way of staying out of it. Yet, in the context of Dickens's novel, the Bumbles' reversal of fortune—from workhouse masters to workhouse inmates—merely effects a long anticipated reconciliation between social status and character. As Oliver is elevated to his rightful and legitimate place within middle-class society, the Bumbles and Monks descend to the workhouse and the prison. In this way Dickens creates a fairy-tale ending in which rapacious bourgeois individualism is symbolically displaced by a just moral order.

Near the end of *Oliver Twist* Mr. Brownlow attributes Oliver's good fortune to "a stronger hand than chance" (328). Providence is thus invoked to sanction a new era of Christian and civic community. Oliver's plan to ensure that his old friend Dick is "clothed and taught" proves too late (341), but the dawn of a pastoral order is signaled nonetheless. Harry Maylie's decision to give up Parliament for a career as a village clergyman signifies more than selfless devotion to Rose. It is also Dickens's final repudiation of a society dominated by competitive individualism and snobbish pretense: a world of "cold and sordid people," eager to punish an "ambitious man" by "sneering" at his wife's family history (226). Through Harry middle-class abilities symbolically shift from national politics to the personal realm of neighborhood pastorship. Thus, in a resounding affirmation of the Christian and civic economy—reinforcing the Habermasian linkage between private and public life—Harry becomes a pastor, while Rose devotes herself to spreading "goodness and charity abroad," and performing "domestic duties at home" (359). By such means the new generation of Maylies will diffuse the bonds first forged between Oliver and his benefactors. Through pastoral relations their charitable efforts will be duly reciprocated by "hearts overcharged with gratitude" and instilled with "love and duty" (210).

Oliver Twist and the Problem of Character

Dickens's novel thus concludes with what appears to be an ebullient portrait of a Chalmers-like social order. Indeed, a reading like D. A. Miller's makes it possible to situate *Twist* as the fictional complement to the civilizing mission of Chalmers, Kay or Tuckerman. Miller has described Oliver's stay with the Maylies as a "domesticating pedagogy," part of "a technology of discipline constitut[ing] this happy family in a field of power relations" (10). Yet, on close inspection, Dickens's fairy-tale ending turns out to depend on several preconditions that run counter to the project of "making the working man like me." Closure is facilitated less by dedicated character building than by innate virtue and a retreat from the urban conditions that Chalmers and Kay were so determined to improve. The absolute moral virtue attributed to Oliver is not fundamentally transformed, and still less "constituted" by, the Maylies' household regime. Indeed, Oliver is no more the product of the Maylie home than he is of Fagin's efforts to inculcate a criminalizing pedagogy.[26] *Oliver Twist*, I suggest, cannot be assimilated to the middle-class civilizing mission, because in various ways the novel undermines the entire premise of character building. Dickens's inability to stabilize a prescriptive notion of character—to uphold the moral improvability of each and every individual and to instate reliable pastorship of some kind as the means to achieving that end—accounts for a novel that is, at once, powerfully radical *and* sentimentally essentialist and reactionary.

Dickens's representation of the working-class condition is, to be sure, as graphic as the reports of his social scientific contemporaries (see Schwarzbach, "Terra Incognita"). But the novel's condemnation of the status quo is, at the same time, so sweeping that it casts doubt on the efficacy of incremental reforms, whether voluntary or statist. In particular, Dickens blurs the normative opposition between hardworking poverty and blamable pauperism. In *Oliver Twist* imiseration occurs both inside and out of the workhouse, and few distinctions are made between law-abiding laborers and criminals. As Sikes carries

Oliver out of London on a housebreaking expedition, they pass a chaotic mass of "unwashed, unshaven, squalid, and dirty figures" (146–47). These wretched workers are fortunate compared to the inhabitants of Jacob's Island, home to "unemployed labourers of the lowest class . . . and the raff and refuse of the river" (332). With the special exception of the rural village, the struggling but sympathetic poor of Dickens's later novels are absent.[27]

Ironically, the only trace of domesticity among London's lower orders is Fagin's den, in which the "'spectable old gentleman" is portrayed as a kind of underworld homemaker—frying sausages, whistling as he makes coffee, and "gently lifting" Oliver into bed (63, 66). After Oliver's brutal passage, Fagin's gang cannot but strike the reader as a viable community within a ruthlessly oppressed class. Hence, the most radical moment in the novel occurs when Oliver's intrinsic middle-class identification is momentarily suspended. As Fagin parodies a Brownlowesque gentleman, Oliver joins in the seditious pleasure, laughing "till the tears ran down his face" (70).[28]

Oliver Twist would be the more subversive novel thus suggested were it not for its contrary investment in essentializing virtuous character. Here is Dickens's bulwark against the embourgeoisement that, in Martineau's tale, reduced middle-class morality to a materialistic display. In the special case of Oliver—who, like the protagonist of a fairy tale, is a dispossessed Maylie cast as a pauper lad—character is presented as an innate, but not necessarily inherited essence. Thus, the long-suffering orphan exemplifies an incorruptible "principle of Good," while his half-brother Monks is a born incorrigible, given "from [his] cradle" to "evil passions, vice, and profligacy" (3, 330).[29] Materialism motivates the coerced marriage of Oliver's father, but elsewhere the novel obfuscates the financial position of genteel exemplars such as Brownlow and the Maylies. Predicated neither on wealth, education, nor any other discernible foundation, the benevolence of these characters simply comports with their station, in glaring but unexplained contrast to corrupt social peers such as Mr. Fang.

Ambiguous though they are, Oliver's innate goodness and Brownlow's essentialized gentility provide Dickens with a crucial antimaterialist way of answering the post–New Poor Law question, "What makes the difference between a poor person and a gentleman?" In this way Dickens figuratively restores the "character test," reversing the tendency to value economic success and respectable appearances without scrutinizing underlying moral qualifications. That said, it is important to stress that Dickens's *essentialist* defense against embourgeoisement is distinct from Chalmers's or Kay's *anti-essentialist* alternative.

For the latter, morality is never innate or mysterious but always the product of tireless self-improvement, nurtured by intimate pastoral bonds.

Oliver's innate possession of the right stuff has, unsurprisingly, interested many critics of the novel. Cates Baldridge, for example, has argued that Oliver's goodness, like that of his near relation Rose, demands a "genetic" explanation (185). But such a reading, for all its thought-provoking nuances, ultimately appeals to an anachronistic notion of genetic determinism. Dickens's contemporaries lacked a consistent theory of biological inheritance and commonly advanced ideas in which nature and nurture were far less distinct than they are apt to be today.[30] Just as important, a genetic position would have contradicted their assertion of individual free will. For most middle- and upper-class Victorians—orthodox Benthamites being obvious exceptions—character was, therefore, too sacrosanct a concept to be reduced to the determined effect either of nature or nurture.

Hence, in essentializing Oliver's goodness, Dickens was not promoting the Maylies' blood, nor middle-class genealogy more generally. But he was, without question, seeking a surer foundation for moral authority. The author of *Oliver Twist* clearly believed in the legitimacy of a Christian and civic community; yet he also questioned the middle classes' self-serving appropriation of the pastoral mantle. By casting doubt on middle-class morality, Dickens problematized the civilizing mission: undermining the process through which would-be middle-class exemplars constituted themselves by professing to elevate the morality of their social inferiors.

These instabilities surface in the contrast between Oliver's innate moral essence and other depictions of character in the novel. Significantly, Dick, another workhouse orphan, represents innate goodness that is not, like Oliver's, linked to secret middle-class lineage. Nancy's gendered moral essence is, by contrast, resilient but vulnerable. Although the remnants of "a woman's original nature" redeem her momentarily, the prostitute's brutal death is finally determined by a "life . . . squandered in the streets" (266). Yet, if these figures suggest the various degrees to which innate virtue resists environmental influence, still others challenge that model entirely. I have already suggested that the Bumbles' character defects are connected to their bourgeois cultural identifications. Bill Sikes's monstrous deviance suggests an ambiguous combination of working-class degeneration and environmental damage. In Fagin's case Jewishness provides a salient racial explanation for moral deficiencies.

Yet another series of ambiguities emerges in relation to Noah Claypole, a "charity-boy" who eagerly represents himself to Fagin as "a regular cunning sneak" (43, 302). Dickens's philanthropic bent might tempt us to speculate that Noah is, like Monks, a born incorrigible—impervious to the wholesome pastorship of the charity school. In fact, Dickens deeply dislikes Noah's school, anticipating his satire on a comparable institution, the Charitable Grinders of *Dombey and Son* (1846). Taunted by "the ignominious epithets" of status-conscious shop boys, Noah has clearly been demoralized by, rather than in spite of, his position as a charity boy (44).

Of course, Chalmers and Kay often criticized the degrading effects of irresponsible charity, and in *Oliver Twist* Dickens obliquely sanctions the activities of a Kay-like philanthropy, the Juvenile Delinquent Society (135). But Dickens's particular hostility to charity schools exceeds Chalmers's critique. It is surely no coincidence that both Noah and Rob, Noah's counterpart in *Dombey*, rise from charity boys to *spies:* as though a sneaking and servile hypocrisy, rather than a robust moral independence, were the end effect of philanthropy.[31] Whereas the personal pastoral relation between Oliver and the Maylies is repeatedly cast as a mutually elevating bond, the charity school is presented as a blatantly coercive institutional device. It is as hostile to the communitarian ideals of Chalmers's parish school as it is unlike Oliver's homely relation to the Maylies. The imperious Dombey, a subscriber to the Grinders, exposes the heart of the problem when he rejects "general education," but insists that "the inferior classes . . . be taught to know their position" (*Dombey* 117). Thus, in the charity school Dickens presents the troubling antithesis of the Maylies' personal pastorship, and a prelude to the dubious philanthropy of *Bleak House*.

There is, however, yet another and even more disturbing sense in which the figure of Noah undermines the novelist's attempt to stabilize a just moral order. Here Dickens once again harks back to Mill's evocation of a modern world in which representation—or what a person "seems"—overshadows what he "is." Dickens's disdain for charity schools is ultimately rooted in a stigmatizing process much like that of Martineau's workhouse. Rob's transformation into a Grinder involves his wearing "a dress and badge" that identify his dependent condition to the world at large (*Dombey* 117). Likewise, Noah's "coat and badge" and "leathers" mark him out for the jibes of the neighborhood shop boys (*Oliver* 282, 44). Such ritualistic markings, including haircuts and parish uniforms, were integral to the reformers' efforts to turn the refugial workhouse of the Old Poor Law into a negative and deterrent social space. As a newborn infant, Oliver "might have been the child of a nobleman or a beggar." Yet once he is "enveloped" in workhouse garments, he, like Noah, is "badged and ticketed." As a marked "parish child," Oliver falls "into his place at once": he is "the orphan of a workhouse," "despised by all, and pitied by none" (19). Here, as with Noah, Martineau's materialistic semiotics return with a haunting power to determine lived subjectivities. Ignominiously labeled "charity" by the local shop boys, Noah "retorts" by calling Oliver "Work'us" (44, 52). For a brief moment, when Oliver's ragged clothes betray his whereabouts to Fagin (117), a materialist epistemology—wherein clothes make the man—ominously asserts itself. Although the novel energetically resists this bourgeois determinism, Dickens's social critique is never more acute than in his rendering of Noah. Noah's intent to repay "with interest" the mortification he has suffered "shows . . . how impartially the same amiable qualities are developed in the finest lord and the dirtiest charity-boy" (44). From the high to the low, the crudest competitive individualism is the debased legacy of a society bent on creating man in the image of self-interested *homo economicus*, "putting entirely out of sight any considerations of heart, or generous impulse and feeling" (87).

Taken in its entirety, Dickens's novel reveals a radical uncertainty about the makings of character—thus undermining the viability of a Maylie-like pastoral community. Character is simultaneously innate and acquired. It is, on the one hand, the inherited effect of race, gender, and genealogy and, on the other, the other, the contingent product of sociocultural inscriptions and bourgeois-materialist signs. At times a predestined state of grace conferred by a providential Nature, character is also the sad casualty of an impersonal universe—a world that dooms all but a fortunate few to the determining effects of inheritance, environment, or both. In all of these ways Dickens clouds the question of agency so crucial to his contemporaries. The individual of *Oliver Twist* is alternately a morally autonomous and self-directing force, and the powerless pawn of larger forces. With such tenuous foundations for individual and social improvement, Dickens's early novel foreshadows his struggle in *Bleak House* to visualize a collective form of pastorship, able to cure the ills of a modern liberal society.

"The Law Is a Ass": Epistemology in Oliver Twist and Frances Trollope's Jessie Phillips

If the law supposes that . . . the law is a ass—a idiot. If that's the eye of the law, the law's a bachelor; and the worst I wish the law is, that his eye may be opened by experience—by experience.   — CHARLES DICKENS, *Oliver Twist*

Law is a matter of business; means and ends are the things to be considered in it.

—JOHN STUART MILL, "BENTHAM"

In an oft-cited passage in *Oliver Twist* Mr. Bumble learns that "in the eyes of the law" he is even more culpable than Mrs. Bumble: "for the law supposes that [his] wife acts under [his] direction." Bumble's reply—"If the law supposes that . . . the law is a ass"—is one in a series of comic episodes through which the imperious beadle is transformed into the most docile of henpecked husbands. Yet, at another and deeper level, Bumble's assessment of the law offers a striking parallel to Dickens's critique of the New Poor Law's legalized politico-economic rationality; its attempt to displace "character" with an impersonal test of financial need. Like a bachelor who presumes to know the married man's condition, the law thus rules by abstraction rather than "experience."

Bumble's observation also illuminates Max Weber's analysis of modern legal (bureaucratic) rationality. According to Weber, the law's authority and utility rest on its calculability: its concentration on what Dickens describes as "worldly considerations and probabilities" (204). "Fully developed bureaucracy," writes Weber, operates impersonally, "without bias or favor." "Its peculiar character and with it its appropriateness for capitalism is the more fully actualized the more bureaucracy 'depersonalizes' itself, i.e., the more completely it succeeds in achieving . . . the exclusion of love, hatred, and every purely personal, especially irrational and incalculable, feeling from the execution of official tasks" (*Law* 351). Although Britain was, as Weber frequently asserted, remarkably resistant to bureaucratization, the New Poor Law typified modern legal rationality in its attempt to depersonalize poor relief—to exclude the "irrational and incalculable" from its function. Particularly disturbing (and, in practice, impossible to enforce) was the law's attempt to replace the old-fashioned "character test" with the impersonal "workhouse test." Under this rule all paupers would be relieved in the confines of the workhouse, irrespective of moral condition. Dickens, I argue, responded to this rationalizing innovation by exposing the irrational effects of formalized reason. The novel demonstrates that any attempt to ground authority in impersonal rules rather than personal experience poses problems for a just moral order—in particular, by thwarting the reading of character.

Indeed, the problem of character in *Oliver Twist* is illuminated by Weber's analysis. As an antimaterialist concept of human individuality, character was predicated on what, in Weber's terms, were two potentially overlapping modes of legitimacy: the *traditional* (derived from hierarchical social relations), and the

charismatic (derived from special qualities of person). So conceived, character was, by definition, unassimilable to the modern legal rationality on which bureaucracies depend (*Economy* 1:212–301). Hence, whether cast chiefly as a "traditional" readiness to fulfill customary obligations to the community, or as a "charismatic" quality of self-originating power, character was precisely that which could not be reduced to objectified, impersonal, and calculable standards. That was true, moreover, regardless of the particular modern criteria in question: whether the forms of a bureaucratic procedure, the privileged material signs of a competitive bourgeois society, or the knowledge-producing categories of the new social sciences. As that which was insistently relational and personal, character was held to be impenetrable to any mode of knowing which, like Weber's modern legal rationality, was based on the exclusion of interpersonal affect. In this way character was a defense against the law's displacement of "sympathy, favor, grace, and gratitude" (*Law* 350–51)—the relational glue of a Christian and civic economy.

In *Oliver Twist* Dickens's assault on legal rationality takes a comic form: one that prepares us to appreciate Frances Trollope's complicated exploration of the modern epistemology in *Jessie Phillips*, another tale of the New Poor Law. When Oliver is discovered in the Maylie household after his unwilling participation in Sikes's burglary attempt, his innocence is determined in a "domestic parliament" overseen by the affable Dr. Losberne. Having heard Oliver's "weary catalogue" of wrongs, Losberne concludes that the boy is an innocent victim (199). The problem is that circumstantial evidence tells against Oliver, while outside authorities (the local constable and the Bow Street Runners) have been summoned to the house.[32] When Rose suggests that "the poor child's story . . . will be sufficient to exonerate him," Losberne deprecates her feminine naïveté. Viewed through the "eyes" of "a practised police-officer," he explains, Oliver's uncorroborated tale has "many ugly points about it" and will fail to satisfy those who "take nothing for granted" (204). In other words, the law, as in Bumble's beleaguered protest, operates without respect to experience.

Losberne concludes that the only way to spare the innocent is, ironically, to conceal the truth. To screen Oliver's "real story," Losberne undermines the credibility of witnesses and uses medical expertise to confuse the facts (204). This morally justified chicanery is facilitated by the authorities' clownish incompetence, the witnesses' lower-class status, and Oliver's fortuitous lapse from consciousness. It is in this compromised fashion that Dickens's "domestic parliament" supersedes its official counterpart, just as the Maylies' personalized charity symbolically displaces the New Poor Law.

In *Jessie Phillips: A Tale of the New Poor Law* (1842–43) Frances Trollope provides an even more sustained representation of epistemological quandaries in the wake of the 1834 act.[33] Like Dickens's Mrs. Maylie, the author of *Jessie Phillips* "would not . . . for the world" invite the law into her domestic sanctum (*Oliver* 205). Indeed, Trollope's Tory-leaning political outlook makes her an even more obvious spokesperson for the Christian and civic economy than was Dickens. Nevertheless, whereas Dickens portrayed rural England as a sanctuary for traditional social relations, Trollope's novel, set in a small country parish, demonstrates the extent to which bourgeois materialism's alien epistemology has penetrated even the quaintest locales.

Narrating a wide range of socially disruptive effects, Trollope merges a domestic novel modeled after *Pride and Prejudice* with the melodrama of a failed *Pamela*, seduced and ruined by an upper-class villain. In the end both plots are resolved through a quasi-gothic romance of illicit sex, murder, and madness. As we shall see, madness—which was itself the object of rationalizing reforms in early-Victorian Britain—provides an important countervailing influence in the novel. Since madness involves the suspension of reason, it provides a privileged vantage point from which to question the limitations of the 1834 act's legalized politico-economic rationality.

Trollope's novel unflinchingly represents the structural origins of rural England's increasing bourgeois individualism. Whereas Dickens's idealized country village featured binding relations between rich and poor, Trollope depicts a social hierarchy in dangerous flux: a waning nobility, a financially straitened gentry, an ascendant professional class, an aggressively mobile commercial class, and a dangerously ambitious laboring class. But Trollope is not without her own ideals. In the rural community of the past, she implies, economic, social, and moral power were harmoniously aligned. As a result, character was transparently knowable, and "respectability" a simple question of filling one's appropriate station. As Trollope sees it, this traditional social structure has been disrupted by two interrelated modern phenomena: first, by accelerated political and economic change; and, second (and more conspicuously), by an alien and depersonalizing form of authority—centralized bureaucracy—and the modern legal rationality on which it is based.

Legal rationality's intrusion into the rural order is symbolized by the arrival of an Assistant Poor Law commissioner. Like his real-life counterpart, Dr. James Phillips Kay, Trollope's commissioner has come from the city to oversee the administration of a law that, as Trollope tells it, undermines traditional social relations, traditional ways of knowing, and the fixed hierarchies thus produced. In this destabilized social context, respectable character (or the power to define it) has become a hotly contested form of symbolic power, not unlike the competitive semiotics displayed in Martineau's tale. Hence, whereas Dickens had created an unimpeachable (if ungeneralizable) fairy-tale essence, unique to privileged figures such as Oliver, Trollope's novel faces the instability of character head on.

In so doing, Trollope represents a heated contest for social legitimacy staged within a pluralistic, multilayered society—much like F. M. L. Thompson's historical account of the "rise" of respectability. For Trollope, as for Thompson, Victorian respectability has become a "variable and relative" concept (*Rise* 354).[34] This relativist clash has damaged the transparency of character, triggering a contest over its definition. Thus, for the traditional ruling classes character is a bulwark against unfettered materialism: a moral currency through which to maintain preeminence in the face of declining economic and political power. For the socially ambitious, character must be either rejected or, as in Martineau's tale, recast in materialist terms to confirm newfound economic gains.

As though to intensify this struggle for social legitimacy, Trollope exempts no one, regardless of rank, from the financial burdens to which modern rural life has become increasingly subject. In contrast to the generic affluence of Dickens's virtuous middle classes, Trollope's novel, written during 1842, the "gloomiest" year in the nineteenth century (Briggs, *Age* 295), represents a ubiquitous financial pinch. Money troubles plague everyone from the laboring classes who, in Malthusian fashion, have overpopulated their prosperous village, to the local duke, whose estates are so encumbered that he lives abroad and seeks a wealthy wife for his son. Emblematic of this endemic financial anxiety is the ignominious, prisonlike workhouse to which—despite its socially excluding effects—the threads of Trollope's various subplots all connect.

The novel opens with the story of Mrs. Greenhill, a former servant of the duke. When Greenhill applies to the parish, her reputable character is invoked to justify outdoor relief instead of the workhouse—an appeal to the traditional reciprocity between deference and patronage. Significantly, Greenhill faces the workhouse because her socially ambitious son has speculated unsuccessfully with her annuity. As Trollope sees it, such ambitions from below, (attempts, in effect, to establish a bourgeois social order), are connected to disruptive "city" influences. Hence, Mr. Baxter, a wealthy brewer "in a sort of transition state between the tradesman and country gentleman," compares unfavorably to the traditional notables with whom he shares a seat on the local Poor Law board. Unlike them, Baxter is a "thorough-going Radical" and hearty supporter of centralized legislation. In contrast to their charitable paternalism, Baxter is a "jocund democrat, who"—with Bumble-like self-importance—is "never . . . so merry as when a pauper [is] the subject of . . . jest." Thus, when "respectable" Mrs. Greenhill appears before the board, Baxter dismisses her connections to the duke. He goes on to invoke the New Poor Law as a valuable "cure for [such] partiality, and all the rest of the old countrified notions about character" (1:128, 150, 208, 223). In so doing, Baxter allies himself with the law's attempt to replace an antimaterialist standard of character with an impersonal test of need.

Of course, such "old countrified notions about character," and the sort of people who hold them, are precisely what and whom Trollope attempts to validate in her "Tale of the New Poor Law." Yet, significantly, Trollope does not reject the notion of the deterrent workhouse out of hand. On the contrary, by emphasizing the expense of modern living—land acquisition and genteel education for the ambitious trades family, and the sheer costs of suitably maintaining large families for the established gentry—the novel tacitly recognizes the necessity of encouraging independence among the lower orders. In contrast to *Oliver Twist*, Trollope's novel is less critical of the call for working-class self-reliance than it is of the act's determination to implement politico-economic nostrums through centralized rules. Trollope's chief concern, then, is that the management of parish affairs be left in traditional local hands—safe from the pernicious influence of London officials and their allies among the neighborhood parvenus.[35]

To achieve this end, Trollope must reaffirm the pastoral qualifications of the traditional ruling classes. Yet, since they are increasingly vulnerable to financial pressures and competition from below, her efforts to reinforce their moral superiority are undermined by the very processes she seeks to reverse. So, for example, the novel glimpses at a clergyman so overworked while supporting his large family that he cannot even spare fifteen minutes to advise his workhouse flock. A more central figure is Squire Dalton, the Mr. Bennet–like father of Ellen, who is the heroine of the domestic plot. Eager to affirm his moral qualifications, the novel declares that "no man living ever placed less undue value upon money." Yet Dalton is also the father of "no less than ten" marriageable daughters. It is not, therefore, entirely surprising to find that it was from Dalton's cottage, managed by a professional steward, that the worthy Greenhill was evicted—leaving the duke's family retainer to face the workhouse, while her home of old was offered to the highest bidder (1:235, 236). Hence, while Trollope prefers to point the finger at extra-rural agencies and ambitious tradesmen, she simultaneously exposes the corruption and complicity of the traditional upper classes.

Trollope's domestic plot concerns the thwarted marriage plans of Ellen Dalton—a model heroine in the style of Jane Austen—and Lord Pemberton, the son of the impecunious duke. Wanting to spare Pemberton the humiliation of finding his former nurse in the workhouse, Ellen secretly pays off Greenhill's debts and restores her to her respectable place in the Dalton cottage. The eventual discovery of these actions helps to resolve the marriage plot: when the duke and duchess recognize in the squire's daughter a worthy wife for Pemberton, they rescind their objections to the match and relinquish their hopes of finding an heiress with considerably more than Ellen's eight thousand–pound dowry. Hence, Pemberton's proposal at the end of volume 2—signaling the nobility's validation of character over wealth and rank, and uniting nobility and gentry— should mark the close of the Austenian marriage plot.

Yet it is here that the domestic plot intersects with the anti-*Pamela* story of Jessie Phillips. Jessie, a beautiful, talented, and intelligent seamstress is repeatedly identified as "the most respected girl in the parish." Only, in Jessie's case, respectability has become a dangerously fluid bourgeois signifier. Looking beyond the virtuous character of "respectable" Mrs. Greenhill, Jessie aims to elevate herself in the manner of Martineau's "respectable" status seekers. Thus, Jessie's "perilous" "delusion"—her ambitious conception of herself as "a *Pamela* sort of exception" to "other girls of her position"—tempts her to fall and ruin. Whereas Trollope celebrates Ellen's Austen-like leap from squire's daughter to future duchess, she roundly condemns Jessie's desire to raise herself from seamstress to "mistress of the Manor House" (2:110–11).[36]

Jessie's eventual tragedy is further hastened by extra-rural agencies. Her seducer, Ellen's villainous brother Frederic, is emboldened by the New Poor Law's bastardy clause, which prevents unwed mothers from holding the fathers of their children accountable. Moreover, when Frederic abandons Jessie, leaving her pregnant and thoroughly disgraced, her obvious resort is the New Poor Law's socially negating workhouse. Only there can the once respected aspirant to gentility "hide [herself] . . . from all eyes," for it alone has "the faculty of obliterating, from the minds of all without, the remembrance even of the names and the existence of those within it" (1:165, 108).

Trollope's workhouse thus becomes the central figure of a vastly transformed and fragmented rural society. Although the traditional governing classes are still nominally in charge, their moral authority has been undermined and corrupted by modern tendencies that the novel is at pains to reverse. Since character has lost its transparency, and respectability its fixed structures of reference, communal life now operates as a relentless policing of others: an anxious and ultimately self-conscious gaze, in contrast to which the workhouse stands as the one place that renders inhabitants invisible. It is thus described in gothic terms as "that barefaced monster of a Union Poorhouse, which seems to glare upon us with its hundred eyes" (1:42). This is not a figurative panopticism, but the projection of the divided community's own anxious surveillance onto the emblem of its most ignominious form of exclusion. For precisely that reason, Trollope's poor law tale shifts midstream from domestic realism to a quasi-gothic critique of modern legal rationality.[37]

Frances Trollope's Critique of Reason

Nothing can be more slightly defined than the line of demarcation between sanity and insanity. . . . Make the definition too narrow, it becomes meaningless; make it too wide, the whole human race are involved in the drag-net.
— *The London Times*, JULY 1853

With the marriage plot on hold and Jessie and her unborn child trapped in the workhouse, Trollope's novel takes on sudden gothic overtures. Immured in the parish "dungeon," "tortured" by the gibes of the "grossly vicious," and subjected to a "frightfully dismal and dreary . . . daily routine," the erstwhile village beauty transforms into a "strange-looking figure, half-ghostly, half grotesque" (2:192–93, 3:62). In this condition Jessie escapes from the workhouse and gives birth to her baby in a secluded shed. Through a series of plot contrivances the baby is murdered by Frederic Dalton under circumstances that make it seem as though Jessie herself is the perpetrator. With remarkably little change in status, Jessie is transferred from the workhouse to the prison, where she awaits her trial. Recollecting nothing of the baby's disappearance, Jessie readily believes herself guilty, concluding that she murdered her child in a fit of insanity. Already "half-ghostly" before the attribution of murder and madness, she now severs all remaining worldly connections and gives herself over to deep penitence and preparation for death.

Trollope's shift from domestic realism to gothic melodrama is fascinating not least because the result is to align the pauper and the lunatic: both outcasts in a society increasingly subject to bourgeois definitions of propriety. In *Madness and Civilization* Foucault describes reason as a dominatory monologue: the effect of a radical post-Enlightenment silencing of "la folie" (x–xi). Yet, according to Peter McCandless, Victorian attitudes toward the insane were complicated and paradoxical. Respectable Britons were, on the one hand, scandalized by the prospect of lunatics at large and strongly in favor of incarceration. Yet they were also far too identified with their legendary national liberties to tolerate the possibility of unjustified loss of freedom. This contradiction was exacerbated by contemporaries' stubborn belief that "a line between the sane and the insane" could "be drawn without a great deal of difficulty" (McCandless, "Liberty" 367). In actuality the "line of demarcation between sanity and insanity" was, as an 1853 article in the *Times* lamented, unnervingly elusive. Depending on where the line was placed, madness, it recognized, might either be stripped of descriptive utility or cast so as to compromise the sanity of the "whole human race" (qtd. in Skultans 172). The early- and mid-Victorian period thus saw fierce debates over the definition of madness: debates waged both within and between the legal and medical professions. Just as the New Poor Law attempted to displace an unreliable character test with an objective economic standard, so legal practitioners vied with medical men, asserting that insanity was a "fact" to be validated "in like manner as any other kind of fact" (McCandless, "Dangerous" 85).

For my purposes what is of interest here is the impact of such debates on contemporaries' state of mind. For Trollope and her readers questions of sanity were as vexingly elusive as questions of character—while in both cases epistemological certainty was the desired end. Trollope's novel follows Dickens's in insisting that personal experience is a more reliable path to knowledge than legal or bureaucratic inquiry. Hence, just as Losberne must conceal Oliver's "real story" from the asinine law, so Trollope is compelled to hide the truth in the service of justice. In so doing, Trollope plays with the extrarational possibilities of madness, subjecting the epistemology of the New Poor Law to a thoroughgoing critique.

As Trollope tells it, Deepbrook's leading male citizens are all too ready to conclude that Jessie is guilty of murdering her baby: the clergymen and landowners following the proto-Gradgrindian lawyers and officials in basing their arguments "*strictly* upon FACTS" (3:163). In this manner the novel shows how the abandonment of a knowledge based on character for one that recognizes only facts, "law and logic," transforms a once harmonious and integrated community into a "deluded crowd" (3:173, 193). But Trollope finds an alternative to these modern authorities by looking beneath and beside the traditional ruling class—in the extrarational knowledge of young women of the gentry. The "eccentric" Martha Maxwell, who suspects Frederic based on personal knowledge of his duplicity and Jessie's goodness, is thus described as possessing "a shrewdness of observation into character, which, like that of a practiced fortune-telling gypsy, often seemed to give her something wonderfully like a powerful divination" (2:98). And, when Ellen, who so far has been noted for her Elizabeth Bennet–like good sense, discerns her brother's guilt simply by reading his facial expression, her state of mind is thus described: "She had not . . . lost her reason, but rather seemed to possess more power than usual. . . . There was no confusion of intellect; all was terribly distinct and clear in the frightful picture thus spread before her, but every feature in it was gigantic, and every feeling, every faculty, seemed stretched and distended into supernatural strength and power, that she might gaze upon and understand it all" (3:242). In this way a "supernatural" and feminine epistemology takes the place of the fairy-tale essence that, in *Oliver Twist*, served to defend true character against the distortions of bourgeois materialism and legal rationality.[38]

Nevertheless, this extrarational female power to see and know cannot operate independently of the ubiquitous struggle for social legitimacy, and its impact on the domestic plot. To conserve its social power, the class that Ellen Dalton represents must jealously protect its claims to moral superiority. As Ellen contemplates the disgrace she and her family would suffer if Frederic's murderous adultery were made known, their social exclusion is tied to Jessie's. "Their future lives must be poisoned by undying shame, and never-to-be-forgotten misery; their country made too full of ignominy to hold them, and their honourable name converted into a stigma and disgrace!" (3:215). This uncontainable shame evokes Jessie's fall, transforming the entire "country" into a workhouse-like locus of ignominy. Similarly, Ellen's query—"where could they all . . . find darkness deep enough to hide them?" (2:188)—directly recalls the question that drove Jessie into the workhouse.

In the end the Dalton family is spared this outcast fate, but only by means of tenuous plot contrivance and, more important, only at the permanent expense of truth. As the weight of pending disgrace drives Ellen to temporary madness, Frederic's guilt undermines his hitherto acute faculties of rational self-preservation. Projecting Ellen's and Martha's supernatural vision onto the whole community, he flees "the eyes that [are] gazing on him" and, ironically, drowns himself believing that the imbecile laugh of Silly Sally, the workhouse idiot, is "the taunting gibe of an accuser, whose voice was the ordained signal for his execution" (3:300, 305). Jessie, meanwhile, is found not guilty by reason of insanity. She dies—still believing that she murdered her child—just moments before the verdict is pronounced. This remarkably ambiguous conclusion neither definitely convicts nor exonerates Jessie from a catalogue of indistinct transgressions, including social climbing, pauperism, sexual impropriety, murder, and madness. Thus, in the absence of a fairy-tale essence like Dickens's, truth is radically compromised for all. Even Ellen, entirely innocent of any crime, suffers the consequences. Believing that Frederic has run away, Ellen gradually recovers from her delirium and is rushed off to Florence to marry Lord Pemberton inexpensively. To preserve her now fragile mental stability, the family withholds knowledge of Frederic's death until months later, and she is never told the circumstances under which he died.

Hence, while modern legal rationality has been discredited, its only viable alternative—the extrarational and, indeed, often irrational knowledge of women—is ultimately undermined. Just as Dickens's fairy-tale ending is haunted by the specter of bourgeois-materialist appearances, so Trollope's critique of reason succumbs to the normalizing pressures of the contest for social legitimacy. The events he has witnessed lead the assistant Poor Law commissioner to the "unphilosophical" conclusion that "common sense" is preferable to bureaucratic uniformity. Yet he is rewarded for this insight, in proto-Kafkaesque fashion, by being transferred so frequently that he is "prevented" from "being useful any where." On the other hand, the narrator relates the marriage of the commissioner's son, a lawyer, to Martha Maxwell with rather inexplicable cheer: the couple moves to London (hitherto a suspect place), where he "devotes" himself to "business" and becomes "greatly distinguished in his profession," hitherto a questionable vocation (3:323, 321–22). Hence, while the novel ends with a plea for a more Christian poor law, and reasserts the "demoralising effect" of centralization, the only processes that it successfully inscribes are those contributing to a volatile culture of respectability constituted on delusive bourgeois-materialist and modern legal-rational grounds.

Assessing the New Poor Law

Oliver Twist and *Jessie Phillips* were part of a multifarious and popular culture of resistance to the New Poor Law. Despite widespread dissatisfaction with the status quo, and easy passage in Parliament, the 1834 act was and remained highly unpopular, repugnant not only to the working classes but also to a wide range of the middle and upper classes. For at least a decade vigorous and widespread opposition to the New Poor Law aimed to overturn the act entirely. The new regime survived this tumultuous initiation primarily because antipathy to the law was second only to the fear of a pauperized working class.[39]

Anti–New Poor Law representations included pamphlets, such as the infamous *Book of Bastiles* [*sic*] (1841), a collection of workhouse atrocities; ballads, sketches, cartoons, and handbills; public protests and riots; and local folklore, such as the belief that "children in workhouses were killed to make pies with" and that aged pauper corpses "were employed to manure the guardians' fields" to "save the expense of coffins" (qtd. in Crowther, *Workhouse* 31). A. W. N. Pugin's "Contrasted Residences" (see fig. 1), from the same series of illustrations which inspired Carlyle and Ruskin, incorporated some of the most notorious practices associated with the new regime. John Walter, the editor of the *Times*, led a vigorous attack, influencing the tone of *Oliver Twist*. Carlyle interrupted a project on Oliver Cromwell in order to excoriate the "Poor-law Prisons" in *Past and Present* (1846). Poor law officials themselves contributed to the notoriety of the workhouse by stressing the instrumentality of the new deterrent mechanisms.

In 1836 Edwin Chadwick, secretary to the Poor Law Commission, pseudonymously published extracts from the commission's first report in the *Edinburgh Review*. Although some version of the deterrent workhouse had by then been introduced throughout much of rural England, the unpopular central commission lacked the power and the technical means to ensure that even relatively cooperative Poor Law unions introduced the workhouse system in its prescribed form. Hence, Chadwick was writing under considerable political pressure when he attempted to demonstrate that the results so far "have fully answered the [Royal Commission's] most sanguine anticipations" ("New" 506). Although the statistics he produced recall Martineau's tale (with the number of able-bodied inmates dropping by as much as 98 percent), Chadwick told a quite different story about working-class transformation. As he portrayed it, the less eligible workhouse was an instrument of social discipline, not an agent of deep-seated cultural change.

For example, Chadwick incorporated the story of Thomas Pocock, a dissolute and rebellious laborer (reminiscent of Martineau's Mr. Monks). To curb Pocock's occasional bouts of drinking, Chadwick reported, Mrs. Pocock told her husband's employer that "there is nothing" Pocock "minds so much as the thoughts of that workhouse." Upon her request he was threatened with discharge so that dread of the workhouse would "keep him to his work" and out of the public house (515–16). Although the story exemplifies the formidable efficiency with which the threat of disciplined confinement deters fecklessness, alcoholism, and insubordination, there is no sense whatever that Pocock cultivated middle-class status—nor even that he found the workhouse an ignominious (rather than merely unpleasant) place.

The difference between Martineau's and Chadwick's propagandistic accounts of the New Poor Law thus compels us to ask whether the post-1834 workhouse operated in the short term, as a coercive deterrent, or in the long term, as a catalyst behind an increasingly dominant bourgeois culture in which economic dependence was thoroughly stigmatized. The answer is that it did both. Crude coercion was always an operative factor, characterizing the early years of reform and then resurfacing in the 1860s, when depression in trade and agriculture once again precipitated a crackdown on "eligible" outdoor relief. But in the long term the law worked by encouraging the respectable poor to dread economic dependence of any kind, no matter the cost.

By 1845 a vivid, almost mythical, but contradictory discourse surrounded the institution of the workhouse. On the one hand, contemporaries were scandalized by barbarous images of little girls locked overnight in mortuaries, of the severe flogging of women and children, of paupers so starved they were compelled to gnaw on the rotten bones that were provided for bone crushing—all of which,

Figure 1. "Contrasted Residences for the Poor," from *Contrasts; or, A Parallel between the Noble Edifices of the Fourteenth and Fifteenth Centuries, and Similar Buildings of the Present Day; Shewing the Present Decay of Taste: Accompanied by Appropriate Text* (1836) by A. W. N. Pugin. Under the "Modern Poor House" Pugin depicts the separation of families; the isolation of the structure from church and community; the prisonlike walls, bars, locks, chains, and cuffs; the threat of corporal punishment (a practice more typical of Old Poor Law policy than new); the regimented, monotonous workhouse diet; and the use of pauper bodies for medical dissection (a feature that, while largely untrue, was widely believed).

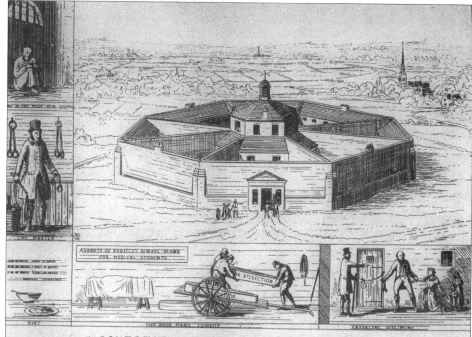

CONTRASTED RESIDENCES FOR THE POOR

ANTIENT · POOR · HOYSE.

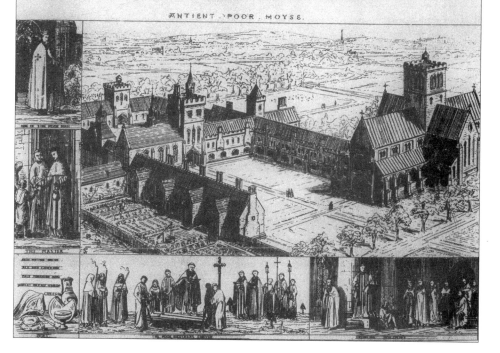

unlike many similar accounts of atrocity, were factual. At the same time, contemporaries recoiled from the depersonalizing regimentation of institutional life: from workhouse diets, workhouse uniforms, enforced silence, and enervating monotony. Thus, the idea of the workhouse as a corrupt, disorderly, and barbaric place was in many respects indistinct from the equally repellent idea of it as a hyperrational, impersonal, efficient instrument of social discipline (Crowther, *Workhouse* 30–32; Wood 81; Henriques, "How" 366). This inconsistent iconography was directly related to the limitations of the central administration, whose members, despite their own notoriety as noxiously interfering bureaucrats, remained incapable of subjecting local unions to their authority (Fraser 53–54). As a result, many historians have devoted their efforts to recovering local experience—sifting through infinite variations of old and new practices, centralized interference, and local resistance—in order to construct composite institutional and social histories (see, e.g., Digby).

Nevertheless, to argue that the New Poor Law was both unevenly implemented and widely disliked is not at all to conclude that it was ineffective. From the working-class point of view the difference between the efficient "less eligibility" principle executed in Martineau's tale, the unabashed coercion advertised by Chadwick, and the barbarism of Dickens's or Trollope's workhouses seems to have mattered less than the combined power of all such representations in marking the workhouse as an outcast place. As Karel Williams has argued, existing data on post-1834 relief rolls do not adequately indicate the impact of the New Poor Law, since, by definition, those who were deterred were neither eligible for outdoor relief, nor willing to enter the workhouse (68–69). Later novels such as Charles Reade's *Very Hard Cash* (1863), Dickens's *Our Mutual Friend* (1862–63) and George Gissing's *The Nether World* (1889) illustrate Williams's point, representing working-class people willing to starve and (in the latter case) go to jail rather than submit to the ignominy of pauperdom. Thus, according to F. M. L. Thompson, the New Poor Law was "the one big success of the century, for the transmission of middle-class standards . . . to the working classes" (*Rise* 355). In this respect the 1834 act functioned as the legal complement to middle-class project of "making the working man like me."

That said, Thompson's overall intent is to stress the relative autonomy of working-class culture. Despite the undeniable effect of deterrent legislation, working-class norms, he argues, are "best seen as a bundle of self-generated habits . . . rather than as being either imitative or imposed from outside or above." Thompson thus refutes the conclusions of the "social control" school of history while, in so doing, pointing to the thwarted pastoral ambitions of bureaucrats such as Chadwick, and voluntarists such as Chalmers (355).[40] In a sense, then, Thompson's arguments suggest that the New Poor Law was successful precisely because its implementation was uneven. By rejecting Chadwick's pastoral agenda, limiting the enforcement powers of the Poor Law Commission, and leaving the largest share of responsibility to local ratepayers and voluntary organizations, Whigs and liberal Tories created the kind of government which suited the popular idea of Britain as a nation of self-governing individuals and communities. Grasping a liberal moment that reached its fullest expression in the mid-Victorian constitutional consensus, they recognized "that if one governed too much, one did not govern at all" (Foucault, "Space" 242).

The early-Victorian reformers who abolished the Old Poor Law, promoted deterrence, and left positive pastorship almost entirely to voluntary agencies thus acted as self-conscious liberals and ardent moralists. So long as the Christian and civic economy was imagined as the self-actualizing ideal of individuals and communities, laissez-faire legislation could be seen as its necessary complement. Unlike paternalism, wrote J. S. Mill, the reformed law treated the poor "as moral agents, influenced by motives," and not "as creatures whom we can feed like pigs or turkeys" ("Proposed" 1072–73). As legislators, the Whigs and their allies preserved local autonomy and curbed bureaucratic excesses; they thus promoted a thriving voluntarist culture that, in many respects, dwarfed the activities of Somerset House.

Yet, while they carefully restrained the powers of centralized bureaucrats, the same reformers did not foresee the consequences of reframing moral questions in modern legal terms. From a Weberian perspective they mistook their arduous curb on bureaucratic powers for an effective check on the spread of a depersonalizing bourgeois-materialist rationality. By promoting atomized, competitive, and materialistic notions of individual status, and objectifying "tests," the same law that stigmatized pauperism also undermined the idea of character as an antimaterialist concept of human individuality. As Ruskin was to put it in *Unto This Last* (1862), the reification of political economy threatened the "social affections," and reduced the human being to a soulless "covetous machine" (168). The 1834 act was thus the chief legislative means through which *homo economicus*—the calculating subject of bourgeois individualism—was concretized and propagated.

Hence, at bottom, what the social texts of Martineau, Dickens, and Frances Trollope illuminate is a historic conjuncture between incompatible modern ends: a self-affirming middle-class desire to "make the working man like me," and a bourgeois call to rationalize, economize, and stabilize. Middle-class identity had been predicated on the moral imperative of a civilizing mission. Yet the New Poor Law, the first piece of social legislation to follow on middle-class enfranchisement, deployed parliamentary power to stigmatize poor relief, without respect to individual character, and with no guarantee of preventive pastorship.

In practice many unions retained the traditional character test: relieving the respectable widow out of doors, and consigning her dissolute neighbor to the stigmatic workhouse. Nevertheless, the law stood for a new and impersonal power to objectify the human condition. How, in its wake, could civic-minded volunteers mobilize their efforts without lapsing into Gradgrindian social science or Pardigglesque philanthropy? How could they remake working people in their own self-image without unmasking their own Bumble-like bourgeois pretensions? How could they reconcile personal knowledge with legal rationality so as to avoid the epistemological quandaries of Frances Trollope's "deluded crowd"? These questions asserted themselves repeatedly in Victorian literature as writers such as Dickens, Mill, Gaskell, Ruskin, Gissing, and many others struggled to stabilize their antimaterialist worldview.

Of course, from the Chadwickian perspective through which the 1834 act is often approached, these century-long conflicts are invisible. Determined eventually to mastermind a far-reaching tutelary state, Chadwick unambivalently strove to enforce the workhouse test. With no allegiance to personalized relations or intersubjective ideals, Bentham's disciple could envision the shift from legislative deterrence to the pastoral state as two consecutive phases—one negative and the other positive—in implementing the same bureaucratic utopia. But for those for whom terms such as *character* conveyed qualities that, by definition, could not be objectified—in other words, for the majority of middle- and upper-class Victorians—pastorship remained a personal, voluntary, and community obligation, not the province of a bureaucratic state. Thus, many who saw the 1834 act's mandate against outdoor relief as part of a self-affirming civilizing mission became vociferous opponents of Chadwick's ambitious Sanitary Idea, a subject to which I turn in the next chapter.

The works of Martineau, Dickens, and Frances Trollope thus provide a textual record of two clashing worldviews in the wake of the New Poor Law. Such fictional representations dramatize the difference between the stalwart moral universe of Thomas Chalmers, woven through with vertical and horizontal social bonds, and the atomized individuals of bourgeois materialism. Behind Martineau's "happy fable" of self-maintaining labor is a disturbing democratization of bourgeois competition and status consciousness: a reduction of character and a hollowing out of the middle-class moral core. For Frances Trollope the fully knowable traditional community has been irrevocably lost. In *Oliver Twist* Dickens imagines a fairy-tale essence impervious to material debasement even while depicting a landscape of shepherdless drudges. To fulfill the problematic project of "making the working man like me," Dickens ends by literalizing it. When Mr. Brownlow sees "something in [Oliver's] face . . . that touches and interests [him]" (76), he ends by exposing the self-serving underside of the civilizing mission. Charity's putative extension of family ties, that is, dissolves into the long-anticipated disclosure of Oliver's actual blood kinship to his middle-class benefactors. As we shall see in chapter 5, the tenuousness of this imaginative defense against bourgeois materialism became all the more evident decades later when, in *Our Mutual Friend*, Dickens returned to the theme of the pauper lad, and made Bradley Headstone the most monstrous victim of character building in British fiction.

CHAPTER THREE

Is There a Pastor in the *House*?

Sanitary Reform and Governing Agency in Dickens's Midcentury Fiction

> Dickens's genius is especially suited to the delineation of city life. London is like a newspaper. Everything is there, and everything is disconnected.
> — WALTER BAGEHOT, "CHARLES DICKENS"

> In sober truth, whatever homage may be professed, or even paid, to real or supposed mental superiority, the general tendency of things throughout the world is to render mediocrity the ascendant power among mankind. In ancient history, in the middle ages, and in a diminishing degree through the long transition from feudality to the present time, the individual was a power in himself; and if he had either great talents or a high social position he was a considerable power. At present individuals are lost in the crowd. . . . The only power deserving the name is that of masses, and of governments while they make themselves the organ of the tendencies and instincts of masses. This is as true in the moral and social relations of private life as in public transactions.
> — JOHN STUART MILL, *On Liberty*

> Don't think it is a part of my despondency about public affairs, and my fear that our national glory is on the decline, when I say that mere form and conventionalities usurp, in English art, as in English government and social relations, the place of living force and truth.
> — CHARLES DICKENS

Charles Dickens's interests in legal and administrative reform are as apparent to readers as the famous depictions of Chancery and the Circumlocution Office in, respectively, *Bleak House* (1852–53) and *Little Dorrit* (1855–57). Dickens's equally profound engagement with sanitary reform is less obvious. In this chapter I argue that the debates about governance engendered by the public health movement—including Edwin Chadwick's groundbreaking "Sanitary Idea"—are important to understanding *Bleak House* as well as underlying questions of pastoral agency in a self-consciously liberal society. In his 1851 preface to *Oliver Twist* Dickens had insisted that sanitary reform must "precede all other Social Reforms," preparing for "Education" and "even for Religion" (qtd. in Butt and Tillotson 190–91). Here sanitary reform becomes fundamentally necessary to the nation's moral and physical well-being. Yet it would be a mistake to infer from such remarks that Dickens had become a staunch proponent of the state's duty to intervene in the lives of individuals and communities.

Bleak House memorably dramatizes the need for pastorship in a society of allegedly self- reliant individuals. But it by no means clearly endorses state tutelage, nor, indeed, any other form of institutionalized authority. Instead, like John Stuart Mill, Dickens testifies to the diminished power of modern individuals, without clearly seeking (as Mill himself attempted to do) collective alternatives to the individual's limited capabilities. As we shall see, Dickens's growing skepticism toward the myth of self-reliant character, epitomized in the 1855 letter cited in the epigraphs, left the novelist without a secure foundation for modern authority. Clearly, by midcentury the idealized pastoral community figured at the end of *Oliver Twist* seemed more tenuous. Walter Bagehot, a staid liberal who accepted the disconnection of "city life" as a matter of course, noticed the frustrated radicalism of Dickens's later novels. For Bagehot, Dickens betrayed an unmasculine "tendency . . . to make men dissatisfied with their inevitable condition," "to make them fancy that its irremediable evils can be remedied" ("Dickens" 87). A more sympathetic reader might have replied that, in *Bleak House*, complacency toward an intolerable status quo is a mark of moral turpitude, no matter how bleak the prospect for social progress. The novel thus represents a society that, at its best, resembles Mr. Snagsby: recognizing the inhumanity of a pastorless nation, but "puzzled" as to how to proceed.

Bleak House is not, of course, reducible to the vicissitudes of the sanitary movement, but it is nonetheless illuminating to trace the novel's response to the manifest failures of the Public Health Act of 1848, a historical context I describe in some detail in the analyses that follow. As historians have suggested, midcentury sanitary reforms stalled because of hardened divisions over technology, finance, ideology, and politics. The crux of the debate was rarely the need for action, but the far more difficult question of in whom and how to vest the authority to act (Fraser 70). In *Bleak House*, a novel saturated with contemporaneous social issues, Dickens represents aspects of Britain's semi-reformed, semi-antiquated institutional foundation in terms of a ubiquitous sociopolitical deadlock (symbolized by the fog, the rain, and the generation and accumulation of meaningless paperwork). Despite the obscurity, it is possible to trace the deadlock to two strains of selfish interest among the governing classes: one archaic and aristocratic, the other modern and bourgeois. Significantly, the relation between the two is not the dynamic class struggle of the French Revolutionary era, but a midcentury standstill favorable both to ancient privilege and to modern exploitation. Nevertheless, whereas the ancien régime is best personified by its moribund establishments (Chancery, Parliament, Chesney Wold), its modern counterpart is represented as the decay of middle-class character (the hypocrisy of Chadband, the pettiness of Guppy, the meanness of the Smallweeds, the parasitism of Vholes, the selfishness of Skimpole, the self-importance of Pardiggle, and the vocationlessness of Richard Carstone). This very decline resonates with Mill's 1836 prognosis of a national character threatened by the "decay of individual energy" ("Civilization" 135); with what, in *On Liberty*, Mill further described as a condition of isolation, powerlessness, and mediocrity.

In this chapter I aim to present a vividly historical picture of Dickens's struggle to defuse threatening forms of power, and to locate a legitimate foundation for pastorship in a liberal society riddled by ideological conflict, institutionally entrenched self-interest, and unnerving epistemological uncertainty. This critical object involves multiple layers of analysis, alternately bringing historical contexts to bear on *Bleak House*, and *Bleak House* to bear on historiography. I begin by describing the important correspondences between the novel and the sanitary movement, a process that entails exploring connections between Dickens's ambivalence and the contrary public persona of Edwin Chadwick. By way of further demonstrating the relevance of such arguments, I move to a reconsideration of D. A. Miller's influential reading of *Bleak House* and the police. In the remainder of the chapter I further describe the complicated social context in which the search for authoritative pastorship unfolds, including the increasing professionalization of Britain's educated middle classes, and the nation's formidable voluntarist tradition. Dickens himself was involved in charitable endeavors of various kinds, but, as readers of *Bleak House* are well aware, the author unsparingly satirized organized philanthropy in the figures of Mrs. Pardiggle and Mrs. Jellyby. I consider this defensive antifeminism at some length, arguing that Dickens's motive is not to shield femininity as such, but to shield feminine domesticity's crucial harborage of the personal. Dickens's imaginative repudiation of charitable practices he publicly and privately supported warrants a sustained contrast between Dickensian deadlock and the corporate voluntarism practiced by the mid-Victorian Charity Organization Society. Although novels such as *Bleak House* and *Little Dorrit* were potentially subversive, Dickens's skepticism toward modern and institutionalized forms of power, his search for an "old-fashioned" but effective social foundation, tended unexpectedly to favor the vision of Britain's organized philanthropists.

Bleak House and the Sanitary Movement

To recognize the profound relation between *Bleak House* and the sanitary movement, it is necessary to revisit the latter's tortuous and ultimately anti-climactic history. From the 1830s on, a combination of vested interests and deep-seated ideological disputes combined to obstruct sanitary reform with effects that, in and of themselves, anticipate the comic-grotesque of Dickens's novel. Whereas the Royal Commission's report on the poor laws had produced substantial legislation within six months, it took six years before an "emascu-lated" Public Health Act followed upon Edwin Chadwick's groundbreaking *Report on the Sanitary Condition of the Labouring Population of Great Britain* (1842) (Fraser 70).

In an exemplary anticipation of *Little Dorrit*'s "How not to do it," Parliament's immediate response to the *Report* was to launch a circumlocutious investigation into disease and squalor that had already been discovered. By 1843 the *Westminster Review* complained that, if "the Reform Bill epoch" had typified "action without reflection," the present era is equally "remarkable for inquiry without results" (qtd. in Lewis 69). Such protests did not obviate the need for a Royal Commission to produce reports on the Health of Towns in 1844 and 1845, nor for Chadwick himself to reiterate his own conclusions in an 1847–48 series of London investigations entitled—as though to emphasize its redundancy—*First, Second, and Third Reports of Commissioners appointed to inquire whether any and what special means may be requisite for the improvement of the health of the metropolis.* Yet, despite the notoriety of the 1842 *Report* and the mountain of collateral documentation that followed, it was not until 1848, when dread of approaching cholera diminished resistance to legislative action, that Lord Morpeth's compromised Public Health bill was enacted.

By this point Dickens had himself been enlisted in the service of the cause.[1] Although Dickens's brother-in-law, the engineer Henry Austin, was of one of Chadwick's faithful allies, the author remained cool to the man whom many Britons still associated with the heartless politico-economic orthodoxy of the

New Poor Law. Dickens was more disposed to support Dr. Thomas Southwood Smith, a less technocratic sanitary reformer whose public career had begun with the protection of factory children (Brundage 95–98). Hence, Dickens's 1850 speeches on behalf of the Metropolitan Sanitary Association—a body formed to raise public support for London reforms, and to quell hostility to centralization—are not those of a committed Chadwickian. But it is important to note that the author who would soon satirize Britain's scandalously inefficient government in the Circumlocution Office was not, like so many of his contemporaries, a dogmatic opponent of centralization (cf. E. Johnson 2:1129).

In fact, Dickens's views on the matter are decidedly ambivalent. In his 1850 speech he declared that the "principal objectors" to sanitary reform are greedy landlords and "less selfish" gentlemen with "a weak leaning to the words 'self-government.'" Yet, in a key passage looking back to Carlyle's *Past and Present*, and ahead to *Bleak House*, the novelist misrepresented a "leaning" that, weak or otherwise, is evident in his own works. Dickens invited those who insist that the affairs of "the next parish [are] no business of theirs" to keep their typhus or smallpox "within [their] own bounds" (*Speeches* 107).[2] This clever conceit conflates Scrooge-like self- interest (or smug Podsnappery) with a sincere conviction in the superiority of local, voluntary, and other characteristically English forms of civic action.[3] John Stuart Mill, for example, while no friend to the tight-fisted "dirty party," had feared that "what is done for the people benefits them only when it assists them in what they do for themselves" (qtd. in MacDonagh, *Early* 68). Lacking Mill's philosophical rigor, Dickens often advocated paternalism. Nevertheless, as Kathleen Blake's recent work on *Bleak House* suggests, Dickens's novels are more in line with the era's mainstream individualism than is commonly realized. In an 1854 letter alluding to his famous caricature of utilitarianism, the author averred that it is Mr. Gradgrind's excesses, and not his intentions, which warrant censure. "Perhaps," he adds, "by dint of his going his way and my going mine, we shall meet at last in some halfway house" (qtd. in Collins 213).

That the Dickensian house, which metaphorically represents the condition of England, is so incurably bleak testifies, I suggest, to the failed materialization of this very halfway house—the British "middle course" later described by Mill in his *Autobiography* (174). In *Bleak House* Dickens attempts to produce an ideological synthesis that, were it successful, would articulate a suitably English relation between the individual and the society: one that is (among other desiderata) stable but democratic, rational but compassionate, authoritative but liberal.

In this respect his novels attempt imaginatively to redress the "fragmentation" and "arrested development" of contemporaneous politics and social policy (Briggs, *Victorian* 91). Yet the antitheses ostensibly at stake in this process are themselves complicated and deceptive. If, for example, we imagine Dickens as favoring humanitarian sympathy while opposing Gradgrindian utilitarianism, that is not necessarily to say that he is for state rather than private action; for Chadwickian centralization rather than local control; for the professional expert as opposed to the well-trained volunteer. Yet these were among the ideological divides that helped to stall the progress not only of sanitary reform, but also of modern governance more generally.

In their superb chapter on *Bleak House* John Butt and Kathleen Tillotson establish the correspondence between Dickens's novel and various contemporary deadlocks. Between 1850 and 1852, as *Bleak House* was planned and begun, readers of the *Times* would have been outraged by the delay and ineffectiveness of Chancery reform, urged anew of the importance of as yet unimplemented sanitary improvements, and advised that Parliament itself—the object of Dickens's "Doodle" satire—was largely to blame. Indeed, the Whig defeat of 1851 left Britain without a government for a period of two weeks as a series of politicians failed to form a viable administration.[4] With stalled sanitary reform in mind, the *Times* opined that "the most serious evil of the political *deadlock* was 'the indefinite postponement or defeat of various measures of great public utility'" (qtd. in Butt and Tillotson 188). These sentiments are epitomized in Dickens's description of Tom-all-Alone's: tied up in Chancery while "fetching and carrying fever, and sowing more evil in its every footprint than Lord Coodle and Sir Thomas Doodle . . . and all the fine gentlemen in office, down to Zoodle, shall set right in five hundred years" (*Bleak* 273). For the *Times* this aristocratic monopoly on parliamentary power was an "insult to a free people." "What becomes of all our numerous institutions for self-government," they editorialized, if "the sacred gift of government, is after all, an heirloom in two or three families?" (qtd. in Butt and Tillotson 188).[5]

Yet, when Chadwick emerged to combat the deadlock, he, rather than aristocratic corruption, became the primary focus of popular critique. Mythologized and demonized, Chadwick was likened to a Prussian autocrat and a host of foreign tyrants including Napoléon, the pope, and the Russian czar. As we shall see, *Bleak House* displays a comparable ambivalence. The novel persistently undermines the modern agencies that might unsettle pernicious deadlock, instead favoring symbolic and impracticable, but suitably British, alternatives.

Overseeing the Social Body: England's "Prussian Minister"

He was determined that the British world should be clean and live a century but on one condition only—that they consented to purchase real patent Chadwickian soap, the Chadwickian officially-gathered soft water, and the true impermeable telescopic earthenware pipe, and when they did die, were interred by his official undertakers in the Chadwickian necropolis.   — *The Economist*

Edwin Chadwick's success in portraying himself as the master agent of an all-embracing Sanitary Idea was one of the most remarkable feats of self-promotion in the nineteenth century. At a time when eulogists of the nation's character lauded self-government, and derided the centralized bureaucracies of the Continent, Chadwick defiantly constructed himself as England's "Prussian Minister."[6] As Bentham's most prominent Victorian disciple, Chadwick's agenda may seem linked to the panoptical designs of his predecessor. But this line of thinking about sanitary reform is potentially misleading. Chadwick's *Report* became the model of a new and controversial technocratic rationality, but neither its rhetorical form (which often resembles journalistic exposé) nor its recommendations precisely illustrates what D. A. Miller has described as panopticism's "hidden and devious discipline" (22).[7]

A historically specific approach to the 1842 *Report* must emphasize its relation to an existing body of social scientific ideas. The discourse of public health had originated in diverse eighteenth-century inquiries into growing urban concerns such as contagious disease, sewage disposal, water supply, housing, and burial practices. Chadwick's *Report* consolidated these materials while making further use of the data collected by the recently established Poor Law Commission. The *Report* thus became the first official document to broadcast an emerging social perspective, in which health, morality, and political stability were linked to environmental factors (Flinn 44, 58; Fraser 64; Childers, "Observation" 411–15). Whereas Bentham had based his legislative ideas on theoretical principles, Chadwick's proposals appealed to a massive empirical database (Lewis 10).

Significantly, these innovations marked a dramatic transition in Chadwick's own career. As a poor law reformer, Chadwick had merely helped to implement an existing body of ideas; but, as author of the sanitary *Report*, he was "radical and original" (Fraser 64; cf. Brundage 79–99). When he first embarked on sanitary research in 1838, Chadwick was still driven by the economizing logic of the New Poor Law: determined to reduce the nation's "Fever Bill" by demonstrating the material costs of ill health. This narrow object was eventually dwarfed by the Sanitary Idea—his sweeping vision of the vast social impact of unregulated dirt and disease.

Ironically, the groundbreaking social view Chadwick thus promoted had roots in a moral conception of society which was ultimately at odds with the Sanitary Idea's rigorous environmental determinism. Chadwick was especially indebted to the researches of three pioneering physicians—James Phillips Kay, Neil Arnott, and Thomas Southwood Smith—who, as assistant Poor Law commissioners, had established authoritative links between urban squalor and disease. As we saw in chapter 2, Kay (later Sir James Kay-Shuttleworth) was the author of an influential treatise, *The Moral and Physical Condition of the Working Classes . . . in Manchester* (1832). Kay's call for mandatory sewerage and drainage, as Chadwick later acknowledged, "foreshadowed" the Sanitary Idea (Selleck 69–70). Yet, unlike Chadwick's *Report*, Kay's text was split between the environmentalist priorities of social science, and the moral priorities of organized charity. The advent of cholera pointed to the need not only for sanitary legislation, Kay believed, but also for a pastoral visiting scheme like that of Thomas Chalmers, the pioneering philanthropist to whom *Manchester* was dedicated. Industrial towns such as Manchester were in crisis because the "natural ties" between governing and working classes had been "disrupted" (11). This emphasis on personalized character-building relationships was utterly alien to Chadwick. For the latter, character was the determined effect of "physical circumstances" and hedonistic conditioning. The "habits" of those "obliged to occupy inferior tenements," he alleged, "soon become 'of a piece' with the dwelling" (*Sanitary* 220, 194).[8] Here the stress on habits betrayed an absolute environmental determinism, antithetical to the "presiding virtues" stressed by Kay (6).

Chadwick's bold Sanitary Idea thus presented a secular, materialist, and deterministic recasting of a hitherto semi-theistic and idealist moral discourse.[9] That said, as the tortuous political aftermath suggests, Chadwick could not dislodge this still influential mind-set from the emerging social sciences, nor radicalize Victorian governance accordingly. On the contrary, Kay's blend of the scientific and personal remained highly influential, anticipating a mid-Victorian movement to organize charity that vied with statist alternatives to pastorship up until World War I. In many respects it was the moderate Kay, rather than the radical Chadwick, who, as education secretary between 1839 and 1849, became, for a time, the most successful model of the public servant as "heroic" expert.[10]

In Kay's development from local volunteer to state official, from private physician to public servant, from charitable visitor to modern professional expert, we find an important (if short-lived) pattern: an early-Victorian approach to the secularization of the religious community's traditional pastoral functions.

By contrast, Edwin Chadwick, for all his reputed Prussian ministerialism, was a maverick who pursued power with such relentless entrepreneurial vigor that he eventually became "the most hated man in England" (qtd. in R. Williams, *Culture* 94).[11] In Chadwick's singular imagination the notion of the social lost its personal undertones, prompting technological and bureaucratic solutions. In an audacious attempt to master the social body, Chadwick envisioned a comprehensive "venous-arterial" system of sewerage and drainage to minister to the nation's sanitary needs. Looking beyond the simple waste removal advocated by the respected physician Southwood Smith, Chadwick called for a continuous water supply, and a vast network of underground pipes. By these unprecedented means noxious sewage might be removed from crowded cities and transported to rural areas, where, as fertilizer for Britain's farms, it would become "liquid gold" (Flinn 60; Chadwick, *Sanitary* 120–24).

Chadwick's controversial plan, sparked by the recent invention of the egg-shaped sewer pipe, enabled him to roil a wide range of vested interests while pitting the authority of civil engineers against that of physicians (*Sanitary* 216). Yet Chadwick's ultimate design was to legitimate his own unique credentials. In an 1842 letter Chadwick explained that Britain's health depended on "applications of the science of engineering of which medical men know nothing," as well as jurisprudential expertise "of which the engineers know nothing" (qtd. in Brundage 84). Who better to superintend the complicated medical, engineering, legal, and administrative dimensions of this intricate plan than the architect himself? As Anthony Brundage suggests, "There was only one man in the kingdom qualified" to oversee the Sanitary Idea (82).

Chadwick is justifiably remembered for his role in attempting to introduce modern bureaucratic methods to a nation that had prided and continued to pride itself on the absence of a Continental raison d'état. Yet, significantly, the manner in which Chadwick urged legal-rational methods on his countrymen—his grandiose planning, zealous bullying, public campaigning, and private jockeying for position—exemplified precisely the kind of individual power that bureaucracy aims to repress. That Chadwick's practical accomplishments "seem minimal," culminating in his retirement from public service in 1854, should not obscure the extent to which he envisioned himself, and succeeded in persuading many of his contemporaries to regard him as a master agency. The eventual passage of an "emasculated" Public Health Act in 1848, establishing what was to be a short-lived Board of Health, embroiled Chadwick in a series of widely publicized contests with an array of powerful adversaries (Fraser 71, 70; cf. Finer 355–482). More than any other contemporary, it was Chadwick who personified the dangerous "monomania" of the expert, hardening popular resolve against the foreign modes of power which seemed to threaten Britain's legendary liberty (Searle 23).

This midcentury controversy was a central context for *Bleak House*. That the novel followed the *Report* in exposing dangerous squalor is as clear as Dickens's scathing critique of the nation's ineffective political, legal, and public health institutions. What is, perhaps, less obvious is the subtle fashion in which *Bleak House* also responds to Edwin Chadwick's public persona: his notorious would-be master agency. Throughout this period supportive characterizations of Chadwick dovetailed with pejoratives in ways that illuminate Dickens's ambivalent representation of modern expertise. One sympathetic portrait, published prior to the passage of the act, described Chadwick as the "one public man living" whose "perseverance nothing can tire," whose zeal "will admit of no hindrance" (qtd. in Brundage 120–21). Such superhuman attributes were scarcely less daunting than the fatally flawed prowess represented by *The Economist* in 1854. In one of the least hostile of a chorus of leading articles trumpeting Chadwick's forced ousting from the Board of Health—a defeat that signaled the effective demise of that controversial body, and the end of Chadwick's official career— the author of the Sanitary Idea was described as a "public man" to whom the nation owes its greatest debt. "His industry is something frightful. His pertinacity is something more terrible still." Unfortunately, the "usefulness" of such "vast" abilities is vitiated by a "mental peculiarity which utterly disqualifies him for the executive services of his country. He is essentially a despot and a bureaucrat." Indeed, the same writer declared that Chadwick's perverse disdain for self-government qualified him for service in bureaucratic countries such as Russia, Britain's foe in the recently commenced Crimean War (qtd. in Brundage 155–56). Such descriptions of Chadwick as an exogenous figure frequently recurred. Rather than conform to British customs, claimed another article, Chadwick would demand "blind, passive obedience to the ukase, decree, bull or proclamation of the autocrat, pope, grand lama of sanitary reform" (qtd. in Lewis 369).

In the early 1850s, as Dickens began to plan his next novel, the recently enacted Board of Health still enjoyed a share of popular support—including that of the author of *Bleak House*. But virulent opposition to un-English legislation was already in evidence and would soon accelerate. What is clear in retrospect is that, while Chadwick's public persona tended to dominate the debate, his groundbreaking Sanitary Idea was, in and of itself, far too radical a plan for a nation that, since the French Revolution, had prided itself on the avoidance of extremes. As John Stuart Mill was to observe in his *Autobiography*, "It is the character of the British people . . . that to induce them to approve of any change it is necessary that they should look upon it as a middle course" (174). The reorganization, technical innovation, unification, and concentration of powers for which Chadwick called was no middle course—no Dickensian halfway house—but a veritable revolution, in technological, political, administrative, and epistemological terms. As Dickens's new novel was bleakly to demonstrate, this was not a revolution that the British public, or, in the final analysis, Dickens himself was prepared to tolerate. To understand *Bleak House*'s profound contradictions—its inability to imagine an appropriate middle course, and its subtle reflections on Chadwickian master agency—further requires a reconsideration of D. A. Miller's influential thesis.

Bleak House and the Police: the Problem of Charisma

According to D. A. Miller, the nineteenth-century novel "shows disciplinary power to inhere in the very resistance to it" (27). This inescapable paradox is exemplified by *Bleak House*, in which the distinction between carceral space (e.g., Chancery) and its putatively liberal antithesis (the middle-class home) is emphasized but ultimately undermined (100).[12] Miller's ingenious reading of *Bleak House* rests on two provocative assumptions. The first is that the "evident archaism" of Chancery symbolizes "a new kind of bureaucratic organization" (75). The second is that the "blatantly modern Detective Police," personified by Mr. Bucket's "master-agency," harks back to "a traditional and familiar model of power" (73, 75). These assertions equip Miller to argue that what *Bleak House* produces is a radical uncertainty about the boundaries and extent of power; one that "facilitate[s] the disposition, functioning, and promotion" of a totalistic disciplinarity (80–81).

Dickens's investment in sanitary reform tells against Miller's thesis. Why, for example, would Dickens confound his own social critique by choosing medieval Chancery, that "slow, expensive, British constitutional kind of thing" (60), to

symbolize *modern* bureaucracy? (cf. Blake 2–3). Describing the recently instituted uniformed police, Dickens is enthusiastic, portraying their efficiency with
the same admiration he displays toward the industrious housekeeping of Mrs.
Bagnet. By contrast, describing another modern innovation, the New Poor
Law's economizing and deterrent workhouse, Dickens is censorious.[13] Since the
novel clearly discriminates between these contemporary institutions, it seems
likely that Chancery's "evident archaism" symbolizes nothing so much as the
pernicious tenacity of that archaism—a problem that, like the aristocratic stran-
glehold over Parliament, posed a tangible midcentury threat to the well-being
of the nation. "To the common apprehension of Englishmen the Court of
Chancery is a name of terror, a devouring gulf, a den whence no footsteps return" (qtd. in Butt and Tillotson 185). These *Bleak House*–like remarks were
printed by the *Times* in March 1851 in response to the Whigs' long delayed and
insufficient Chancery reforms. It is true that Dickens, like many contemporaries,
sometimes conflates old and new forms of "circumlocution." It is also true that
he was skeptical of progress and ambivalent toward the modern tendency to approach social problems through bureaucratic means. Nevertheless, it is important to distinguish between Dickens's critique of the "Old Corruption"—
Britain's as yet unreformed legacy of vested interests, medieval forms, and
nepotism (Rubenstein 55)—and the kind of ambivalence that Dickens himself
displays when he undermines modes of modern agency which might mitigate
the paralyzing effects of the latter.

A more illuminating aspect of Miller's reading is his description of the "traditional" power attributed to the modern detective police as personified by Inspector Bucket. Introduced just ten years before *Bleak House*, London's small detective force had been widely acclaimed, even mythologized, with Dickens
himself repeatedly publicizing detective activities in *Household Words* under such
striking rubrics as "The Modern Science of Thief-taking" (see Butt and Tillotson 196–97). By *traditional* Miller perhaps has in mind Max Weber's paradigmatic distinction between modern legal-rational (bureaucratic) authority, and
its traditional precursor. Yet an even more suitable Weberian analogue for
Bucket's agency, explaining the detective's "superhuman" and "magical" qualities (Miller 79), is *charismatic* authority. Charisma is, for Weber, a special mode
of power which arises in response to crisis, whether the society in question is
modern, traditional or, as I am arguing of Dickens's midcentury Britain, locked
in a stalemate between the two. Because charisma purports to inhere in qualities of person (rather than in institutional position or traditional status), Weber's

concept corresponds to the "individual energy" and "influence" cherished by Mill. Thus, if Dickens displays a kind of nostalgia toward Bucket, it is perhaps because he, like Mill, laments an overall decline in the very quality that shrewd Harold Skimpole attributes to the detective: his "peculiarly directed energy" (886).

Indeed, from a Weberian perspective we might say that, while Chancery represents the corruption of traditional power, the uniformed police—efficient and impersonal—provides a rare Dickensian viewpoint on bureaucracy at its best. Inspector Bucket, by contrast, is a decided personality as well as a peculiar blend of public employee and private eye (Miller 79). He thus stands apart from Chadwick's demands for bureaucratic rationality even while approximating the powerful agency attributed to Chadwick personally. Understanding Bucket as representing a Millite desire for charismatic authority illuminates what is most valuable in Miller's reading. For Miller, Chancery's diffuse chaos produces a desire for the detective police—for a master agency to solve such discernible mysteries as the murder of Tulkinghorn.

Miller argues further, however, that the detective police ultimately obliges the reader by arresting itself. Delineating its own ostensible limits, it provides a profoundly desired *"representation of the containment of power"* in a system in which power is, in actuality, "total" (75). One problem with such a reading is that *Bleak House* is not, like *The Moonstone* (1868), a prototypical detective fiction—not least because Dickens's murder plot is not (like the theft of the diamond in Collins's work) consistently foregrounded. That is not to say that Dickens does not play with several conceits that were eventually to become standard detective fare.[14] Nevertheless, Dickens's far-reaching novel makes no pretense of Bucket's capacity to solve the entrenched social problems at its heart. However much the death of a blackmailing lawyer, and the arrest of a foreign lady's maid with a murderous axe to grind may first titillate and then satisfy, the novel never ceases to identify its raison d'être in the far more complicated sanitary plot. It is the latter aspect of the novel that, like the social scientific mind-set that takes the social body for its object, assimilates problems of poverty, morality, and contagious disease, figuring them as the conspicuous by-product of England's deadlock: Tom-all-Alone's.

Nowhere is Miller's application of the Foucauldian paradigm more misleading than in his analysis of this crucial metonym for the ailing social body. For Miller, Tom's is a "delinquent milieu," "saturated" and "penetrated" by Bucket in a way that circumscribes (rather than represses) delinquency, so as to subject it more effectively to "power." By thus arguing that the purpose of "Tom-all-

Alone's is that it *be* all alone" (77), Miller obscures the moral of Dickens's 1850 speech, of Esther's smallpox-ravaged complexion—the moral, in fact, of Chadwick's sanitary *Report*. Tom's "revenge" is precisely the impossibility of containment: physical, moral, or otherwise. "There is not an atom of Tom's slime, . . . not one obscenity or degradation about him, not an ignorance, not a wickedness, not a brutality of his committing, but shall work its retribution, through every order of society, up to the proudest of the proud" (683).[15]

Of course, it is possible to argue that this moral imperative—the "body-ness" of the social body—is, like the sanctity of the middle-class home, a mere rhetorical deception. But, even were that the case, it would not change the fact that the novel's representation of Bucket's agency is subsumed under this very normative critique. Hence, while Bucket's charisma is electrified by the detective plot, it is positively unplugged by the sanitary plot. The detective's reputation among the denizens of Tom's (his visible power to intimidate and coerce) turns out to be far more daunting than his panoptical knowledge *of* them. This point becomes especially evident in the famous scene in which Bucket shines his "lighted bull's-eye" on Tom's "undrained, unventilated," "stinking ruins," and questions the brick makers' wives. Unlike the technocratic Chadwick or the philanthropic Kay, Bucket indifferently surveys what are, to the sociological imagination, the environmental causes of moral effects. (Neither detective nor social scientist, Mr. Snagsby's untutored response to the same scene is to "sicken in body and mind," "as if he were going . . . into the infernal gulf.") Confronting the battered women, Bucket high-handedly repudiates Liz's wish to see her Christlike infant die rather than suffer poverty, disease, and brutality. As he advises her to "train him respectable" (364–67), his proximity to Chadbandian hypocrisy becomes clear. Indeed, he is so far unlike the master agency of the detective plot as to recall Mrs. Pardiggle, another "inexorable moral policeman," "pouncing on the poor" (158, 479). The same motif is repeated when Bucket misrepresents the much-sinned-against Jo, as a much-sinning "Toughey"— "trouble enough, and well enough away from London"—hounding him quite literally to death in order to help conceal Lady Dedlock's secret (830–31).

Such developments make clear that, unlike the forward-moving sanitary reformer, Bucket polices for the status quo: his precious charismatic agency ultimately channeling back into deadlock. This is not a Foucauldian paradox but an exploitative deployment of disciplinary power with material foundations in the unholy midcentury alliance between bourgeois and aristocratic interests. Privately serving an upper-class clientele, while publicly enforcing a post–New

Poor Law bourgeois order in which poverty signifies moral degeneracy, the "art" of the police officer, as Skimpole discerns, entails "a strong faith in money" and its "useful[ness] to society." Bucket's willingness to bribe Skimpole is, the text implies, as "blameable" as the deplorable weakness that enables the latter to justify his Judas-like betrayal of Jo (886). Thus, the underside of Bucket's desirably masterful allure is his being, in fact, a tool of Sir Leicester, on the one hand, and, on the other, of such "profound philosophical prescriptions" (Dickens's ironic term for politico-economic nostrums) as require Jo to "move on" for the convenience of those who thrive off of his exploitation (320).[16]

I have argued against a Foucauldian reading of *Bleak House* in which Bucket's delimited master agency is understood strategically to enhance the totality of disciplinary power. Anachronistically reading Chancery as an emblem for a fully-fledged modern bureaucracy—a tutelary state that, in midcentury Britain, had yet to emerge—Miller concludes that the limitations on Bucket's agency are but a screen. The irony is that Bucket's inadequacies are part of a social critique through which Dickens points to the insufficiency of tutelage—whether public (e.g., the workhouses and hospitals that decline to help Jo; the courts and Parliaments that fail to eradicate menaces to public health) or private (e.g., the "telescopic philanthropy" of Mrs. Jellyby). While the sanitary movement did, as Peter Logan has argued, establish "an apparent need for sustained" attention to the working-class condition (147), what *Bleak House* contributes to that project is a palpable sense of frustration, conflict, and dismay. To be sure, Inspector Bucket's coercive presence in Tom-all-Alone's, like the barbaric penality Dickens was to represent in *Great Expectations* (1860–61), testifies to the functioning of an official police, however blatantly crude and repressive.[17] One might plausibly argue that Jo's delusion of an omniscient Bucket—"everywhere" hastening him to flee, "cognizant of everything"—suggests the latter's panoptical power. It is, however, significant that Allan Woodcourt, Esther's heroic physician and husband-to-be, attributes that singular fancy to a social cause: Jo's "ignorance" (693).

Writing with a conscious intent to hasten sanitary reform but maintaining deliberate distance both from Chadwick and specific legislative mechanisms, Dickens represents the need (if not the will) for a positive tutelary authority; for what, in his later works, Foucault retheorized as modern governmentality's secularized pastoral function. What *Bleak House* figures are not the docile objects of panoptical discipline, but the unfed, unwashed, untreated, unschooled, and (morally, physically) dangerous bodies of Dickens's quasi-sociological imagination. Like Mrs. Jellyby's neglected progeny—"tumbled about," "perfect little calendars of distress"—the last recourse of England's children is to be apprehended by the police (109). Although Dickens variously represents them as charismatic, efficient and forceful, he is no less certain that the modern police are neither sufficiently empowered nor appropriately qualified to care for Britain's ailing social body.

In fact, Dickens's refusal to acknowledge the police as an appropriate institutional base for pastoral authority speaks directly to the history of policing in nineteenth-century Britain. Dickens and his contemporaries admired the efficiency of the Metropolitan force, and romanticized the exploits of the new detectives; but Britain continued to lack the uniform police apparatus of post–Napoleonic France. In his 1839 Constabulary Report, Chadwick had tried unsuccessfully to modify French precedents and Benthamite prototypes in suitably English ways. His incomplete recommendations on policing culminated in a "timid," which is to say permissive and decentralized, act (Finer 164).[18] More than three decades later the Metropolitan commissioners defined police function in explicitly negative terms: "at best" to prevent "a certain portion of crime" and thus "make clean the outside of the platter." What the police do not even attempt to undertake, they insisted, is "the improvement of the morals and manners of the people" (qtd. in Jones 141). Chadwick himself addressed these deficiencies in 1855, when, having lost his position on the Board of Health, he drafted a series of questions and sought to resume his constabulary researches. Chadwick asked: "What offences admit of prevention by the action of a police alone?" and "What offences must be prevented if at all by the care taken by the public themselves?" (qtd. in Finer 167). These searching questions, directly bearing on the legitimacy of pastoral agency in a liberal society, remained unanswered by Chadwick, who was never again to serve the British public in an official capacity. Needless to say, the questions were no less compelling for Britain's novelists.

Hero-Experts, Old Boys, and Mr. Tulkinghorn

In the early phases of the sanitary movement, physicians such as James Phillips Kay and Thomas Southwood Smith typified the ideal of the public servant: part hero, part expert. Both doctors were men of the self-making classes: religious dissenters, with family connections in commerce and industry. Like Chadwick's, their credentials were predicated on zealous dedication to a social cause and, consequently, on unique and hard-won expertise. Yet, in contrast to Chadwick's revolutionary thinking and unbending will, these men were able, within limits, to accommodate themselves to a hidebound system of upper-class patronage in which deference and connection often counted for more than a thoroughgoing knowledge of "How to do it." It is tempting to see in Kay's transition, from local hero to expert official, a blueprint for the modernization of Victorian governance. But that would be entirely to underestimate the entrenched upper-class interests so vividly depicted by *Bleak House*. Whereas Chadwick's most powerful adversaries were the radicals and local powerbrokers among Britain's urban elite, Kay's career demands that we shift our focus from London fogs to the genteel mildew of Chesney Wold.

The fact is that by midcentury the charismatic middle-class hero-expert was already being supplanted by a decidedly different breed of civil servant (see Johnson, "Administrators"). This was the public school and Oxbridge educated "old boy"—the genteel (upper- or upper-middle-class) professional man whose prominence in the civil service was institutionalized after 1870 (see chap. 4). According to this elite variation on the professional ideal, service was defined in terms of gentlemanly character, not specialist expertise. Epitomizing the post-Chadwickian backlash against the latter, a contemporary asked, "who is to check the assertion of experts when the government has once undertaken a class of duties which none but such persons understand?" (qtd. in Searle 23). Significantly, the Balliol old boy who posed this telling question was Ralph Lingen, the man who replaced Kay-Shuttleworth in the Education department when the latter was "very shabbily" driven out in 1849 (Gowan 12).[19] Public school–educated administrators—bred to value social distinction, and to disparage zealous innovation and technical knowledge—helped to sustain upper-class political power, not least by avoiding controversial measures.

In this way displacement of heroic middle-class experts by old boys entailed a renewed repudiation of raison d'état. Rather than vigorously pursue pastoral ambitions, the mid-Victorian state would instead govern in the indirect manner described in Foucault's later works on liberalism. Paradoxically, then, Dickens's most trenchant plea for tutelage coincided with the onset of the mid-Victorian era's resurgent laissez-faire-ism: not the origin but the consummation of the "moment it became apparent that if one governed too much one did not govern at all" (Foucault, "Space" 242).

Dickens's relation to this important historical development is, as so often, complicated and contradictory. In 1852, while writing the first number of *Bleak*

House, Dickens was helping the wealthy Miss Coutts to choose a real-life Tom-all-Alone's to be cleared: a classic example of Victorian voluntarism. Significantly, Dickens rejected the expert advice of Mr. Field—the real-life model for Inspector Bucket—in favor of Dr. Southwood Smith, a member of the General Board of Health. While the author was "disposed to doubt the efficacy" of the policeman's "peculiar sort of knowledge," he was certain that the physician knew "all about" the people and "how [they] live" (qtd. in Butt and Tillotson 197–98). Yet, although Dickens's respect for Southwood Smith's well-rounded knowledge suggests a model sanitary agency, *Bleak House* almost entirely refrains from representing it. Bucket's circumscribed and negative power is the novel's only fleshed-out representation of official agency. While the latter is an obvious tribute to Field, there is no comparable attempt to portray Southwood Smith's role as physician-reformer—no picture of the charismatic, semi-entrepreneurial/semiprofessional heroic expert, appointed to an embattled board, but determined to push through deadlock in order to provide much-needed pastoral care.

What Dickens represents, instead, is Allan Woodcourt, who, significantly, attempts to rescue Jo from disease, deprivation, and Bucket's hounding. A "sea-going doctor," Woodcourt is proud to have the bearing of a naval officer. The eccentric Miss Flite hails him (as though he were a prototype for civil service reform) as a "meritorious, distinguished, honourable officer" (692–93). Yet Esther's future husband is, in the end, one of the least developed characters in *Bleak House*. The doctor's role in the sanitary plot is ultimately displaced; his affinity to early-Victorian hero-experts symbolized by an episode that occurs thousands of miles from Tom-all-Alone's. Following a shipwreck in the East Indian seas, Esther's "dear physician" "saved many lives, never complained in hunger and thirst, wrapped naked people in his spare clothes, took the lead, showed them what to do, governed them, tended the sick, buried the dead, and brought the poor survivors safely off at last!" (556).

Here is precisely the comprehensive pastoral agency necessary to implement sanitary reform. It is all the more significant, therefore, that Dickens neither installs Woodcourt in the civil service or military, nor depicts him as a citizen-activist for local or voluntary sanitary improvements. For all his symbolic potential Woodcourt is no more (or less) than an exemplary neighborhood doctor, his "patient ministration" cherished by rich as well as poor. While this view of the physician emphasizes the professional's likeness to the female domestic ideal, it retrogresses on Dickens's public support for the state's appropriation of the pastoral function. Hence, like the revitalization of Sir Leicester's noblesse oblige, and the stress on Esther's sentimentalized feminine domesticity, Woodcourt's private paternalism—representing what is least modern in the "heroism" of Southwood Smith—is conservative. In this respect the conclusion of *Bleak House* favors the normative self-reliance, local autonomy, and ardent voluntary ethic of the Gladstonean liberal era to come.

Of course, Dickens's reneging on his support for bureaucratic authority is hardly surprising. Although the public speaker mocked the Englishman's provincial fear of "centralization," the novelist created works that "as a whole [are] not centralized" (Arac 183). On the one hand, *Bleak House* implies that reforming antiquated institutions such as Chancery is crucial to the nation's physical and moral well-being. On the other, the novel's implicit wish for an England resembling the interior of Bleak House—"pleasantly irregular," and "old-fashioned rather than old" (116)—strikingly recalls Blackstone's well-known defense of the English law as "an old gothic castle": "venerable," "cheerful and commodious" despite its "winding and difficult" approaches (qtd. in Stone 128–29). From the unambivalent legal-rational perspective of a Bentham, gothic relics are, like Chancery, indefensible fortresses of Old Corruption. Thus, Dickens's inability imaginatively to render a modern pastoral agency like Southwood Smith's or Kay-Shuttleworth's suggests a consciousness trapped between the incompatible worldviews of Bentham and Blackstone.

Dickens's imaginative deadlock is further tied to the class context I have outlined, in which administrative power shifted from middle-class experts to old boys. In George Rouncewell's devotion to the humbled Sir Leicester, Dickens rejuvenates the traditional bond between master and servant, symbolically balancing the loss of Rosa, Lady Dedlock's maid, to the upwardly mobile (entrepreneurial) branch of the Rouncewells. Yet Dickens looks askance at contemporary efforts to recast noblesse oblige as an institutionalized pastoral base for a modern society. In particular, he casts aspersions on the genteel pretensions of the upper middle classes, and the old boy network's efforts to monopolize professional careers. Samuel Smiles's description of the "pitiable" eagerness of his young contemporaries to pursue "poorly paid and routine, though 'genteel' occupations" was not published until 1859 (*Self-Help* 335–36). But the trend lamented by the author of *Self-Help*—in which Britain's best-educated middle-class men were drawn away from "ordinary industry," and toward genteel professionalism—is fully evident in *Bleak House*. To maintain his class position the hapless Richard Carstone must secure a professional place—in pursuit of which John Jarndyce at one point seeks out the influence of Sir Leicester. Richard's

fundamentally pecuniary interest in medicine, the military, and the law is ironically reflected in his eventual victimization by Vholes—a lawyer who justifies
his professional parasitism by constant reference to family expenses (590).

These representations link social deadlock to the compromised moral fiber
of Britain's educated elite. Although the novel does not probe the merits of public school education—a theme Dickens pursued in *Our Mutual Friend*—*Bleak
House* nonetheless adumbrates Smiles's distaste for the degenerative effects of
place seeking. In this way Dickens offers a prescient comment on the developing norm of the civil servant as old boy: not *Little Dorrit*'s vitriolic attack on the
Barnacles, but a diffused yearning for the Daniel Doyce–like charisma of the independent hero-expert. Through the squandered youth of Richard Carstone,
Bleak House anticipates *Little Dorrit*'s dire prognosis of dwindling national vitality after the author's "depressing" experiences with administrative reform.[20]
Indeed, from this vantage point Richard's indifferent shifting from one professional berth to another may be read as the cause, rather than the symptom, of
his self-destructive absorption in Jarndyce and Jarndyce. Richard's susceptibility to Chancery's corruption is, in other words, predetermined by the "mere
form and conventions," the status-driven careerism, to which Britain's educated
middle-class men were increasingly encouraged to submit themselves (Dickens,
qtd. in Cotsell 198–99 n. 4).

By far the most terrifying modern agency represented in *Bleak House*, however, is that of Mr. Tulkinghorn, who, as a self-employed legal professional, displays protobureaucratic attributes that are curiously underemphasized by
Miller.[21] If Bucket personifies the potentially charismatic qualities of modern
expertise, the more insidious Tulkinghorn represents its latent instrumentality
at its most dangerously inhuman. Lady Dedlock's chilling description of Tulkinghorn suggests the very type of bureaucratic impersonality: he is "mechanically faithful without attachment," and "too passionless" to be either friend or
enemy (567). Foreshadowing the baneful status anxiety that destroys Bradley
Headstone in *Our Mutual Friend*, the novel emphasizes Tulkinghorn's social sub-
servience to his "fashionable" employers, implying that he resentfully "treasures
up slights and offences" (457–58). Such a reading of Tulkinghorn—socially inferior but functionally superior to those whom he nominally serves—casts ominous aspersions on the pastorlike confidentiality enjoyed by the legal professional. Hence, it is through Tulkinghorn that Dickens's most serious misgivings
toward Chadwickian expertise are symbolized.

As exemplified either by Chadwick or Tulkinghorn, expertise is even more unaccountable than the do-nothing aristocratic regime it aims to supplant. Here Dickens registers a concern much like that of Ralph Lingen: how is the public to police the pastoral power it entrusts to experts, when expertise consists precisely in knowledge beyond the public ken? Bentham had believed that official power could be safely monitored by public vigilance. But, in Dickens's Millite world of diminished individual agency and increasing specialization, the public—ever more dependent on "the general arrangements of society" (Mill, "Civilization" 129)—is as clueless as Mr. Snagsby. Tulkinghorn's professional *savoir* thus belies the commonplace Victorian notion of bureaucracy as a foreign mode of power, visited only on populations incapable of self-government.[22] The lawyer's ominous capacity to "melt" between his legal chambers and Chesney Wold symbolizes the compromised autonomy of the home (639). Here Tulkinghorn is less Chancery's appendage than a private harbinger of atomized modern power, battening off of profitable expertise in society's complicated "arrangements." Hence, while midcentury Britain lacked the centralized state apparatuses of the Continent, it did not, as Mill's analysis suggests, lack the tendency to render individuals dependent on agencies beyond their control.

Doubtless, for some readers, these signs of uncontainability—the muddied distinction between Chancery's institutionalized archaism and Tulkinghorn's expertise for hire—may justify a return to D. A. Miller's thesis (in which modern disciplinary power is total). I suggest, however, that Dickens is prone to magnifying Tulkinghorn's threat (prior, at any rate, to murdering it) because the novel's unstable epistemology problematizes modern pastorship of any kind. We have seen how *Bleak House* is torn between Benthamite and Blackstonean legal conceptions, between personalized and bureaucratic forms of pastorship—deepseated rifts that impeded the ardently sought-after halfway house. The same is true of the novel's ideological conflicts: the admiration, on the one hand, of robust Rouncewellian individualism and the wish, on the other, for a Christian pastoral community such as that figured at the end of *Oliver Twist*. Indeed, but for its defensive sentimentalization of the home, it would be clear that *Bleak House* evinces a deep philosophical skepticism.

It is therefore useful to compare Dickens's acute distrust of modern agency to James Phillips Kay's vigorous pastoral ambitions. In his work on *Manchester* Dr. Kay was able confidently to recommend legislative as well as "personal" interventions because, like Chalmers before him, he envisioned himself within a providential (morally as well as materially sound) cosmology. In a way that is unimaginable for Dickens, Kay simply believed that a tenable collective purpose—*"the united exertions of the individual members of society"* (12)—was in reach. Just as Dickens lacked the providential convictions of the Manchester reformer, so he lacked, as Matthew Arnold was to say of Britons generally, the secular "notion . . . of the State." For Arnold, one of the first self-styled liberals to endorse Continental modes of governance, a statist philosophy of some kind was crucial to visualizing "the nation in its collective and corporate character, entrusted with stringent powers for the general advantage" (83–84).

Dickens thus failed to imagine a collective foundation (either religious or secular) on which safely to predicate the deployment of modern expertise. Instead, he fell back on the family, a private institution, supplemented only by domesticated relationships between neighborhood physicians and their patients. Although Dickens recognized the limitations of individual and family self-reliance, he could not envision a supra-individual authority that would not threaten the latter's autonomy and purpose. As figured in *Bleak House*, atomism and impotence are less the direct institutional effect of Chancery and its ilk than the sign of pervasive self-interest, inside and out of bureaucratic institutions, archaic as well as modern. This is true whether the suspect agency in question is Bucket's policing on behalf of the ruling-class elite, or Tulkinghorn's even more terrifying policing on his own behalf. "Indifferent to everything but his calling" (567)—a calling that might be characterized as a dangerous perversion of pastoral power—Tulkinghorn's accumulation of "secrets" represents a modern tendency, the power of the expert, detached from any but the most narrow and isolated of bourgeois interests.

Britain's "Inexorable Moral Policeman"

Under these circumstances Dickens's desire for charisma's personal legitimacy, his refusal to institutionalize a desirable pastoral agency such as Allan Woodcourt's, becomes completely intelligible. Indeed, it is even possible, up to a point, to read the novel as powerfully resistant rather than skeptical: on the one hand, a Mill-like unmasking of liberalism's putative empowerment of the individual and, on the other, a prescient refusal of the statist compromises to come. Recalling George Bernard Shaw's characterization of *Little Dorrit* as "a more seditious book than *Das Kapital*," *Bleak House*, like its successor, "reveals the essential sickness of the entire political and social system" (see Page 171). As Dickens represents it, midcentury deadlock so fundamentally favors selfish interests—the elite privilege of the aristocrat or professional, the acquisition of the entrepreneurial bourgeois—that no pastoral authority can escape capitulation in one form or another.

There is, however, another important dimension to *Bleak House*'s representation of agency: one that, by exemplifying uncompromised pastoral care, works to undermine the novel's "seditious" resistance and to perpetuate the contradictions I have described. Selfless feminine domesticity, especially as personified by Esther, represents a seemingly irreproachable form of guidance—relatively autonomous from the selfish interests served by Bucket and antithetical to the expert will-to-power of Tulkinghorn. In this privileged, gendered form, the ostensibly apolitical pastoral function of the home—including Mrs. Bagnet's suitably working-class variation on the theme—represents Dickens's most optimistic viewpoint on the social order.[23] It is therefore unsurprising to find the novel striving to defend the home along with the gender mythologies on which the home's exceptional qualities are predicated. This defense, I will argue, further involves Dickens in satirizing the professional ambitions of female philanthropists such as Mrs. Jellyby and Mrs. Pardiggle. Ironically, Dickens's conservative domesticity thus pits him against a movement that, in the mid-Victorian era, attempted to realize a halfway house much like that sought by the novelist himself.

To explore this idea further we must first recall that *Bleak House* concludes with a symbolic domestication of the professional. As a private physician of modest means, overseeing the health and welfare of a local community, Woodcourt's medical practice is harmoniously aligned with the feminine domesticity of his wife. Here Dickens deliberately overlooks the extent to which Victorian physicians, including Southwood Smith, aggressively pitted scientific expertise against feminine domestic authority (see Poovey, *Making* 42; 194 n. 51; and S. Shuttleworth). Moreover, by stressing Woodcourt's homeliness, Dickens distances his ideal from the new emphasis on professional gentility. By thus muting the most modern and contentious aspects of the professional ideal, Dickens endows Woodcourt with the cultural capital of Victorian domesticity, creating an unimpeachable mode of pastoral agency.

Yet, for all its ideal qualities, Woodcourt's homely male professionalism has limited practical application to Britain's vast social quandaries. Hence, more significant than this parting gesture is its reactionary underside—Dickens's antifeminist assault on middle-class women's extradomestic activities. Unsurprisingly, the same imagination that attributes the special aura of female homemakers to male physicians and evokes detectives who enthuse over "domestic bliss" anathematizes the professional ambitions of women (732). In particular, Dickens is at pains to satirize the organized philanthropy of women such as Mrs. Jellyby and Mrs. Pardiggle, emphasizing their derelict domestic duties, and futile public endeavors.[24]

It is therefore absolutely crucial to recognize that the notion of Mrs. Pardiggle as an "inexorable moral policeman" was far less absurd to Dickens's contemporaries than the novel's burlesque treatment implies. Rather, Mrs. Pardiggle's activities illustrated a venerable Christian and civic tradition with origins in Thomas Chalmers's early-nineteenth-century precedent. The practice of home visiting not only expanded throughout the nineteenth century; it also became increasingly rationalized, organized, and ambitious—a process of legitimation which was enhanced by deliberate links to the growing authority of social science. Victorian Britain's multifarious philanthropies performed a substantial, if demonstrably inadequate, pastoral function, employing nearly twice as many paid workers as were employed by the Poor Law (Prochaska 384–85).

Women, including such noteworthy figures as Mary Carpenter, Octavia Hill (the granddaughter of Southwood Smith), Helen Bosanquet, and Beatrice Webb, were eventually involved at every level of this formidable enterprise. Indeed, it seems likely that one of the most important pastoral developments of the prewar era—the turn-of-the-century transition from charitable volunteer to modern social worker—depended on the kind of ideological overlap between feminine domesticity and professionalism which Allan Woodcourt exemplifies.[25] Hence, in satirizing Mrs. Pardiggle (as well as Miss Wisk and Mrs. Jellyby), Dickens pitted himself against one of the most prototypical—"old-fashioned rather than old"—pastoral practices of the Victorian era. Organized philanthropy—blending modern science with familiar Christian, civic, and domestic discourses—was, to the minds of many, the halfway house that Dickens himself had sought. An unmistakably British hybrid of voluntarism and professionalism, private and public agency, collectivism and self-help, the figure of the mid-Victorian visitor–cum–social worker—including the iconic lady visitor–cum–social worker—provided a crucial ideological synthesis around which alternately statist, localist, or voluntarist versions of modern pastoral agency might flourish.

Dickens's antagonism to this important development is illuminated by contrast to a contemporaneous voluntary organization: the Ladies' National Association for the Diffusion of Sanitary Knowledge, founded in 1857. In an unmistakable attempt to contain professional men's assault on women's domestic credentials, the association insisted on the gendered segregation of sanitary duties. Whereas men's strength and intellect qualify them to "devise schemes for draining and cleansing . . . towns" (read Chadwick's technocratic engineering, rather than Kay's or Southwood Smith's medicalized domestic interventions), women's experiences as mothers, housewives, and teachers qualify them to "effect those urgently needed changes in infant management, domestic economy, [and] education . . . without which humanity could never attain to its destined state of bodily perfections, *though all injurious external circumstances were changed*" (qtd. in Behlmer, *Friends* 56–57; emph. added). By thus delegating the most mechanical (Chadwickian) aspects of sanitary reform to men, the Ladies' National reappropriated the crucial moral components of sanitary reform for themselves, arguing that only women (and not physicians or engineers) are qualified to minister to the internal social body. Yet, while the Ladies' National Association thus invoked the same mystified femininity that Dickens aimed to preserve, the creator of Mrs. Pardiggle and Mrs. Jellyby would doubtless have cautioned them, after the manner of the latter's neglected husband, "Never [to] Have a Mission," feminine or otherwise (477).

In other words, the heart of *Bleak House*'s antifeminism is not to shield femininity as such, but to shield feminine domesticity's crucial harborage of the personal. That quality is vitiated once domestic functions take on the cast of administrative machinery. For all their professed femininity the Ladies' National Association, like Mrs. Pardiggle, exemplified a philanthropy that consists in "moving declaratory resolutions . . . at public meetings" (478), rather than in unobtrusive, spontaneous, and sympathetic domestic care. Hence, Dickens's complaint against organized philanthropy was articulated as a normalization of gender, but it was motivated by an antimaterialist impulse very like Thomas Carlyle's. In "Signs of the Times" (1829) Carlyle had excoriated the modern philanthropist's tendency to dismiss society's "mere natural organs" in favor of calling "public meeting[s], appoint[ing] committees," issuing "prospectuses," and eating "public dinner[s]" (467). For Dickens, as for Carlyle, such activities represented a bureaucratization of social life, favoring "machinery" at the expense of the familylike relations that charity ought to extend.

Whether reposed in homely doctors, or devoted housekeepers, pristine domesticity was thus, for Dickens, the last preserve of Carlyle's "natural organs." Domesticity's personal relations were a bulwark against the atomization and mechanization of the social body, and a means to preserving individual autonomy. Thus, Dickens commends Esther's motherly care for Charley and sisterly care for Caddy Jellyby while likening Mrs. Pardiggle's wholesale "benevolence" to "a strait waistcoat." Thus, on the very same grounds, he contrasts Wood-

court's compassionate "habit . . . of speaking to the poor" to Bucket's domi-
neering officialism, and to the "patronage" and "condescension" of England's
self-appointed philanthropic police (479, 684). Thus, as almoner to the wealthy
Miss Coutts, Dickens preferred "personal charity" to "impersonal public relief"
(Crowther, *Workhouse* 68).

Yet, lest we underestimate Dickens's extraordinary contradictions, we must
also note that the author was positively fascinated by reformatory institutions
such as prisons, hospitals, asylums, and schools—praising those establishments
that respected the individuality of the inmate.[26] As a public-spirited citizen,
Dickens was at the vanguard of mid-Victorian Britain's budding interest in institutional rehabilitation: a positive approach to illness or delinquency, to challenge the negative functions ascribed to the deterrent workhouse and punitive
prison (see Crowther, *Workhouse* 63; Walton). In his fiction, however, Dickens
refrained from delegating the home's sanctified pastoral functions to the suspect
space of the curative institution. Just as *Bleak House* features no model civil servant like Southwood Smith, so it omits the kind of modular establishments supported by Dickens and Miss Coutts. Although the novel includes many homes
that resemble institutions—Tulkinghorn's Lincoln's Inn chambers, Mrs. Jellyby's
home–as–office space—the only benevolent institution it figures is the home.
To be sure, the tendency to disclaim institutionalized pastorship is nothing new
in Dickens's fiction, which includes a roster of children morally and physically
stunted by benevolent establishments.[27] In *Bleak House*, however, it is chiefly
through overt hostility to women's organized philanthropy that Dickens expresses profound skepticism toward the curative institutions he privately helped
to support.

Dickens's inability to embrace Mrs. Pardiggle, like the absence of a fictional
Southwood Smith, is, therefore, symptomatic of the paradoxes that pervade his
midcentury novels and, more generally, the self-consciously liberal society these
novels represent. Britain's social body manifestly lacked the kind of order,
method, and efficiency which makes the Bagnet family thrive. But neither Dickens nor his contemporaries was prepared to vest such comprehensive powers
in any but the most homely, personal, and charismatic of agencies. Dickens's
ideal of a world that is "pleasantly irregular" requires a catachrestic supervisory
power: one that is rational but unbureaucratic, personal but omnipresent,
charismatic but institutionalized, authoritative but liberatory, efficient but
English. Incapable either of realizing this antithetical ideal, or of recognizing
the "seditious" implications of his own critique, Dickens falls back on a conserv-

ative mystification of domestic and feminine personality. *Bleak House* thus demonizes Mrs. Pardiggle in order to stave off the protobureaucratic modes of governmentality she portends. Underlying this defensive antifeminism, moreover, is a Millite anxiety about modernity's diminution of individual autonomy.

Dickens and Mid-Victorian Liberalism

In 1873 a utilitarian-minded contemporary characterized the British social order in a way that recalls *Bleak House:* "If anyone were to attempt to say what the internal government of England is, . . . he would be smothered in the attempt under a chaos of acts, charters, commissioners, boards, benches, courts, and vestries of all sorts and conditions, which have no unity, are subject to no central control in most instances, and are suffered to atone for all their other defects by what Frenchmen praise as 'le self-government,' which not infrequently means the right to misgovern your immediate neighbours without being accountable for it to anyone wiser than yourself" (qtd. in Searle 16). Citing this noteworthy passage from James Fitzjames Stephen, Geoffrey Searle argues that the midcentury reaction against Chadwick set back reforms for a generation, perpetuating "administrative arrangements that made no pretence to functional efficiency" (16). Yet there is no question that, in the prosperous decades after Chadwick's fall, Britain's liberal constitutional consensus was stabilized and strengthened, culminating in an era famous for equipoise. As Searle demonstrates, it was not until the very different historical circumstances of the fin de siècle—including the prospect of Britain's declining world power—that the quest for efficiency became sufficiently broad to weaken the nation's profound anti-statism. Dickens's seditious, skeptical, and paradoxical novels of the 1850s were thus vindicated by the late-century backlash against liberalism, and by historians' reconstructions of the era's "confusion" and "incoherence" (Clark, *Making* 206–7). Nevertheless, Dickens's immediate contemporaries were far less sympathetic: prone to questioning the novelist's masculine rational faculties (Walter Bagehot), lamenting his lack of psychological realism (George Eliot), and satirizing his stylistic excesses (Anthony Trollope).[28]

With such criticism in mind, it is tempting to align Dickens's literary career with the hero expertise of the early-Victorian era. Hence, like Sir James Kay-Shuttleworth, Dickens found himself superseded in the 1850s by a newer, more dispassionate breed of literary professional: for example, by Trollope's "steady observation," and Bagehot's aloof composure (Briggs, *Victorian* 87). As a heroic professional who, Chadwick-like, exposed the nation's dysfunctional social body, Dickens's midcentury critiques anticipated those of a later generation. Yet there is also no denying that, despite his indictment of midcentury deadlock, Dickens was himself complicit in perpetuating the liberal myths that helped to keep such criticism at bay.

Indeed, to the more complacent mid-Victorian mind, the aftermath of the fallen Sanitary Idea might appear "old-fashioned rather than old." Although the 1848 Public Health Act had failed either to mandate or substantially regulate local sanitary practices, it did succeed in expediting improvements on a voluntary and regional basis (Fraser 72–77).[29] To a latter-day utilitarian such as Stephen, the irregular patchwork created by "self-government" of this kind was indistinguishable from Chancery's ineffective archaism. Nevertheless, that enthusiasts of Britain's liberal traditions might actually "boast of this state of affairs" (Brundage 159) is, as we have seen, evident in Dickens's own ambivalent representations. However much he might lampoon Podsnap's disdain of "un-English" government in *Our Mutual Friend,* the creator of Tulkinghorn and Mrs. Pardiggle had done his share to solidify the British predisposition to favor the "pleasantly irregular" over the rational and bureaucratic.

Hence, while Trollope's fiction better represents the contemporary preference for a moderate literature, Dickens's midcentury novels are more in tune with mid-Victorian liberalism than the author was likely to have realized. In chapter 6 I turn to the fascinating turn-of-the-century clash between members of the Charity Organization Society and Fabian socialists: a contest for control over national pastorship between ardent voluntarists and would-be official experts. Here, however, I want to close my discussion of *Bleak House* by contrasting Dickens's desire for a catachrestical pastoral agency to the early ambitions of the Charity Organization Society, founded in 1869, just a year before Dickens's death.

Mrs. Pardiggle and Miss Hill

The object of the Charity Organization Society was nothing less than to transform society through well-coordinated voluntarism. Operating locally, but reporting to the London-based Central Commission, COS volunteers and their salaried assistants would subject Britain's labyrinthine charities to systematic oversight. In this way they would reinforce the New Poor Law's deterrent policies by eliminating the pauperizing effects of indiscriminate charity. Trained volunteers would, in effect, not only supplement but also supervise Poor Law officials. Through their trademark case study method COS members would distinguish authoritatively between the incorrigible pauper (who must bear the brunt of deterrent poor laws), and the deserving candidate for charity. Assistance to the latter would vary widely, with primary emphasis placed on minimizing dependence, encouraging thrift, and, consequently, building character. In all of these ways, but especially in their emphases on charity's ostensibly personal qualities, the COS harked back to the ideas of Thomas Chalmers, "almost the patron saint of the C.O.S" (Mowat 10).

This vision of a thoroughly systematic philanthropy, cooperating on a semi-official basis with existing Poor Law authorities so as to reinforce the law's rigor, entailed much to repel the author of *Oliver Twist* and *Bleak House*. Nevertheless, I suggest that Dickens's deeply contradictory stance—insisting on the moral necessity of pastorship while casting aspersions on modern pastoral agencies—worked in favor of the corporate voluntarism envisioned by the COS. As Jane Nardin has argued, Victorians of many stripes sought to forge "a consensus about the ends of action that would heal their divided society, by uniting men in the pursuit of a single moral goal" (13–14). Dickens's novel, we have seen, founders precisely because it cannot imaginatively sustain collective purpose of this kind. But novels such as *Bleak House* and *Little Dorrit* nevertheless incite desire for such a purpose. Skeptical and conflicted, Dickens's midcentury legacy was a harrowing display of paralyzed individual agency: Mr. Snagsby's disempowered citizenship, Daniel Doyce's thwarted invention, John Jarndyce's circumscribed benevolence. In effect the COS attempted to reverse this Mill-like modernity by systematically updating what, in a more heroic era, Dr. James Kay had envisioned as *"the united exertions of the individual members of society."*

Hence, despite the un-Dickensian stress on bureaucratic organization, COS rhetoric, deeply influenced by Chalmers, often reads as though written by studious disciples of the "old-fashioned rather than old." Indeed, Dickens's phrase illuminates what one historian has characterized as the "essential duality" of a movement that was "professionally pioneering but ideologically reactionary" (Fraser 131; cf. Mowat xi). Nowhere is the similarity between Dickens's novels and the COS stronger than in their mutual privileging of the personal. COS papers repeatedly contrast the impersonal state to the sympathetic knowledge of charitable volunteers. In 1870 Sir Charles Trevelyan, an early COS supporter, argued against any perversion of the charitable relationship: "By passing through official hands," he insisted, charity "loses the redeeming influence of personal kindness" (qtd. in Behlmer, "Character-Building" 59). Octavia Hill, a founding COS member, concurred: "no radical cure of those who have fallen low can be effected" "without a strong personal influence" (qtd. in Maurice 257). Hence, it is ironic, but not at all surprising, that the COS's primary defense against the welfare state should be the "personal" qualities of an organized corps of Pardiggles.

It is possible to imagine Dickens's ambivalence toward a voluntary bureaucracy instituted in the name of personalized charity. In many respects the COS's hallmark case studies produced individualized philanthropy of the kind Dickens tended to endorse. Octavia Hill's 1869 inaugural paper, "The Importance of Aiding the Poor without Almsgiving," recalls the paternalistic relations implicit in Allan Woodcourt's homely professionalism. Like a latter-day Cheeryble or Rose Maylie, Hill urges her prosperous audience to promote "mutual help" among "neighbors," and to regard the poor as family members, not "as a separate class" (qtd. in Bell 108). Although Dickens might have balked at her Jellyby-like "mission," and Pardiggle-like public resolutions, he is likely to have commended the model housing project she undertook with John Ruskin's financial support (known by the quaintly Dickensian address of Paradise Place, Marylebone). Moreover, Hill herself, as though an attentive reader of *Bleak House*, recruited only women whose "own homes came first and their [volunteer] work second" (Nord, *Apprenticeship* 121).

Appointed to the COS's Central Commission in 1875, Hill's priorities shifted from neighborhood casework to bureaucratic oversight.[30] Unsurprisingly, Hill's voluntarist efforts to impose centralized uniformity over Britain's multifarious philanthropies were no more successful than had been her grandfather's attempt to regulate sanitary reform twenty-five years before. Local clergymen and poor law officials resisted COS meddling, and tensions flared up even between the COS's Central Commission and its own district committees (Bell 112–13; Mowat 22–23). Although Dickens would have probably joined those critics who accused the society of heartless bureaucracy, he might nevertheless have appreciated Hill's appeals to volunteers with "deep sympathy for the poor," and her efforts to prevent the COS's becoming "a dry, ineffectual machinery for enquiring about people" (qtd. in Boyd 112).

"Something Is Wrong, Somewhere . . ."

Emphasizing henpecked men and officious women, Dickens's midcentury caricature of organized philanthropy conveys the impression of a marginal and

obnoxious social practice with little mainstream credibility. No one would conclude from reading *Bleak House* that, by the turn of the century, the Charity Organization Society would be sufficiently prominent to secure six out of nineteen
places on a prestigious Royal Commission; much less that philanthropic ladies
would be advising Parliament on questions of national importance.[31] Nevertheless, in his novels (as well as his own charitable activities) Dickens repeatedly
contrasted a personal ideal of pastorship to various official alternatives, within
and outside of the state. As J. S. Mill had shown in "Civilization," Victorian
Britain adulated the self-reliant individual while encouraging modern tendencies that diminished individual power. Through his commitment to personalized
community bonds, Dickens attempted imaginatively to transcend this paradox,
but ended by oscillating between radical critique and defensive capitulation.

Without a viable collective agency (such as Chalmers's religious network or
Arnold's state) Dickens could not imagine a safe means of institutionalizing
modern power. Like Chadwick's famous *Report*, Dickens's novel publicized the
need for pastorship, but, unlike the committed technocrat, the novelist refused
to authorize the means. Dickens's final refuge was the sentimentalized domesticity through which he evoked an impossible form of pastoral power: rational
but unbureaucratic, personal but omnipresent, charismatic but institutionalized,
authoritative but liberatory. In this sense Dickens's genius in *Bleak House* was
to vivify the paralyzing social deadlock that ensued when powerful class interests exploited ideological conflict and political indecision for their mutual advantage. Conversely, Dickens's limitation was to end by rehearsing some of liberalism's most entrenched and self-justifying mythologies.

Although Dickens himself would probably have disliked organized charity,
his novels tended nevertheless to legitimate the COS's voluntary alternative to
statist pastorship. In their distinctly British blend of voluntarism and professionalism, private and public agency, collectivism and self-help, COS members
visualized a halfway house like that sought by Dickens. But, just as Dickens had
declined to create a fictional counterpart to Dr. Southwood Smith, so, in Mrs.
Pardiggle, the novelist rejected the kind of rationalized philanthropy which Octavia Hill promoted. Like Mill, but in a more symbolic fashion, Dickens seems
to have discerned that bureaucratic specialization and depersonalization advances even where the state's power is, as in Victorian Britain, jealously guarded.

In chapter 6 I argue that the movement to organize charity was less a bona
fide individualism than a professionalized and quasi-collective pastoral strategy,
cloaked in the defense of a certain rhetorical tradition. This tradition, sometimes

celebrated in Dickens's novels, included foundational British notions such as character, entrepreneurial spirit, and self-reliance. But, because the professed cradle of this tradition was the home, and because the home, in turn, enshrined a domestic ideal of great symbolic importance to the nation's expanding professional population, the same mythos that applauded self-help also nurtured professionalism. "Despite their dislike of state intervention," writes Perkin, the COS's methods led "to the development of the professional, and eventually state-employed, social worker" (*Rise* 24; cf. Mowat 101–2). When the Charity Organization Society upheld Octavia Hill as a model of personalized but scientific philanthropy, its members did not realize that they were laying the ground for the vastly empowered technocratic state of the post–World War I era. Dickens, the creator of Mrs. Pardiggle and Mr. Tulkinghorn, seemed to foresee that eventuality. At any rate, he remained resolutely unwilling to entrust any official, inside or out of the state, with the powers he so confidently bestowed on Esther Summerson and Allan Woodcourt.

In the preceding analyses I have emphasized the perceived dangers of various contenders for a modernized pastoral function that would eventually become necessary to the growth of industry and empire. From a Millite point of view, however, the most conspicuously foundering agency is that of the would-be citizen whose independence, democratic participation, and moral growth are crushed by modern civilization's massifying, specializing, and commodifying tendencies. From this Millite point of view *Bleak House* is the story of Mr. Snagsby's representative inability to practice, or even imagine, effective citizenship. Shaken by a single witness of Tom-all-Alone's, Mr. Snagsby simultaneously pronounces on the detective story and the sanitary plot that subsumes it when he apprehends his own powerlessness and complicity: "Something is wrong, somewhere; but what something, what may come of it, to whom, when, and from which unthought of and unheard of quarter, is the puzzle of his life" (409). From this foggy and guilt-ridden vantage point *Bleak House* only incidentally tells the story of Chancery's Old Corruption, Chesney Wold's "deadened" noblesse oblige, Richard Carstone's blighted youth, Bucket's venal police power, Tulkinghorn's threatening expertise, and Mrs. Pardiggle's unfeminine delusions of grandeur. Rather, from the Millite perspective the novel's symbolic detective finger ultimately points to such commonplace middle-class homes as Mr. Snagsby's, and the disabled civic agency of Britain's ordinary middle classes.

CHAPTER FOUR

An Officer and a Gentleman

Civil Service Reform, and the Early Career of Anthony Trollope

For the superior situations endeavours should be made to secure the services of the most promising men of the day, by a competing examination on a level within the highest description of education in this country. In this class of situations there is no limit to the demands which may ultimately be made upon the abilities of those who, entering them simply as junior clerks, gradually rise to the highest posts in them. To obtain first-rate men, it is obvious that recourse should be had to competition.
— NORTHCOTE-TREVELYAN *Report on the Civil Service*

The [Northcote-Trevelyan] reporters . . . clearly want to have the article, namely, a good Government clerk, ready-made to their hand, so that they may have no trouble with him after his appointment. He is to walk up to his desk on his first morning, armed at all points for every description of official fight, prepared to settle difficult points of international law in French or German, or to work out correctly any abstruse calculation required by the Chancellor of the Exchequer; to draw out a new constitution in elegant English, or if needs be . . . to quote . . . Latin and Greek. . . . He is, moreover, to be of excellent moral character, a member of some Christian community, certified as to age, sound of wind and limb, ambitious as regards the civil service, but humble and docile as to his own feelings, serious and sedate, though under twenty, punctual in attendance, and not too much given to heavy lunches at two o'clock.
— ANTHONY TROLLOPE, "THE CIVIL SERVICE"

In early 1855, as the *Times* headed up a remorseless exposure of gross incompetence in the Crimea, the British nation was rocked by a crisis of leadership which Dickens's *Bleak House* could but foreshadow. As an army of journalists telegraphed uncensored accounts of military disaster to London, the public responded with cries for "efficiency," antiaristocratic furor, and, in Parliament, a radical-leaning Select Committee to investigate ministerial mismanagement.[1] If 1848, the year of revolutions abroad and Chartism in Britain, had marked the high point of the working-class challenge to the existing order, then 1855, the year in which John "Tear 'em" Roebuck forced the resignation of Lord John Russell, represented a middle-class challenge, both entrepreneurial and radical, to what remained a nation politically dominated by its upper ranks. By February 1855 the famous diarist Lord Greville was, for the first time in his life, "really and seriously alarmed at the state of affairs"—by which he meant at the *Times*'s assault on "the aristocratic elements of society and the Constitution" (qtd. in Briggs, *Victorian* 61). Such views were not confined to the nobility. In an unpublished manuscript a struggling author waxed Carlylean as he lamented the corrupting effects of newspapers on the "over-strained public mind" (*New Zealander* 180). Significantly, the same author, one Anthony Trollope, had already produced a more temperate critique of midcentury popular culture in his first semisuccessful novel, *The Warden* (1855).

The short-lived crisis over administrative reform was part of a longer historical narrative that began in 1832 with the enfranchisement of middle-class men, and culminated in the solidification of the liberal constitutional consensus of the mid-Victorian years. One of the most important political manifestations of that consensus was a trade-off in which Britain's dynamic middle classes ceded the nation's leadership to an upper-class elite in exchange for free rein over business and local affairs. To achieve this end, Whig-Liberal strategists of the 1850s struggled to stabilize government, quell radical unrest, and fill a political void that one historian has likened to a "centre of indifference" (Clark, *Making* 43). In this chapter I approach this subject through a fascinating convergence between Victorian literature and the Victorian state: between, on the one hand, the Northcote-Trevelyan civil service reforms forwarded by William Gladstone, Benjamin Jowett, and Sir Charles Trevelyan, and, on the other, the early works of Anthony Trollope.

Civil service reform in the age of Gladstone's liberal economic policies, Trevelyan's colonial legacy in India, Jowett's university reforms, and Trollope's early novels was a complicated and long-evolving affair. As I argue in the first part of this chapter, it involved a shift from the early nineteenth century's prescriptive notion of character, a teleological definition of character implying the limitless improvability of all human beings, to a far more conservative descriptive notion of character, focused on the unique attributes of the born-and-bred

gentleman. In Trollope's Barsetshire novels gentlemanly character is richly nuanced and deftly naturalized. Such a literature was auspicious for mid-Victorian
political consensus: able to sublimate the nation's bold entrepreneurial spirit by
integrating it within the crucial imagining of a "classless class of well-bred men."
Yet my purpose in this chapter is to look at the genesis of this hallmark fiction.
Trollope's first Barsetshire novels coincided with the writing of two very different kinds of texts, each of which responded to civil service reform and the surrounding social context. In the unpublished *New Zealander* and in *The Three Clerks*
(1858), a novel with a Dickens-like stance on contemporary affairs, Trollope de-
parted from the Barsetshire mold. The latter relates a disturbing allegory in which
wrongheaded civil service reforms exacerbate destructive modern tendencies.
What is at stake, I argue, is the balance Trollope had achieved in his first Barsetshire novels and would go on to achieve in his own developing professional persona. This same symbolic balance—between entrepreneurial self-making and
genteel solidity—was the foundation of the mid-Victorian era's fabled equipoise.

A Few Good Men

Who are so successful in carrying off the prizes at competing scholarships, fel-
lowships, &c. as the most expensively educated young men? Almost invariably,
the sons of gentlemen, or those who by force of cultivation, good training and
good society have acquired the feelings and habits of gentlemen. The tendency
of [recruitment by open competition] will, I am confident, be decidedly *aristocratic*, but it will be so in a good sense by securing for the public service those
who are, in a true sense, [the most noble].   — SIR CHARLES TREVELYAN

The fanciful pedantic tests which the Reverend B. Jowett gladly discerns in the
scheme of Sir Charles Trevelyan would secure many qualities of the fine gentleman; but in trying to secure those qualities, it would exclude many persons from
the public service who possess qualities still more essential to the practical conduct of business.
   — "COMMON SENSE OF THE CIVIL SERVICE QUESTION"

Few aspects of Victorian history are as complicated as the administrative reforms unfolding in the decades after the landmark Northcote-Trevelyan *Report
on the Civil Service* (1853–54). Contemporaries and modern scholars alike have
often mistakenly regarded the *Report* as a solidly middle-class development: "part

of the general rise of the bourgeoisie's influence on government, linked to the steady progress of democratization, the increasing complexity of administration, technological change and so forth" (Gowan 8).[2] That misleading impression was, in fact, deliberately cultivated by the authors of the *Report*, who criticized the aristocracy's use of the civil service as a "Foundling Hospital" to provide for incompetent "Waifs and Strays" at the public's expense (Trevelyan, qtd. in Hernan 24). The same impression was reinforced by the Gradgrindian reputation of Sir Charles Trevelyan—the original of Trollope's Sir Gregory Hardlines in *The Three Clerks*—a man renowned, as his brother-in-law Lord Macaulay was to put it, for "rigid integrity" (qtd. in Hernan 16).

Dickens's famous satire on the "Circumlocution Office" in *Little Dorrit* (1855–57) was, of course, a direct response to Crimean blunders. Indeed, Dickens was a prominent spokesman for the Administrative Reform Association (ARA), a pressure group demanding that politicians and administrators emulate the nation's entrepreneurs in learning "How to do it." Yet, while the Northcote-Trevelyan reformers had proposed competitive examinations as a means to recruiting meritorious officials, neither Dickens nor the ARA advocated the *Report* (O. Anderson, "Administrative" 274–76). On the contrary, there is much evidence to suggest that the original of Tite Barnacle, the nepotistic aristocrat depicted in *Little Dorrit*, was none other than Sir Charles Trevelyan. As head of the Treasury, Trevelyan had incurred Dickens's disfavor not only for his role in the Crimea but also for his tight-fisted resistance to sanitary improvements (see Philpotts).

The influence of Trevelyan—a colonial official in India and Ireland as well as a Treasury official and founding member of the Charity Organization Society— must not be understated. But it is also important to recognize that the *Report* was commissioned by William Gladstone, then chancellor of the Exchequer. As we shall see, Gladstone's Coleridgean notions of liberal governance, amplified by Benjamin Jowett's ambitious university reforms, influenced his stance on administrative reform. Hence, despite conspicuous deployment of utilitarian principles and entrepreneurial rhetoric, the deliberate aim and ultimate effect of the *Report* was, in fact, to dislodge the middle-class foothold in the Victorian state, to diminish Bentham's legacy, and to do so in the interests of an elite class of public school and Oxbridge-educated "gentlemen" (Gowan; Mueller 167–223; Dowling 64–66, 150).

The idea that an upper-class Coleridgean rather than middle-class Benthamite vision drove mid-Victorian civil service reforms rests partly on biographical foundations: on Jowett's persuasive scheme of a civil service "clerisy"; on Gladstone's predicating liberal economic policies on a Coleridgean philosophy of governance; and on Trevelyan's eventual consent, culminating in his readiness to abolish Haileybury, a Benthamite training institution, in 1853. As we saw in chapter 3, dwindling enthusiasm for intrusive pastoral programs such as Kay-Shuttleworth's educational agenda or Chadwick's Sanitary Idea had left an alarming void within Whig-Liberal policy, evident in the political deadlocks of *Bleak House.* John Stuart Mill had already articulated a powerful case for Coleridge. Mill urged enlightened progressives to "rejoice" over Coleridge's demonstrating the importance of established institutions, and his "vindicat[ing] against Bentham and Adam Smith" the notion of a "clerisy": "an endowed class, for the cultivation of learning, and for diffusing its results among the community" ("Coleridge" 207, 208, 212).[3] As a young Peelite, Gladstone had written *The State in Its Relations with the Church* (1838), a Coleridgean critique of utilitarianism and the individualist bent of Evangelical Christianity. This youthful allegiance to the Anglican Church was soon succeeded by an almost religious conviction in the unifying potential of liberal social policy including free trade, low taxation, and strict controls on government spending (Stansky 38–43, 77–83).

Significantly, Gladstone's transition from resolute Tory to arch-liberal did not necessitate his abandoning the quest for a Coleridgean clerisy. On the contrary, a clerisy-like civil service would, as Gladstone saw it, cement the consensus between middle-class industry and upper-class statesmanship while solving the vexing problem of providing pastoral guidance for a dynamic liberal society. With this end in mind the Northcote-Trevelyan reformers proposed to match the entrepreneur's Smilesean ethic with a cultivated, as well as competitive, Oxbridge complement. Hence, while entrepreneurial rhetoric clearly infiltrated the reformers' notions of gentlemanly merits—a subject of great weight for Anthony Trollope—that is not to say that civil service "competition" reflected the interests of entrepreneurs. While privately inciting the *Times* to attack the nepotism of "our high Aristocracy," Trevelyan just as privately assured one upper-class skeptic that the effects of open competition would be "decidedly *aristocratic*" (qtd. in Hughes 72). Sir Stafford Northcote concurred, convinced "that the advantages which a university training would give in . . . competition would almost insure the selection of a large majority from among those who have received it" (qtd. in Mueller 204). Gladstone, meanwhile, assured Lord John Russell that open competition would "strengthen and multiply the ties between the higher classes and the possession of administrative power" (qtd. in Compton 266).

Competitive examination was, in fact, a controversial idea that, despite its superficial resemblance to entrepreneurial culture, was repudiated by Samuel Smiles. In *Self-Help* (1859), the holy writ of Britain's industrious classes, Smiles insisted on the "thoroughly demoralizing" effects of "cramming" for examinations, and warned that, with so "little room left" for "free" mental action, "a functionarism as complete as" ancient China's might ensue (335–36). Nor was Smiles the only middle-class figure to realize that written examinations based on Oxbridge curricula would favor upper-class interests, promoting what the *Daily News* described as the "sophistries and pedantries of the Trevelyan school" (qtd. in O. Anderson, "Administrative" 278). Dickens was also skeptical. In an 1855 *Household Words* essay Dickens assumed the persona of a plain-speaking and, indeed, rather Trollopian civil servant, disdaining the notion of examining clerks "as if they wanted to take high degrees in learned professions" (qtd. in Philpotts 284).

In fact, the most important precedent for competitive recruitment was not in Britain's entrepreneurial culture but in its colonial service in India.[4] Thomas Babington Macaulay, a high-ranking Indian administrator had championed competition since the 1830s. For a Whig such as Macaulay the impetus was partly political: competition provided a means of curtailing the unpredictable effects of patronage as well as ensuring the competence of recruits. That said, Macaulay was doubtless sincere when in 1833, and again in 1853, he enunciated a "pious belief that academic success ensured, if it was not directly related to, good character" (Compton 268; cf. Moore, "Abolition" 247). In Parliament, "at the Bar, at the Bench, [and] at the Church," Macaulay insisted, "those who attain high distinction in the world are generally men who were distinguished in their academic career" ("Government" 708). In so arguing, Macaulay articulated a view of education which, like that of his brother-in-law Charles Trevelyan, had been shaped by his experiences in India promoting a policy of English education.

Dialectics of Empire and Home

[Trevelyan] has no small talk. His mind is full of schemes of moral and political improvement, and his zeal boils over in all his talk. His topics, even in courtship, are steam navigation, the education of the natives, the equalization of the sugar duties, the substitution of the roman for the Arabic alphabet in the oriental languages.   —THOMAS BABINGTON MACAULAY

The political education of a nation is the work of time; and while it is in progress, [the British in India] shall be as safe as it will be possible for us to be. The natives will not rise against us, we shall stoop to raise them. . . . [T]he national activity will be fully and harmlessly employed in acquiring and diffusing European knowledge, and in naturalising European institutions. . . . The change [to Indian independence] will thus be peaceably and gradually effected; there will be no struggle, no mutual exasperation; the natives will have independence, after first learning how to make good use of it. . . . Trained by us to happiness and independence, and endowed with our learning and political institutions, India will remain the proudest monument of British benevolence; and we shall long continue to reap, in the affectionate attachment of the people, and in a great commercial intercourse with their splendid country, the fruit of that liberal and enlightened policy which suggested to us this line of conduct.

— CHARLES TREVELYAN, *On the Education of the People of India*

In her important work on British imperialism Gauri Viswanathan has persuasively argued that it is necessary "to consider English culture first and foremost in its imperial aspect" ("Williams" 49). To illustrate the pitfalls of an insular Marxist criticism, Viswanathan turns to Raymond Williams's analysis of Mill's "Coleridge" essay. In *Culture and Society* Williams offers a far-reaching genealogy of the Coleridgean meaning of *culture*, defined as "a court of appeal" through which to "condemn" the narrowly instrumentalist aims of capitalism and utilitarianism (63). But, argues Viswanathan, Williams locates the origins of this romantic critique exclusively within England, ignoring the likelihood that a two-way relation between colonizer and colonized both enabled and shaped this crucial discourse. She contrasts Williams's one-sidedness to the more inclusive approach of Eric Stokes. In *The English Utilitarians and India*, Viswanathan believes, Stokes presents utilitarianism as "a construction of imperial rule, its principles of governance being constantly tested and challenged" in a "dialectic of empire and home" ("Williams" 60, 62).

Mid-Victorian civil service reforms were also shaped by such a dialectic, I shall demonstrate, and one that relates to Stokes's and Viswanathan's research into Anglo-Indian education. Indeed, demonstrating the Northcote-Trevelyan agenda's roots in colonial experience helps to explain why it was that a particular notion of gentlemanly character dominated the reformers' program throughout the century. In midcentury Britain, as in India, the prescriptive discourse of character was displaced by a more politically restrained, descriptive discourse.

Colonial experience thus provided an important foundation on which to craft an ideal of disinterested governance suitable to Britain's self-consciously liberal and increasingly conservative society.

In *Masks of Conquest* (1993) Viswanathan details the fascinating history of English education as it developed in early-nineteenth-century India as part of a strategy for British rule. In the late 1820s "'Indian character' suddenly became a subject of immense importance" in debates over colonial governance. Whereas hitherto the education of Indians had been secondary, and arguments had centered on the conduct of British rulers, the debate now began to focus on the moral development of the colonized. Rather than superimpose English civilization onto the essentialized India constructed by Orientalist discourse, the British would instead deploy a deliberate course of anglicization directed toward transforming Indian character from within (*Masks* 34–35; cf. Stokes 26–27; Jan-Mohamed 80–81; David, *Rule Britannia* 18, 33). "To trade with civilised men," declared Macaulay, a leading proponent of anglicization, "is infinitely more profitable than to govern savages" ("Government" 717).

The metropolitan counterpart to this important colonial development was the increasing middle-class obsession with building working-class character. As we saw in chapter 2, reformers sought to halt what was perceived as the demoralizing dependence encouraged by the Old Poor Law. To insist on the duty to build working-class self-reliance was implicitly to assume that human character was prescriptive—that it could and, indeed, should be elevated and improved. Hence, just as the object of reformed colonial policy was to anglicize Oriental subjectivities, so the movement to reform the English poor laws expressed an early-Victorian prescription to "make the working man like me." Both the 1833 Charter Act, curbing the protectionist commercial dominion of the East India Company, and the 1834 New Poor Law, seeking to remove the evils of a pauper dole, were perceived as liberalizing policies that would culminate in the improvement of popular character.

At the center of anglicist colonial policy in India was Charles Edward Trevelyan, the man who both shaped and promoted Macaulay's 1835 "Minute." Trevelyan has been described as an archetype for his times—epitomizing the era's distinctive fusion of Evangelicalism, Whig-liberalism, political economy, and (to a degree) Benthamite utilitarianism (Stokes 46; cf. A. D. Webb 20, 25). If, in certain respects, the man that Trollope was to caricature as "Sir Gregory Hardlines" matched the zealous public service of Edwin Chadwick and Sir James Kay-Shuttleworth, in others he personified their nemesis.[5] Trevelyan and Chadwick clashed bitterly over the latter's midcentury sanitary agenda. As a close-fisted Treasury secretary, Trevelyan had "little use for Chadwick," decrying him as a reckless spendthrift determined to squander the public purse (Brundage 160).

Much of what divided these administrative mavericks was the deep rift between their respective Benthamite and liberal positions.[6] Trevelyan and Macaulay were second-generation Evangelicals who, like Thomas Chalmers, sought to elevate human character through idealized pastoral relations between rich and poor. Utilitarian emphases on efficiency and economy were, to a degree, compatible with this end. But the views of prominent Benthamites such as Chadwick and James Mill were, in other respects, antithetical to their liberal agenda. Colonial rule had provided the elder Mill with opportunities to promote the most bureaucratic aspects of Bentham's legacy, including centralized legislative interventions that the majority of Britons—as Chadwick eventually discovered—refused to tolerate.

Although the clash between liberals and Benthamites took many forms, one of the most crucial contests concerned the education of Indians. James Mill's views typified the mechanistic model of human subjectivity so objectionable to many of Bentham's critics. For Mill the idea of gradually anglicizing Oriental character to prepare Indians for self-government was irrelevant when a system of comprehensive laws would immediately and permanently ensure their optimal happiness. This bureaucratic approach offended the liberals' cherished moral and religious convictions. Macaulay and Trevelyan saw anglicization as part of a sacrosanct civilizing mission. By transforming character from within, English education would produce more genuine converts than the missionary school (Viswanathan, *Masks* 88, 116; Stokes 46–47).

Hence, at bottom what English education provided was a pastoral device suitable to the liberal bent of early-Victorian colonialism. In articulating a relation in which Britons "stoop[ed] to raise" their colonial subjects in exchange for the latter's "affectionate attachment" and "commercial intercourse" (qtd. in Stokes 47), Trevelyan set forth the foundation of an imperial identity still hallowed in Keith's 1937 history of India. According to Keith, "It was the aim of the greatest among the early British administrators in India to train the people of India to govern and protect themselves . . . rather than to establish the rule of a British bureaucracy" (qtd. in Chatterjee 14).

These liberal assumptions underlay the 1835 "Minute," Macaulay's famous call to create an English-educated class of Indians "who may be interpreters between us and the millions whom we govern—a class of persons Indian in colour and blood, but English in tastes, in opinions, in morals, and intellect" (729). This ostensibly anti-essentialist prescription presented Englishness as that which is cultivated rather than born. Hence, while character was deeply embedded in the history of individuals and nations, a penetrative pastorship such as that ascribed to English literature study could, "in the fulness of time," retexture a nation's moral fabric ("Government" 716). By training an Indian elite, the British might thus inject a powerful shaping force into Oriental history: a seminal class through whom to advance the blood of Indian genealogy by dint of English mind.

Significantly, this civilizing strategy was not presented as a long-term paternalistic relation between colonizer and colonized, but as a process of diffusion which, once initiated, would become self-acting. English-educated Indians would not only disseminate Western knowledge, but also "refine" and "enrich" native vernaculars, creating "fit vehicles" for elevating the masses ("Minute" 729). Anglicization was thus presented as a liberal character-building process with democratizing effects. Macaulay could, when necessary, justify colonialism by asserting the "immeasurable" superiority of British culture. A "single shelf of a good European library," he infamously declared, "was worth the whole native literature of India and Arabia" (722). Yet so far from forecasting permanent British rule, both he and Trevelyan looked forward to a still more desirable future in which colonial domination was superseded by trade. "That would, indeed, be a doting wisdom," Macaulay told Parliament in 1833, "which would keep a hundred millions of men from being our customers in order that they might continue to be our slaves" ("Government" 717). "Our object," wrote Trevelyan a few years later, is "to rouse the mind and elevate the character of the whole [Indian] people"; for, "as far as capability of acquiring knowledge is concerned, the native mind leaves nothing to be desired" (299–300, 289). In thus foregrounding a rhetoric of reciprocity and liberalization while, in effect, stabilizing colonial inequalities, Macaulay and Trevelyan once again resembled their contemporaries in urban Britain. The latter also drew on liberal ideas to present their mission to "make the working man like me" as a mutually uplifting exchange between potential moral equals.

That said, Trevelyan's multifaceted career was also a veritable lightning rod for the shifts that occurred within British liberalism in the years between the late 1820s, when he championed English education in India, and the 1870s, when he variously worked to implement Northcote-Trevelyan reforms, and, as a COS member, to organize British charities. Trevelyan's 1838 return to Britain coincided with the close of a liberal era in Indian reforms. By 1854, coincident with the transfer of ruling power from the East India Company to the Crown, education policy saw a decided revision. Anglicization had in a sense been too successful since the colonial state, denying Indians' access to high-ranking positions, refused to gratify the "Western" ambitions that English literature had helped to cultivate. Sir Charles Wood's 1854 dispatch thus signaled a more pragmatic approach to colonial rule. Henceforth education policy would take advantage of India's indigenous hierarchy, establishing discrete tiers of schooling, prescribing "practically useful" subjects for the masses, and abandoning the premise of a universal humanist curriculum (Viswanathan, *Masks* 142–65). These policies were concretized after the military and civil rebellion of 1857–58, in the wake of which, as Bernard S. Cohn writes, "a theory of authority became codified, based on ideas and assumptions about the proper ordering of groups in Indian society, and their relationship to their British rulers" (165; cf. Stokes 258, 264). Significantly, then, the idea of a stratified curriculum corresponding to analogous divisions in the colonial service germinated within the very same political coterie that was beginning to see the *English* service as a lynchpin of lasting constitutional stability.

Trevelyan's early commitment to character building thus differed, at least in theory, from Wood's straightforward rule. Yet, in the years between Trevelyan's 1838 departure from India and Wood's 1854 dispatch, the two Whigs closely collaborated in yet another colonial enterprise. Between 1845–49 Wood, then chancellor of the Exchequer, gave Trevelyan, then secretary of the Treasury, a free hand in applying a laissez-faire policy to famine-stricken Ireland.[7] Trevelyan's readiness to insist that negligent Irish landlords were to blame for the social crisis highlights an important point about the liberal mind-set he epitomized in the 1820s and 1830s. As the implicit paradox of a "liberal" imperialism doubtless suggests, liberal ideology and social hierarchy were not, as the rhetoric often implied, antithetical, but, to the contrary, deeply interdependent. Hence, the change within liberal policy which took place in the 1850s can be understood as an intensification of hierarchical investments that hitherto had remained muted by the prescriptive rhetoric of character building.

Testifying before Parliament in 1853—the year of the civil service *Report*—Trevelyan stood out as an "unswerving champion" of early-nineteenth-century liberalism, still committed to English education in India (Stokes 253). Yet his insistence that "the inevitability of self-government in India was to be consciously worked for and welcomed" had "paled into a stress that the British would have to remain in India indefinitely to ensure good government" (A. D. Webb 18).

How much that shift reflected a drift toward Wood's pragmatism and how much the influence of Jowett's views on civil service reform is open to question. What is certain is that, once removed from a colonial setting in which anglicization had dominated his thinking, Trevelyan's philosophy of governance was reoriented toward metropolitan contexts.

Wood's 1854 dispatch ultimately strengthened the Benthamite position in colonial India. This turn of events was so antithetical to liberal principles that, when Trevelyan returned to India in 1859, his public opposition to British policies resulted in his immediate recall (A. D. Webb 23). Yet, while Benthamite bureaucracy was accelerating in India, in England the failure of Chadwick's sanitary program amounted to a categorical rejection (see chap. 3). Benjamin Jowett's vision of a civil service clerisy thus provided a timely and serendipitous strategy for elite liberals such as Gladstone, Trevelyan, Wood, Sir Stafford Northcote, Robert Lowe, and Ralph Lingen. By replacing the discredited Benthamite expert with the Oxbridge gentleman, Jowett offered a means by which not only to respond to popular demands for effective pastorship, but also, in so doing, to curb middle-class aspirations to administrative power.

For my purposes the most salient aspect of the shift from the liberal politics of the 1820s and 1830s to that encouraged by the Northcote-Trevelyan agenda was the concomitant change in the discourse of character. Whereas the prescriptive mission "to make the Indian like me" had been predicated on the unquestioned excellence of British national character, the plan to institute a national clerisy entailed a rather different descriptive strategy. No longer trained exclusively on Orientals, the Irish, and the working classes, the project of moral improvement was refocused on the British ruling class. This shift—from examining the defects of those below to cultivating the virtue of those above—eventually enabled upper-class liberals to create a powerful myth of disinterested governance.

"A Classless Class of Well-Bred Men"

In India efficiency is quite of secondary importance; it indeed bores the natives desperately. But a high tone, quite down to the drummer-boys, is everything, at least to the stability of the British Government in the country.
— G. C. M. BIRDWOOD, *On Competition and the Indian Civil Service*

The simple question [in evaluating the quality of an institution] must be whether a particular institution harmonises with other institutions, and with a certain rude, vague, yet quite intelligible something, which may be called the English scheme of life. The great endowed schools are less to be considered as educational agencies, in the intellectual sense, than as social agencies.

— CITED BY ANTHONY TROLLOPE, "PUBLIC SCHOOLS"

One of the most important features of the midcentury realignment of liberal political culture and the emergence of a conservative constitutional consensus was, therefore, a profound shift in the meaning of character. As we have seen, the idea of character which prevailed in the 1820s and 1830s described an individual and social force of great magnitude. Character in this form entailed a theoretically limitless potential for inner development, catalyzed by interpersonal relations—by what Evangelicals and secular idealists alike conceptualized as the potential impact of "a direct assault on the mind" (Stokes 30). Compared to this formidable transformative possibility, the new discourse of character—which began to take hold in the 1850s, but peaked in the mid-Victorian era—was noticeably stationary, if in theory responsive to the long-term effects of painstaking nurture.

The potentially momentous difference between the two is suggested by a late remark from Trevelyan. In 1838 Trevelyan had exhorted his countrymen to "stoop to raise" benighted Indians to an ideal form of character signified by Englishness. In 1863 his evocation of a rather different notion of character betrayed his investment in social hierarchy both in India and in Britain. No longer cast as novices on their way to developing anglicized characters of their own, Indians were now endowed with a shrewd capacity to judge the character of their rulers: to know "instinctively the difference between the English gentleman, courteous, considerate and commanding respect, and those 'brought to the front from obscure corners of society,' boorish, contemptible and disgusting" (qtd. in Compton 269). If in its prescriptive form character had promised breathtaking forward motion, in its newer descriptive form it privileged incremental change, constitutional conservatism, and established hierarchy.

Yet, as Trevelyan's comment also makes clear, the burden of this shift rested on "the English gentleman," the much-touted excellence of whom quite deliberately invited the discerning gaze of the governed. Not surprisingly, the price for this privileged superiority was to generate considerable anxiety and debate regarding the determinants of gentlemanly status. It is one thing to declare, as G. C. M. Birdwood did in 1872, that "a high tone" was more important than efficiency in maintaining "the stability of the British Government" (qtd. in Compton 269). It is another to warrant the precise description of that tone.

Although the definition was always arguable, there is no question that the same historical circumstances that produced a descriptive view of character also favored a restrictive usage of *gentleman*. That such developments were tied to contemporaneous civil service reforms is manifest in W. L. Burn's situating of the gentlemanly ideal as a "safeguard against" the zealous expert (263). With a concern like that which prompted Trollope to write *The Three Clerks*, H. S. Tremenheere, himself a civil servant, feared that open competition would result in recruiting "uncommon clever fellows from some third rate place of Education, who will sell public documents to the first newspaper that offers a good price" (qtd. in Brundage 161). Tremenheere was seconded by no less a personage than Queen Victoria, who also worried that competitive recruitment would "fill the public offices with low people without the breeding or feelings of gentlemen" (qtd. in Briggs, *Victorian* 111). Northcote-Trevelyan supporters had therefore to convince such critics that a reformed civil service would meet entrepreneurial demands for sound government by safeguarding the quality of gentlemanly recruits, not by recruiting entrepreneurs. Gentlemanly character was thus made to convey a tense polyvalence: on the one hand, sufficiently competent to steward the nation's business interests and, on the other, sufficiently cultivated to transcend the latter's manifest limitations.[8]

In creating a political framework for this end, the writers of the *Report* closely followed the lead of the Oxford tutor Benjamin Jowett. If Macaulay and Trevelyan typified the terrific importance of Evangelicalism among the British ruling classes, Jowett, in turn, suggested the increasing sway of Broad Church thinking with its emphasis on Christian manliness and German-Romantic philosophy. "Victorian churchmen," writes Richard Dellamora, "attempted to form a clerisy whose plan of action combined a belief in divine telos with a program of Liberal political reform" (198; cf. Crowther, *Church* 30–31; Dowling xiii). It was Jowett who persuaded the reformers to abolish Haileybury, the respected Benthamite college where Trevelyan himself had prepared for a career in the Indian service—a move that signaled the Whigs' "decisive break" with the utilitarian tradition in England (Gowan 16; cf. Moore, "Abolition" 248). Haileybury's disappearance meant that Oxford and Cambridge would alone supply the most desirable civil servants both in India and at home. Such "almost incalculable" advantages, Jowett argued in a Coleridgean vein, would "replace Oxford in its true relation to the Church & the Country," or, in Trevelyan's analogous terms, "replace our two great Universities . . . *in relation* with the active life of the country" (qtd. in Moore, "Abolition" 250, 254).

Hence, while the Northcote-Trevelyan agenda was publicized as a plan for administrative efficiency, its more far-reaching, if often abstract, goal was to provide gentlemanly pastorship for a metropolitan society envisioned in conservative liberal terms. Gladstone's landmark economic reforms of 1853 were of a piece with the *Report*. Liberal economic policies would "not only . . . develop the material resources of the country," but also "knit the hearts of the various classes of this great nation yet more closely than heretofore to that Throne and to those institutions under which it is their happiness to live" (qtd. in Stansky 78). Thanks to the confluence of Jowett's ideas and the legacy of anglicist policy in India, "those institutions" might now be imagined to include a civil service clerisy, staffed by the nation's best-educated gentlemen.

In this way the Northcote-Trevelyan agenda professed to fill a crucial void. Its underlying philosophy of governance was sufficiently positive to mobilize the political ambitions of the Whig-Liberal elite, but also sufficiently neutral in appearance to facilitate the emerging consensus between them, their professional allies, and the entrepreneurial middle classes. Gladstone quietly assured Russell that a service divided into mechanical and intellectual ranks would enable Britain's aristocrats to prove their "immense superiority." Trevelyan privately envisioned the civil service as an "'Imperial University' whose existence . . . would powerfully affect society at every level" (qtd. in Compton 266). In public, however, the allegedly disinterested government of "men of independent character" involved a barrage of Royal Commissions devoted to improving the armed forces, the church, the nation's charities, and, above all, the educational foundations of their own privileged sphere (Wood, qtd. in Parry 180). Such character-forming institutions, wrote a commentator whose views on public schools won the approval of Anthony Trollope, secured that "rude, vague, yet quite intelligible something, which may be called the English scheme of life" (qtd. in Trollope, "Public Schools" 480). While Jowett provided budding Oxonians with "a moral counsel so capacious . . . that it became a 'pastoral supervision,'" at Cambridge tutors such as Leslie Stephen improved undergraduate character by introducing sports, and cultivating ties of "respect and affection" (Dowling 33; Rothblatt 188–89, 189 n. 1). The 1864 Taunton Commission advocated competitive admissions to strengthen endowed schools for the middle classes, while the 1861 Clarendon Commission on public schools sought to "mould . . . the character of English Gentlem[en]," equipping them with "vigour and manliness of character," and teaching them to "govern others and control themselves" (qtd. in Parry 181).

Hence, while competitive recruitment was publicized as a triumph for entrepreneurial principles, insiders such as Gladstone, Trevelyan, and Jowett saw that the integration of public schools, Oxbridge and the civil service would amount to a powerful institutionalized elite to preside over a three-tiered liberal society. The highest-ranking posts would be reserved for Trevelyan's "true" aristocracy: the very best of those "expensively educated young men" who by birth and education had "acquired the feelings and habits of gentlemen" (qtd. in Hughes 72). Beneath them would be a tier of subordinate positions earmarked for the well-educated members of the "great *Middle Class*" (Trevelyan, qtd. in Compton 266). Finally, the availability of thousands of low-level clerical positions would, it was believed, "induce the 'lower orders' to educate their children and impress them with the importance of a good character" (Compton 266).

It is important, however, to bear in mind that, at least in the nineteenth century, the Northcote-Trevelyan agenda was more successful in enhancing the cachet of genteel credentials (e.g., public school education) than it was in establishing the importance of the civil service in England, either practically or symbolically. Like most Victorian reforms, the adoption of Northcote-Trevelyan recommendations in England occurred piecemeal, through the voluntary compliance of individual units. There was, as Peter Gowan stresses, "nothing automatic and organic about the implementation" of Jowett's program, which was, rather, "consciously fought for" over several decades (11). Unification of the service, enabling professional mobility between branches, was not, by and large, achieved until the twentieth century. As late as 1875, five years after the Order of Council that at long last mandated competitive examinations, contemporaries continued to contrast the "supreme importance" of administrators on the Continent and in India to the negligible status of their English counterparts (Scoones 349).[9]

Nevertheless, while the mid-Victorian civil service enjoyed only modest short-term gains, in the long run the Northcote-Trevelyan *Report* was immensely successful in establishing a puissant mythology of liberal governance by an enlightened administrative class. That Jowett's agenda should produce a powerful mythology rather than, first and foremost, a coherent bureaucratic machine was, in fact, entirely predictable. The entire notion of Coleridgean governance was predicated on a "Platonic Idea": the diffused pastoral effects of established institutions, and the cultivated men who staffed them (Gallagher, *Industrial* 193; cf. Dowling 33). As J. M. Compton has observed, the perceived gentility of British administrators often functioned as a "deus ex machina," obviating "all necessity for any serious thinking about problems of government" (270).[10] Well-bred public servants could, it was believed, exercise an effective pastoral role without recourse to the controversial interventions of centralized legislation or philistine experts. In this way the Northcote-Trevelyan program, in conjunction with public school, university, and colonial reforms, created a new mythology, translating the upper classes' monopolization of administrative power into an ideal of disinterested governance. Indeed, that ideal still resonated more than a century later in a modern scholar's description of the British civil service as "a classless class of well-bred men" (qtd. in Marion 481).[11]

Drawing on Coleridge, as well as colonial experience, the *Report*'s exponents believed that the disruptive side effects of a vigorous capitalist economy could be tempered by superlative example from above. As we have seen, the idea of diffusion had been central to anglicist colonial policy, and further linked to a prescriptive and, therefore, potentially democratic notion of character. By contrast, the idea of a civil service clerisy was made possible by a descriptive and, therefore, discriminating notion of character. In the first case diffusion was seen to exercise a potentially radical and transformative effect. In the second case its far more conservative function was gently and indirectly to stabilize and civilize, to diffuse the sweetness and light that Matthew Arnold would eulogize in *Culture and Anarchy* (1869). Liberal governance in this form was, in turn, predicated on the legendary, if also anxiety-provoking, status of the English gentleman.

In the years following the *Report* Britain's public schools, "those great ateliers for turning out well-made characters," became the primary vehicle for the development of men able to control themselves and govern others (Collini, *Public* 114; cf. Gagnier, *Subjectivities* 174). Even solidly middle-class authors such as Elizabeth Gaskell chimed in, praising the character-building effects of the public school ("Visit to Eton" 2). Robin Gilmour has argued that the schools resolved the tension between middle and upper classes, "broadening the basis of gentility" by making public school education a veritable trademark of gentlemanly qualification (*Idea* 7). By thus authenticating the gentleman's credentials, public schools facilitated the symbolic work of transforming the nation's elite into a "classless class of well-bred men."

That said, to broaden the base of gentility, even in so exclusive and deliberate a fashion, was inherently to revisit a prescriptive notion of character in which every human being was, in theory, endowed with the potential to develop the most ennobling governing qualities. In chapter 5 I explore this contradiction as it reverberated in Dickens's *Our Mutual Friend,* a novel in which public school–educated Eugene Wrayburn both has, and does not have, gentlemanly attributes that his working-class rival, Bradley Headstone, fundamentally lacks. In the remainder of the present chapter I turn to works by Dickens's midcentury contemporary, Anthony Trollope. Although Trollope persistently criticized specific Northcote-Trevelyan recommendations, his novels and other writings ultimately—unlike Dickens's—made an important contribution to stabilizing the descriptive notion of gentlemanly character upon which the new civil service mythology depended.

Anthony Trollope and the Domestication of "Excelsior"

A competing examination in itself is no bonus in these worldly days. Men do not now stride through all the dust of an Olympic race-course for a laurel-wreath. The glory of having his name written in the first place of honour on Mr. Jowett's list, will not entice the most promising youth of his age into permanent service under the Crown; there must be other inducements than these.

— ANTHONY TROLLOPE, "THE CIVIL SERVICE"

Excelsior! It is very nice to be a Commissioner, and to sit at a Board at Sir Gregory's right hand: much nicer than being a junior clerk at the Weights and Measures. . . . But there are nicer things even than that; there are greater men even than Sir Gregory; richer figures than even £1,200 a year!

— ANTHONY TROLLOPE, *The Three Clerks*

In his memorable exploration of the mid-Victorian era through its celebrated personalities, Asa Briggs points to Anthony Trollope as one of the two writers whose works best portray the "superficially secure and comfortable England" of an era in which sanguine expectations of progress were "tinged with expediency." At the height of the Crimean debacle in 1855 J. A. Roebuck headed a landmark investigation into the highest echelons of government. A contemporaneous pamphlet asked *Whom Shall We Hang?* Yet by 1857 the war was over, and Lord Palmerston's government had won the nation's confidence. Britain's fleeting infatuation with populist radicals was superseded by a preference for "average churchwardens" (*Victorian* 37, 90, 85–86). That characterization was applicable not only to Palmerston, but also to a host of Trollopian gentlemen, from Barsetshire's clergymen to the self-possessed statesmen of the Palliser novels. With upper- and middle-class Britons united behind a conservative liberal agenda—one equally purged of expert interference and democratic ambition— the ground was laid for a novelist apt to familiarize the world they claimed as their own. Trollope's genius for subtleties of character charmed, where Dickens's broad strokes antagonized. Whereas others "roundly condemned," Trollope "gently pricked" (Rhodes 216). What D. A. Miller has described as "The Novel as Usual" (107–45), what Jane Nardin has called a privileging of commonsense morality over moral prescriptiveness (28), what David Skilton has seen as a tendency to describe social ills rather than to cure them (*Trollope* 58–78), all point to the qualities that made Trollope the premier novelist of a period of relative political quiescence. Such critical assessments also suggest how richly Trollope was able to contribute to what I have so far described as an emerging myth of disinterested governance stressing social hierarchy and the legitimating powers of descriptive character.

For an example one need look no further than Trollope's first Barsetshire novel, *The Warden* (1855). Mild-mannered Mr. Harding undeniably holds the kind of sinecure which a modern society must teach itself to renounce in the interests of progress. But, for all that, he is a gentleman through and through, "the moral center of the Barsetshire novels" (Nardin 9). As the narrative progresses, it becomes clear that to distort Harding's character is even more grievous an error than to tolerate the antiquated practice of the placeholder. Not since Jane Austen's works played a similar role in comforting a society shaken by the French Revolution had the English novel invested so much symbolic weight in the self-improving potential of genteel society.[12] According to J. Hillis Miller, "Trollope's narrator watches his people with an equable sympathy, a sympathy so perfect and so neutral in temperature that it insinuates itself into the reader's mind" (*Form* 85). This neutral temperature, and this subtle power to insinuate, precisely anticipate what Britain's most intellectual advocate for the civil service, Matthew Arnold, sought to establish in an "impartial" state.

That said, my purpose in the present discussion is to analyze a distinct phase in Trollope's early career, sparked by the Northcote-Trevelyan *Report*, and its reverberations in popular responses to the Crimea. In *The New Zealander*, a series of essays drafted during the height of the Crimean scandal in 1855–56, Trollope struck an uncharacteristically admonitory note—more like Carlyle's diatribe than the calm observation for which the chronicler of Barsetshire is famous.[13] Just as *The New Zealander* seems to take its cue from Carlyle, so *The Three Clerks* (1858), a fictional rejoinder to the Northcote-Trevelyan *Report* and the clamor for administrative reform, bears the impress of such dark Dickensian fictions as *Bleak House* and *Little Dorrit*. Trollope's early works are thus noticeably split between the stridently critical and the profoundly composed. While *The Three Clerks*, in the manner of Dickens's novels, testifies to the moral anarchy of a pastorless liberal society, Trollope's inimitable Barsetshire novels affirm the aegis of well-bred men. What is particularly at stake, I will argue, is a balance or synthesis between two mid-Victorian popular ideals: the upper-class myth of the born-and-bred gentleman, and the entrepreneurial myth of the self-made man. In the following analyses I read *The Three Clerks* as an allegorical domestication of *Excelsior*, Trollope's ironic term for the destructive powers of energy and ambition in a modern bourgeois society.

Energy and Ambition

We are launching into boundless competition with the recklessness of men who should start a balloon without ballast.

— W. BAPTISTE SCOONES, "THE CIVIL
SERVICE OF ENGLAND"

Over and above the money view of the question I wished from the beginning to be something more than a clerk in the Post Office.

— ANTHONY TROLLOPE, *An Autobiography*

In *An Autobiography* Trollope methodically relates the payment he received for each and every published work, ridiculing the idea that artists and men of letters ought to care less for money than do barristers or bakers. All "material progress," he avers in a restatement of the popular politico-economic doctrine, has originated in "man's desire to do the best he can for himself." Indeed, "the more a man earns the more useful he is to his fellow men." If *An Autobiography* thus evokes the perspective of contented professional prosperity, *The New Zealander* may be said conversely to betray that its author had so far earned a paltry "£55 for the hard work of ten years" (*Autobiography* 71, 69). Yet Trollope's grievances as an obscure public servant and undiscovered writer do not fully explain the distinctive qualities of *The New Zealander* and *The Three Clerks*. The fact is that both *The Warden* and *Barchester Towers*, two veritable classics, were written during the very same period, with the latter novel drafted "more or less concurrently" with *The New Zealander* (Super 76).

Immersed in its present-day context, *The Three Clerks* is, like *The New Zealander*, more intelligible as a response to the world of *Little Dorrit* and the Northcote-Trevelyan *Report* than as the follow-up to Trollope's Barsetshire novels. Although *The Warden* famously satirizes the excesses of Victorian popular culture, Barsetshire's imaginary terrain nonetheless rests securely on the character of men like Mr. Harding and Archdeacon Grantly. *The Three Clerks*, by contrast, lacks this underlying stability. It is a study of the "corruption of modern life," a disquieting morality tale in which stark contrasts and quasi-Dickensian carica-tures abound (Halperin 8; cf. Bareham 57, 80). If, as Briggs avers, Trollope was, in the 1850s and 1860s, the aloof chronicler of a self-satisfied age content to traf-fic in expedience, *The Three Clerks* is the glaring exception to that rule. Less chronicler than scourge, Trollope here anticipates the vitriolic critique of an-other distinctive work, *The Way We Live Now* (1875).

Trollope's early novel tells the story of three government clerks—Harry Nor-man, Alaric Tudor, and Tudor's cousin Charlie Tudor—and their relations to three sisters, Gertrude, Linda, and Katie Woodward, the daughters of a cler-gyman's widow. Private and public narratives intersect, with Harry's and Alaric's professional rivalry at "the Weights and Measures" (a Treasury-like department) reproduced in their contest for the hand of the beautiful but flawed Gertrude. The basic structure of the novel is thus a series of contrasts between different characters, especially "Norman" and "Tudor" strains of the English gentleman. "What were the faults of [each] character," the narrator announces at the out-set, "it must be the business of this tale to show" (5; cf. 10). Harry Norman, the younger son of a landed family, attended public school and Oxford prior to be-coming a clerk. By contrast, "ambitious" Alaric Tudor, the son of a squandering army officer, has no family income to supplement his clerk's salary. Although "not perhaps superior to Norman in point of intellect," Tudor is "infinitely su-perior in having early acquired a knowledge of how best to use such intellect as he has" (7).

In the early stages of the novel Norman, the better financial prospect, courts the worldly and self-willed Gertrude, while Alaric, "literally destitute" apart from his salary, flirts with Linda, a passive female paragon. All is well until Sir Gregory Hardlines, head of the Weights and Measures, is appointed to a North-cote-Trevelyan-like civil service commission, with his replacement to be chosen through an office-wide competition. As Trollope sees it, the best senior man deserves the position according to the existing practice of seniority and the improving principle of "detur digno": let it be given to the worthy. Although Trollope disagrees with the Northcote-Trevelyan principle of "detur digniori"—let it be given to the *more* worthy—he does let on that Harry Norman is deemed the "most useful man in the office" (63). Significantly, then, the victor of "Mr. Jobbles"'s grueling examination is neither a senior man, nor Harry, nor Mr. Minusex ("who could do as many sums . . . as a learned pig"), nor the prolific Alphabet Precis. It is, rather, the least senior man in the office: the self-assured and ambitious Alaric Tudor (63).[14] Alaric soon rises to a position on the Civil Service Commission and wins Gertrude for his bride. In this way Hardlines's wrongheaded principles are shown to favor qualities that are already dangerously unchecked. Once in a position of power, Alaric is blinded by ambition and tempted by the unscrupulous Undy Scott, a parasitic Scottish aristocrat. He rapidly descends "the Slope of Hell." A hypocrite and a "rogue," Alaric is as guilty as Bill Sykes, the underclass criminal of *Oliver Twist*, only more personally blamable for his downfall (341, 345–46).

Trollope's novel thus formulates a deliberate response to the Northcote-Trevelyan *Report* and the post-Crimean clamor for administrative reform. As a post office official, Trollope was, from the start, critical of several Northcote-Trevelyan proposals. Apart from his bitter opposition to open competition (*detur digniori*), one of Trollope's most persistent complaints was that the plan was impracticable, a utopian "dream of perfection." Such youthful prodigies as the reformers sought to recruit were unlikely to exist anywhere in the kingdom ("Profession" 225; cf. "Civil Service" 112). Even more important, the public had no "right" to demand "energy" and "ambition"—"the luxuries of the labour market"—without any plan for rewarding them (*Clerks* 561). In a chapter originally drafted as part of *The New Zealander*, and interpolated into the first edition of *The Three Clerks*, Trollope declaimed:

> Ambition seek the Civil Service, or energy waste in so unprofitable a garden the muscles and vigour of its youth! No, not while there be bishops and judges in the land; not while physicians ride in chariots, and write themselves baronets; not while there be glory to be won in the field, and a gallant name in the wars; not while there is a pen for ambition to use, or even a plough for energy to follow!
>
> . . . [R]ailway shares, low as such be, have more to offer ambition than Downing Street. Manchester, with her millions of miles of Calico, will be a better mart for energy than Somerset House. (561)[15]

As in all of his writings on the subject, Trollope's viewpoint here is recognizably that of a hardworking public servant, for whom the long-standing injury of low pay and limited advancement has been aggravated by the insult of outside censure. "The civil service is a stepmother," Trollope quipped, "and has no right to expect affectionate, heart-given offices from her children" ("Civil Service" 420; cf. "Profession" 214–15). The way to draw top men into the service, he argued, is not obsessively to examine those who apply, but, rather, to reward those who enter by providing ladders to the highest and most lucrative echelons of administrative power ("Civil Service" 412; "Profession" 226).

Trollope may thus be said to have advocated the ostensible ends of the *Report*—a more efficient service staffed by qualified men—while strongly dissenting as to the means. He agreed that patronage was "a great evil" that ran counter to the "spirit of the age" ("Civil Service" 422). But, like many contemporaries, he saw competitive examinations as reflecting a misguided entrepreneurial emphasis. Unlike Smiles, Trollope was misled into believing that the *Report* had been designed to favor men "from a class educated in a less costly . . . manner than those who fill our universities" (417). Like the latter, however, Trollope believed that the system would encourage "cramming" rather than warrant knowledge or intellect (*Clerks* 4). Trollope was thus entirely unable to perceive the *Report*'s underlying assault on middle-class expertise, and its attempt to constitute a civil service on Coleridgean grounds. On the contrary, he portrayed the reformers as uncompromising zealots who, more like than unlike the notorious Chadwick, were driven by impracticable theories. Trevelyan was a self-styled "governor of Utopia" and his fictional counterpart, Sir Gregory Hardlines, a "Civil Service Pharisee" ("Civil Service" 413; *Clerks* 58). Benjamin Jowett was also cast in a Gradgrindian light: "Mr. Jobbles had divided the adult British male world into classes and subclasses, and could tell at a moment's notice how long it would take him to examine them all" (*Clerks* 125). Such caricatures, representing Northcote-Trevelyan as a utilitarian measure, reveal how Trollope's understanding of the *Report*, like that of many contemporaries, fell wide of the actual mark. Certainly by the time of the *Autobiography* Trollope was ready to say that, while he "never learned to love competitive examination," he "became and [is], very fond of Sir Charles Trevelyan" (75, cf. 29–31).

Yet it is precisely Trollope's dread of competitive examination, that "much loathed scheme" (*Autobiography* 75), and not his distaste for the pharisaical reformers who promoted it which makes *The Three Clerks* such a distinctive novel. Sir Gregory Hardlines is narrow-minded and self-important in the manner of the Evangelical Mr. Proudie; but at bottom the threat he presents to the social order is no more grave than that of Barsetshire's bishop. It is, in fact, one of the ironies of *The Three Clerks* that as Alaric becomes increasingly hardened and corrupt—a narrative anti-*Bildung* that is one of the novel's great achievements—Sir Gregory becomes an almost sympathetic figure. Although his schemes are dangerously naive, the Hardlines professional ethic is sound. So long as one subordinates one's own interests to "those of the public service," Sir Gregory tells Alaric, one "will not fail to receive the praise such conduct deserves" (152).

But, by the time he hears it, Alaric Tudor—drunk with newfound power, and blinded by ambition—has already violated this rule. With Undy Scott as his mentor, Alaric has begun to profit illicitly from his official position. He soon becomes a thoroughgoing hypocrite, with Sir Gregory's principles controlling his "outward conduct," and Undy's expedience ruling "the inner man" (152). In the end Sir Gregory is nearly hoisted with his own competitive petard. As Alaric's insatiable drive impels him to seek parliamentary power in direct contravention of Hardlines's ethics, the latter despondently watches his ungrateful protégé "climb above his head" (403).

Clearly, then, it is not utilitarianism, Evangelicalism, or any other narrow-minded creed that poses the most serious threat to social well-being. Rather, it is energy and ambition themselves—the "luxuries of the labour market"—which disrupt the Novel as Usual. *The Three Clerks* thus strikes the entrepreneurial ideal at its very heart: casting ominous aspersions on what Samuel Smiles was soon to immortalize as the "indomitable spirit of industry," that "spirit of self-help . . . [which] has in all times been a marked feature of the English character" (*Self-Help* 40–41, 18). This distinctive theme is encapsulated in the reiteration of *Excelsior*, a "watchword" invoked ironically at various stages of Alaric's self-destructive climb (399).[16]

Trollope's defensive curtailment of the entrepreneurial spirit will, perhaps, strike some readers as a surprise. In his autobiography Trollope hastened to bridge the divide between professional and entrepreneurial ideals which, as Harold Perkin has shown, pervaded Victorian culture (*Rise*). While Matthew Arnold contrasted the enlightened professional to the philistine man of business, for Trollope the man of letters was neither more nor less than an exemplary entrepreneur, "do[ing] the best he [could] for himself and those about him" (*Autobiography* 71).[17] Indeed, to the mind of one recent critic *An Autobiography* was "an aid to self-reliance, and a supplement to Samuel Smiles's famous" work (Skilton, "Introduction" xiii). In writing his own life, Trollope thus synthesized the entrepreneur's competitive self-interest and the professional's dedicated service.

This autobiographical synthesis, moreover, looks back to the equipoise of the Barsetshire novels. In *Barchester Towers* Mr. Harding and the Archdeacon are "cast in different moulds," for Grantly, a flawed but rock-solid gentleman, is endowed with a "spirit and energy and power of combating" that the quietistic warden utterly lacks (456). Yet in Barsetshire the Hardings and Grantlys are united, despite temperamental differences, by bonds of common gentility. Like Mrs. Gaskell's Etonians, they form "a strongly-united brotherhood" ("Visit to Eton" 4). In the contemporaneous London of *The Three Clerks* this class-based camaraderie is disrupted by competition, both professional and amorous, culminating in a disturbing breach between placid Normans and aggressive Tudors. The pernicious effects of competition are thus epitomized by Mrs. Woodward's ominous Darwinian prophecy: "The world . . . will soon be like a fishpond, very full of fish, but with very little food for them. Every one is scrambling for the others' prey, and they will end at last by eating one another" (121).

Significantly, Barsetshire's Archdeacon is, in many respects, as ambitious a man as the rising young star of the Weights and Measures. In the opening chapter of *Barchester Towers* the "proud, wishful, worldly" Grantly sinks to his knees in prayer. His sin is to hope that his father's death is not so prolonged as to thwart his own professional advancement (3). Yet in *The Three Clerks*, written less than a year later, Alaric Tudor's "spirit and energy and power of combating" are not only the root of his personal downfall but also, symbolically, a serious threat to the nation as a whole.

Trollope's seeming volte face—his dyspeptic assault on the entrepreneurial spirit—is, I argue, deeply tied to the same contemporary crises that motivated *The New Zealander*. Alaric Tudor's ignoble rise and precarious fall speak directly to the post-Crimean clamor for administrative reform, and the cult of the self-made man which the latter helped to foster. Both *The New Zealander* and *The Three Clerks* thus provide a fascinating textual record of Trollope's efforts to confront disruptive cultural forces that threatened to negate the very imaginative possibility of Barsetshire.

The Way We Live Now

The past two years have certainly been prolific of the most serious and saddening mercantile crimes. Men of the highest standing, of seemingly stainless character, have been found to have been for years in the practice of the most systematic and heartless fraud. We have had religious embezzlers, philanthropic connivers at forgery, felons of taste, education, and public spirit.

— *London Times*, FEBRUARY 1857

Alas, alas! how is it that in these days such men become rogues? How is it that we see in such frightful instances the impotency of educated men to withstanding the allurements of wealth? — ANTHONY TROLLOPE, *The Three Clerks*

Perhaps nowhere else in his vast oeuvre is Trollope's morality as conspicuous and unironical as it is in *The New Zealander*. With an earnest that Trevelyan himself would have lauded, these essays on the condition of England exhort individual self-improvement as vigorously as the works of Smiles or Harriet Martineau, look to an aristocracy of worth in the manner of Carlyle, and express a distaste for the leveling effects of democracy worthy of Tocqueville (see, e.g., *New Zealander* 11, 13, 20, 37).

By 1855 such ideas had a decidedly old-fashioned ring, as Trollope himself had suggested in his satire on Carlyle ("Dr. Pessimist Anticant") in *The Warden*. Yet other aspects of *The New Zealander* are decidedly more timely. "Of all the beautiful creations of man's fancy," Trollope asserts, "freedom is the most lovely" (9). Like J. S. Mill, soon to elaborate further on such ideas in *On Liberty* (1859), Trollope describes the disempowering and demoralizing effects of a modern bourgeois society. For Trollope the decay of individual character is tied to the influence of the popular press, particularly the *Times*, a newspaper "that no man may attempt to moderate with impunity" (35).[18] With mediating figures such as Barsetshire's gentleman-pastors nowhere in evidence, the *Times* stands to tyrannize and corrupt an entire nation (39).

This sense of imminent decline and urgent contemporaneity deeply reverberates in *The Three Clerks*. Like the essays, Trollope's 1858 novel depicts a world in which modern decay is unchecked by exemplary character, gentlemanly or otherwise. The novel extends *The New Zealander*'s critiques of civil service reform and the commercial scandals of the mid-1850s—both themes that had also loomed large in *Little Dorrit*. Although the Crimean outrage of 1855 and the vehement middle-class radicalism it engendered are not explicitly described, they provide a crucial key to Trollope's intense curtailment of the energy and ambition personified by Alaric Tudor.

As Olive Anderson has observed, the Crimean debacle "provoked an outburst of overt class bitterness and impatience with prevailing institutions far more comprehensive and alarming that anything which had been seen since the early 1830s or was to be seen again for many years, and served to convince many . . . observers that the admired English body politic was at last in decline." At its inception the Administrative Reform Association expressed a moral outrage akin to *The New Zealander*'s, demanding not only an end to aristocratic cronyism, but also a broad-based reform "of public life in its widest sense" (*Liberal* 97). Yet, as the outcry escalated, the movement was increasingly dominated by J. A. Roebuck's strident radicalism, and the bourgeois "cult of commerce." This class-conscious attack pitted aristocratic incompetence against the ostensible virtues of commercial experience and the "mystique of business" ("Janus Face" 233, 241–42). Critics asked whether "the great railway administrators and contractors, the men who manage lines of packets, who own and direct successfully the operation of whole fleets of merchant ships," might not make far better ministers than Britain's "blundering" aristocrats (Briggs, *Victorian* 63–64). Although Dickens was no advocate of the crassly commercial, *Little Dorrit*'s contrast between the Barnacles and Daniel Doyce—between aristocratic inertia and middle-class enterprise—could not but fuel such fires. Certainly, from Trollope's perspective, Roebuck's harangues, Dickens's satire on the Circumlocution Office, and the renewed interest in open competition as a panacea produced the impression that a narrow-minded entrepreneurialism, fomented by demagogic newspapers, was carrying the day.

And yet if, in this regard, Dickens and the *Times* seemed allied in a regrettable campaign for shortsighted commercial values, in at least one important respect these popular voices were in line with Trollope's thinking. "The past two years have certainly been prolific of the most serious and saddening mercantile crimes," wrote the *Times* in February 1857. "Men of the highest standing, of seemingly stainless character, have been found to have been for years in the practice of the most systematic and heartless fraud" (qtd. in Weiss 72). With similar thoughts in mind Trollope closed *The New Zealander* with a reference to John Sadleir, the notorious swindler whose 1856 suicide inspired *Little Dorrit*'s Mr. Merdle. "Could the career of that wretched man . . . have been possible," Trollope asks, "had falsehood, dishonesty, pretences, and subterfuges been odious in the eyes of those who came daily in contact with his doing?" (211).

The very same question provides the central theme of *The Three Clerks*, a novel that makes explicit reference to Sadleir and several other "felons of taste, education, and public spirit." Trollope represents the widespread tolerance for falsehood in quasi-Dickensian fashion: as a landscape of grotesque artifice, and a commodification of the human. In a faint echo of *Dombey and Son* railroads have turned the countryside into a city (*Clerks* 21). Undy Scott and his brothers engage in "matrimonial speculation," selling their titles to wealthy wives, for "needy" aristocrats "cannot afford to associate with [their] fellow men" except by "making capital of them" (83, 88). In a subplot that may have inspired a similar scenario in *Our Mutual Friend*, Alaric and Undy conspire to arrange a marriage between Charlie Tudor and an heiress so that they, as her trustees, can safely speculate with her fortune.

Given such a backdrop, frauds such as Sadleir—or, for that matter, Alaric—are not aberrations, but, rather, symptoms of what Trollope calls the "pernicious wind" of expediency. "Every great man, who gains a great end by dishonest means, does more to deteriorate his country . . . than legions of vulgar thieves" (345–46). Yet more impressive than such lapses into sermonizing is the psychologically convincing representation of Alaric Tudor's ruin. Through this complex narration Trollope translates the era's gusto for energy and ambition into an allegory of the entrepreneur-turned-rogue. In so doing, the novel revisits the middle-class radicalism fomented by Roebuck, situating itself with regard to the popular myths that ultimately paved the way for consensus: the born-and-bred gentleman and the self-made man.

According to Olive Anderson, the middle-class radicalism of the post-Crimean period was Janus-faced: simultaneously looking back to the republican constitutional ideals of the old English gentry, and ahead to the modern cult of the businessman ("Janus Face"). The same Janus-face, I suggest, expressed itself in the two myths that facilitated the transition from midcentury crisis to mid-Victorian consensus. Although Trollope misunderstood the intentions of the Northcote-Trevelyan *Report*, his Barsetshire novels gave popular form to Jowett's Oxbridge-educated ideal. By touting the qualities of the English gentleman, novels such as *The Warden* idealized the qualities of genteel breeding, quelling middle-class doubts as to the merits of the nation's political and administrative elite. At the other side of Anderson's Janus-faced radicalism was a mandate to empower practical men of business. The popular reply to that mandate—and the obverse of the ideal of the born-and-bred gentleman—was epitomized by the self-made man as eulogized by Samuel Smiles.

Published just a year after *The Three Clerks*, Samuel Smiles's *Self-Help* became one of the best-selling works of the nineteenth century. Smiles's text originated in an 1845 series of lectures, which was itself derivative of still earlier works. Significantly, in the 1850s Smiles at first failed to find a publisher for his dated homilies just as Trollope failed with *The New Zealander*. It was not until the Crimean scandal and the Indian Mutiny had produced widespread dissatisfaction with "English officialism" that a paean to "the determined energy and self-reliance of the national character" was deemed a marketable commodity (*Self-Help* 214).[19]

It is thus reasonable to expect Smiles's text to evoke the dynamic liberalism of the 1830s. In terms that cannot but recall Trevelyan's Anglicist policy, or the middle-class civilizing mission discussed in chapter 2, Smiles stresses "Self-Culture," defining it as "the power to elevate the character and expand the spiritual nature" (325, 334–35). At the same time, however, *Self-Help* also differs from such character-building discourses as Trevelyan's. Whereas the latter typically presented self-reliance as the effect of improving relations between colonizer and colonized, prosperous and poor, Smiles's emphasis is on a wholly autonomous power of self-making. Significantly, Smiles, a Scottish-born radical, turned to self-help after deciding that working-class politics were untenable "in an atmosphere of ignorance and poverty" (Briggs, *Victorian* 120). *Self-Help*, in other words, articulates an intensely idealist, even transcendentalist, philosophy in which "the free industrial energy of individuals" is held to "counteract" hostile circumstances, including not only poverty but also "laws" and constitutional "imperfections." Hence, what Smiles describes as "that active striving of the will," that "intense anticipation [that] itself transforms possibility into reality," does not depend on the pastoral guidance of the morally exemplary (40–41, 205). Smiles's political origins thus assert themselves in a radically individualist recasting of the prescriptive view of character. In *Self-Help* the social hierarchies and character-building relations that underlay prescriptions such as Trevelyan's are all but irrelevant to a profoundly individual project of self-realization.

It is easy to understand why such a text appealed so strongly to a nation shaken by military ineptitude, and discontented with its upper-class leadership. What Smiles provided was a fantasy of limitless individual autonomy. Better still, since such "indomitable spirit" was alleged to be "a marked feature" of English national character, Smiles's readers, by virtue of their Englishness, became privileged heirs to this desirable personal endowment (18). Smiles thus masterfully blurred the distinction between prescriptive and descriptive views of character, suggesting that the prized human potential of the former was also a national treasure of sorts, appertaining especially to British heritage and race. Although the author of *The Three Clerks* could not have read Smiles's 1859 best-seller, the unfettered individualism eulogized in *Self-Help* would have been familiar to

Trollope as the post-Crimean cult of the entrepreneur. Hence, something very like the "determined energy" of Smiles's "indomitable" self-makers lies everywhere behind the novel's dark rumination on moral decay.

Normans and Tudors

Alaric's education was going on rapidly. . . . He had already learnt the great utility, one may almost say the necessity, of having a command of money; he was beginning also to perceive that money was a thing not be judged of by the ordinary rules which govern a man's conduct. In other matters it behooves a gentleman to be open, above-board, liberal, and true; good-natured, generous, confiding, self-denying, doing unto others as he would wish that others should do unto him; but in the acquirement and use of money . . . his practice should be exactly the reverse; he should be close, secret, exacting, given to concealment, not over troubled by scruples; suspicious, without sympathies, self-devoted and always doing unto others exactly that which he is on his guard to prevent others from doing until him—viz., making money by them.

—ANTHONY TROLLOPE, *The Three Clerks*

Hence, while mid-Victorian consensus depended on a balance between Smiles's populist myth and its genteel Barsetshire obverse, throughout most of *The Three Clerks* Trollope assumes a far more disruptive stance. In a telling passage Alaric pragmatically courts the favor of the Woodwards' Uncle Bat, a retired naval officer, while discussing the maladministration of government offices. Tudor, aware that the old man harbors a grudge against the navy, echoes the Administrative Reform Association, urging "pressure from without . . . [to] do the work." Norman, who is too high-minded to seek favor, bluntly describes such rhetoric as "trash" (45). The result is that Uncle Bat determines to help Alaric marry Gertrude, even though Harry has long courted her, and Alaric has made overtures to Linda. Later, while contemplating the merits of Harry's superior education, Alaric invokes the transcendentalist wish fulfillment so central to Smiles's popular success: "Education is nothing—mind, mind is everything; mind and the will" (76). Encouraged by such sentiments, Alaric's ambition devolves before our eyes into self-deluding expedience, diverging ever more sharply from Norman rectitude—a split between the self-made man and the gentleman which ultimately damages both sides.

The irony, of course, is that Alaric, unlike the Scottish Undy or the demonized Jews of other Trollope novels, is in no sense racially marked as a born scoundrel. Education thus counts for a very great deal, indeed. As the motherless son of a spendthrift father, Alaric has had none but a "very miscellaneous" schooling (8). Tony Bareham has likened Alaric Tudor's "broken domestic circle" to that of another youthful A.T., Anthony Trollope (67). On the whole, however, the novel highlights the social provenance of Alaric's defects. Like Bradley Headstone in *Our Mutual Friend*, a different kind of self-made man, Alaric has internalized the bourgeois values of a status-conscious society.

At bottom, then, Alaric is corrupted by a pervasive culture of expedience, what Matthew Arnold later described as an anarchic penchant for "Doing as One Likes." Modern men resort to dishonesty, Trollope explains, because they overvalue their "object" (346). As an obscure clerk, Alaric lusts after "power, station, rank, [and] wealth" until he is tempted to procure them at any cost (102). Trollope thus demystifies what Smiles exalts as that "intense anticipation [which] itself transforms possibility into reality." Behind the cult of the self-made man Trollope discerns a world of Tudors driven by a ruinous fetish: "Excelsior!" Competitive schemes such as Trevelyan's thus fuel a hazardous fire, spurring self-deluding egotists to envision themselves as glory-bound prodigies, while they learn, in effect, to "wallow in the mire" (186).

Trollope reinforces the Tudor-Norman contrast through a complementary alignment between the Woodward sisters. Linda's "soft" and passive femininity represents Trollope at his most conventional (24). Her most impressive feat is to master her disappointment when she is jilted by Alaric, enabling her to transfer her affections to Harry. By contrast, Gertrude provides a dramatic female counterpart to Alaric's unbridled energies. Haughty and unsentimental, she has imbibed the reformist tenets of the day: "a competitive examination in every service," she enthuses, "would make young men ambitious" (121). When Mrs. Woodward praises Norman's generosity, Gertrude calls him "spoony" and "Quixotic." "I think every man is bound to do the best he can for himself," she says, proving herself the ideal wife for a self-made man (136–37). Hence, by pairing Gertrude's aggressive femininity with Tudor, and Linda's conventional alternative with Norman, Trollope sets the stage for a conclusion in which staid gentility outlasts reckless ambition, self-sacrifice bests self-promotion, and civilized hierarchy asserts its advantages over anarchic individualism.

And yet, in the end, *The Three Clerks* falls short of achieving that effect. To be sure, toward the end of the novel Tudor is tried and imprisoned for his crimes, while Norman unexpectedly rises to his brother's place as heir to the family seat. As Harry bids farewell to the Tudors, who are bound for a hard life in Australia following Alaric's release, he reflects on the difference between them: "Harry was Mr. Norman of Normansgrove, immediately about to take his place as the squire of his parish, to sit among brother magistrates, to decide about roads and poachers, parish rates and other self-absorbing topics, to be a rural magistrate, and fill a place among perhaps the most fortunate of the world's inhabitants. Gertrude was the wife of a convicted felon" (508). Trollope's brief idyll on the rural gentry, "perhaps the most fortunate of the world's inhabitants," cannot but recall Barsetshire, which, for all its ostensible remoteness from *The Three Clerks*, must surely have beckoned to the man about to write *Doctor Thorne* (1858), the third of the series. In this brief passage "Mr. Norman of Normansgrove" is called up, Barset-like, to preside over poor laws, policing, and civic improvements—the very same issues that provoked a century-long debate over the nature of pastorship in a modern liberal society. Doubtless those who promoted a clerisy-like civil service sought to uphold precisely such well-bred men as Mr. Norman of Normansgrove, and to eschew such discreditable "rogues" as Alaric Tudor.

In the end, however, *The Three Clerks* does not leave us savoring the gentility of Normansgrove's scion, not least because he himself suffers from invidious comparison. Although his devotion to Alaric early on is engaging, over the course of the novel he is, by turns, visibly embittered by failure, and relegated to the margins of narrative interest. According to Bareham, Norman is "marked by an unshakeable if not always superficially attractive honesty" (55). Increasingly, the reader's sympathy for him depends largely on Mrs. Woodward's long-standing preference. "How infinitely greater are truth and honesty than any talent, however brilliant!" declares the clergyman's widow, in a statement that must also explain Trollope's devotion to this priggish Norman (339).

As though to amplify Harry's weakness, Gertrude, so far from deformed by Alaric's ambition, ends by ascending to tragic grandeur. Loyal and "cheerful" despite poverty, disgrace, and expatriation, Trollope can hardly find sufficient language to ennoble her. He must content himself to declare that the "heroism of the Roman, who, for his country's sake, leapt his horse into a bottomless gulf, was as nothing" to her (544). It is surely significant that, having so thoroughly appraised "the true ring of [Gertrude's] sterling metal," the best Trollope can say of Linda is that "at Normansgrove, with a steady old housekeeper at her back, and her husband always by to give her courage," she had found "the very place for which she was suited" (547, 539).

Fittingly, then, it is Gertrude who voices the most telling comment on Norman debility. In the novel's most remarkable moment Gertrude introduces her sons to Harry just before leaving for Australia. "These are the little men," she says, "that in good times coming will be managing vast kingdoms, and giving orders to this worn-out old island of yours" (510). The narrator concurs: "There was no longer an excelsior left for talent and perseverance in this effete country. She and hers would soon find room for their energies in a younger land" (513).

Similarly, when Gertrude speaks her mind on Trollope's own pet subject, the civil service, Alaric's fall is seen from an entirely new standpoint. "A government office in England is thraldom," she complains, for civil servants must "sacrifice [their] individuality" to "a lumbering old machine" (513). In his 1855 response to the Northcote-Trevelyan *Report*, Trollope had reluctantly agreed with Sir James Stephen that, as "dullness . . . is the lot of the civil service," the idea of recruiting "the ambitious and the gifted" was absurd ("Civil Service" 424). A related point is made in the excised civil service chapter in *The Three Clerks*. In an obvious rejoinder to *Little Dorrit* Trollope insisted that there is "no insaner cry than that raised against routine," without which discipline modern life is impossible (558–59).

In *An Autobiography* Trollope is rather less resigned to office routine: "from the beginning," he admits, he wished to be "something more than a clerk in the Post Office" (72). In describing his official duties, Trollope portrays himself as an autonomous actor: a self-starting, outspoken, and "thoroughly efficient" public servant (89). He takes care, in other words, to distance his autobiographical persona from such dull routine as the "keeping of books," and "the necessary manipulation of multitudinous forms" (47; cf. 62, 90). In this way Gertrude's plaint on the lot of the clerk—in Stephen's terms, "entombed for life . . . in a Public Office" (qtd. in Pellew 13)—is recognizably meaningful to the author of *An Autobiography*. Through Gertrude, Trollope thus presents a view very unlike the novel's own domesticating process. Indeed, Gertrude sounds much like Samuel Smiles on the subject of the civil service: it is "a most pitiable sight," Smiles lamented in *Self-Help*, to see educated young men eager for the "routine, though 'genteel' occupation of a government office" (335–36). Like Gertrude, Smiles evokes the specter of an effete country with no space for the boundless ambition of self-made men. Hence, Gertrude's proud embodiment of a noble entrepreneurial spirit situates Trollope's own domestication of "Excelsior!" as that which will doom Britain to an undistinguished future.[20] It does not help matters that, for the moment, the final words on the subject are left to the uncharismatic heir to Normansgrove: "I always liked the Civil Service," he says, "and now I leave it with a sort of regret" (513).

The Third Way

> Many a young clerk became bad in character under the auspices of the [Civil] Service. Many a lad placed alone in London, with six hours' work to be done in the day and with no amusements provided for his evenings, has gone to shivers on the rocks of Metropolitan life.
>
> —ANTHONY TROLLOPE, "THE CIVIL SERVICE"

But Trollope's novel is, of course, a tale of three clerks, not two. It is through the third clerk—Alaric's cousin Charlie Tudor—that the novel attempts to create a middle ground, alleviating what would otherwise be a devastating split between Tudor ambition and Norman placidity. The story of Charlie Tudor is also the most autobiographical in the novel, based on Trollope's discreditable start as a lone nineteen-year-old post office clerk going "to shivers on the rocks of Metropolitan life." Charlie's character is therefore, in many ways, alien to the oppositional logic of the Norman-Tudor allegory. As an "Infernal Navvy"—a clerk in the notoriously lax department of Internal Navigation—Charlie leads a dissolute lifestyle. He is deeply in debt and, worse still, romantically entangled with Norah Geraghty, an Irish barmaid. Charlie is thus thorough enough a gentleman (in a way that Alaric is not) to prefer debtor's prison to marrying a wealthy heiress; yet these scruples do not preclude his falling prey to disreputable society. Like Trollope (and unlike Harry Norman), he is sufficiently energetic and ambitious to pursue a literary career in addition to his clerkship. Yet for the greater part of the novel he lacks nearly all of the qualities necessary either to the ideal gentleman or entrepreneur: he has "no self-respect, no self-reliance, [and] no moral strength" (*Clerks* 340). What Charlie requires above all is discipline, the "law of life" which Trollope himself allegedly lacked as a solitary youth (*Autobiography* 27–28).

Hence, through Charlie, Trollope grafts his own developing professional persona onto an allegory of civil service reform in a turbulent age. This autobiographical move enables Trollope eventually to figure a comic compromise like those in his Barsetshire novels. Thanks partly to Sir Gregory Hardlines, Charlie, who assumes Norman's place at the Weights and Measures, finds the discipline he needs. At the same time, Charlie becomes the first clerk to "enter . . .

without the strictest examination" (536). Hence, with Alaric's expulsion having symbolized the domestication of "Excelsior!" Hardlines's rigorous ethic, purged of its competitive obsession, takes its place in a London world that, at long last, begins to resemble Barsetshire.

To be sure, part of that resemblance is made possible through a conventional Victorian device: the domesticating influence of genteel women such as Mrs. Woodward and her youngest daughter, Katie. One suspects that Elizabeth Barrett Browning and Trollope himself were not the only contemporaries to be "wrung to tears" by Katie's deathbed plea for her beloved Charlie's reform (*Autobiography* 75, 95; Bareham 72). Too young to recognize her own dangerous attachment, Katie is spared the ignominy of female immodesty by a serious wasting illness. In the kind of paradox that Victorian readers loved, Katie's imminent death—brought on by emotional repression—liberates her to declare her otherwise unspeakable love for Charlie. That declaration, combined with some luck, eventually stirs Charlie to escape the "moral suicide" of marrying a barmaid (374). After a full recovery Katie weds the man to whom she has openly avowed her love (541).

What is especially significant about this familiar feminine terrain is its having to stand in for the descriptive qualities of gentlemanly character which, in *The Three Clerks*, are so conspicuously lacking. In the absence of an unimpeachable exemplar like Mr. Harding, Trollope resorts to reifying gentility by cruder means. As Charlie struggles to disentangle himself from debt and vague promises to Norah, Trollope contrasts Katie's angelic form to the barmaid's dirty nails and cheap-smelling pomatum (226, 374–75). A gentleman who marries beneath him, Trollope insists, does so at his own moral peril. Although working women may well be virtuous, their low "habits, manners, and ideas" will inevitably disgust the "palate" of the cultured husband and ensure his moral decline (374). Such ham-fisted classism betrays an anxiety—a fear of degeneration—seldom evident in the Barsetshire novels. As he contemplates an alliance with Norah, Charlie asks himself, "What miserable reptile on God's earth was more prone to crawl downwards than he had shown himself to be?" (221).

Trollope comes closer to reproducing Barsetshire's equanimity in a memorable scene involving Undy Scott. When the latter attempts to exonerate himself at his club, "a discreet old baronet" is moved to make a cameo appearance: "one who moveth not often in the affairs around him, but who, when he moveth, stirreth many waters; a man of broad acres, and a quiet, well-assured fame which has grown to him without his seeking it" (521). Here is a gravitas like Mr. Harding's—as though the warden were momentarily transferred to the pages of *The Three Clerks* to stand for a moral authority that neither Norman nor Charlie Tudor can command. Significantly, in proposing that Undy Scott be expelled from the club, the baronet speaks "in a voice of unusual energy" and sits down (521). With the special exception of Charlie's budding literary career, and in spite of Gertrude's impassioned counternarrative, the novel remains true to its impulse to regard "energy" as a dangerous and destructive force.

That said, Charlie's literary career dominates the final pages of *The Three Clerks*. Indeed, the novel closes with a scene of domesticated literary enterprise. When we last see him, the erstwhile Infernal Navvy is not only "Mr. Charles Tudor, of the Weights and Measures," but also a "distinguished master of modern fiction" (541). As the extended family gathers together to read a review of Charlie's third novel (in reality a practical joke planned by Linda), we are reminded that Anthony Trollope "never put pen to paper" until he married (*Autobiography* 48).

Trollope's quaint and domestic conclusion thus reintegrates energy and ambition in a form that looks back to the tempered worldliness of Archdeacon Grantly and ahead to the literary entrepreneur of the *Autobiography*. Indeed, in an 1883 review Trollope's *Autobiography* was lauded precisely for its synthesis of entrepreneurial qualities ("the daring of manliness") and gentle breeding ("the quietness of equanimity").[21] Charlie's story—that of a clerk who saves his "character as a gentleman" by turning to professional writing and marrying a born-and-bred lady—serves as a metanarrative of sorts. Through Charlie, Trollope prefigures his own experience as he shifted from quasi-Dickensian writing to the stream of mainly temperate fiction to come.

Early in Charlie's literary career a magazine editor recommends a number of marketable subjects for serialized fiction, including the Divorce Bill, the Crimean War, and the Indian Mutiny. Consisting precisely in the kind of charged social themes which had led Trollope to sermonizing and portentous allegory, Charlie rejects these suggestions. In so doing, he foreshadows the wisdom of *An Autobiography*. Unlike the clergyman or moral philosopher, Troliope warns, the novelist must teach by "charm[ing] his readers instead of wearying them." To teach readers "that things meanly done are ugly and odious, and things nobly done are beautiful and gracious," the novelist has but to represent character realistically: "to 'hew out some lump of the earth'" (*Autobiography* 143, 96). Such unobtrusive tactics soon earned Trollope the reputation of a man who "always writes like a gentleman" (qtd. in N. Thompson 156). Be that as it may, Charlie Tudor does not disdain to respond on a practical note by raising the subject of "Payment" (535). Hence, in writing himself as Charlie—or writing Charlie, in effect, as the future author of *An Autobiography*—Trollope sought that harmonious balance so crucial to the tenor of his most popular novels and, not incidentally, to the stability of mid-Victorian politics and society.

Culture and Anarchy

> I think that no youth has been taught [in my novels] that in falseness and flashness is to be found the road to manliness; but some may perhaps have learned from me that it is to be found in truth and a high but gentle spirit.
>
> — ANTHONY TROLLOPE, *An Autobiography*

In his introduction to *Barchester Towers* Robin Gilmour contrasts Anthony Trollope to Walter Scott. Scott's novels, as Coleridge once observed, stage a grand-scale contest between "adherence to the past" and the "passion" for progress (qtd. in Gilmour, "Introduction" xxii). For Gilmour, Trollope provides a comic counterpart to this historical dialectic: whereas Scott accommodates progress, Trollope comically reverses "the forces making for change" (xxii). Gilmour is not, of course, wrong to accent this conservative impulse in Trollope. Yet to describe *Barchester Towers* solely in terms of its allegiance to the past is to overlook the important contemporary role such novels played. From the standpoint of mid-Victorian liberals such as Gladstone and Jowett, Britain's timeworn institutions were the key to the future as well as a link to tradition. Hence, Trollope does indeed provide a comic counterpart to Scott's romances; but, in so doing, he offers precisely a Scott-like fantasy of England's "glorious 'middle way,'" tailor-made for mid-century dilemmas.[22] Although gentle-hearted Mr. Harding may lack a "force of character" sufficient "to stand against the spirit of the times" (*Barchester* 456), the Archdeacon's mettle, supplemented by his wife's, is sufficient to keep Barchester's *parvenus* at bay. In a different way, at the close of *The Three Clerks*, Anthony Trollope's alter ego emerges, Ivanhoe-like, to suggest a stabilizing balance between Norman civility and Tudor ambition. For Gladstonean liberals such narratives balanced two sides of the same constitutional ideal, facilitating consensus between the nation's enterprising middle classes and its governing elite.

In the 1850s, I have argued, Britain underwent a turbulent transitional period, "a centre of indifference," during which the governing authority of the nation's hereditary aristocracy was seriously questioned. The eventual alliance between the upper and middle classes was facilitated by the displacement of the early nineteenth century's prescriptive view of character: a concept at once too democratic and too exhortative to facilitate a conservative consensus based on laissez-faire economics and social hierarchy. Smiles's contribution to this transition was a radically individualized yet nationalistic recasting of the old character-building ideal. In Smiles's popular myth no British male lacked the power and autonomy to become a self-made man.

Civil service reformers contributed something at once distinct from and complementary to Smiles's populist myth. The backbone of their philosophy was a hierarchical principle, long fundamental to liberal thinking though often muted by the progressive rhetoric of prescriptive character. Even so radical a liberal as John Stuart Mill acknowledged it when, in the 1830s, he supported anglicization, arguing that the character of those "classes possessed of leisure and natural influence, ultimately determines that of the whole people" (qtd. in Viswanathan, *Masks* 149). A "Gospel for the educated," wrote Benjamin Jowett, is necessary, "because the faith of the educated is permanent, and ultimately affects the faith of the poor" (qtd. in Crowther, *Church* 32). Mid-Victorian liberals thus implemented laissez-faire economic policies while invoking a powerful notion of diffusive pastorship which had effloresced in colonial India. Armed with this distinctive philosophy of governance, Gladstone and his supporters set out to implement what Matthew Arnold would describe as the "action of a diligent, an impartial, and a national government" (*Culture* 17).

One of the challenges of studying liberal governance in this mid-Victorian form is to make sense of the inevitable gap between contemporaries' perceptions and the empirical record. As we saw in chapter 3, Jowett's influence first asserted itself in the Education department, where his Balliol protégés (including Arnold) were instrumental in undermining the ambitious agenda of Sir James Kay-Shuttleworth, a middle-class expert. While it is easy to discern the negative motives behind this upper-class curb on popular education—fiscal retrenchment, political conservatism, and the avoidance of controversial state policies—it is difficult, at first, to discern a positive philosophy at play. Hence, in an illuminating analysis of Arnold's views on working-class education, D. M. Mason observes that the meaning of Arnold's writings on the subject "is not altogether clear." Whereas for Kay-Shuttleworth the state's duty to elevate working-class children through schools was plain, for Arnold "the State's role [was] much more distant." As Arnold saw it, culture would "somehow" be conveyed from afar: not by teachers and clergymen in the classroom but by civil servants and aristocrats (184).

Clearly, what was behind this ostensible obscurity was a belief in the diffusive powers of gentlemen-administrators (the same "first plane" of men to whom, in his testimony before the Taunton Commission on middle-class schools, Arnold attributed "fine and governing qualities" [qtd. in Perkin, *Rise* 83]). But that belief need not—as it would for Bentham, James Mill, or Chadwick—express itself in a bureaucratic structure. As Susan Zlotnick has argued, Arnold represents the very apogee of antimaterialist social critique: "Arnoldian culture, the Arnoldian man of culture, and Arnold's conception of class all rest somewhat precariously upon an absent material base" (58). Indeed, these "extraordinary dematerializing tendencies" (59) were precisely the stuff of which mid-Victorian myths were made.

In 1861 Arnold warned that Britain's aristocracy was no longer sufficiently "superior" to justify its hold on political power ("Democracy" 4–5). What was needed, in other words, was a new governing-class mythology: the aristocracy reborn in the diffusive powers of a classless class of well-bred men. By 1866 Leslie Stephen was prepared to declare that Britain was "still an aristocratic country"—for Britons of every class had retained their "instinctive liking for the established order of things." That "instinct," he went on to explain, can never be "boosted up" by legislation (qtd. in Briggs, *Victorian* 254). The "mass of English people," wrote Walter Bagehot in 1867, yield to "what we may call the *theatrical show* of society," including "a certain pomp of great men" (*English* 248). Such contemporary insights help us to see why diffusion, rather than legislation—a dematerialized idea rather than a concrete bureaucracy—is the underlying form of the state as conceptualized in *Culture and Anarchy* (1869). As the modern successor to a hereditary aristocracy, the function of the Arnoldian state was, like the function of criticism, to disseminate "sweetness and light" (66; cf. 98–101). To be sure, such ideas might, in practice, be invoked to justify legislative initiatives of many kinds. Yet it is impossible to mistake Arnold for a statist of the Chadwickian or Fabian stripe. Arnold's idealism, inspired by Coleridge and Jowett, found its purest expression in the mythic cultivating powers of well-bred men—a myth to which Arnold himself became a principal contributor.

In a somewhat less obvious way Anthony Trollope, I have argued, was another such contributor. Trollope was not himself a self-styled Coleridgean,[23] but his proximity to Jowett's and Arnold's ideal reached a peak in the 1860s. Indeed, the *Fortnightly Review*, "the most intellectual" journal of its day (Super 188), was founded by Trollope and others in response to Arnold's 1864 call to cultivate a "disinterested love of a free play of the mind on all subjects" ("Function" 35).

It was in that high-minded venue that Trollope published an 1865 essay on public schools. As though to play music to Jowett's ears, Trollope asked, "Who can define the nobility that has attached itself to Englishmen as the result of their public schools; or can say whence it comes, or of what it consists?" ("Public Schools" 480).

Such starry-eyed homages to the cradle of Britain's ruling elite were, in the 1860s, commonplace. But in Trollope's case they were voiced by a man who eventually recounted a very different kind of public school experience. In *An Autobiography* Trollope describes the "ignominy" and "daily purgatory" he "endured" when, as the son of an impoverished farmer of "gentle standing," he was admitted to join Harrow's "aristocratic crowd" (9, 8). Reading of such experiences, one cannot but think of "Excelsior!"—of Alaric Tudor's ruinous haste to acquire power, station, rank, and wealth. "The indignities I endured," Trollope chillingly adds, "are not to be described" (*Autobiography* 14).

And, indeed, in the lofty pages of the *Fortnightly Review* Trollope chose not to describe them. What he did, instead, was to offer yet another Barset-like portrait of England's glorious middle way. "In almost every [English] bosom," he averred, "there sits a parliament in which a conservative party is ever combating to maintain things old, while the liberal side of the house is striving to build things new" (477). Fittingly, Trollope's professed political affiliation was "advanced Conservative-Liberal" (*Autobiography* 188; cf. Glendenning 383). Trollope thus cautioned moderation on the subject of public school reform, reminding his readers that the principal contribution of such institutions was social, not intellectual: "The son of the squire of the parish and the son of the parson are placed together at the same school, are educated in the same way, enjoy an equal footing, so that in after life they meet together with mutual sympathy, and on an absolute equality as gentlemen" (486–87). Trollope appears to have seen no contradiction between his own painful social exclusion, and the public school's professed function in producing cohesive upper ranks: men united (like Mr. Harding and Archdeacon Grantly) by their common descriptive capacity to "govern others and control themselves."

In his illuminating history of mid-Victorian Britain, Geoffrey Best asserts that the "only sure way of knowing you were a gentleman was to be treated as such" (270). Yet to define the gentleman's mythic qualities Best turns reflexively to Trollope. In *The Last Chronicle of Barset* (1867) Josiah Crawley, an impoverished clergyman, transcends his shabby garments as Trollope, the self-described "Pariah" of Winchester, emphatically did not (*Autobiography* 12). Armed with

Oxbridge connections that Trollope was too poor to afford, and academic distinction that the young Trollope lacked the wherewithal to achieve, Crawley eventually manages to pass muster in Barsetshire for precisely the reasons that old boys, according to Benjamin Jowett, made the best civil servants.[24]

"In England," a French contemporary remarked, "boys begin swaggering about their social position as soon as they leave the nursery, and if you would have some fun, you should follow groups of public school boys . . . on their way home" (qtd. in Best 272). Such accounts of schoolboy snobbery bear out Trollope's recollection of "those dreadful walks" to and from school, during which he "might have been known among all the boys, at a hundred yards' distance" by his unpresentable clothing (*Autobiography* 16). Too poor to dower his daughter, the fictional Josiah Crawley tells her future father-in-law, "I would we stood on more equal grounds" (*Chronicle* 885). (Crawley's demeanor, his "shaggy eyebrows," "long nose and large powerful mouth," suggest Trollope himself in much the same way that Alaric Tudor's youthful hardships recall the author's.) Archdeacon Grantly, ever honorable despite his flaws, tells Crawley: "We stand . . . on the only perfect level on which such men can meet each other. *We are both gentleman*" (180, 885; emph. added).

Behind the premier novelist of the age of equipoise, the age of civil service reform, was an experience of intense social ostracism: a goad to energy and ambition of novelistic proportions. In Smiles-like fashion Anthony Trollope transcended this early experience and, what is more, did so by imaginatively producing the mid-Victorian obverse of the self-made man. On this "first plane," first articulated in the Northcote-Trevelyan agenda, and later elaborated by Matthew Arnold, gentlemen effortlessly recognized one another and, in so doing, diffused civilization to those beneath them. The Novel as Usual thus helped to popularize a notion of civil servants as the natural pastors of a modern liberal society—disinterested governors and bastions of culture. The idea was sufficient to persuade the Victorian commercial classes of its value, and, indeed, to withstand the leap in the dark to come.

CHAPTER FIVE

A Riddle without an Answer

Character and Education in *Our Mutual Friend*

> Let the soldier be abroad, if he will; he can do nothing in this age. There
> is another personage abroad . . . the schoolmaster is abroad; and I trust to
> him, armed with his primer, against the soldier in full military array.
> — HENRY, LORD BROUGHAM

> I have very seldom seen, in all the strange and dreadful things I have seen
> in London and elsewhere, anything so shocking as the dire neglect of soul
> and body exhibited among these [ragged school] children. And although I
> know; and am as sure as it is possible for one to be of anything which has
> not happened, that in the prodigious misery and ignorance of the swarm-
> ing masses of mankind in England, the seeds of its certain ruin are sown, I
> never saw Truth so staring out in hopeless characters, as it does from the
> walls of this place.
> — CHARLES DICKENS

In an 1870 exemplum of *Words and Their Uses* Richard Grant likened character
to "an inward spiritual grace of which reputation is, *or should be*, the outward and
visible sign" (qtd. in Collini, *Public* 106; emph. added). Grant's wish for precise
correspondence between the inner qualities denoted by character and the outward signs that constitute worldly reputation perfectly illustrates the haunting
tensions of the 1860s, a decade that saw renewed agitation for franchise, educational, and poor law reform. As I argued in chapter 2, the 1834 Poor Law
Amendment Act threatened the ideal of character by attempting to solve a moral
problem—the pauperization of laborers—through impersonal politico-
economic and legal means. In seeking to dismiss the claims of character, and to
reduce reputation to a single economic criterion, the law challenged a worldview
in which Christian and civic values had been seen as preeminent. In place of a
charitable community, united by personalized character-building bonds, critics
of the law discerned the hardening of a bourgeois social order. In such a world
atomized individuals would vie for material assets, while character devolved into

the superficial signs of "respectability." Nowhere was this challenge to Christian and humanist ideals more evident than in Dickens's *Oliver Twist* (1837–38). In the figure of Oliver—untainted by exposure to the brutal, the vulgar, and the iniquitous—Dickens imagined character as an inviolate principle of good. But elsewhere the novel portrayed a world already dominated by narrow bourgeois interests, and debasing environmental influences.

Whether read for its assertion of the transcendent potential of human goodness, or for its dark materialist critique, *Oliver Twist* thus revealed the cast of Dickens's developing social imagination, depicting the deep-seated problems of a modern liberal society. In *Twist*, as in *Bleak House* (1852–53), Dickens sought to indemnify the individual against depersonalization and embourgeoisement through the extension of familylike pastoral relations: epitomized by the union of the Maylies (a clergyman's family) and the Woodcourts (a physician's family) at the close of each novel. As I argued in chapter 3, *Bleak House* presented personalized pastorship of this kind as the only means by which to guide Britain's shepherdless multitude without raising the insidious specter of dehumanizing institutional authority. In this way the author of *Bleak House* was visibly trapped by the puzzles of a modern liberal society. How might one attempt to build self-reliant character without quashing it? How to instruct the working classes without reducing them (and, ultimately, oneself) to the status of objects? How to elevate the "swarming masses of mankind" without breeding the vulgar bourgeois conceits prized by humbugs of the Bumble, Pardiggle, and Chadband variety? How, in other words, to foster the "inward spiritual grace" of character without capitulating to a cult of respectability predicated on superficial display? In *Bleak House*, as in *Oliver Twist*, Dickens's only consistent answer to such questions was the family, spontaneously extended through personal charity and domesticated professionalism.

In *Our Mutual Friend* Dickens's pastoral emphasis shifts from sanitary reform to education, but his expectation of finding "a Pastor in the House" is more bleak than ever. In *Bleak House* Dickens retreated from various collectivist possibilities because he dreaded the institutionalization of authority as much as he rued the suffering of the poor. In *Our Mutual Friend*, written after the midcentury backlash against centralized reforms, the symbolic threat of master agencies is much diminished. Mrs. Pardiggle's philanthropic "pounce" has been succeeded by the smugly dismissive Podsnap and the garishly unconcerned Veneerings. Mr. Inspector, as his anonymity implies, lacks Bucket's infamous depths and, unsurprisingly, fails to solve his case. Atomized and privatized, the world of this novel is inaccessible to the master manipulations of a Tulkinghorn, although Silas Wegg, a cartoon villain, is quite possibly his parody. Hence, the novel's subversion of an educational mission that Dickens publicly supported is related to, but not identical with, the overturning of the Sanitary Idea in *Bleak House.*

In *Oliver Twist* the resort to a defensive essentialization of character marked the novel's rejection of education as a viable solution to the problem of Britain's working-class condition. Yet throughout his career Dickens voiced strong public support for popular education. *Twist* thus provided an early indication of Dickens's skepticism toward the prescriptive view of character which underlay early-Victorian liberal thinking, especially the middle-class project of "making the working man like me."[1] Hence, in many respects *Our Mutual Friend* stages a return to the themes of *Twist*—a reexploration of the foundations of character and an attempt to test their relation to education.

As such, the novel is positively saturated with pedagogy of various kinds. Bella Wilfer, Dickens's favorite pupil, learns that domestic bliss is not for sale. Lizzie Hexam, one of Bella's moral guides, enrolls her brother Charlie in a ragged school, hoping he will "rise to be a master full of learning and respect" (72). Eugene Wrayburn, himself a public school graduate, urges Lizzie to accept his patronage; he arranges for Lizzie and Jenny Wren to be tutored by the venerable Riah. Bradley Headstone, who is training Charlie as a pupil-teacher, unsuccessfully attempts to claim the job for himself. But Headstone also provides "occasional evening instruction" for Sloppy, a pauper youth employed by the Boffins (444). Boffin himself seeks to acquire the cultural capital befitting his elevated station through tutorials with Silas Wegg. Yet by far the most formidable educational process of all is the one through which Bradley Headstone has been transformed from "pauper lad" into "highly certificated stipendiary schoolmaster" (267, 265).

As a pauper-*cum*-schoolmaster, Headstone represents the very epitome of the early-Victorian liberal imperative to educate the working classes. As a public school graduate, Eugene Wrayburn, Bradley's rival, is the emblem of a very different liberal moment: a mid-Victorian focus on strengthening the nation's governing classes. Headstone and Wrayburn thus dramatize the midcentury shift I described in chapter 4: from a potentially democratic prescriptive notion of character to a relatively static descriptive notion that justified social hierarchy. The charged contest between schoolmaster and old boy thus serves to illustrate Dickens's deepening skepticism regarding character in either form.

Dickens's public embrace of popular education was emphatic. As a public speaker, he promoted the idea that education held the key to producing "sweet accord and harmony among all classes" (qtd. in E. Johnson 2:622). In addition, the author closely followed the work of the early-Victorian era's most influential educational reformer, Sir James Kay-Shuttleworth, secretary to the newly established Committee of the Privy Council on Education between 1839 and 1849. Dickens was, for a time, sympathetic to Kay-Shuttleworth's plan to remove pauper children to special "district schools." He also considered collaborating with the latter on a model school for the poor (Collins 87). That said, from Mr. M'Choakumchild of *Hard Times* to the murderous schoolmaster of *Our Mutual Friend*, Dickens was a strident critic of Kay-Shuttleworth's most determined effort: the training of working-class, often pauper-born, schoolmasters.[2]

Dickens's fear that the wrong kind of education would dehumanize the working classes was memorably foregrounded in *Hard Times* (1854). His return to that theme in what is arguably the most complex of his novels, results in a profound narrative split: *Our Mutual Friend* is effectively divided into two major plots, one sentimental and the other realist. As Mary Poovey has argued, the sentimental tale of John Harmon and Bella Wilfer is, by the end of the novel, "almost completely cordoned off from the other plots." The Harmons' idyllic union is powerless to rectify the entrenched social problems elsewhere described in more realist terms (*Making* 164).[3] This narrative split exercises a significant impact on the novel's exploration of character and education. In the nostalgic sentimental plot, in which tutelage is figured in familial terms, Bella's reform is the sign of education's redemptive potential. But elsewhere the novel recoils from a formal educational mission that, as Dickens narrates it, has become inextricable from the dubious middle-class project of "making the working man like me."

As the sentimental plot consists in nothing so much as a fantasy of education without recourse to any extradomestic pastoral authority, I turn first to a discussion of Bella's triumphant moral regeneration and its *Twist*-like foundations. In the next sections I describe the educational reforms necessary to understanding the face-off between schoolmaster Bradley Headstone and old boy Eugene Wrayburn. I conclude the chapter with a discussion of the epistemological context in which Dickens's exploration of education and character takes place.

A Sentimental Education; or, Charity, the Novel, and the New Poor Law Revisited

O 'tis love, 'tis love, 'tis love, that makes the world go round!
—CHARLES DICKENS, *Our Mutual Friend*

I have been called upon to admit that I would give Poor Law relief to anybody, anywhere, anyhow. Putting this nonsense aside, I have observed a suspicious tendency in the champions to divide into two parties; the one, contending that there are no deserving Poor who prefer death by slow starvation and bitter weather, to the mercies of some Relieving Officers . . . ; the other, admitting that there are such Poor, but denying that they have any cause or reason for what they do. . . . [T]hat my view of the Poor Law may not be mistaken or misrepresented, I will state it. I believe there has been in England, since the days of the STUARTS, no law so infamously administered, no law so often openly violated, no law habitually so ill-supervised.
—CHARLES DICKENS, POSTSCRIPT TO *Our Mutual Friend*

If *Our Mutual Friend* were reduced to its sentimental plot alone, we might describe it as an attempt to update *Oliver Twist* by introducing education (of a kind) into a charitable social order. John Harmon, whose miserly father became wealthy in the scavenging trade, stands to inherit his father's lucrative dust mounds on the condition that he marry Bella Wilfer. Bella, selected by old Harmon for her defective temper, describes herself as having "money always in [her] thoughts and desires" (521). The aim of Dickens's sentimental education is thus to transform Bella from her mother's daughter into a domestic angel like Rose Maylie, a symbolic prelude to securing a "Harmonized" social hierarchy.

Hence, like *Twist* and another anti–New Poor Law fiction, Frances Trollope's *Jessie Phillips*, Dickens's late novel details the ways in which Christian and civic ideals are disrupted by bourgeois social ambitions. If one aspect of this story is the scathing satire on the Veneerings, a more subtle feature is the sentimental plot's quiet foreclosure on upward mobility. Boffin's attempt to cultivate himself in the manner of a gentleman thus introduces him to the villainous impostor Wegg. Similarly, the Boffins' plans to educate a working-class boy as a gentleman (already marked as a problematic project in *Great Expectations* [1860–61]) are abandoned for the more conservative end of turning Sloppy, a workhouse orphan, into a respectable cabinetmaker.[4] Moral fiber is thus improved through the curbing of social mobility, and the affirmation of a stable hierarchy in which individuals are, like the Boffins, content to develop within the bounds of their native rank. As we saw in the last chapter, this was precisely the kind of tiered society that conservative-leaning liberals had, since the 1850s, sought to cultivate under the aegis of well-bred gentlemen. In Dickens's version "Harmony Jail," like *Bleak House* before it, becomes an exemplary foundation for the extension of homely social bonds.

Nevertheless, in subjugating wealth to ideal pastoral qualifications, Dickens's late novel by no means aims to strip money of its social power. To the contrary, wealth's power takes on a conspicuous form of its own: the ominous, even scandalous, dust mounds that have fascinated so many critics.[5] It is therefore important to recognize that "dust" is not, like Mrs. Wilfer's pretentious desire for it, banished from the plot, but, rather, purified. John Harmon's succession to his father's property entails a veritable transubstantiation in which the old man's "money . . . turn[s] bright again" (849). This process includes the visible deconstruction and sorting of the mounds: their monetary worth extracted and distributed to the exemplary, while the filthy remains are carted off into the margins along with undesirables like Wegg. Significantly, "Mr. and Mrs. John Harmon had so timed their taking possession of their rightful name and their London house, that the event befell on the very day when the last wagon-load of the last Mound was driven out at the gates of Boffin's Bower" (849). Just as gold is purged of sordid debris, so noble ends are carefully distinguished from the monetary means on which they often depend.

This process of moral and physical purification cannot but recall us to the sanitary debates of the *Bleak House* era. In that novel Dickens insisted that "Tom's slime" would penetrate the very highest ranks of society unless personalized pastorship such as Esther's cured Britain's ailing social body. The author of *Bleak House* steered clear of the middle-class determination to "make the working man like me"—a suspect project that he delegated to the likes of Mrs. Pardiggle. Dickens was clearly aware that the campaign for sanitary reform might devolve into a pompous moral crusade, the effect of which would be to reify boundaries, rather than strengthen bonds, between rich and poor. Indeed, works such as Kay's *Moral and Physical Condition of the Working Classes . . . in Manchester*, and Chadwick's sanitary *Report* hardened the divide between the ascendant middle classes and the increasingly proletarianized working classes. As Steven Marcus has noted, the human excrement and other refuse documented in Chadwick's *Report* became a "virtual objectification" of the working-class social condition (*Engels* 185; cf. Stallybrass and White 125–48; Childers, "Observation"; Logan 143–65; Poovey, *Making* 115–31).

Dickens's infamous mounds may thus be seen as an attempted sentimental intervention against the objectifying gaze of middle-class moral crusaders. If his excremental vision provides a "virtual objectification" of any class, it is, without question, his own. For, as Dickens sees it, middle-class submission to bourgeois materialism has reduced social life to mere surface display. There is, as I will argue later, a difference between the sentimental plot, where dust figures the middle classes' compromising embourgeoisement, and the satire on the Veneerings, where wealth lacks even the undeniable substantiality of waste matter. Nevertheless, old Harmon's heaps clearly betray the arrogance of a Podsnappian middle class that, as Stallybrass and White have shown, liked to pretend that its own mounds didn't smell (139–40).

In thus figuring the danger of objectifying social relations, Dickens's famous dust is one of two central elements that connect the sentimental plot to the darker realist elements of *Our Mutual Friend.* The second of the two is the novel's revisiting of another Twistian theme: the deleterious effects of the New Poor Law. As he apostrophizes "my Lords and Gentlemen and Honourable Boards" (248), Dickens harks back to his early censure of economizing poor laws.[6] Nevertheless, an important change had taken place between 1837 and 1864. Whereas *Twist* had insisted that a deterrent and laissez-faire-ist poor law would fail to meet working-class pastoral needs, *Our Mutual Friend* goes farther, representing the results of such policies after more than a quarter of a century.

The early 1860s, years of severe urban hardship, saw a renewed interest in the poor laws. Critics, including Dickens, pointed out that workhouses were largely occupied by those unable to support themselves by any other means: orphans, the elderly, and the physically and mentally disabled.[7] On the other hand, the rise in outdoor relief and charitable aid for the unemployed led to renewed fears of the "Pauper Frankenstein" (M. Rose 60). These contrary attitudes—simultaneously condemning and ratifying the principles of 1834—were further complicated by wide variations between the theory and practice of the New Poor Law. Although most Poor Law Unions had, from the outset, preferred the old-fashioned "character test" to the stipulated "workhouse test," pauperism was nevertheless deterred because both practices successfully amplified the stigma of economic dependence (see chap. 2). As one French observer remarked, "the poor consider it a point of honour" to avoid the workhouse, even though, in cities such as Manchester, it is "a palace compared with the kennels in which the poor dwell" (Taine, qtd. in Wood 102). Hence, for all its intent to implement a rationalized policy of "less eligibility," the New Poor Law worked primarily by making pauperism a mark of personal disgrace.

Dickens dramatizes this theme in the story of Betty Higden, the impoverished washerwoman who agrees to give up her grandson for adoption by the Boffins. Determined to maintain self-reliance at any cost, Betty's "highest sublunary hope" is to die "untouched by workhouse hands" (566; cf. 247–48). Betty's obsession drives her into exile and hastens her grandson's death. Dickens thus points to the irrational excess always implicit in a policy that, in seeking to dispauperize the able-bodied, had shamed the helpless. Decrying the "Gospel according to Podsnappery," he joins John Ruskin and other concerned contemporaries in declaring, to cite Betty's requiem, that "all [is] not quite right between us and our sister—or say our sister in law—Poor Law" (577).[8]

Dickens's solution to this problem, however, is fundamentally Twistian. Were *Our Mutual Friend* reduced to its tightly sealed sentimental plot, the novel would conclude with a Maylie-like picture of domesticated harmony and stability: the dawn of a new social order, purged of pernicious bourgeois desire. Harmon's patronage of Sloppy—who will be taught a respectable trade—obviates the law by constituting close personal bonds between high and low. Upward mobility is curbed; replaced by a just social hierarchy.

Yet Dickens's novel, read in its entirety, compels us to read against the grain of sentimental narrative. In particular the novelist's inability to stabilize the character distinctions on which a just social hierarchy depends ultimately tells against the viability of a "Harmonized" nation. Indeed, by picturing education as a family affair, consecrating Betty's death, and securing Sloppy's future, the sentimental plot may be said to exercise its own form of Podsnappian gesture—dismissing further consideration of the poor with its unrelenting drive toward closure. Only the most tenuous of threads lead us outside of Dickens's harmonious sanctum: compelling us to contemplate the position of workhouse boys without wealthy patrons; of laboring poor who, in their desperate quest for respectability, refuse to be martyred like Betty Higden. Tenuous though such connections might be, they are sufficient. For Dickens equips us to recognize that, if Sloppy were unloosed from sentimental caricature—if he were rendered as a pauper lad striving to raise himself above workhouse stigma by means of education and a respectable profession—he would no longer be Sloppy, but, instead, Bradley Headstone: the villainous schoolmaster of *Our Mutual Friend*.

The Schoolmaster Is Abroad

All must tell the State
She has no right to educate. —ANONYMOUS

I am so dreadfully jaded . . . by the supernatural dreariness of [Sir James Kay-
Shuttleworth], that I feel as if I had just come out of the Great Desert of Sahara
where my camel died a fortnight ago. —CHARLES DICKENS

Perhaps nowhere in Victorian history is the ambivalence toward pastorship
in a liberal society more evident than in the attitudes toward popular education.
Lord Brougham's confident 1828 declaration that "the schoolmaster is abroad"
was, to say the least, decidedly premature. Resistance to popular education came
partly from conservatives, many of whom believed that education would make
the working classes discontent with their lot. Liberals, on the other hand, saw
education as integral to building character but clashed among themselves as to
ways and means.[9]

Nevertheless, beginning in 1833, the Whigs found a way to strike a compromise with opponents of state-supported education. The state determined
to provide grant money to any school that met certain minimal conditions. For
my purposes the most important aspect of this statist wedge into education was
the appointment of Sir James Kay-Shuttleworth as secretary to the newly
established Committee of the Privy Council on Education. Yet, while Kay-
Shuttleworth's efforts "to remake the working-class child in the middle-class
image" are central to my understanding of *Our Mutual Friend* (Sutherland, "Education" 129), it is important to clarify their limits. Government grants subsi-
dized schools where private resources were available, but they did not provide
schooling in areas where such resources were lacking. Hence, before 1870, when
the rudiments of a more comprehensive system were introduced, the largest
number of working people had at best limited access to formal education of any
kind. As F. M. L. Thompson avers, "the schoolmaster as policeman did not
work": the school never became "the dominant or decisive element . . . in shaping the [working-class] outlook" (*Rise* 151; cf. "Social Control" 192–95).[10]

Ironically, one of the only ways to receive a state education was to be a pauper child—like Bradley Headstone. While the state's interference in educating
the children of self-reliant Britons was vigorously opposed, the idea of educating pauper children—orphans and the children of dependent adults—was less

contentious. As an assistant Poor Law commissioner, Kay-Shuttleworth had persuasively argued that the doctrine of less eligibility was inapplicable to pauper children, who could not be blamed for "their misfortunes" (*Training* 3; cf. 14).

Although historians have demonstrated the limits of Kay-Shuttleworth's official authority (e.g., Paz, "Limits"), there is no question of his impact on early-Victorian attitudes to popular education, including Dickens's.[11] In previous chapters I have described Kay-Shuttleworth's exemplary relation to an urban middle class that perceived its pastoral obligations in philanthropic terms while avidly exploring modern social scientific methods. As a disciple of Thomas Chalmers, Kay-Shuttleworth sought to build working-class character through personalized charitable bonds. Nevertheless, his voluntary work in Manchester also involved statistics and other methods of objectifying the working-class condition. This blend of moral ends and bureaucratic means was also evident in his thinking on working-class education.

Kay-Shuttleworth justified the leap from a laissez-faire poor law to a state-supported educational agenda by emphasizing the unique circumstances of the pauper child. To break the cycle of hereditary pauperism, children must be removed from workhouse "stigma," insulated from adult paupers (including their parents), and relocated to special "district schools" under the supervision of dedicated schoolmasters (*Training* 6–7, 14). Yet what thus began as a strategy to serve a "special class" of children was subtly extended to include working-class children as a whole. In *The Training of Pauper Children* (1838), a Kay-Shuttleworth report published by the Poor Law Commission, the idea of shielding infant paupers from the pernicious influence of the workhouse became an analogue for the mission of schools in general. Schools for the working classes, Kay-Shuttleworth explained, "separate" children "from the contaminating influence of the street or lane in which [their] parents reside." They serve an intensive pastoral function, "rearing . . . hardy and intelligent" workers" and, in so doing, securing "the property and order of the community" (*Training* 27, 17).

Although his debts to Thomas Chalmers remain evident, Kay-Shuttleworth thus altered the framework in which his mentor had situated the school's character-building mission. As we saw in chapter 2, Chalmers's parish school, with its manifest nostalgia for the traditional rural community, was presented as a collective social space through which to unify and integrate a socioeconomically diverse community. Teachers would join their prosperous neighbors in visiting the homes of the poor, thus proliferating the ties between the local school and neighboring families of all ranks. By contrast, Kay-Shuttleworth's writing on education tended to present the working-class neighborhood as a hostile environment, detrimental to the school's improving effects. Family visiting—a principal feature of his early work in Manchester—was displaced by a growing emphasis on the pastoral potential of the school itself, "a little artificial world of virtuous exertion."[12] Kay-Shuttleworth thus tended to portray the school as an institutional alternative to, rather than a vital center of, communal bonds between rich and poor. He increasingly articulated a strong statist position: eager to elicit the support and supervision of local patrons, but convinced that voluntarism alone could not discharge society's "great collective duties" (qtd. in Digby and Searby 85–86).

But that is not to say that Chalmers's apostle had become an advocate for impersonal disciplinary institutions. To the contrary, Kay-Shuttleworth was deeply impressed by the liberal educational innovations of Scotland and the Continent. Under their influence Kay-Shuttleworth imagined the teacher as a substitute parent for the working-class child, a committed educator who would "deserve" and "obtain the reverence and the love of his charge" ("Punishment" 15). Such presumably progressive ideas ran counter to the "monitorial humbug" then prevalent in working-class schools (qtd. in Fraser 83). Repudiating the regimented rote learning of the monitorial system, Kay-Shuttleworth urged the "intimate moral rapport" described by Switzerland's Pestalozzi and Scotland's David Stow, another Chalmers disciple (R. Johnson, "Educational Policy" 112; Selleck 134–39, 160–71). Corporal punishment, he argued, was a sign of incompetence, destructive of the mutual respect on which the "wise and able Teacher" depended ("Punishment" 13–14). Indeed, learning motivated by "the fear of punishment, the hope of reward, or the desire of personal distinction" was positively "mischievous." Rather than resort to such demoralizing incentives, the well-trained schoolmaster would cultivate a "natural craving after truth," enabling students to "infer" knowledge for themselves (*Training* 31, 27). His methods would resemble those "with which a kind mother surrounds the instruction of her child" ("Punishment" 17).[13]

The disciplinary aims of this recognizably modern educational philosophy are profoundly complicated. Like much else in his thinking, Kay-Shuttleworth's embrace of Scottish and Continental methods was inconsistent. The emphasis on "training"—on cultivating the understanding rather than drilling—implied a sincere desire to enhance students' autonomy. There is also no question that Kay-Shuttleworth aimed to personalize the teacher-student relation. Like the clergyman's role upon which it was tacitly modeled, the teacher's pastoral abilities depended largely on personal attributes—native abilities that would be amplified through teacher training. Neither stern disciplinarians, nor inert vessels of facts, Scottish educators were, in Kay-Shuttleworth's phrase, "missionaries of the true faith in teaching" (qtd. in Selleck 138). In all of these ways Kay-Shuttleworth's educational philosophy gestured toward liberalism's intersubjective ideal: mutual recognition between equals.

Nevertheless, Kay-Shuttleworth's invocation of Scottish and Continental innovations cannot be disengaged from the underlying project of bringing working-class habits in line with middle- and upper-class social objectives. As Richard Johnson has demonstrated, the ostensible goal of enhancing working-class moral autonomy was riddled by and even contingent on the assumption that the working classes lacked this very faculty.[14] To demonstrate the need for liberal education, Kay-Shuttleworth and the inspectors denounced working-class culture, insisting on the deficiencies of working-class parenting ("Educational"). Interspersed with Kay-Shuttleworth's liberal rhetoric were prominent reminders that education would serve ruling-class interests, rearing "suitable god-fearing men" and curtailing "a race of prostitutes and felons" (*Training* 5–6).

Such contradictions were also evident in the teaching philosophy itself. At times Kay-Shuttleworth commended the kind of disciplinary routine which led many contemporaries to decry the tyrannizing effects of Continental education. In school, he averred, the working-class child "learns to rise, to sit, to march, to beat time in concert with his fellows; . . . [and] to sing" (*Training* 7).[15] More typically, Kay-Shuttleworth emphasized the importance of granting students liberty, developing student intellect, and minimizing punishment. Nevertheless, in so doing, he implied that the necessary counterpart to such liberalizing measures was to amplify teachers' vigilance. In such passages the goal of enhancing working-class autonomy culminated in an anxious desire to endow teachers with panoptical powers like those described in Foucault's *Discipline and Punish*.[16]

Yet, if working-class character building were to depend on the schoolmaster's vigilance, it followed that the selection and training of teachers would be of paramount importance. Significantly, this issue had been of little moment to Chalmers, who seemed simply to assume that Scotland's teachers were competent to exercise a high "moral power" over students and their families (1:54).[17] By contrast, the inadequacy of suitable teachers, and the need to supervise teachers closely, was a recurring theme both during and after Kay-Shuttleworth's tenure in education. That anxiety clearly stemmed from the necessity of employing working-class teachers to instruct their peers; for middle-class professionals would not condescend to the lowly status of "teachers of the poor" (Kay-Shuttleworth, qtd. in Fraser 265).

As a result, the training of teachers became, by necessity, the most concrete manifestation of an otherwise often utopian project of educational character building. The schoolmaster's alleged moral autonomy was not a distant end but a professional necessity upon which his pastoral authority was to be predicated. Teaching apprenticeships were the subject of the landmark 1846 "Minutes," typically seen as the high point of Kay-Shuttleworth's influence on educational policy. In addition, when he found himself unable to raise either government or charitable support for a model training institution, Kay-Shuttleworth and his colleague E. C. Tufnell established Battersea Training College at their own expense. The "main object" of such an establishment, Kay-Shuttleworth explained, was "the *formation of the character of the schoolmaster*" (qtd. in Selleck 160).

The 1846 "Minutes" created a five-year "pupil-teacher" apprenticeship. Boys of thirteen would be instructed by a qualified schoolmaster, after which they might compete for a coveted place as a "Queen's scholar" at a training college. By such means, Kay-Shuttleworth declared, a "poor man's child may . . . enter a profession at every step in which his mind will expand, and his intellect be stored, and, with the blessing of God, his moral and religious character developed." As this inviting rhetoric suggests, the purpose of the plan was not only to qualify teachers, but also, in so doing, to amplify the attractions of teaching. With the unskilled monitorial method still prevalent, there was, according to Kay-Shuttleworth, "little or nothing in the profession of an elementary schoolmaster . . . to tempt" any working man "having a respectable acquaintance" (qtd. in Fraser 264–65).

Yet, putting rhetoric aside, the idea of raising the status of schoolmasters—in effect, promoting working-class men to positions of social authority—produced predictable conflicts and anxieties. To mitigate this unusual sanctioning of social mobility, the Education department sought, in effect, to un-class teachers, locating them in "a no man's land" (Digby and Searby 42). Teachers would be raised well above their working-class charges, but kept thoroughly subordinate to the local elite. The department thus called on the voluntary efforts of clergymen and prominent families to supervise schools, "infus[ing] that spirit which cannot be looked for from our present race of teachers" (qtd. in R. Johnson, "Educational" 115). Hence, teachers were, on the one hand, authorized "agent[s] of civilization," and, on the other, objects of governing-class scrutiny (qtd. in Selleck 160).[18] In this way the working-class schoolmaster both was and was not endowed with faculties that were fast becoming the established hallmark of the English gentleman. Just three years prior to the appearance of *Our Mutual Friend*, the Clarendon Commission on public schools had defined the gentleman's character as an ability to control himself and govern others—a point to which I will return.

Kay-Shuttleworth's most distinctive contribution to the schoolmaster project was the influential Battersea Training College. Determined to raise lowly pauper lads to the ranks of the respectable, Kay-Shuttleworth was aware that schoolmasters so educated would be the products of "hot-house training." If a teacher's mind "were not thoroughly impregnated by a religious principle, or if a presumptuous or mercenary tone had been given to his character, he might go forth to bring discredit upon education by exhibiting a precocious vanity, an insubordinate spirit, or a selfish ambition." Battersea aimed to provide an institutional solution to this problem, preparing teachers for a "humble and subordinate position" of "modest respectability" (qtd. in Collins 169). The college's inaugural class—composed mainly of orphaned pauper boys—maintained a rigorous, almost monastic regimen of gardening, study, teaching, and religious worship. Adapting the ideas of another Swiss educationist, Kay-Shuttleworth sought to instill budding schoolmasters with the qualities of the "peasant father." The ideal graduate would acquire not only knowledge and pedagogical ability but also "an honest pride in the labour of his hands, in his strength, his manual skill, his robust health, and the manly vigour of his body and mind" (qtd. in Selleck 161; cf. 159–71). Clearly, Kay-Shuttleworth saw peasant masculinity as a means to developing moral autonomy—the ability to control oneself and govern others—without poaching on the charged social terrain of the so-called gentleman.

These intentions notwithstanding, the efforts to train working-class schoolmasters produced a new cultural stereotype, "the over-educated, conceited, ambitious teacher" (Collins 153). At the same time, teachers themselves were at pains to define their social position: insecure of the superior status to which their educational attainments and reputable character seemed to entitle them. In *A Schoolmaster's Difficulties* (1853) one teacher contrasted the established status conferred by various occupations—from laborers and mechanics to tradesmen and professionals—to the unnerving ambiguity of the schoolmaster. As Philip Collins has noticed, it is this vulnerable social position, rather than the classroom itself, which is of greatest interest to Dickens in *Our Mutual Friend* (160, 166). Indeed, Dickens's portrait of Bradley Headstone, an obvious product of Kay-Shuttleworth's hothouse training, is, as I will argue, one of the most telling indictments of the middle-class character-building project in the whole of Dickens's oeuvre.

Dickens satirized the Kay-Shuttleworth-era schoolmaster in *Hard Times* (1854), his famous attack on utilitarianism. The formidable Mr. M'Choakumchild appeared just as the first crop of pupil-teachers was emerging from the process laid out in the 1846 "Minutes." Presented as a product of "Her Majesty's most Honourable Privy Council's Schedule B," M'Choakumchild was cast, rather misleadingly, as a dehumanizing fact dispenser and politico-economic doctrinaire (1:47; cf. Collins 144–59). Symbolizing Dickens's entrenched dislike of bureaucratization—in this case, the standardization of teachers' knowledge—the "stony" and overtaught M'Choakumchild foreshadows his counterpart in *Our Mutual Friend*.

Yet the figure of Bradley Headstone also responds to a mid-Victorian educational context that *Hard Times* could not have entirely anticipated. By the time Dickens returned to the subject in *Our Mutual Friend* Kay-Shuttleworth's controversial early-Victorian educational policies had been substantially modified. Under the Revised Code of 1862 a new and more conservative breed of mid-Victorian liberals touted the advantages of the free market, reversing the zealous interventions of their predecessors.[19] This shift in educational policy was part of the larger cultural dynamic I described in chapter 4: the stabilization of a mid-Victorian consensus in which the middle classes delegated political power to the upper-class elite in exchange for free rein over commercial enterprise. In the wake of Chartism, commercial scandals, the Crimean debacle, rebellion in India, and the fall of the Sanitary Idea—to name just a few contemporary controversies—the ideal of a stable social hierarchy presided over by the "disinterested" government of born-and-bred gentlemen had gained wide currency. It is in this context that an early-Victorian educational agenda that claimed to build working-class character was superseded by a mid-Victorian agenda that aimed to strengthen the governing credentials of the nation's elite through public school and university reform.

Hence, whereas Kay-Shuttleworth had envisioned a far-reaching elevation of working-class character, the antidemocratic liberals of the 1858–61 Newcastle Commission on popular education were content simply to stabilize the social hierarchy on which their political interests depended. This new-model liberal agenda—with its broad appeals to economy, efficiency, and local control—enjoyed considerable middle-class support. Civic-minded and philanthropic middle classes were free to pursue the self-affirming project of "making the working man like me"; only their exertions were no longer likely to result, as had Kay-Shuttleworth's, in official position. Although high-minded liberals such as Benjamin Jowett sought to refashion the civil service, their conservative vision focused on fortifying and diffusing the character of British gentlemen, not educating the poor.

Hence, under the Revised Code of 1862 working-class education was subjected to a no-frills experiment in "free trade." The system of "payment by results" aimed to promote "cheap" and "efficient" schooling, but would settle for either. As it was neither "possible" nor "desirable" to aspire to anything beyond basic literacy for the masses, the state would content itself to reward those schools in which reading, writing, and arithmetic were effectively taught (Fraser 85, 265–66). With little investment in raising the status or "forming the character" of working-class educators, the Revised Code cut off the grants to pupil-teachers and abolished Queen's Scholarships. The schoolmaster was abroad, but the state now concerned itself primarily with rewarding his efficiency.[20]

From the standpoint of the Revised Code it is therefore possible to view Bradley Headstone—whose personal history looks back to the 1846 "Minutes"—as the product of a short-lived experiment in social engineering. Dickens doubtless disliked the penny-pinching economies of the Newcastle Commission, including the Gradgrindian examination of children, and the retreat from policies that, however minimally, had recognized the pastoral obligations of the state. Nevertheless, his arguments in favor of popular education were, on the whole, free of high-minded claims to developing working-class intellect, or raising working-class social standing. As Philip Collins has demonstrated, Dickens's main educational stress was to provide indigent children with sound "industrial" preparation for their livelihood: a trade or military service for the boys and domestic service for the girls (81).

In *Our Mutual Friend* Dickens attempted to resist the elitist notion that old boys were the bearers of British character in its highest form. Yet even as he did so he simultaneously cast further doubts on the potentially democratic prescriptive view of character. Nowhere—least of all in the depiction of Bradley Headstone—do Dickens's novels look forward to widespread social mobility premised on the limitless improvability of all humankind. To the contrary, Headstone's career is, as we shall see, a veritable cautionary tale in which teacher training threatens to create a breed of hothouse aberrations.

"The Manly Vigour of His Body and Mind"

What then is [the schoolmaster's] calling? Whereabouts in the sliding scale of
society is his position? . . . The labourer, the mechanic, the tradesman, the professional man, the clergy, all have their place and calling in the great hive:
whereabouts is the schoolmaster's, and what is it?

— ANONYMOUS, *A Schoolmaster's Difficulties*

Bradley Headstone, in his decent black coat and waistcoat, and decent white
shirt, and decent formal black tie, and decent pantaloons of pepper and salt, and
with his decent silver watch in his pocket and its decent hair-guard round his
neck, looked a thoroughly decent young many of six-and-twenty.

— CHARLES DICKENS, *Our Mutual Friend*

In their illuminating account of Victorian society Stallybrass and White describe education as the process through which middle-class urbanites affected
to transcend the limitations of their lowly physiology, distinguishing between
their own civilized culture and the gross materiality of working-class life. Education sanitized, elevated, and ultimately erased the middle-class body as the
child learned bowel control, cleanliness, correct posture, and polite speech
(144–45). To borrow Pierre Bourdieu's important concept, education thus entailed the acquisition of a middle-class "habitus," ensuring the integration and
signification of a deeply classed identity.

From this standpoint Kay-Shuttleworth and his allies may be seen to have
urged a potentially transgressive departure from the stabilizing logic of high and
low. Their educational agenda sought, in effect, artificially to impose a middle-
class habitus on children who would otherwise be marked by the lowly influences of workhouse or working-class family. Playground drills would subject
children's bodies to domesticating discipline, while liberal pedagogical methods
enlivened their intellects and raised their moral tone. Although this educational
process ultimately reinscribed the social difference it sought to mitigate, it is
crucial, nevertheless, to contrast Kay-Shuttleworth's progressive intentions with
the conservative bent of his mid-Victorian successors. In the 1860s, as prominent
Whigs and Liberals determined to strengthen the educational qualifications of
their own class, they simultaneously lowered the goals of popular education.
Rather than aspire to raise working-class children to middle-class standards, the

Newcastle commissioners determined, instead, to reduce their schooling to the barest minimum.

Dickens, a conflicted liberal much attached to the ideal of the close-knit charitable community, could not be content with either position. Although he was attracted to the pastoral elements of the Kay-Shuttleworth agenda, he disliked the secretary's social scientific thinking and bureaucratic methods. Even more crucial to understanding *Our Mutual Friend*, Dickens recoiled from Kay-Shuttleworth's most ambitious experiment in upward mobility: the intensive training that claimed to transform pauper lads into "highly certificated stipendiary schoolmaster[s]" (*Mutual* 265). Hence, Bradley Headstone's radically destabilized body is the expression of Dickens's antipathy toward social engineering. In this way Headstone represents the monstrous failure of the middle-class project of "making the working man like me": a project that, as Dickens represents it, entails a pernicious blend of bureaucratic depersonalization and bourgeois arrogance.

Dickens's palpable contempt for Headstone has led Collins to remark on the author's lack of compassion for mid-Victorian schoolmasters, subject to the indignities of ambiguous social position (166). In her fascinating analysis of the contest between Headstone and his public school rival, Eugene Wrayburn, Eve Kosofksy Sedgwick has argued that "contrasts of class" here appear "under the guise of contrasts of personality and sexuality" (166). Such observations ring true to a point but ultimately suggest a still deeper level of analysis. Dickens declines to compassionate with Headstone's vulnerability because it is precisely the pretense of upward social movement which he means to condemn. That condemnation, moreover, stems from a stark pronouncement on the inescapable effects of class. Thus, Headstone's personal and sexual weaknesses are not a guise for his lowly origins, but a testimony to them. To wit, Bradley Headstone is a freak of nurture: his ineradicable lowborn nature stultified and perverted by hothouse experimentation.

Dickens's attitudes are illuminated in a contemporaneous account of a visit to a model workhouse school, where Kay-Shuttleworth's influence remained evident. There the author was delighted to find pauper children of both sexes trained (without corporal punishment) for gainful employment in the military or domestic service. Commending the students' excellent "moral health," Dickens assured his readers that military drills did not extinguish the boys' individuality. Yet, although Dickens was thus eager to affirm the moral autonomy of paupers trained for subservient employment, he was far less enthusiastic about the pupil-teacher training reserved for the school's most talented scholars. Indeed, Dickens paused to warn one such prodigy that "a cold eye . . . and a hard abrupt manner, are not by any means the powerful engines that [his] innocence suppose[d] them to be" ("Short-Timers" 318, 316). Here, in a sense, is a key to Bradley Headstone: a man on the verge of discovering that the "engines" he has sedulously acquired are far less "powerful" than he has been led to believe.

When we first meet Headstone, he is described through a proliferation of "decent" surfaces—decent shirt, tie, pantaloons, watch, and hair-guard (266). Yet Dickens's point is not that, like the Veneerings, the schoolmaster lacks depths. To the contrary, Headstone's distinctive condition is one of ineffaceable (lowborn) depths in perpetual revolt against the artificial imposition of (socially ambitious) surfaces. This dynamic is figured as a profound antagonism between Headstone's embodied nature and his clothes. Although he "was never seen in any other dress," the narrator observes, "there was a certain stiffness in his manner of wearing this, as if there were a want of adaptation between him and it, recalling some mechanics in their holiday clothes" (266). That Headstone's body resists the clothing of a schoolmaster symbolizes an irreconcilable conflict between the born-and-bred aspects of his habitus.[21]

Clearly, whereas Bella's education entailed a deep, domesticating appeal to her womanly nature, Headstone's training does the very opposite. "He had *acquired mechanically* a great store of teacher's knowledge." "From his early childhood up, his mind had been a place of *mechanical stowage*" (266; emph. added). As the italicized language suggests, Headstone's training is alien to his born depths. Here Dickens echoes other contemporary critics who described pupil-teachers as "overlaid with facts," "unwholesomely stimulated," and "stunted and baffled" (qtd. in Collins 152). Hence, as Dickens tells it, Headstone has been positively violated by the artificial introduction of "teacher's knowledge." Indeed, "unwholesome stimulation" puts the rape thematics identified by Sedgwick in yet another context, shedding different light on why "the schoolmaster behaves socially like a man with a hungry rat in his bowels" (166).

Headstone's dysfunctional body thus makes a mockery of Kay-Shuttleworth's ideal of the "peasant" schoolmaster. The latter's "honest pride" in manual labor, the secretary believed, would prevent his desiring to emulate the class pride of the aristocrat or middle-class professional. Yet, as Dickens tells it, teacher training destroys the schoolmaster's "manly vigour of . . . body and mind." Indeed, Headstone would have been as robust as any peasant if only he had avoided the pupil-teacher system: "there was enough of what was animal . . . still visible in him, to suggest that if young Bradley Headstone, when a pauper lad, had chanced to be told off for the sea, he would not have been the last man in a ship's crew" (267).

Hence, whereas Dickens typically ties moral turpitude to bourgeois self-interest (e.g., Mrs. Wilfer's materialism, Podsnap's indifference, Fledgeby's greed), Headstone's crimes derive from deep-seated, almost physiological disturbance. His predicament is rendered through a language of punishing physical discomfort: *suppression, constraint, stowage, smouldering*, and, eventually, *blowing up*. Once again, Sedgwick's observations—intended to illustrate the novel's anal eroticism—lend themselves to yet another meaning. "Sphincter domination," she argues, "is Bradley Headstone's only mode of grappling for the power that is continually flowing away from him" (169). Her comment elucidates Dickens's masterful use of physiological imagery to connote the tenuous class status of the hothouse schoolmaster: Headstone "had toiled hard to get what [he] had won, *and . . . had to hold it now that it was gotten*" (267; emph. added). The same striking image recalls the importance of bowel control in the bourgeois educational process described by Stallybrass and White. From this view Headstone's sphincter-centered physiology represents an arrested development, in contrast to the effortless self-control of the middle-class body. Like a child who has not yet fully mastered his first round of training, Headstone "always seemed to be uneasy lest anything should be missing from" him (267).

In the final analysis Headstone fails miserably to incarnate the middle-class habitus. Still less can he make the grade of the public school gentleman: able to control himself, and thus govern others. Indeed, as he is pitted ever more intensely against his tony rival, Headstone devolves into utter incontinence. In one critical encounter with Lizzie the schoolmaster's mouth becomes dry, his teeth set, and, as though teacher's knowledge were being zealously stowed on the spot, his hands exercise "a curious tight-screwing movement . . . like the action of one who was being physically hurt, and was unwilling to cry out." "Some of us," he tells her, "are obliged habitually to keep it down" (399–400). As the drama further unfolds, Headstone becomes subject to involuntary tics and bodily emissions: uncontrollable sweating (401), spasms of pain (402), insomnia (609), the bursting of blood vessels (704), and fits (821). After he attempts murder—as though, having at last erupted under pressure, his mortal coil disintegrates—he is described as a disembodied head (608, 610).

In the sunny world of the sentimental plot Dickens implies that the happiest lot for a pauper lad is that of Sloppy, secure in the patronage of kind-hearted, gentlemanly John Harmon. In that sheltered context Sloppy's caricature—his utter psychological vacuity—attracts little notice. But Dickens's determination to condemn the character-building project through a tale of teacher training gone awry ultimately bears on Headstone's sentimental double. Dickens would have us believe that Headstone's innate capacity for working-class self-realization has been destroyed by overambitious experimentation. He would have us believe that patronized cabinetmakers—like the pauper lads who march in perfect time at model schools—are autonomous individuals who thrive under the nurturing pastoral care of their benefactors. Clearly, Dickens was himself more subject to the contradictions of Kay-Shuttleworth's philosophy than he was wont to realize. In the end Dickens's insistence that working-class men could be individuals so long as they recognized their subordinate station is quite as paradoxical as Kay-Shuttleworth's insistence that working-class men could achieve the self-command of their social superiors so long as they first subjected themselves to middle-class tutelage and surveillance. Indeed, it is possible to argue that neither man had any real confidence in the potential for moral autonomy among the lowly and pauperized. One begins to notice that Sloppy, despite his sympathetic treatment, already is what Headstone degenerates into being: an eccentric composite of physical quirks such as his trademark howl and bursting buttons.

Yet, if one side of Dickens's refusal to "make the working man like me" implies the insufficient moral potential of the lowborn and impoverished, the other side speaks to middle-class deficits. Dickens's satire on Podsnappery and the Veneering social milieu goes far to discredit middle-class pastoral authority. Less obvious but just as damaging is Dickens's ambivalent representation of the genteel professional. In his depiction of Eugene Wrayburn, Dickens has yet another tale to tell about education—one that ties the novel to the mid-Victorian shift away from prescriptive character building and toward a conservative cult of the born-and-bred gentleman.

"A Riddle without an Answer"

Out of the question to marry her . . . and out of the question to leave her.
The crisis!   — CHARLES DICKENS, *Our Mutual Friend*

Like Bradley Headstone, the character of Eugene Wrayburn speaks to a specific, if less overtly polemical, educational context. Wrayburn and his companion Mortimer Lightwood, who were "once boys together at a public school" (61), are clearly products of what one historian has called "an archetypal national institution" (Wiener 21). According to F. M. L. Thompson, by the 1860s public school education was becoming the definitive marker of marriageability in middle- and upper-middle-class circles. Hence, he notes, the "public-school type," with its codified "speech, manner, dress, and behaviour," was instantly recognizable to Victorian mothers—and also, no doubt, to readers of Victorian novels (*Rise* 145; cf. 103). Even so solidly middle-class an author as Elizabeth Gaskell was ready to vouch for the old boy's mystique: "there is a *je ne sais quoi* in an Eton man," opines one Gaskell character, "which distinguishes him wherever he goes, and stamps him as a gentleman at once" ("Visit to Eton" 3).

By contrast, Dickens's decidedly mixed attitude toward public schools cannot be detached from his class position. As Collins has noted, neither public school nor university was within the social reach of the young Dickens, a circumstance the author did not seek to change for his own sons (9, 24–25). Dickens's novels occasionally feature sympathetic old boys, such as the affable Mr. Pocket of *Great Expectations;* representations that arguably counterbalance Steerforth and Gowan, the villainous old boys of *David Copperfield* and *Little Dorrit.* In the years prior to the writing of *Our Mutual Friend,* both public schools and the ancient universities had been reformed under the auspices of Coleridgean liberals such as Benjamin Jowett, the Oxford classicist. Reformers promised to diffuse "manly spirit, moral strength, and . . . public service orientation," thus re-legitimating the notion of a governing-class elite (Mueller 183–84). A related motive was the establishment of objective qualifications for positions in the civil service, slowly undergoing reform in the wake of the 1853–54 Northcote-Trevelyan *Report.* As we saw in chapter 4, Dickens disputed the *Report*'s recommendations, arguing for a more practical and democratic breed of public servants.

Nevertheless, in *Our Mutual Friend* Dickens is more interested in the question of class than in the civil service per se. Eugene Wrayburn and Mortimer Lightwood are lawyers rather than clerks, and both men are so strikingly unambitious that even Trollope's Harry Norman is a dynamo by comparison.[22] Instead, Dickens here revisits a theme first broached in the story of Richard Carstone in *Bleak House.* In that novel Richard's flaws derive from his connections to the Chancery suit. Nevertheless, as Esther points out, his public school "education had not counteracted those influences, or directed his character" by finding "out what his natural bent was, or where his failings lay, or . . . adapt[ing] any kind of knowledge to *him.*" Here Esther contrasts the public school's uniform approach to the kind of personalized attention which John Harmon devotes to Bella's reform. As a result, Richard suffers from a fatal "indecision of character" (218)—a profound vocationlessness that leads him from one profession to another before culminating in his ruin. Tellingly, Benjamin Jowett had alluded to a similar problem of vocation when he argued that the civil service would provide "an answer to the dreary question which a college tutor so often hears 'what line of life shall I choose, with no calling to take orders and no taste for the bar, and no connections who are able to put me forward in life?'" (qtd. in Mueller 194–95).

In *Our Mutual Friend* Wrayburn's and Lightwood's lack of any demonstrable "taste for the bar"—their Richard Carstone–like vocationlessness—is explicitly tied to their class position. Eugene openly mocks the notion of "calling," avowing that seven years after his call to the bar he has "no business at all, and never shall have any." Both men have had their careers "forced upon" them by family ambitions, a form of captivity expressed in their "dismal," "dungeon-like" legal chambers (62, 335). Indeed, "M.R.F."—Wrayburn's "respected father"—has selected a prestigious profession for each of his younger sons without respect to their individuality, decreeing that one be "a little pillar of the church," another be "pitch-forked into the Navy," and so on (193–94). Dickens thus exposes the self-serving practices of an entire class—the same class demarcated by public school education—the social status of which depends largely on professional callings and mercenary marriage. As though to cast doubt on the public school's pretensions to producing public-spirited leaders, he presents Wrayburn as having been born expressly to exercise and sustain the prerogatives of his rank.

Nevertheless, while Eugene is thus subject to the idleness of the nouveau riche Veneerings, Dickens endows him with a psychological depth and moral potential that they utterly lack. It is therefore crucial to recognize just how great a stake this novel has in Eugene Wrayburn, who is the realist plot's counterpart to John Harmon—indeed, the realist counterpart to a long line of Dickensian benefactors from Mr. Brownlow to John Jarndyce. Were Wrayburn's character to justify the old boy's social consequence—as Headstone's is seen to demarcate the lowly limits of the pauper lad—then Dickens would have imagined a stable foundation for a hierarchical society led by gentlemen. Dickens's novel would, like Anthony Trollope's Barsetshire series, provide a persuasive vision of a world secure under the governance of men of character: born-and-bred gentlemen such as Mr. Harding and Archdeacon Grantley.

But Dickens's support for Wrayburn's character is profoundly ambivalent, "a riddle without an answer." In many respects the old boy and the schoolmaster are less autonomous creations than classed antitheses—interdependent constructions whose qualities emerge through constant juxtaposition. In thus representing them, the novel tends to reify a classist double standard that both troubled and fascinated the author. For, while Headstone's limitations are unambiguously determined by his birth and perverted by his breeding, the foundations of Wrayburn's character remain irreducible and mysterious. That is precisely why, as Sedgwick puts it, the "moral ugliness of Eugene's taunts against the schoolmaster" is never as damning as "the unloveliness of the schoolmaster's anxiety and frustration" (167).

Whereas hothouse experimentation deforms Headstone's nature, the public school—despite its failure to personalize or to motivate—seems perfectly to calibrate birth with breeding. Here (if not elsewhere) Dickens is at one with Trollope, who described the public school as a social institution, the main purpose of which was not to educate, but to unify men of a certain class. Mid-Victorian reformers had stressed the merit of competitive examinations in public schools, universities, and the civil service. Yet the author of *Our Mutual Friend* is indifferent to such propaganda. Headstone's schoolboy prizes merely confirm his childish inferiority. Meanwhile, the "utterly careless Eugene," so far from seeking laurels, coasts on the sheer indubitability of his genteel credentials (339). Hence, with Eugene the novel betrays a certain awe of the old boy's symbolic power: his ease in exuding airs beyond the reach of any pauper lad. As Collins has noticed, in writing *Our Mutual Friend*, Dickens labored to reproduce the "tones of Old Boy camaraderie and persiflage" (24), that buoyant upper-middle-class habitus so instantly spotted by matchmaking mothers.

As a result, the contest between the old boy and the schoolmaster is so unequal that we might forget that Dickens was not himself a product of the public schools; that he, more Headstone-like than Wrayburnian, was an ambitious self-made man; that he, not unlike an erstwhile pauper lad, had endured the ignominy of the debtor's prison and blacking factory. Dickens first emphasizes their inexorable antagonism—"some secret, sure perception between them, which set them against one another in all ways" (341)—only to reveal that Headstone is constitutionally inferior to the rival he cannot resist. Thus, Wrayburn's "composed smoking" and "perfect placidity" are contrasted to Headstone's "raging jealousy and fiery wrath" (341–42; cf. 465). Here, as everywhere, Headstone's body-bound working-class habitus is dominated by infantile physical and emotional responses, while Wrayburn's gentleman's habitus exemplifies effortless self-mastery. Thus, Headstone sweats profusely, decrying his own weakness "in a very agony"; Wrayburn, in turn, blows his ash, tosses away his cigar, and considers his antagonist "rather an entertaining study" (344–45). Later, as the men pursue one another in a dangerous game of public school cat versus pauper lad mouse, Wrayburn's delight in "the pleasures of the chase" contrasts with Headstone's "baffled . . . exhaustion"; Wrayburn's imperturbable sleep with Headstone's dreadful insomnia (606–9).

Of course, the upshot of these relentless oppositions is always their foundation in class. Thus, Wrayburn boasts of "tempting" Headstone to follow him, taking cabs so as to "drain the [schoolmaster's] pocket" (606). Yet the hardworking teacher lives within his modest means, while Wrayburn, clientless and living beyond his income, has fallen prey to Fascination Fledgeby. The effect, however, is to epitomize the gulf between them. Wrayburn may be in debt to a ruthless moneylender, but, as a public school gentleman, he is implicitly above the issue of "drained pockets" in a way that Headstone, no matter how industrious, will never be. This double standard—so entrenched that Dickens seems hardly to notice it—harks back to the gentleman's origins in aristocratic privilege. According to the old-fashioned "code," gentlemen were honest "to other gentlemen, though not necessarily to servants and inferiors"; were honorable toward ladies, "though not necessarily [toward] mere women and serving-girls"; and paid their debts to fellow gamblers, "but not necessarily . . . to tradesmen and shopkeepers" (Perkin, *Origins* 274).

Of course, Dickens supplies us with ample grounds on which to indict a man whose gentlemanliness so manifestly consists in breeding and social privilege rather than virtuous character. Wrayburn's indolence and carelessness are glamorized sufficiently to discredit Headstone but never actually condoned. Hence, upon seeing Jenny Wren brought to tears by her father's insobriety, Wrayburn "was sorry, but his sympathy did not move his carelessness to do anything but feel sorry" (596). (How little moved was his carelessness is later demonstrated when Wrayburn helps "Mr. Dolls" to drink himself to death by paying him to spy on Lizzie's whereabouts.) On the whole Dickens displays a wonderful ambivalence toward Eugene: unflinchingly exposing his moral defects, yet loath, nonetheless, to discount the value of his cultural cachet.

Significantly, it is Lizzie Hexam, a sentimental character in a realist plot, who mediates on Eugene's behalf, investing him with an otherwise inexplicable redemptive potential. Describing himself to Jenny Wren as a "bad idle dog," Eugene explains that he cannot "reform" for the simple reason that "there's nobody who makes it worth [his] while" (285). Dickens thus sets the stage, however improbably, for a moral regeneration like Bella's. In so doing, he promises, in effect, to endow a dark realist narrative with the sentimental power to turn dust into gold. It is one thing for Dickens to transform selfish, dimpled, fretful Bella Wilfer into "the Complete British Family Housewife" with a waive of his sentimental wand. But can Dickens reform Eugene Wrayburn—bored, arrogant, selfish, dissolute, anti-Semitic, and bent on ruining the working-class woman he loves?

In at least one important sense Dickens does not want to: for through Eugene he challenges a powerful mid-Victorian myth, suggesting that public schools breed men who, for all their masterful deportment, fall far short of the moral qualifications for governing others. Yet in another sense this is the character question that Dickens has all along wanted to pose: the riddle without an answer. Formulated as a social critique, the question is, How far short of moral integrity does Eugene's superior breeding fall? The same question, formulated as an artistic problem is, Can Eugene Wrayburn change when Bradley Headstone cannot?

That Bella's zealous plunge into homemaking will not suffice is a point Dickens ironically concedes in the important chapter from which I have taken the title of this chapter (bk. 2, chap. 6). When Mortimer reproaches Wrayburn for having purchased superfluous kitchen utensils, Wrayburn explains that he has surrounded himself with homely objects in the hopes that their "moral influence" will help him to cultivate "domestic virtues" (337, 347). Pressed further by Mortimer to declare his intensions toward Lizzie, Wrayburn's indecision becomes the riddle without an answer. The stage is set for Wrayburn's test of character to consist in his conduct toward the woman he describes as the best "in all this London" (347).

As most readers recognize, Wrayburn is on the verge of failing miserably when he is beaten senseless by his schoolmaster rival. That said, Wrayburn's reprehensible conduct is somewhat obscured by Lizzie herself, Dickens's chief spokeswoman for the awesome symbolic power of the public school. As a beautiful woman, privy to the idealized femininity usually reserved for middle-class figures, Lizzie transcends the body-bound habitus that circumscribes Headstone. Like Nancy in *Oliver Twist*, her speech improves over the course of the novel, testifying to her rising feminine grandeur. Hence, no Dickens reader will be surprised to find Eugene ready to assert Lizzie's worth. "There is," he tells Mortimer, "no better [girl] among my people at home; no better among your people" (347).[23] Yet, by thus repudiating the substance of the social difference that divides them, Wrayburn confounds his unwillingness to court Lizzie in the manner of a gentlewoman. Half-besotted by love and half-inflamed by his "wonderful power over her," the idle dog remains bad to the last, unsure whether marrying a penniless woman with "no station" will preclude his becoming "bored" (764–65). In the end Lizzie is reduced to begging Wrayburn to spare her, to grant her "the full claims of a lady" on his generosity. Wrayburn selfishly disregards her plea: "base indeed," he presses his advantage, kissing the unprotected factory girl, and forcing her to declare her love (761).[24]

Hence, even without having ruined Lizzie, Eugene fails the test of his character. His last words before the assault are: "Out of the question to marry her . . . and out of the question to leave her. The crisis!" (766). Yet, despite his manifest deficiencies, Lizzie herself remains the champion of what is irreducible in his makeup. Lizzie's first response is to regard Wrayburn's "lightest touch, his lightest look . . . [as] glimpses of an enchanted world" (465). Such effusions arguably represent a naive working woman's first exposure to one who, as a "gentleman," is "not of [her] sort" (403). Yet it is surely significant that Lizzie's inflated perception of Eugene's character persists even as he drives her to flee and beg for mercy. In the novel's most uncritical support for the myth of the born-and-bred gentleman, she tells Wrayburn, "If my mind could put you on equal terms with me you could not be yourself" (763).

Of course, Lizzie's eventual marriage ostensibly overturns the classist double standard she has helped to authenticate. When obnoxious Veneering guests presume to articulate the "voice of Society," condemning Eugene's marriage to a "a horrid female waterman," the sympathetic Twemlow rises to his defense. In so doing, he articulates a democratic ideal of the gentleman, in opposition to the old boy network's exclusivity: "I beg to say, that when I use the word gentleman, I use it in the sense in which the degree may be attained by any man" (888, 891).

But is *Our Mutual Friend* the product of a democratic imagination? The problem with Twemlow's conclusion is its obvious dependence on the vilification of Bradley Headstone, whose monstrosity justifies the novel's otherwise egregiously antidemocratic foreclosure on the upward mobility of working-class men. For, if class is to be stripped of the magical properties imputed to it by Lizzie, and if Lizzie herself can transcend the debasing effects of low birth and squalid environment, why is Bradley Headstone so entirely constrained by his working-class origins? To a degree Kay-Shuttleworth takes the blame: for, through Headstone, Dickens indicts the specific effects of the hothouse variation on the character-building theme. But even if we are ready to believe that the schoolmaster's monstrosity figures a very particular threat to social well-being, how can we explain Charlie Hexam? Why is Charlie morally destroyed, long before his exposure to the pupil-teacher system, by his sister's selfless efforts to raise him?[25] Clearly, the specter of bureaucratic impersonality was but one aspect of Dickens's evident recoil from the democratic potential of education.

On the other hand, Dickens was hardly reconciled to the mid-Victorian conservative agenda: the static hierarchy favored by the Newcastle commissioners. He could idealize that hierarchy, dreaming of the faultless, familial paternalism of a Brownlow, Jarndyce, or Harmon. And he could even betray his own awe of the public school charm: that disarming *je ne sais quoi* that enchants Lizzie, and makes Jenny Wren "sparkle" at the mere mention of "Mr. Eugene Wrayburn" (403). But in the final analysis, for all his susceptibility, Dickens could not bring himself to stand behind the old boy's mid-Victorian call to govern the nation. While the schoolmaster literally embodies Dickens's skepticism toward the prescriptive view of character, Wrayburn figures the deceptive allure of class credentials which, in the 1860s, were increasingly invoked to justify a static descriptive view.

In a kind of poetic justice, then, Dickens's underlying resistance to the myth of the public school gentleman ends by impressing itself directly on the body of Eugene Wrayburn. When we last see the schoolmaster's body, it is locked in a struggle-to-the-death with Rogue Riderhood, yet another of Headstone's working-class doubles (see Farrell 779–80). When we last see his rival, "the once gallant Eugene," we find him "wan and worn," "resting on his wife's arm, and leaning heavily upon a stick." His medical attendants are pleased to declare "that he might not be much disfigured by-and-by" (883). The man once pronounced for his effortless self-possession has become as physically infantilized as was his dead rival.

In the end, then, Headstone and Wrayburn—representing two sides of Dickens's deepening skepticism toward the foundations of character—merge symbolically into one and the same damaged body. As though finally to repudiate the double standard, Eugene's disfiguration evens the score between redeemable old boy and irreclaimable schoolmaster. The highly improbable Wrayburn marriage, signaling Eugene's moral repentance, is managed through a variety of special narrative devices including deathbed regeneration, sentimental enclosure, and social retreat. But these all proceed from the violence done to Wrayburn's body.[26] Hence, the price paid for Wrayburn's ascendancy to a higher moral plain is the loss of what Dickens has all along admired from afar: that habitual ease that, in mid-Victorian Britain, increasingly symbolized the old boy's authority to rule a nation and, indeed, an empire.

"No Established Character"

As is well known to the wise in their generation, traffic in Shares is the one thing
to have to do with in this world. Have no antecedents, no established character,
no cultivation, no ideas, no manners; have Shares. . . . Where does he come
from? Shares. Where is he going to? Shares. What are his tastes? Shares. What
squeezes him into Parliament? Shares.

— CHARLES DICKENS, *Our Mutual Friend*

But it is different with commodities. . . . There it is a definite social relation
between men, that assumes, in their eyes the fantastic form of a relation
between things. — KARL MARX, *Capital*

In a remarkable 1843 letter to the philanthropist Angela Burdett Coutts,
Dickens described his visit to a ragged school. Commending the venture, Dickens praised the "moral courage" of the schoolmasters and their use of the "excellent" Glasgow instructional method, "reach[ing] the boys by kindness." This
was, of course, the same method that Kay-Shuttleworth had embraced for state-
supported pauper education; the same method that led Dickens to give the
unlovely M'Choakumchild his conspicuously Scottish surname. Perhaps, then,
it is not surprising to find that, even as he urged Coutts's financial support, Dickens cast doubts on the possibility of educating the ragged. "I have very seldom
seen . . . anything so shocking as the dire neglect of soul and body exhibited
among these children," he declared. Whereas similar experiences spurred the
likes of Thomas Chalmers, Kay-Shuttleworth, and Octavia Hill to feats of organized pastorship, Dickens's response was despairing and even fatalistic. "The
children in the Jails are almost as common sights to me as my own; but these are
worse, for they have not yet arrived there, but are as plainly and as certainly trav-
eling there, as they are to their graves" (qtd. in E. Johnson 1:461–62). Dickens's
pessimism foreshadows the paralyzing deadlocks of *Bleak House* and the educational failures of *Our Mutual Friend*.

Dickens's letter also betrays an anxious fear of working-class progeny, little
evident in his sympathetic portrait of Jo. In another 1843 letter on ragged
schools Dickens wrote that "the dangerous classes of society" are "in a state so
miserable and so neglected, that their very nature rebels against the simplest religion" (qtd. in E. Johnson 1:463). A decade later he struck a similar note in
Household Words, arguing for "the compulsory industrial education of neglected

children" on the grounds that such measures were necessary to precluding a volcanic eruption of crime (qtd. in Collins 71, 235 n. 5). Dickens's nonfictional writings thus articulate an anxious readiness to subject certain elements of the working class to institutional authority. Yet in the novels Dickens reverses this relation, eliciting compassion on behalf of helpless orphans, and representing schools, as Patrick Brantlinger has noted, as "places of tyranny and miseducation" ("Oliver" 59).

Written during a turbulent period that saw growing agitation for expanded male suffrage, *Our Mutual Friend* betrays something of Dickens's anxiety toward the "dangerous classes." The "prodigious misery and ignorance of [England's] swarming masses" are deeply imprinted on such unsavory figures as Charlie Hexam, Gaffer Hexam, Mr. Dolls, and Rogue Riderhood. The ragged school that Charlie attends is "pervaded by a grimly ludicrous pretence that every pupil was childish and innocent" (263). Yet, even while the novel thus insists on the damaging effects of the working-class environment (another feature harking back to *Oliver Twist*), it is as powerless as its precursors to represent the systematic pastoral redress evoked in the nonfictional writings. In the end formal education is endowed with the dubious power to deform Bradley Headstone and to polish Eugene Wrayburn's manners. In neither case does it provide a means to shaping or otherwise ensuring the moral fiber at either end of a just social hierarchy. Here, then, as in other Dickens novels, the problematic relation between character and pastorship points to underlying fractures in the author's worldview.

In the preceding discussion I have argued that the Headstone/Wrayburn rivalry figures two sides of Dickens's profound skepticism toward the foundations of character. On the one side, Headstone's born limitations tell against the prescriptive potential of human character, implying the existence of a natural hierarchy. Yet, on the other side, Wrayburn's public school charm amounts to far less than the descriptive qualifications to govern the nation. The novel thus flummoxes the would-be social improver, who is left eager to authorize a class of Harmons, but unable to affirm a means through which to educate or otherwise locate such exemplary pastors. In so doing, it reveals that character was very far from that comforting transparency envisioned by Richard Grant in 1870: "an inward spiritual grace" legible to others through the outer garment of "reputation."

Ironically, the novel's most transparent certitude is the humble telos of Bradley Headstone—whose lowborn nature is distorted by the artifice of hothouse training, whose very body betrays the impropriety of schoolmasters' clothes. So far from transparent, Wrayburn's upper-middle-class character remains a riddle without an answer up until the fated moment when Headstone literally bashes the double standard, triggering his rival's penitence and rebirth. Wrayburn's riddle thus takes us to the heart of Dickens's skepticism in ways that elucidate the underlying philosophical struggle.

To invoke character in the nineteenth century was, typically, to regard the individual's spiritual condition as inseparable from collective purpose of some kind. Throughout the century this moral worldview vied with its materialist antithesis, a competing foundation for modern truth claims in which character lost its transcendent and intersubjective possibilities and was reduced to the product of external determinants, bourgeois competition, and representation. Grant was calling, in effect, for a correspondent truce when he insisted that worldly reputation "is, or should be," an index to "inward spiritual grace." John Ruskin cast the very same problem as the central paradox of modern times. Bourgeois materialism, he wrote in *Unto This Last* (1862), "is apt to undermine . . . manly character," yet material value cannot thrive without "developing" the latter. For "wealth," as Ruskin defined it, depended on the priority of an empowered moral agent: on "THE POSSESSION OF THE VALUABLE BY THE VALIANT" (262, 263).

This desired subordination of the material to the moral had been weakened by the New Poor Law, which enhanced the importance of representation, and disordered the personal relations on which traditional knowledge had been predicated. Critics such as Mill described a society so massified, atomized, and depersonalized that reputation was fast becoming a manufactured commodity, like newspapers and advertisements. A similar idea is related under a different aspect in "A Reference to Character," an 1853 article in *Household Words*. There a London tradesman relates his experience extending credit to a "perfect stranger." At first chastising himself for his "unjust suspicions," he eventually discovers that the stranger is a practiced swindler. Disabused of his naïveté, the narrator hastens to enlist the services of "Perry's Bankrupt and Insolvent Registry Office," in which a "complete key to each person's character and career" may be found indexed in "a vast collection of ponderous tomes." The moral of the story is that one cannot be too suspicious, nor too reliant on organized documentation, in a world in which character checking of this kind has become "a daily necessary of commercial life" (390–92).

For my purposes what is most interesting about the article (and Dickens's editorial relation to it) is its subversion of the sound epistemology looked for by Ruskin and Grant. In "A Reference to Character," as in Mill's "Civilization," modern bourgeois social life conflates moral and worldly attributes while rendering both subject to materialist objectification: whether the surveillant record keeping of the credit bureau, or the self-promoting antics required to call attention to one's "marketable qualities" ("Civilization" 133). What is entirely supplanted in either case is the very crux of the moral worldview: character as a manifestation of the potential for humanist or Christian development.

In the sentimental plot, where Dickens's moral vision holds fast, bourgeois priorities are symbolically reversed as material "value" is safely entrusted to stewardship of the "valiant." In this way the transformation of dust into Harmon gold affirms Grant's epistemology: forging an indivisible link between outer reputation and inner character.[27] But elsewhere the novel undermines this link, testifying to the reduction or superseding of morality and, consequently, the riddling of human character. Before our very eyes the notion of divine or natural sanction, the ultimate safety net of the moralist, becomes a self-serving rhetorical strategy, invoked by Podsnap to justify his apathy toward the poor. "It is not for *me*," Podsnap pompously insists, "to impugn the works of Providence" (188).

Nowhere, however, is the threat of uncontested bourgeois materialism more apparent than in Dickens's satire on the Veneerings. Through the Veneering crowd Dickens portrays a depthless world predicated on the exchange-value of commodities: a world of "bran-new people" whose great-grandfathers come packed "in matting," and whose guests are "dinner-furniture" to be rolled out on "castors" and stuffed with "leaves" (49). Significantly, Marx was formulating his distinction between exchange-value and use-value in *Capital* (1867) at around the same time that Dickens was writing *Our Mutual Friend*. Hence, Dickens's evocation of commodified dinner guests and human furniture was nearly contemporaneous with Marx's discussion of bourgeois capitalism as that which propagates vivified products and dehumanized labor (71–83).[28] Worldly reputation so little corresponds to transcendent humanist depths that Veneering society reduces individuals to synecdochic instances of the former: they are "a Member, an Engineer, a Payer-off of the National Debt, a Poem on Shakespeare, a Grievance, and a Public Office" (49). Depthless superficiality is further figured in the grotesque Lady Tippins: "you might scalp her, and peel her, and scrape her, and make two Lady Tippinses out of her, and yet not penetrate to the genuine article" (164). By thus making the human body into a "capitalist emblem," writes Sedgwick, Dickens problematizes the relation of parts to wholes: "the parts swell up with accumulated value" and, as with Marx's vivified commodities, "take on an autonomous life of their own" (170).

Yet Dickens's most memorable achievement in figuring the effects of an economy fueled by the circulation of signs is surely the personification of "Shares." As the mark of the phantasmatic value assigned to paper in a capitalist economy unleashed from personal accountability, "Shares" not only undermines the transcendent moral value sought by Ruskin and Grant; it also undermines the stable material value required by the tradesman in "A Reference to Character." In the wake of limited liability legislation and its impact on capitalist speculation, "Shares," that is to say, stands for the speciousness and contingency of mid-Victorian prosperity (cf. Hilton 255–97; Poovey, *Making* 155–81). Through a modern capitalist economy in which "valuable possessions" are made subject to the reign of paper, the overlapping humanist projects of Dickens, Ruskin, and even Marx are radically undermined. Wealth can neither be stewarded by the valiant nor appropriated for human needs, for, under the reign of "Shares," dust itself has been reduced to signs. For Dickens, as for Marx, then, commodity fetishization ultimately entails, in Patrick Brantlinger's terms, "the production of something from nothing, gold out of paper or mere credit"—a condition so "pervasive and profound that . . . there is no longer any clear outside to the belly of the whale called 'capitalism'" (*Fictions* 149).

In the end, then, Dickens is flummoxed by the prospect of a world unable to distinguish between exchange-value, a value measured as the relation between things, and the value of nurturing human potential. With so nullifying a vision of social life in mind, it is little wonder that Dickens remained powerless to imagine education as a collective human enterprise. Nor can we be surprised to find him fascinated, however transiently, by that special symbolic value imputed to the public school. The "traffic in Shares"—which have "no antecedents, no established character, no cultivation, no ideas, no manners"—stands for the radical displacement of human potential in a world manifestly unready to solve the riddle of collective purpose.

CHAPTER SIX

Dueling Pastors,
Dueling Worldviews

Perhaps no characteristic of the present efforts for social reform are [sic]
more hopeful and more important than the deepening emphasis now
placed . . . on the moral element in social reform. . . . Today the key-word
in reform is "cooperation" and in economics "character." If this may seem
to some too optimistic a view, we remind them that individualist, socialist,
and even anarchist reformers all seek cooperation, while in economics the
reason why individualist economists fear socialism is that they believe that
it will deteriorate character, and the reason why socialist economists seek
socialism is their belief that under individualism character is deteriorating.
—*The Encyclopedia of Social Reform*

We are becoming idiotic about character.
— H. G. WELLS, *The New Machiavelli*

"Energy of will—self-originating force—is the soul of every great character,"
wrote Samuel Smiles in 1871. In so doing, he reiterated the main theme of his
enormously popular *Self-Help* (1859), presenting "character" as the rock-solid
foundation of British liberty and British progress during a century of tumultuous
change (*Character* 27–28). Smiles's populist myth, endowing every Briton with
the potential for radically transformative self-making, was, as I argued in chapter 4, the ideal panacea for a nation traumatized by Crimean blunders and weary
of the leadership of do-nothing aristocrats. By 1860 middle-class industry and
upper-class statesmanship had reached a stable consensus, symbolized by the
balance between Smiles's self-made men and the myth of disinterested governance by well-bred gentlemen. Inseparable from this mythology, however, was
its sustaining material underside: economic prosperity, constitutional conservatism, and the informal collectivism of countless philanthropic, voluntary, and
self-help organizations. My purpose in this concluding chapter is, therefore, to
address the crisis of character and the backlash against liberalism which began

at the end of the century and culminated in the New Liberalism of the pre–World War I era.

In the preceding chapters I have described a number of ways in which Britain's liberal mythologies were, throughout the century, threatened by ominous undercurrents: the depersonalization of the New Poor Law; the manifest inadequacies of voluntarism, localism, and individual self-reliance; and, more generally, the disempowering, homogenizing, and commodifying effects of modern civilization. These tensions, long simmering beneath the placid surface of mid-Victorian equipoise, were exacerbated by the momentous changes of the fin de siècle. After decades as the world's leader in industry and empire, Britain, by now a mass (male) democracy, was forced to acknowledge the importance of efficient pastorship in a competitive world economy.

In the following chapter I focus on two highly influential voluntary associations, both of which sought to meet this demand. The Charity Organization Society and the Fabian Society offered two contrasting strategies through which to impose order and authority on what had long been celebrated as a nation of self-reliant individuals and communities. In actuality the COS's voluntary casework had a great deal in common with the bureaucratic expertise urged by the Fabians. Nevertheless, the COS drew on Idealist philosophical foundations and sought to enlarge organized voluntary initiative, while the Fabians drew on materialist philosophy and aimed to justify state intervention along socialist lines.[1] Hence, COS and Fabian proposals emerged from within two disparate worldviews.

The debate between Idealist proponents of the COS and Fabian socialists manifested itself in the idiosyncratic disciplinary development of British sociology. The contemporaneous political contest reached a head in the 1905–9 Royal Commission on the Poor Laws. These competing positions prepared the ground for the New Liberal middle course of David Lloyd George and Winston Churchill. As we shall see, the New Liberal political agenda temporarily resolved a crisis concerning character and social policy by inventing a new national tradition: the National Insurance Act of 1911.

Unsurprisingly, the same dueling worldviews and the same quest for pastoral solutions figured in late-Victorian and Edwardian literature. Late-Victorian novels such as George Gissing's *The Nether World* (1889) idealize character's self-originating force even while depicting a world of isolated individuals dominated by sordid necessity and impersonal economic forces. H. G. Wells's utopian writings, which set out to create a mandate for Fabian-inspired social policies, end by reinscribing the Millite paradox of the powerless individual in a mass society.

Responding to Fabian dystopia, E. M. Forster's story "The Machine Stops" calls for a renewed linkage between matter and spirit, the real and the ideal. I conclude the chapter by describing the very different way in which New Liberalism attempted both rhetorically and institutionally to resolve the philosophical contradictions of the era.

Dueling Pastors: The Charity Organization Society and the Fabians

I do not . . . belittle material conditions or deny that insuperable misfortune may destroy the industrial qualities and drag a man down among the invertebrate Residuum. Still less, in maintaining the main evil to be moral, do I suggest the indolent and vulgar evasion—"It is all their own fault." On the contrary, the fault, I am persuaded, lies in great measure at our door; but the suffering—the suffering is *inevitably* theirs.

—BERNARD BOSANQUET, "CHARACTER IN
ITS BEARING ON SOCIAL CAUSATION"

What we have to do is apply the scientific method to facts of social life.

—BEATRICE WEBB, ADDRESS TO THE
LONDON SOCIOLOGICAL SOCIETY

The contest between organized charity and the Fabians' statist agenda can be represented through the careers of two prominent married couples: the COS's Helen and Bernard Bosanquet and the Fabians' Beatrice and Sidney Webb. The chief goal of the Charity Organization Society, founded in 1869, was to promote individual and family self-reliance by voluntary means. District by district, COS committees would organize Britain's labyrinthine charities, providing individualized assistance for the deserving and eliminating the "pauperizing" effects of indiscriminate handouts. The Fabians, by contrast, sought to eradicate Britain's unsystematic philanthropic legacy, replacing it with a "rationalised two-way relationship between the individual and the state" (Harris, "Society" 63). The COS thus harked back to the negative (deterrent) function of the 1834 New Poor Law. Minimal public provision for the destitute was a "necessary evil" that must never be permitted to encroach upon the norm of the self-maintaining family (B. Bosanquet, "Socialism" 303–4). The Fabians drew, instead, on the long-suppressed positive (technocratic and interventionist) aspects of the Benthamite tradition—aspects that had been in abeyance since the mid-century failure of Edwin Chadwick's sanitary reforms.

These oppositions crystallized in the landmark divisions of the 1905–9 Royal Commission on the Poor Laws. The COS-dominated Majority Report urged rigorous application of the deterrent policies set forth in 1834. This legal strategy would be supplemented by charitable but scientific assistance for the "helpable" poor, based on "careful study of the characters and circumstances" of each "case" (Dendy 169–70).[2] The Fabian-dominated Minority Report instead urged dissolution of the existing poor laws and foresaw no meaningful role for philanthropy. Social problems must instead be broken down, classified and systematically remedied by means of specialized intervention and institutional rehabilitation.

Significant though they are, the differences between the COS and the Fabians did not, as they appear, strictly conform to Harold Perkin's important distinction between the individualist entrepreneurial ideal and its pro-collectivist professional rival. Rather, the COS represents an interesting complication of Perkin's argument, since they advanced proto-professional methods through entrepreneurial rhetoric.[3] The difference between the COS and the Fabians, therefore, is better understood as that between two strains of self-consciously "sociological" but implicitly paternalistic thinking, both of which mandated collective and professionalized responses of some kind. Both groups addressed themselves to what the 1897 *Encyclopedia of Social Reform* described as the "moral element in social reform," invoking "cooperation" in order to ameliorate "character" (qtd. in Collini, *Liberalism* 49 n. 24). In so doing, both presented a distinctive vision of national pastorship yoked to the authority of modern science, including a discernibly postindividualist philosophy of the state and a notion of collective moral purpose embedded in evolutionary design. That said, to a remarkable extent the COS and the Fabians represented two distinct fin-de-siècle worldviews, with competing claims to the emerging discipline of sociology.

British Sociology

Britain's idiosyncratic sociological development—its failure to produce a "classical sociology" such as Emile Durkheim's or Max Weber's—has long been a "commonplace" among scholars (Collini, "Sociology" 4; cf. Hickox; den Otter 120–48). The present discussion bears on this question because the COS's casework approach to poor relief and the Fabians' non-Marxist variety of socialist analysis represent a substantial part of what Britain did produce when it was not producing a theoretical and "value-free" sociology such as Weber's (see Schroeder). The subject is complicated by the fact that, while the British academy was exceedingly slow to institutionalize the discipline, a wide variety of figures, inside and out of the academy, characterized their work as "sociology."[4] This idiosyncratic disciplinary history testifies to late-Victorian Britain's as yet fluid epistemological foundations.

Although both the Fabians and the Charity Organization Society frequently described their respective activities as sociology, their place in the complicated history of that discipline has become somewhat obscure. In 1903 the COS established the School of Sociology for the systematic training of charitable volunteers. In doing so, they contemplated collaborating with the Fabian-controlled London School of Economics, where courses were already being offered in the "new knowledge of the natural history of society, of social philosophy, social economics and individual and social psychology" (Mowat 113). Yet, in his illuminating exploration of the Idealist contribution to British sociology, Stefan Collini describes the COS as "anti-sociological" while devoting only one footnote to Beatrice and Sidney Webb ("Sociology" 44, 45 n. 128). Clearly, to speak of sociology in Britain during this period is, in effect, to speak of sociologies. As Sandra den Otter has explained, "political science, economics, social philosophy, social surveys, social work, psychology, and sociology spilled into each other" during this period (121).

Collini's reference to the COS's antisociological tendencies relates to two disparate but well-established aspects of Britain's diverse sociological precedents. The most popular exponent of mid-Victorian sociology was Herbert Spencer, editor of *The Economist* and architect of a wide-ranging positivist, evolutionary, and radically individualist theory of the social organism.[5] From the Fabian point of view Spencer's laissez-faire political deductions, but *not* the impersonal evolutionary assumptions on which they were premised, had ceased to be valid. Conversely, for Idealists such as Bernard Bosanquet, Spencer's opposition to state intervention was welcome, but his atomized and depersonalizing evolutionary theory was unacceptable. Hence, neither position is entirely compatible with Spencerian sociology.

When Britain's idiosyncratic pre-sociology is not aligned with Spencer's positivism, it is instead equated with the "crude empiricism" and "narrow" reformist agenda of the "Booth-Rowntree tradition of social enquiry" (Hickox 2). Charles Booth's seventeen-volume *Life and Labour of the People in London* (1889–1903) and Seebohm Rowntree's York-based *Poverty: A Study of Town Life* (1901) are widely recognized as having innovated important methods for social scientific analysis (Fraser 135–36). From a modern disciplinary perspective, however, these ad hoc surveys lack the sociologist's explanatory and theoretical rationale—charges that have been similarly leveled at the Webbs (Simey 106). Indeed, Beatrice Webb's "apprenticeship" as one of Booth's social investigators and her subsequent affiliation with the COS point to the strong affinities between Booth's and Rowntree's social inquiry, COS casework, and Fabian social analysis. Despite many differences, all were concerned to provide moral guidance—that is, pastorship—and, for the very same reason, all claimed sociological legitimacy while diverging from the theoretical and apolitical criteria that were defining the discipline outside of Britain.

Insofar as they were antisociological in Collini's terms, what the COS objected to was not Booth's and Rowntree's casework methods but, rather, the environmentalist interpretive frame and interventionist politics to which their results were soon harnessed. Evidence that as much as one-third of Britain's population lived in a state of grinding poverty tended to discredit the position that self-reliant character, aided by organized philanthropy alone, was a sure path to social progress. Yet it is important to recognize that, in battling the environmentalist camp, what the COS opposed was not collectivism per se but the depersonalizing (statist and materialist) collectivism envisioned by the Fabians. In this respect the COS looked back to an important pre-Victorian precursor: the early-nineteenth-century scheme of neighborhood visiting introduced by Thomas Chalmers, "almost the patron saint of the C.O.S." (Mowat 10). As we saw in chapter 2, Chalmers had sought to abolish the poor laws entirely, arguing that neighborhood charity would build laboring-class character and encourage self-help. For Chalmers charity was fundamentally pastoral: a gift of "judgment," "time and attention," as well as monetary aid (qtd. in Young and Ashton 78). Like Chalmers before them, members of the COS believed that this personal element was crucial to improving character.

As committed collectivists, the Webbs also rejected the atomism and hedonism of Manchester school political economy (Simey 120). Beatrice admired the "persistent service" and "personal responsibility" of the COS, but believed that their Chalmers-inspired service ethic was obsolete (*My Apprenticeship* 1:199; cf. Nord, *Apprenticeship* 122–25, 185–213). Instead, the Fabians' technocratic designs looked back to Chadwick's ambitious public health agenda—an environmentalist approach to improving the nation's moral and physical condition. The Webbs saw themselves, in the words of H. G. Wells, as the "unpaid precursors" of an emerging "class" of "expert officials" (*Machiavelli* 153). In this way Fabian ambitions diverged from the mid-Victorian civil service ideal discussed in chapter 4: the model administrator was, for the Webbs, a hands-on expert, not a genteel diffuser of sweetness and light.

Liberalism during and after the Fin de Siècle

The whole effect upon the mind of a cool observer was of a covey of unsubstantial jabbering minds drifting over a series of irrational economic cataclysms, prices and employment tumbled about like towers in an earthquake, and amidst the shifting masses were the common work-people going on with their lives as well as they could, suffering, perplexed, unorganised, and for anything but violent, fruitless protests, impotent.   — H. G. WELLS, *In the Days of the Comet*

None of the strong men in the strong ages would have understood what you meant by working for efficiency . . .   — G. K. CHESTERTON, *Heretics*

In forwarding competing claims to sociological authority, the COS and the Fabians thus drew on the past in order to envision the future. The "scientific charity" of the COS originated in the character-building pastoral ideal of a Glasgow clergyman and moral philosopher. The state-of-the-art technocracy urged by the Fabians had, in Chadwick's day, been rejected by a generation of Britons who believed with Smiles that "Heaven helps those who help themselves" (*Self-Help* 1). But the fin-de-siècle world into which these ideas were reintroduced was dramatically unlike that of Chalmers or Chadwick. The late-Victorian and Edwardian eras were periods of intense massification: liberalism's core mythologies were subjected to pressures generated by the increasing scale of commercial enterprise, the growth of a mass reading culture, the introduction of advertising, and, of course, the advent of mass politics. Just as liberal claims to a genuinely deliberative democracy were undermined by the rise of party discipline, so the myth of classless progress was challenged first by demands for (male) working-class enfranchisement and then for a labor-oriented political agenda. Demographically, these massifying trends expressed themselves in a shift away from provincial communities and toward the metropolis. No longer synonymous with Smiles's self-made entrepreneurs, Britain's middle classes were increasingly composed of corporate professionals, commuting to and from London's booming suburbs (Harris, *Private* 19–20; Perkin, *Rise* 26–61).

These dynamic shifts coincided with a steady ebbing of Britain's uncontested position as the nineteenth century's preeminent world power. As Geoffrey Searle has argued, mid-Victorian liberalism depended on a national supremacy that most Britons simply took for granted. Only while the nation dominated world markets, outstripped competitors, and ruled the seas could strict adherence to liberal principles simultaneously operate as moral imperative and sound national policy. Britons were rudely awakened to the nation's declining standing by trade depression in the 1880s, Booth's and Rowntree's disturbing revelations, and the humiliating military blunders of the Boer War in 1899. The truth, however, is that British predominance had already been challenged by 1875, when, under the systematic pastoral state of Otto von Bismarck, the newly unified Germany became a serious contender for world dominance (Searle 1–33, 55–106; Fraser 132–43; Perkin, *Rise* 166–67). Writing in 1906, H. G. Wells, a Fabian sympathizer, described British society as consisting in "forty-one millions of people, in a state of almost indescribably aimless economic and moral muddle that we had neither the courage, the energy, nor the intelligence to improve" (*Comet* 602).

Searle describes the subsequent backlash against mid-Victorian liberalism as a mandate for "national efficiency." Rather than liberalism's aloof gentlemen administrators, proponents of efficiency urged a corporatist approach that, like Germany's, would actively promote military power, imperial expansion, social welfare, technological progress, and industrial prosperity. The state they envisioned would, in the words of one Edwardian enthusiast, institute "savoir faire," not "laisser faire" (J. L. Garvin, qtd. in Searle 97). Such an agenda appealed not only to the Fabians, but also to enthusiasts of imperialism, eugenicists, technophiles, large-scale industrialists, Darwinian evolutionists, and professional experts of many kinds. Nevertheless, such an agenda amounted to an about-face on liberal principles that had become synonymous, even for many conservatives, with Britain's national identity. Efficiency discourses tended to promote state intervention of the kind Britain had long abjured, collectivist notions antithetical to self-help, and technocratic specialism at odds with the nation's entrepreneurial and gentlemanly ideals. Unsurprisingly, many Britons opposed and/or were made anxious by these un-English proposals, even as they lamented the national decline that had precipitated them.

These national concerns led to renewed interest in reforming a poor law system that had been fashioned according to stringent liberal economic principles. In their respective approaches to reform both the Charity Organization Society and the Fabians offered a means to satisfying the popular demand for efficient pastorship in some form. As we shall see, character was an operative category for each position as well as a telling sign of disparate worldviews.

"Mind and Will"

When we say . . . that the problem is moral rather than economic, we are not to be understood as adopting any vulgar answer to the vulgar question, "Did this man sin, or his parents, or society?" A moral point of view does not to us mean a point of view which holds a question as solved by apportioning blame to the unfortunate; it does mean a point of view which treats men not as economic abstractions, but as living selves with a history and ideas and a character of their own.

— BERNARD BOSANQUET, "CHARACTER IN ITS
BEARING ON SOCIAL CAUSATION"

Your incapable person is like a London garden, it takes a most extravagant amount of attention to get absurdly small results, but we are very proud of what we do get.

— HELEN DENDY, "MEANING AND
METHODS OF TRUE CHARITY"

As a gradual convert to collectivist thinking, John Stuart Mill was an important precursor for the Fabians. But, as the propounder of a humanistic utilitarian ethic and a major influence on T. H. Green and later exponents of the British Idealist school, Mill also was a crucial figure for members of the Charity Organization Society.[6] Green's Kantian and Hegelian critique of Mill, further developed in Bernard Bosanquet's *Philosophical Theory of the State* (1899), promulgated the crucial transitional notion of "positive freedom." According to this view, government is morally charged to promote human liberty in active fashion. Yet, while Idealists thus repudiated orthodox laissez faire, neither Green (an advanced Liberal) nor Bosanquet (an ardent voluntarist) advocated the investiture of a tutelary and interventionist state. Hence, in retrospect Idealism looks more like a late-Victorian offshoot of Mill's philosophy than the radical break postulated by contemporaries (cf. Nicholson 485–88). Bosanquet ambiguously insisted on the state's "moral purpose," but argued that the "best life" is chiefly realized through "consciousness." From this view the Fabian delight in state intervention and the socialist determination to redistribute wealth fundamentally misunderstood human character. Such material improvements avail nothing, argued Bosanquet, unless they are "charged with mind and will" (*Philosophical* 188, 169–70).[7]

In revising utilitarianism, Mill had forged a synthesis between a too-deterministic Benthamite materialism and a too-metaphysical "Germano-Coleridgean" tradition. To improve on these antitheses he had experimented with Comtean positivism, including Comte's sociology, in an attempt to create an empirical but nondeterministic foundation for social progress. The Idealist tradition revised this humanist project, demoting empirical criteria to secondary importance, and drawing on Darwin and Hegel to supplement the classical teleology that had been so important to Mill (den Otter 29). Hence, the society whose interrelations Mill had theorized in revised utilitarian terms and for which he had sought a positive basis in Comtean sociology was, in Bosanquet's Idealist view, a "social organism" that endowed each member with "a function which is the essence of his being" ("Character" 113). Bosanquet's German-Romantic and evolutionary influences, along with his debts to Chalmers's charitable ethos, imbued his writing with a teleological certitude that Mill, a steadfast critic of a priori assumptions, had been unable to achieve.

This teleology was evident in the Bosanquets' practical proposals for poor law reform. Writing in 1893, Helen Dendy "picture[d] humanity as a great army pressing on towards an invisible goal, and guided by a wisdom not its own." Organized charity must aid the weak and selfish, not by minimizing the pain of falling but by enabling them to "keep step with their comrades" (179). The key to achieving this pastoral aim was the COS's famed casework method: the germ of modern professional social work. Trained to investigate the "difficult question of character," the COS caseworker would recognize that a "little wholesome starvation" at the onset of defective conduct is preferable to the "moral degradation" of dependence (171, 173).

These tenets assumed a more up-to-date Darwinian cast in the contemporaneous writing of Bernard Bosanquet. The continued advance of civilization, he warned, was threatened by any scheme that "suppresses" the "personal struggle for existence" ("Socialism" 306). For this reason organized charity would enhance nature, while a socialistic state would obstruct it. The latter, by discouraging family self-reliance, would commit "an abuse fatal to character," undermining community "efficiency" (290, 306). Left to itself, natural selection would be inherently progressive. That is, in the absence of state interference (or, for that matter, unscientific charity), only those willing to assume the moral and material responsibilities of bourgeois domestic life would marry and, consequently, reproduce the species. Here, by alleging the individual's freedom to choose between respectable domesticity and celibacy, Bosanquet recast what was at bottom the old Malthusian precept that those too poor to maintain a family had better practice "moral restraint " (see Laqueur, "Sexual"). The principles of 1834, he believed, would facilitate this process, further deterring the reproduction of uncompetitive "stock" ("Socialism" 296). Organized charity would play a pastoral rather than primarily humanitarian role. Its chief purpose was to distinguish between the helpable and the incorrigible pauper, facilitating the former's self-reliance while relegating the latter to the tender mercies of the workhouse.

It would be a mistake, however, to reduce Bosanquet's poor law philosophy to a straightforward application of laissez-faire economic principles. Scientific charity involved a full-blown professionalization and bureaucratization of philanthropy, including the preparation of *Annual Reports*, the collection of statistics, and the training of caseworkers. Writing in support of the Majority Report in 1910, Bernard Bosanquet called for "an army of social healers to be trained and organised" (qtd. in S. and B. Webb 280). The historian Simon Gunn has described the organized charity movement as a "spreading network of institutional filiations," staffed "by a burgeoning lay bureaucracy," and providing "islands of authority in a sea of godlessness and profligacy" (32–33). Indeed, COS goals were so systematic that it is possible to argue that the society sought simply to consolidate in private hands the pastoral powers that the Fabians would appropriate for the state.

But here, too, would be a serious misrepresentation. Central to the society's philosophy was a devout belief in the Chalmers-inspired premise that charity, however necessarily scientific, preserved individual and family autonomy in a way that state interference could not. Bosanquet's voluntary army would be trained to approach economic failure as a fundamentally "moral" problem—"a defect in the citizen character" which affects the entire community (qtd. in S. and B. Webb 280). Hence, while the COS envisioned a nationwide network of caseworkers, invested with multifarious pastoral powers, and cooperating with Poor Law authorities on a semiofficial basis, they simultaneously believed that the relation between workers and their "cases" was *personal*. Invidious comparisons between the inert, even harmful agency of the public official and the attentive pastorship of the charitable caseworker surfaced repeatedly in COS writings. When, for example, a 1906 act provided school meals, the COS exhorted volunteers to carry out the state's new responsibilities. For, if the aid to poor schoolchildren were "managed by officials," the society insisted, it would "almost inevitably lose most of the characteristics that . . . make [it] useful to so-ciety" (qtd. in Mowat 154–55). Ironically, then, the COS's foremost defense against Fabian technocracy was the personality of an organized corps of Dick-ensian Mrs. Pardiggles.

It seems clear, therefore, that the late-Victorian and Edwardian organized charity movement was less a bona fide individualism than a professionalized and quasi-collective paternalism, cloaked in the defense of a venerable liberal rhetor-ical tradition. Enshrined in the COS's distinctive point of view was the faith in civil society and the "self-originating force" of character. These still powerful liberal myths, and the moral assumptions that sustained them, legitimated the COS's confident distinctions between the state's inability to "consider the needs of the individual," and the charitable caseworker's unique capacity to "foster" family character (1895 *Annual Report*, qtd. in Mowat 101).

To be sure, the COS's claims on behalf of caseworkers were not purely rhetorical. COS methods strove to deliver a level of personalized service which might conceivably exhaust even the Victorians' formidable voluntary resources. COS casework was remarkably individualized: depending on circumstances, the society might seek pensions for the "respectable" elderly, subsidize emigration, make loans, purchase clothes, apprentice children, or acquire surgical boots for the handicapped (see Mowat 100). Octavia Hill, a long-standing member of the COS Central Commission and a signatory of the Majority Report, urged case-workers to cultivate "deep sympathy for the poor," lest the society devolve into a "dry, ineffectual machinery for enquiring about people" (qtd. in Bell 108; Boyd 112). More imperiously, but no less in earnest, Helen Dendy warned that char-ity work requires "months of patient care, and a determination that if we are to fail it shall not be for want of either time or money" (301). Yet the fact remains that the Fabians sought to establish comparable (and arguably greater) pastoral agencies in the specialized services of the state. Hence, it is significant that, in sparring with their Fabian rivals, the COS did not, by and large, adopt the tra-ditional voluntarist defense against state intervention. Rather than insist on the unconstitutionality of Fabian designs, they preferred to impugn the relation be-tween the government official (whether local or national) and the poor. Virtu-ally ignoring the Fabians' terrific emphasis on specialized training, the COS dogmatically held that state officials were incapable either of understanding or relating to the family and the personal questions of character which sustain it.

This ardent rhetorical privileging of personality was part of a more ambitious attempt to cordon off cherished spheres of social knowledge—to claim the burgeoning field of sociology for organized charity. The COS envisioned sociology as a science of civil society, emphasizing the relations between individuals, families, and communities. Hence, the charitable caseworker was an expert insofar as she was scientifically trained and rationally organized. But she was also a bulwark against bureaucratic impersonality insofar as charity itself remained anchored to a vehemently antimaterialist Victorian worldview.[8]

For the COS long-venerated concepts such as the neighborhood, the home, the family, and, of course, character thus retained their capacity to realize human autonomy. That is why the attack on Fabianism rarely took the form of a polemic against the general principle of collectivism. On the contrary, organized charity was itself envisioned as a collectivizing force, a corporate voluntarism of sorts, positioned as an alternative to statist bureaucracy. Like J. S. Mill before them, COS members perceived the diminution of individual power in a mass society; but, unlike Mill or Dickens, they saw organized charity as a path to transcending modern isolation and to revitalizing character building.

Employing classical republican ideas much like Mill's, Bosanquet described fin-de-siècle civilization as a "modern wilderness of interests." Unlike the ancient Greeks, who recognized their positive duty to govern, modern citizenship had been undermined by multiple "divisions and estrangements" ("Duties" 5, 2). To overcome this fragmentation, Bosanquet urged, Britons must put aside class differences, professional affiliations, regional identities, and even, when required, domestic obligations. Most of all, they must dismiss the pernicious distinction between "official" government—a mere simulacrum—and the self-government that ought properly to realize itself from within civil society. In its current semi-dormant condition the latter is reduced to a "mass of unofficial persons who . . . regard themselves as mere units among millions of their like" (2). Against such pictures of pastorless, liberal dysfunction, the COS positioned the corporate voluntarism alone afforded by organized charity.

This utopian stance was epitomized by C. S. Loch, secretary of the society between 1877 and 1913, self-styled sociologist, and another member of the 1905–9 Royal Commission. Writing in 1903, Loch explained:

> If I were asked why I joined the Society I should answer that through its work and growth I hoped that some day there would be formed a large association of persons . . . who, disagreeing in much, would find in charity a common purpose and a new unity.
>
> . . . Such an organisation might bear on the removal and prevention of evils a

combined force that would far exceed in weight and influence any yet existing. It could make legislation effective, could see that it was enforced. Apart from all legislative interference and with the use of means and influences more far-reaching it could renew and discipline the life of the people by a nobler, more devoted, more scientific religious charity. . . . It would open to many a new path for the exercise of personal influence. (Qtd. in Mowat 81)

While individual agency is clearly constrained, the "combined force" Loch imagines is personalized, charismatic, pluralist, and self-actualizing. It is a "large association of persons," rather than Bosanquet's fragmented "units" or, for that matter, the anonymous evolutionary juggernaut envisioned by the Fabians. Minimizing the importance of "legislative interference," Loch's formulation promised to indemnify the "exercise of personal influence." In this way organized charity secured much-needed pastorship ("the removal and prevention of evils") in a form that neither subjugated, homogenized, nor dehumanized the individual members of the social organism.

In effect the COS attempted to create a pastoral agency that would overcome the paradox of institutionalized authority in a society of putatively self-reliant individuals. Because the relationship between the caseworker and the family was personal and voluntary, rather than official and prescribed, organized charity's "combined force" could have its cake and eat it too. As described by various proponents, it was, on the one hand, systematic, rational, efficient, and affirmative and, on the other, personal, moral, humanizing, and liberatory. The Idealists thus rejected the determinism of their Fabian rivals while simultaneously warranting a positive basis for human progress. Bosanquet's teleology married evolutionary forces with mind and will, repudiating any program that privileged one without the other. Neither the individualist's laissez faire nor the determinist's "mechanical pressure of circumstances" availed until the Idealist's synthesis was first asserted. For Bosanquet positive liberty, the actuation of "some plan or value in the circumstances that press upon us, in relation to which we can assert ourselves," completed the teleology sketched by Mill ("Duties" 5–6). Character, what George Behlmer describes as "that aspect of mind which enabled the [Idealist's] individual to impose order on social circumstances," was the human medium of such progress ("Character Building" 63). Citizen pastorship, an army of "social healers," specially trained but "disciplined and animated with a single spirit and purpose," was the unique corporate agency capable of translating Idealist philosophy into pragmatic social policy (qtd. in S. and B. Webb 280).

"Unconscious Socialism"

It is surely the worst of all forms of national waste to allow the ravages of preventable sickness to progress unchecked; and this not merely because it kills off
thousands of producers prematurely (burdening us, by the way, with the widow
and the orphan), but because sickness levies a toll on the living and leaves even
those who survive crippled, debilitated, and less efficient than they would otherwise have been.

> — MINORITY REPORT OF THE ROYAL COMMISSION
> ON THE POOR LAWS

Of course, from the Fabian point of view what the Bosanquets proposed was
a retrograde philosophical mystification. Practically speaking, Idealism like
Bernard Bosanquet's obstructed the state's modern pastoral potential, and promoted old-fashioned moralizing and inefficient policy in its stead. The COS-
dominated Majority Report, wrote Beatrice Webb, was "an amazingly useless
document" (*Diary* 3:99). Just as the COS never seriously acknowledged Fabian
determination to install qualified social workers in the state, so the Fabians ig-
nored COS determination to achieve a similar end through organized voluntarism. Hence, any analysis of these alternative approaches to social welfare must
look beneath programmatic differences, and query basic assumptions.

Although I have already suggested that the Webbs were heirs to Edwin Chadwick's long-suppressed technocratic interventionism, it is important to recognize that the Fabians envisioned themselves within a much broader historical
narrative. In contrast to Bernard Bosanquet's evolutionary worldview, attendant
on the "personal struggle for existence," Fabian evolution was forwarded by
"blind social forces" and staged at the mass level of societies and nations. Writing in 1889, Sidney Webb credited Auguste Comte, Charles Darwin, and Herbert Spencer with demonstrating the perpetual "dynamism" of civilization. The
ideal of socialism, he argued, was immanent in late-nineteenth-century developments, but it was not the end of history ("Historic" 27–28). Yet Webb's quite
specific present-day purpose was to account for and justify collectivist measures
that a previous generation of liberals (including Spencer) had repudiated. With
this polemic in mind, Webb narrated a history of "irresistible progress" (29). Just
as feudalism was dissolved by the laissez-faire tenets of the industrial revolution,
so this "creed of Murdstones and Gradgrinds" would be superseded as a matter
of course. Individualism, Webb argued, with its atomistic and anarchistic ten-

dencies, must be and, in fact, already was in the process of being displaced by a new "intellectual and moral revolt" (40).

Webb traced the decline of individualism in a panoramic sweep, including references to the Romantic poets, Thomas Carlyle, Charles Dickens, and, of course, John Stuart Mill, whose gradual shift from laissez-faire political economy to collectivism represented a veritable microcosm of evolutionary forces at work (40–41). Yet, so far from exalting these proto-socialist heroes, Webb's ultimate purpose was to subordinate their efforts to the determination of supraindividual forces. In a passage that elucidates the cardinal differences between COS and Fabian philosophies, Webb conceded that the "Zeitgeist" cannot itself "pass Acts of Parliament," or "erect municipal libraries."

> Though our decisions are moulded by the circumstances of the time, and the environment at least roughhews our ends, shape them as we will; yet each generation decides for itself. It still rests with the individual to resist or promote the social evolution, consciously or unconsciously, according to his character and information. The importance of complete consciousness of the social tendencies of the age lies in the fact that its existence and comprehensiveness often determine the expediency of our particular action: we move with less resistance with the stream than against it. (44)

Here Webb offered a bare minimum of free will. Individuals retained the power either to promote or resist progress; to render their actions expeditious or obstructive. Unsurprisingly, Webb's strategy was not to insist on the importance of such negligible advocacy, but to win support by very different means. Webb's far more controversial premise was that socialism was already a fait accompli: immanent in the era's large-scale municipal projects, and in the expanded purview of state and local government. "Such is the irresistible sweep of social tendencies," argued Webb, that the most ardent liberals have worked unconsciously "to bring about the very Socialism they despised" (44).[9] Thus, Webb solicited support for Fabianism not because civilization's progress depends on active mind and will but because skepticism in a universe determined by larger forces is all but meaningless.

Interestingly, the Webbs' deterministic tendencies most clearly emerged when they attempted to prove that they did not, as their critics alleged, ignore "personal character" (S. and B. Webb 304). In their 1910 history of *English Poor Law Policy* the Webbs acknowledged the great extent to which indigence is caused by "personal defects." Yet they proceeded to connect these defects to in-

fant neglect, disability, and unemployment, thus translating personal character
from the cause of pauperism into the effect of theoretically preventable circumstances (305). From there the Webbs were situated to invoke their corporatist notion of joint responsibility, an "indissoluble partnership" between the
individual and the community. In this Fabian version of the social contract, liberalism's hallowed boundary between civil society and government entirely evap-
orates as "new and enlarged obligations," "unknown in a state of *laisser faire*,"
are imposed on individuals (270).

In essence what the Webbs proposed was a preventive as well as curative pastorship, enjoining individuals either to measure up to minimum standards, or
submit themselves to the state's vigorous tutelage. As historians have often
noted, this turn-of-the-century Fabianism had more to do with rationalizing social welfare, and empowering the professional middle classes, than implementing socialism (Perkin, *Rise* 130; Searle 238, 253; Himmelfarb, *Poverty* 353–55).
Needless to say, the Webbs dismissed Idealism's stress on character as a potentially autonomous force. Rejecting charity's inefficiency, the Webbs detailed a
totalizing disciplinary program.

This vision was reproduced (but also critiqued) in the futuristic fiction of H.
G. Wells, who, between 1903 and 1908, was an enthusiastic Fabian. In *A Modern Utopia* (1905) Wells detailed a "World State" administered by a self-elected
elite of highly disciplined "samurai." Providing a wide range of preventive and
curative services, Wells's state ensured proper housing, nourishment, and health-
care for all. To facilitate these pastoral ends Wells envisioned quasi-panoptical
surveillance techniques, eugenics, and the exile of incorrigibles: tutelary policies
that, as Wells portrayed them, did not necessarily impede the goal of maximiz-
ing individual liberty. To the contrary, bureaucratic supervision was necessary
precisely because the personal relations hallowed by the COS were obsolete:
"the homely methods of identification that served . . . when everyone knew
everyone" no longer functioned in a modern mass society (162). Although Wells
was in fact a deeply conflicted Fabian, a point to which I will return, *A Modern
Utopia* confirmed the Fabian view of character as that which must be engineered,
whenever necessary, through timely interventions. Detailing many of the policies described in Wells's fictional utopia, the Minority Report, drafted by the
Webbs, urged preventive strategies too invasive for all but the most zealous enthusiasts of efficiency (Searle 241–43).[10]

Edwardian Deadlock

While the problem of 1834 was the problem of pauperism, the problem of 1893 is the problem of poverty; that a man ought not to be allowed to live in a bad home, that extreme poverty ought to be regarded, not indeed as a crime, but as a thing so detrimental to the State that it should not be endured.

— ALFRED MARSHALL

The 1905–9 Royal Commission's failure to produce *any* legislative response remains "one of the major mysteries of Edwardian political history" (Searle 237). "Never," writes Derek Fraser, can so important a Royal Commission have produced so little in the way of immediate action" (161). What is nonetheless clear is that the Minority Report—much like Chadwick's sanitary *Report* of yore—was simply too un-English to win popular confidence. L. T. Hobhouse exemplified the kind of core liberal resistance which helped to defeat Fabian technocracy. Challenging the era's cult of expertise, Hobhouse may have subtly alluded to the fall of the Sanitary Idea when he reprobated those who believe "that the art of governing men is as mechanical a matter as that of laying drain-pipes" (qtd. in Searle 82). Yet, if Britons recoiled from Fabian plans to engineer character through state pastorship, they simultaneously expressed ambivalence toward the Majority Report's proposal to build character through the combined efforts of deterrent laws and organized voluntarism. Clearly, Alfred Marshall, Cambridge professor of political economy (and disciple of J. S. Mill), had enunciated a growing perception when, in his 1893 testimony before a commission on the aged poor, he distinguished between the blamable pauperism of 1834 and the compassionable poverty of modern times (see epigraph). By the same token Marshall's remarks indicate the extent to which the liberal mythology had been damaged.

In retrospect it is clear that the liberal constitutional consensus had depended on an unquestioned correlation between the self-originating force of character and material prosperity. Britain's declining world standing weakened this foundational myth. Thus, Marshall's new politico-economic construction of the impoverished masses reflected the growing perception of individual powerlessness and environmental influence: a shift from the morally culpable universe of 1834 (wherein pauperism signaled defective character) to the morally neutral universe of 1893 (wherein poverty was determined by social forces beyond the individual's control). Like the Fabians, then, Marshall located individuals in an environment dominated by impersonal forces, a condition of impotence from which only the state's intervention might rescue them. In so doing, he echoed George Gissing's fictional evocation of a working-class nether world, the denizens of which were doomed helplessly to watch "men and women perish before [their] eyes" (*Nether* 102).

To counter this anathematic political economy, C. S. Loch returned to the polemics of the early nineteenth century, arguing that nonstigmatic provision for the relief of poverty would, like the Old Poor Law of yore, "weaken moral obligations" ("Controverted" 244). More than a decade later the Majority Report that he signed insisted that "the causes of distress are not only economic and industrial; in their origin and character they are largely moral" (qtd. in Fraser 160). Britons raised to believe that "Heaven helps those who help themselves" may well have felt a powerful predisposition to favor such arguments. To be sure, few of them were likely to join Sidney Webb in welcoming the prospect of the vanishing "personal element" in business, or any other aspect of everyday life ("Historic" 43). Nevertheless, the material prosperity and global dominion on which Loch's moral claims had once securely rested had visibly deteriorated. While fantastic fictions such as Bram Stoker's *Dracula* (1897) and H. G. Wells's *War of the Worlds* (1898) dramatized Britain's vulnerability to foreign invasion, realist novels such as *The Nether World* (1889) implied the irrecuperability of Smiles's mythic character, at once a self-generating force and a secure moral foundation. Given these uncertainties, the COS's vision of corporate voluntarism could not but appear to offer Idealist abstractions when what was wanted were practical programs to improve national efficiency and ensure national security.

Literature of this era—from fin-de-siècle gothic and social realism to E. M. Forster's 1909 dystopia of a world run by a master machine—illuminates the deep popular ambivalence, helping to explain the failure of both COS and Fabian agendas. "In the last years of the nineteenth century," writes Stephen Arata, British writers anxiously depicted "the collapse of culture, the weakening of national might, [and] the possibly fatal decay . . . of the Anglo-Saxon 'race' as a whole" (1). Late-century gothic novels such as *Dracula*, *She* (1887), and *Trilby* (1894) feature collaborative efforts to ward off foreign threats to British autonomy. But, unlike the COS's combined force for betterment, these posses disband aimlessly just as soon as the gothic villain has been defeated (cf. Stasiak; Wilt; Brantlinger, *Rule* 227–53). More fundamentally, literature of this period attests to the widening gulf between the real (the world of an ever more depersonalized and hostile materiality), and the ideal (the self-originating force, robust industry, and collective purpose on which British national character had long been predicated). What in novels is often represented as "reality, drained of spiritual depth" (L. Anderson 32) thus reproduces the philosophical split between Fabian materialism and COS Idealism; between physical environment and the human telos.[11] Hence, just as fictions of this era recoil from the Fabians' fetishization of machinery, so they remain skeptical of the Bosanquets' promised synthesis.

Late-Victorian and Edward literature thus testifies to the breakdown of Victorian Britain's mythic character. Would-be Nietzschean Over-men are humbled by insurmountable obstacles. When individuals are more convincingly masterful, they evoke unsettling qualities of mechanism, monstrosity, un-Englishness, and decadence. When, on the other hand, humanistic values prevail, they founder in a Millite universe of atomized powerlessness. The realist novels of Gissing and Arnold Bennett enact a disturbing counterpoint between cultured dwarfs and ruthless philistines. Edwin Reardon, the weak but refined protagonist of Gissing's *New Grub Street* (1893), is both contemptuous of and utterly defeated by his commercially successful rival, Jasper Milvain, "a man of his day." In *Clayhanger* (1910) Arnold Bennett translates historical decline into a generation gap, contrasting the crude but effectual mastery of an early-Victorian father to the refined impotence of his mid-Victorian son. In the following sections I turn to readings of specific works by Gissing, Wells, and Forster in order further to demonstrate literature's relation to problems of pastorship, character, and worldview.

Mind and Will in George Gissing's Nether World

The disease inherent in her being, that deadly outcome of social tyranny which perverts the generous elements of youth into mere seeds of destruction, developed day by day, blighting her heart, corrupting her moral sense, even setting marks of evil upon the beauty of her countenance.

— GEORGE GISSING, *The Nether World*

George Gissing's *Nether World* (1889) offers a striking literary instance of the era's dueling worldviews. The novel yearns for a self-originating force like Smiles's even while representing a world in which individual will is mercilessly crushed. Raymond Williams has located the novel in the context of Gissing's youthful political disenchantment; a backlash against "adolescent socialism." There is, to be sure, much justification for such a reading. Yet whatever his recoil from the nether world, Gissing also passionately identified with several of his tragic working-class protagonists.[12] By representing the paralysis of "mind and will" as it is overwhelmed by material necessity, *The Nether World* provides an important fictional complement to the great social debates of the era.

Depicting the "brute forces of society" in scenes as graphic as any portrayed in Charles Booth's social investigations, *The Nether World* presents poverty and degradation as the almost inescapable effects of "social tyranny" (392, 86). Gissing both adopts the viewpoint of the empirical sociologist *and* submits that privileged position to scathing antibourgeois critique. "Observe the middle-aged women" of the nether world, he directs the educated reader. "It would be small surprise that their good looks had vanished, but whence comes it they are animal, repulsive, absolutely vicious in ugliness? Mark the men in their turn: four in every six have visages so deformed by ill-health that they excite disgust" (109). At such moments the reader's presumed repulsion is made inseparable from a countervailing consciousness of complicity ("whence comes it . . . ?"). In another memorable passage Gissing demystifies the supposed moral foundations of middle-class propriety. "Genuine respect for the law" he observes, "is the result of possessing something which the law exerts itself to guard" (217).

Nevertheless, such radical insights can only be sustained by a viable political agency, and in *The Nether World* no such agency is possible. As an uncompromising social realist, Gissing was too conscious of material constraints to attribute a powerful force to mind and will in the manner of the Idealists. Yet, at the same time, Gissing's commitment to the liberal ideal of individual self-determination was too strong to permit enthusiasm either for Fabian or working-class collectivism. As a result, the novel's acute materialist perceptions dissolve into isolated battles between beleaguered individuals and invisible economic forces (cf. Keating 83). Ironically, it is because Gissing so highly prizes the human spirit, and so unflinchingly condemns the capitalism that exploits it, that intellectual development is, to his mind, the cruelest of working-class fatalities. Hence, Clara Hewett's "unfortunate endowment of brains" dooms her to futile defiance and perilous fall. "How can we any of us help what we're driven to in a world like this?" asks Sidney Kirkwood, the artisan whom Clara deserts to try her luck on the stage (79, 102).

Yet in other respects Gissing reveals himself to be as deeply attached to the idea of character as any member of the Charity Organization Society. Michael Snowdon, the novel's tragic working-class visionary, "expresse[s] himself in the tone of one" who, "if the aid of books has been denied to him, still has won from life the kind of knowledge which develops character" (45). Not only Michael, but all Gissing's working-class figures are, no matter how hedged and deformed by circumstance, creatures, partly, of their own making. Although he illustrates the severe limitations on individual autonomy, Gissing nonetheless shares Bosanquet's resolve to view the working classes as "living selves with a history and ideas and a character of their own" ("Character" 105).

Hence, Sidney Kirkwood was saved from the hazards of "unstable character" when the death of his father prompted a "course of self-discipline of which not many are capable" (52). Hence, John Hewett fatefully amplified his daughter's "fierce, unscrupulous rebellion" by teaching her to set her sights too high (86). Hence, Scawthorne, the clerk who hastens Clara's ruin, was a "grave, gentle boy . . . with a great love of books" until semi-starvation and overwork corrupted his moral nature (194). Hence, Jane Snowdon, Michael's granddaughter, was "an ill-used, ragged, work-worn child" but retains, nevertheless, a "moral force" and "power for good" (224, 139). Of course, such examples fall far short of, and even challenge, the myth of character as a self-originating power. Yet the selves they epitomize are, nonetheless, irreducible to the passive products of nature and nurture at play. Individual histories like these—with moral tissue here yielding to, there resisting, the pressure of external forces—constitute the human telos as Gissing saw it.

In an ironic aside Gissing affirms the possibility of progress while revealing himself to be the most disheartened of humanists: "To humanise the multitude two things are necessary—two things of the simplest kind conceivable. In the first place, you must effect an entire change of economic conditions . . . ; then you must bring to bear on the new order of things the constant influence of music. . . . For work as you will, there is no chance of a new and better world until the old one be utterly destroyed" (109). Here, more primary even than the repulsed bourgeois or political cynic, is the frustrated liberal humanist: his still vital conviction in character building implied by music's power to exalt. Surveying the attractions at a popular fair, Gissing denigrates the low appeals to "patriotism" and bitterly laments the absent encouragements to "mind" and "love of beauty" (107). By the end of the novel Sidney's "circle of . . . interests" has "shriveled" entirely to the struggle for subsistence; the artist and thinker loses the will to draw and read (374). Thus, not humanity itself, but an "order of things" which "mar[s] the purposes of Nature" is what prompts Gissing's skepticism and despair (109, 1).

Yet we cannot be surprised to find Gissing expressing little interest in the kind of state pastorship urged by the Fabians. The progress they sought efficiently to forward was the same material juggernaut that Gissing wished away. Already implicit in *The Nether World* is a disaffection for technological advance which eventually propelled him to describe "science" as the "remorseless enemy of mankind" (*Private* 163; cf. Beauchamp 53). The world of the novel is the liberal constitutional order as seen from below. Policemen and prisons exist side by side with the squalid lodgings of the poor. But, apart from protecting property, the Victorian state can hardly be said to exist at all.[13] Gissing, however, is notably indifferent to the absence of institutionalized pastorship: an implicit laissez-faire-ist as well as an explicit ex-radical. Aggrieved to find the human spirit so poorly nourished, he is nevertheless free of paternalistic ambition. In *Thyrza* (1887) Gissing rejected the idea that humanist education might ennoble the working classes. There is no sense in *The Nether World*, as so often in *Bleak House*, that the sufferings of the masses originate in the failed obligations of cabinet ministers, lord chancellors, or the nation's ruling classes.

That said, *The Nether World* has a great deal to say about charity. Although Gissing's attitude to middle-class philanthropy is, at best, ambivalent, there are striking likenesses between his views and those of the Charity Organization Society. In his essay on *Oliver Twist* Gissing adopted the typical COS position on poor relief: the 1834 act, he argued, "awaken[ed] self-respect" in a population that had been pauperized by the Old Poor Law (*Immortal* 63). In "The Soup-Kitchen," an important chapter in *The Nether World*, Gissing produces a dictum to delight C. S. Loch: "Of all the forms of insolence there is none more flagrant than that of the degraded poor receiving charity which they have come to regard as a right" (253). Sounding more like James Phillips Kay or Harriet Martineau than an erstwhile socialist, he at times implies that the nether world's most serious problem is the ineffective "domestic management" of working-class women (56; cf. 15).

Philanthropic efforts of various kinds play a significant role in *The Nether World*. Michael Snowdon, the heir to his son's ill-gotten Australian fortune, has returned to England to find his abandoned granddaughter, Jane. Michael's dream is to use the money to turn Jane into a working-class Lady Bountiful. A woman of the upper world "may do good," he allows, "but she can't be the friend of the poor" (178). The irony is that Jane already plays the role of home visitor to a troubled family, just as Sidney has long looked after the Hewetts. Jane has befriended the hapless Pennyloaf, neglected wife of the Hewett's son Bob. As she instructs Pennyloaf to scrub her lodgings in order to introduce her husband to the comforts of a respectable home, Jane appears to offer little more than the familiar bromides of middle-class philanthropists. Yet, while she is powerless to turn a drunkard's daughter into a model housekeeper, and while Bob is manifestly indifferent to such reputable lures, Jane's "soothing influence" over Pennyloaf offers precisely the genuine friendship that Michael hopes to foster (132).

The eventual failure of Michael's dream, therefore, does not so much repudiate working-class philanthropy as expose the perils of any enthusiasm for social change in the nether world. Just as John Hewett's soapbox oratory culminates in self-shattering "frenzy," so Michael's "noble idea" gradually becomes an idée fixe with "dehumanizing" consequences (182, 137, 255). Jane's nature, Sidney surmises, is suited to "obscure and happy" homemaking. Not "conscious philanthropy," but the spontaneous influence she exercises over Pennyloaf is the appropriate outlet for her moral powers. Sidney himself, meanwhile, is neither "hero" nor "enthusiast." His "old artist-self revived," he can "imagine no bliss so perfect" as to marry Jane and escape the "echo of the suffering world" (234–35, 233). Of course, Sidney's recoil from heroic philanthropy cannot fail to remind us of Gissing's own retreat from radical politics.

Ironically, Michael's obsession with compassionate aid originates in a sad tale of self-help gone awry. As a young husband, he was fatally influenced by a Samuel Smiles–like lecture attributing the sufferings of the poor to thriftlessness. In his subsequent quest for respectability Michael starved himself and drove his wife to drink and suicide. He concludes his story with a sharp rejoinder to philosophies such as that of the COS: "They talk about thriftiness, and it just means that poor people are expected to practise a self-denial that the rich can't even imagine, much less carry out!" (174–75).

In spite of that conviction, to prepare Jane for her duties, Michael turns to Miss Lant, a middle-class philanthropist who vaguely resembles the COS's Octavia Hill. Gissing describes her as the representative of a new secular philanthropy, replacing the old religious piety with "a narrow and oppressive zeal for good works" (229). Miss Lant's involvement thus implicates Michael's ideal in the condescending charity he had sought to displace. Under Miss Lant's mentorship, and with Michael's approval, Jane is soon involved in the operations of a soup kitchen where she can serve the poor "not with aid of money alone, but by her personal influence" (250). Here, of course, is the familiar rhetoric of the personal: the keynote of the middle-class charitable mission since Chalmers's time.

In a story Gissing recounts in lieu of "abstract comment" on philanthropy, Miss Lant and other "conscientious" ladies anger the neighborhood poor by removing the long-standing operators of the soup kitchen, and changing to a more economical recipe. Mr. and Mrs. Batterby, they reason, were "of too coarse a type" to exert "a humanising influence" (251). The installation of "refined" servers (including Jane) to replace the Batterbys typifies the COS's philosophy. Sir Charles Trevelyan, an early supporter of the society, had insisted that "the gift loses the redeeming influence of personal kindness" if it is not passed directly from donor to recipient. Only unmediated contact facilitates the crucial character-building bond (qtd. in Behlmer, "Character Building" 59). But Gissing is as contemptuous of Miss Lant's power to humanize as he is certain of Jane's power to soothe. The novel does not hesitate to distinguish between the self-serving humanist rhetoric of the middle-class zealot, and the unaffected humanity exemplified by Jane.

Hence, the irony of the soup kitchen episode is its demonstrating the validity of Michael's (increasingly destructive) vision. Jane, a "daughter of the people," does in fact understand what the middle-class ladies do not (392). When the ladies are shocked by the ingratitude of the poor, Gissing addresses them directly, reminding them that "this nether world has been made by" people like themselves. "Do *you* be grateful," he warns, "that these hapless, half-starved women do not turn and rend you" (252). This uncharacteristically foreboding passage is a rare instance of Gissing's ascribing the economic system that oppresses the working classes to a human (middle-class) agency. Yet, in this instance, the specter of class conflict serves to vindicate Michael's deluded vision. For, in response to Jane's influence, the Batterbys are returned.

The much greater irony, however, is that, as Gissing sees it, the COS's primary mission has already been fulfilled. Shunning the poor law even more than the police, Gissing's working classes themselves prefer a "little wholesome starvation" to the "moral degradation" of pauperdom (Dendy 171, 173). Mrs. Hewett, once an impoverished pieceworker in an empty garret, starved for three days before being driven to pawn her employer's goods. Years later she is still haunted by the shame of having been tried for theft. Yet the option of the workhouse—stigmatic but legal—does not appear ever to have occurred to her. When John Hewett's burial club, his "one stronghold against fate," is defrauded, he dreads the ignominy of a pauper's grave (185). The workhouse looms over the aged and weak, as when John becomes too rheumatic to be employable. Yet not once in the novel does any laborer consider applying to the parish to appease hunger or lessen toil.

Hence, in *The Nether World* a passionate but despairing belief in the liberatory potential of self-developing character, and an environmentalist view of poverty like Alfred Marshall's, is entangled with unexamined individualist assumptions that reproduce the harsh logic of the New Poor Law. Nonetheless, the novel also shows that economic self-reliance is no guarantor of character in a world in which, as in *Oliver Twist*, the struggle to survive is itself morally injurious. In spite of such crucial demystifying insights, Gissing's only alternative to the shortsightedness of the New Poor Law is the help of the poor for one another—advocated by Thomas Chalmers almost a century before. Jane's marriage prospects are ruined by a fortune she never inherits: although she will never realize her grandfather's ideal, she devotes her life to selfless struggle against the "dangerous despair" of her neighbors (136). Sidney marries Clara, whose face has been disfigured by a rival actress. Neither "an artist, nor a leader of men in the battle for justice," he devotes himself wholly to supporting her and the rest of the Hewett family (391).

Raymond Williams aptly describes this conclusion as a "Victorian solution: a dedication to charity shrunk to an almost hidden scale, within an essential resignation" (*Culture* 175). That resignation—the impact of "brute forces" on the isolated mind and will—is the sign of Gissing's political disenchantment. Sidney's long lost belief in utopian politics is temporarily replaced by the prospect of marrying Jane: rather than collective redemption, he dreams of private retreat into nature, art, and domesticity. Ultimately, however, Sidney is compelled to find purpose in a grueling stoic martyrdom. The reader is left to wonder. Why should such passive sacrifice be preferable to the alter of "tumultuous politics"—the "battle for justice" from which Sidney continues to shrink (143)?

Early in the novel Sidney is "astonished" and "amused" to find John Hewett convinced of the transformative potential of the franchise (53). Yet adult male suffrage and the rise of the Labor Party, still unfolding as Gissing composed his novel, were hardly irrelevant to the nether world. Even the modest entitlements of New Liberalism—school meals, old-age pensions, unemployment insurance—were, as Winston Churchill was to call them, "lifebelt[s]" to supplement the "strenuous exertions" of workers like Sidney and John (82, 210). "What a vile, cursed world this is," Sidney laments, where "men and women perish before your eyes, and no more chance of saving them than if they were going down in mid-ocean!" (102). Undoubtedly, this overwhelming sense of individual powerlessness, the crisis of individual will anticipated in Mill's prescient works, explains Gissing's pessimistic insistence that political involvement leads inevitably to "social bitterness" (143).

Gissing inhabited the moral universe of the Idealist but saw little to romanticize and much to reprobate in the organized voluntarism of self-styled pastors. With the empiricist's acuity and the socialist's materialist critique, he exposed the crushing structures that increasingly led other, less dispirited men and women to think beyond the limits of self-reliance and voluntary aid. In *The Nether World* a single image of collaborative action links Gissing to that forward-moving vision. Near the close of the novel Pennyloaf, now a widow, joins with another single mother. With financial aid from Miss Lant and Jane Snowdon's friendship, the two women open a shop, earn their living, and raise their children together. Here, as so often in this period, the voluntary but proto-professional services of women both originate in and look beyond the manifest limits of "charity, shrunk to an almost hidden scale."

H. G. Wells: Dystopic Fabian

That great empire was no more than a thing adrift, an aimless thing that ate and
drank and slept and bore arms, and was inordinately proud of itself because it
had chanced to happen. It had no plan, no intention; it meant nothing at all.
— H. G. WELLS, *In the Days of the Comet*

Socialism . . . is to be served by thought and expression, in art, in literature, in
scientific statement and life, in discussion and the quickening exercise of propaganda; but the Socialist movement, as one finds it, is too often no more than a
hasty attempt to secure a premature realization of some fragmentary suggestion
of this great, still plastic design, to the neglect of other aspects.
— H. G. WELLS, "SOCIALISM AND THE MIDDLE CLASSES"

Gissing's vision of creating a new order through the humanizing power of music is but a passing and deeply ironic moment in a novel that ends by dismissing the possibility of large-scale social change. By contrast, H. G. Wells— Gissing's friend and sometime member of the Fabian Society—was the author of numerous utopian texts, including *A Modern Utopia* (1905), with its clear applications to Fabianism, and *In the Days of the Comet* (1906), a scientific romance. Critical interest in *Utopia* has generally overshadowed the later work so that the substantial differences between the two have not been elaborated. In the *Comet* social change is precipitated by a sudden cosmic event: a giant comet induces atmospheric changes that result in a physiological transformation of human "nerve and brain" (658). Utopian living in the *Comet* thus derives from the innate self-governing capacities of a reconstituted humanity; not, as in *A Modern Utopia*, from the technocratic pastorship of a self-authorized elite.

In the Days of the Comet is, therefore, antithetical to the Fabian-inspired vision set forth in *A Modern Utopia*. Less like the Webbs than like his Victorian precursor, J. S. Mill, the author of the *Comet* aimed to liberate human individuality, not to maximize material efficiency. More optimistic than Gissing with regard both to politics and science, Wells was caught, nevertheless, between dueling worldviews. Although drawn to the Fabians by a horror of waste and disorganization, and though lacking Dickens's sentimental attachment to the home, Wells was ultimately as confounded by the problem of instituting pastoral authority as was the author of *Bleak House*. At the bottom of his conflict was a Millite perception of the diminished individual in a modern society. This vision was further developed in *The New Machiavelli* (1911), a political novel in which Wells recast his experiences with the Fabians.

Wells's contemporaneous lectures illustrate some of the major differences between himself and the Webbs (with whom he was to part in 1908 after an unsuccessful attempt to seize control of the Fabian Society). In 1905 Beatrice had urged the London Sociological Society to "apply the scientific method to the facts of social life" (qtd. in den Otter 136). A year later Wells told the same audience that it was "nonsense" to view sociology as a positive science (qtd. in Hellegas 58). True socialism, Wells declared, was "the form and substance of [an] ideal life," and, indeed," "all the religion [he] possess[ed]" ("Socialism" 5).[14] Sociology, which Wells conceived as the educational precursor to socialism, must blend art and science to produce "knowledge rendered imaginatively, and with an element of personality; that is to say . . . literature" (qtd. in Hellegas 58). In so saying, Wells articulated a socialist ideal with palpable connections to the aestheticism of William Morris or Oscar Wilde.[15] Not aspiring bureaucrats but artists and "the better sort of" scientists must precipitate the "quickened imaginations and unsettling influences" required to realize a fully-fledged socialism ("Socialism" 18–19).

Wells thus made two important moves, both of which illuminate his utopian romances. First, he placed literature at the heart of a modern sociological project. Second, he made clear that the aim of that project was fundamental change: not material amelioration but a "reconstruction of human life" and a "change of spirit and substance" ("Socialism" 6, 8). Wells's language here situated him as a committed antimaterialist, or quasi-Idealist. *In the Days of the Comet*, in other words, is the work of a man more committed to an ideal of individual and community self-realization than to a comprehensive policy agenda. In it Wells makes his most consistent effort to explore the Mill-like premise that the "final hope" of a "modern Utopia" is "the evolving interplay of unique individualities" (*Modern* 33).

Like Dickens's Bradley Headstone, William Leadford, the narrator of the *Comet*, falls in love with a woman of his own class (his cousin Nettie) only to lose her to an upper-class rival (Edward Verrall, the heir of the family in whose service Nettie's parents are employed).[16] Yet Wells's conscious socialism complicates this Dickensian theme. Although Verrall and his ally Lord Redcar are depicted as potent, even "Homeric," agents in a world of disempowered masses (598), Wells, unlike Dickens, exposes the class origins of their superiority. By Leadford's own account, his upper-class foil "took with a light confidence, as a matter of course, advantages that I would have faced the rack to get, [though] I firmly believed myself a better man than he." That belief notwithstanding, Verrall, complete with Wrayburnian cigar, coolly manages their first confrontation, while Leadford is reduced to Headstonian self-shattering: "I felt like a bombshell of swearing that must presently burst with some violence" (587).

Leadford's determination to avenge himself by murder thus becomes an analogue for explosive class conflicts that were largely submerged in Dickens's novel. Indeed, through a series of narrative convergences the situation of Wells's hero becomes a microcosmic instance of the individual in an unstable global capitalist society. Leadford's personal antagonisms—toward his employer as well as Verrall—take place in "a year of world-wide economic disorganisation" (577). Local employment relations have been aggravated by reckless overproduction overseas. Thus, Leadford's rebellion against the economic and sexual prerogatives of the rich coincides with a miners' strike and employer lockout. As these tensions heighten, and with the mysterious comet already in the periphery, Leadford's predicament is amplified still further by the outbreak of war between Germany and Britain. The narrative thus builds toward a climax in which the comet effectuates the Great Change: a "change of spirit and substance" which Wells had elsewhere ascribed to socialism ("Socialism" 8).

In creating this cogent analogy between atmospheric and socialist transformation, Wells's intent was clearly to write fiction that would "quicken" stultified bourgeois imaginations. The English middle classes, Wells told his Fabian audience, were so entirely unready for socialism that they would "be lost in Utopia" ("Socialism" 15). Nevertheless, in the *Comet* this consciousness-raising intent is undermined by a number of countervailing tendencies. As the narrative approaches its multipronged climax—Leadford's murder attempt, the battle between Britain and Germany, and the impact of the comet—Wells increasingly diverges from materialist critique. Forgetful of capitalist instability, he ends by equating the "irrational obsession" of imperialistic nations at war to the "egotistical wrath" of his murderous hero. As competition is recast as "jealousy," what was first presented as the historical determinants of human suffering becomes the by-product of ineradicable flaws in male sexuality.

One way to explain this shift concerns Wells's well-known penchant for wrangling with sexual indiscretions through thinly veiled autobiography. The story of his adulterous relationship with Amber Reeves, a young member of the Fabian Society, has been documented by many Wells scholars (see, e.g., Huntington). This scandalous affair, which played a part in Wells's acrimonious break with the Webbs, provided the basis for *The New Machiavelli*, a novel in which a Wells-like hero sacrifices political ambition to an illicit sexual passion. In the *Comet*, by resituating capitalism and imperialism as male nature, Wells prepares the ground for an evolutionary and sexual rather than materialist reading of history. By making divisive sexual urges a "rough universal truth" of the species, Wells creates an obvious exculpatory context for his personal misdeeds (688).

That said, there is more to Wells's reflections on gender and sexuality than self-serving apologia. Wells repeatedly urged socialists to acknowledge the hypocrisy of existing sexual mores and to provide for the "full citizenship and economic independence of women" ("Socialism" 11; cf. *Modern* 175–213). It seems likely, then, that autobiographical motives are insufficient to explain the unsettling trajectory of the *Comet*. Autobiography aside, why does Wells set out to "quicken" bourgeois imaginations, only to befuddle them further with a vision of a world ineradicably vitiated by the evolutionary residue of male sexual conquest?

The answer, I suggest, is found in Wells's response to the era's dueling worldviews, including his visible allegiance to a liberal-humanist ideal like Mill's. Wells portrays the Edwardian working classes as a pastorless mass in a nation as dangerously divided into two as it was in the time of Disraeli's *Sybil*: "There on the one hand in a crowded darkness, about the ugly factories and work-places, the workers herded together, ill clothed, ill nourished, ill taught . . . uncertain even of their insufficient livelihood from day to day, the chapels and churches and public-houses swelling up amidst their wretched homes like saprophytes amidst a general corruption, and on the other, in space, freedom, and dignity, scarce heeding the few cottages . . . in which the labourers festered, lived the landlords and masters who owned pot-banks and forge and farm and mine" (567). Wells's damning equation between religious institutions and pubs—both likened to scavenging forms of plant life—puts emphatically to rest Thomas Chalmers's ideal of uniting communities through the parish church. Similarly, Wells's insistence that the patriarchal family is obsolete neutralizes Dickens's vision of domestic pastors such as the Maylies and the Woodcourts. And yet Wells's ostensibly recoupable nether world also stands in contrast to Gissing's. Whereas Gissing's poor were assailed by impersonal forces beyond human control, Wells insists that the "dark world" of the present is "full of preventable disorder, preventable diseases, and preventable pain" (561).

The iteration of *preventability* cannot but recall the Webbs and their eagerness to install a comprehensive pastoral state. But the Webbs were also willing heirs, as Wells was not, to sociological positivism and Chadwickian technocracy. Thus, the interventions that Wells saw as (at best) a means to an end were, for the Webbs, justifiable ends in themselves. In *A Modern Utopia* Wells acknowledged that a Fabianesque world order could only "come about by . . . co-ordinated effort and a community of design" (128). This cautious allusion to the role of a powerful elite was, in the 1906 address, articulated as an appeal to a professional vanguard including doctors, teachers, architects, and engineers. Yet Wells also displays deep discomfort with the idea of empowering an elite to manufacture "informed and disciplined minds" ("Socialism" 22–23). Significantly, *A Modern Utopia* offers almost no account of the means by which the samurai, a "voluntary nobility," came to establish their technocratic and eugenicist regime (259). In *When the Sleeper Wakes* (1897–98), one of his earliest scientific romances, Wells envisioned a totalitarian dystopia: a corporate society ruthlessly dominated by a despotic elite.

Hence, it is no accident that, in the *Comet*, humanity is regenerated precisely by chance and not by the "co-ordinated effort . . . and design" of a pastoral vanguard. Leadford rejoices to narrate the speed with which the post-comet society overcomes its outmoded fears of the "danger to liberty," and realizes hitherto impossible plans for communal living (692). In this way atmospheric change provides the functional equivalent of evolutionary progress: within hours the whole of humankind ascends to the level of *A Modern Utopia*'s self-governing samurai. Herbert Spencer, the influential evolutionary theorist, believed that society was gradually evolving toward a "social state" in which government functions would be entirely superseded by a "social" individual: an "individual . . .

hav[ing] such desires only, as may be fully satisfied without trenching upon the ability of other individuals to obtain like satisfaction" (62–63). By instantaneously producing a world of such exemplars, the comet ostensibly facilitates a vision like Spencer's: utopian emancipation in the absence of pastorship.[17]

That said, Wells's ambivalence is discernible even toward the comet, which, on close examination, exacts a price he is reluctant to pay. The comet transforms society by enabling "a new detachment from the tumid passions and entanglements of . . . personal life"—including male sexuality as Wells conceives it (650). Here he wavers ambiguously between portraying the comet as fulfilling human nature (a liberalizing process), and subduing it (an artificial disciplinary process). In the first case the betterment he describes recalls Mill's elevated humanist ideal: "We live now . . . in a time when everyone is being educated to a sort of intellectual gentleness, a gentleness that abates nothing from our vigour" (563). In the second case the comet's effects are presented in more Huxleyan terms, as a civilizing process that suppresses divisive aspects of the "essential self." "All passion . . . is madness," Leadford declares, only to "[fall] into a doubting of those words" (689, 683). "Nothing was lost from my nature," he insists, "only the power of thought and restraint had been wonderfully increased" (681). Resembling nothing so much as a powerful narcotic, the comet's "pouring mist and suffocation" mollify human strife, producing a deathlike calm (646). Although none "would dare to dream" of returning to it, the pre-comet world included "moments of a rare and evanescent beauty that seem no longer possible," "perceptions of a keenness . . . now altogether gone out of life." The same emotional restraint and intellectual enlargement that has enabled utopia has simultaneously "robbed life of its extremes" (561).

To return to *A Modern Utopia* after reading *In the Days of the Comet* is, therefore, to find new insights into hitherto obscure tensions. With no supernatural comet in sight, Wells is left to employ pastoral interventions to foster samurai-like self-discipline. As he openly wrestles with this paradox, Wells unsurprisingly resembles his COS contemporaries: "We must have a clear common purpose, and a great and steadfast movement of will" (*Modern* 128). We are reminded that Wells's samurai are "voluntary noblemen," not state officials (129). This seeming distaste for statism became even more stark after his break with the Webbs. In *The New Machiavelli* Richard Remington, the Wells-like narrator, contrasts the Fabian stress on "functionaries, legislative change, and methods of administration" to his own desire to promote a "growing collective understanding." The "shapes of our thoughts were the same," Remington declares, "but the substance quite different. It was as if [the Fabians] had made in china or cast iron what I had made in transparent living matter" (153–54).

In *A Modern Utopia* Wells's liberal allegiances surface as the "final hope" to which a Fabianesque world order must look forward: "the evolving interplay of unique individualities." "It does not follow," he insists, "that a man is more free where there is least law and more restricted where there is most" (33). Here Wells recalls the precarious balancing act described in Mill's *Autobiography*: the careful steering between too much and too little reliance on the authority of the state (116). With surgical precision the state must "effectually [chip] away just all those spendthrift liberties that waste liberty, and not one liberty more" (*Modern* 34). In contrast to the *Comet*, in which disruptive passions were sacrificed to achieve a higher level of civilization, Wells here implies that it is possible both to mold character (to chip away "spendthrift" liberties), and to emancipate it (to facilitate "unique individualities"). Here civilizing and liberalizing processes are, at least potentially, mutually reinforcing.

The Eye of a Prince Diffused: Wells's Theory of Modern Power

My political conceptions were perfectly plain and honest. I had one constant desire ruling my thoughts. I meant to leave England and the empire better ordered than I found it, to organize and discipline, to build up a constructive and controlling State out of my world's confusions. . . . The problem that most engaged my mind during those years was the practical and personal problem of just where to apply myself to serve this almost innate purpose. How was I, a child of this confusion, struggling upward through the confusion, to take hold of things? Somewhere between politics and literature my grip must needs be found, but where?   — H. G. WELLS, *The New Machiavelli*

The comparison between H. G. Wells and John Stuart Mill is an important one. Although Mill consistently stressed the need to balance civil and state authority, he also came increasingly to believe that the diminished power of individuals was an inevitable product of modern historical conditions. Homogenization and disempowerment advanced with the scale and complexity of modern societies, whether or not disciplinary power was concentrated in the state. In *A Modern Utopia* Wells evades Mill's prophesy by imagining the samurai who, he speculates, derived from a "great succession of persons of extraordinary character and mental gifts" (260). By contrast, the world of the *Comet* is precisely that of Mill's diminished individuals. Although the wealthy and well-educated enjoy disproportionate powers, these are squandered on self-preservation. The masterful will of *Utopia*'s samurai is neither abundant in their nature, nor cultivated by their nurture. For the common man individual power is a risible, even dangerous, fantasy, as when Leadford, having decided to commit murder, imagines himself as a Nietzschean "Over-man" (625–26). In yet another delusion of grandeur Leadford temporarily imagines himself as a "second French Revolution," confronting Verrall's mother when she comes to remunerate Nettie's parents for their daughter's moral ruin (615).[18]

Hence, beneath Wells's readiness to attribute social problems to men's incurable sexual nature is a stalled class critique, and, beneath that, a Millite perception of the modern individual's diminished agency. As Wells depicts it, modernity's diffusion of power eludes utopian efforts to seize power and mobilize it on behalf of individual or collective agency. In the *Comet* this Mill-like phenomenon is most powerfully articulated in the discussion of mass culture, especially newspapers. Like "other great monstrous shapes" in an age of empire and advanced capitalism, the popular press flourishes "because there [is] no clear Will in the world to bring about anything better." As newspapers translate "blind tumult" into "screaming headlines," the potential for truth is radically undermined (603, 597).

Wells's representation of mass culture thus anticipates a particular kind of poststructuralist critique. Power is not, as in *A Modern Utopia*, concentrated in the bureaucratic organs of a ruling elite, or directly accountable to the class that Verrall and Lord Redcar represent. Newspapers are managed by "youngish men of that eager, rather unintelligent type"—a lesser version of Gissing's Jasper Milvain comes to mind—"that . . . never . . . detect[s] itself aimless, that pursues nothing with incredible pride and zeal" (603). Power is thus both everywhere and nowhere. Like everything else in "this mad era," newspapers are the product of a "strong aimless energy"; sites of "collisions, curses, [and] incoherencies"; "complex lunatic machine[s] working hysterically" without guiding intelligence (604, 605).

From these anarchic sites of mass production Wells constructs a

> vision of dispersal. You see those bundles hurling into stations, catching trains by a hair's breadth, . . . breaking up, smaller bundles of them . . . , and then everywhere a division of these smaller bundles into still smaller bundles, into dispersing parcels,

into separate papers, and the dawn happens unnoticed amidst a great running and shouting of boys, a shoving through letter slots, opening of windows, spreading out upon book-stalls. For the space of a few hours you must figure the whole country dotted white with rustling papers . . . ; men and women in trains, men and women eating and reading, men by study-fenders, people sitting up in bed, mothers and sons and daughters waiting for father to finish—a million scattered people reading . . . or feverishly ready to read . . .

Nonsense! The whole affair a noisy paroxysm of nonsense, unreasonable excitement, witless mischief and waste of strength—signifying nothing. (604)

This pervasive print culture—"paroxysm of nonsense" though it may be—is sufficiently powerful to instigate war between Germany and England, "two huge multitudes of people" (603). Perusing the newspaper beside his very own hearth, Leadford temporarily experiences himself as a "corpuscle" in an imagined community, "the big amorphous body of the English" nation.[19] Under the erroneous intelligence of the press, which hypes the war and buries learned scientific opinion on the comet, Leadford momentarily forgets Nettie and "dreams of battles and victories . . . and the heaped slaughter of many thousands of men." Yet the very next morning, recalled to his personal predicament, Leadford sets out to murder Nettie and Verrall, "oblivious of comets, strikes, and wars" (604, 605).

Wells's representation of the popular press thus illustrates the analysis of liberal governance offered in chapter 1. While clearly integral to processes of atomization, commodification, and ideological interpellation, Wells's newspaper, a directionless "lunatic machine," is neither Foucault's omniscient panoptical device, nor Althusser's dominatory institutional state apparatus. The newspaper-reading populace—further described as "forty-one millions of people, in a state of almost indescribably aimless economic and moral muddle that we had neither the courage, the energy, nor the intelligence to improve" (602)—is, as in Mill's prescient essays, and Foucault's late works on governmentality, enmeshed in a vast network of normalizing relations: what Wells calls a "waste of strength." But, for all that, they are not reducible to the docile bodies of *Discipline and Punish*, or the constituted subjects of Althusser's "Ideology and Ideological State Apparatuses." Rather than an instrument of direct domination, or the productive knowledge-making power of Edwardian science, the press functions as a nation-making ritual, inciting a "paper ferment" in what is mythologized as a pluralistic and self-governing society (604). In so doing, it functions indirectly as a "mode of action . . . upon [others'] actions" (Foucault, "Subject" 220).

Wells, I have suggested, saw utopian literature as a sociological means by which to heighten middle-class imaginations and pave the way for socialist transformation. Yet, caught between dueling worldviews, he ultimately declined to affirm the Fabians' technocratic pastoral agenda. *In the Days of the Comet* is thus both a would-be utopian critique of Fabian dystopia, and a troubling reflection on problems of agency in modern society. Like many of his contemporaries, Wells looked forward to socialist emancipation, without fully embracing the pastoral policies that aimed to achieve it. Hence, in the *Comet* what begins as an uncompromising critique of class society and global capitalism culminates in a paralysis of will, both individual and collective. Wells's utopian romances are marked by a distinctive tension between an autobiographically satisfying submission to evolutionary destiny, and a sobering Mill-like insight into civilization's foreshortening of human agency.

Nowhere is this peculiar Wellsian tension more fully developed than in *The New Machiavelli*, the ironic title of which points not only to Wells's debts to Mill but also to their mutual anticipation of Foucault's later works. In his essay on "Governmentality" Foucault describes the historical opposition between the "transcendent singularity of Machiavelli's prince"—his concentrated sovereign power—and a modern notion of the "arts of government" in which governing practices become pluralized, multifarious, and immanent (91). Wells's hero, spurred by a vision of social betterment, confronts this historical difference in the novel's opening pages. Although he is as driven by the "white passion of statecraft" as was Machiavelli, Remington recognizes that the French Revolution has "altered absolutely" the means by which a "thinking man . . . might do the work of state-building." Whereas Machiavelli had but to influence the Prince, his modern-day counterpart faces a far greater challenge—a challenge Remington accepts with Nietzschean ardor: "The days of the Prince who planned and directed and was the source and centre of all power are ended. We are in a condition of affairs infinitely more complex, in which every prince and statesman is something of a servant and every intelligent human being something of a Prince." This diffusion and leveling of power, familiar to readers of Mill's essay on "Civilization," has, according to Remington, exercised a twofold effect. While the Prince's negative power to suppress has "vanished," power itself has increased; it has, as in Foucault's "Governmentality" essay, become "multitudinous," "dispersed," and "specialized" (*Machiavelli* 4–6). Naively optimistic, Remington at first concludes that modernity has furnished an opportunity to exercise productive power on a scale unimagined in Machiavelli's time.

His goal is to write "a book that catches at thousands of readers for the eye of a Prince diffused" (7). Hence, Remington's COS-like ambition to mobilize an entire nation around collective purpose is fused to the idea of a unifying and edifying mass culture—most unlike the "lunatic" newspaper of the *Comet.*

Yet, before Remington has the chance to impose order on the "world's confusions," the white passion of statecraft is supplanted by a scarlet passion for forbidden female fruit (145). His political prospects wrecked by sexual scandal, Remington realizes that he has "aspired too high" and "mocked [his] own littleness." Posing a question that might also have harried Gissing's Sidney Kirkwood, or Dickens's Arthur Clennam, he asks, "Why do I care . . . when I can do so little?" (359, 362). As though in reply, Remington realizes that he has never "suspected the stupendous gap between the chaotic aims, the routine, the conventional acquiescences, the vulgarizations of the personal life, and that clearly conscious development and service of a collective thought and purpose at which my efforts aimed" (358). Here again is the familiar split between Edwardian real and utopian ideal, expressed in the distinctive Wellsian form of a conflict between personal life and collective purpose.

Unable to reconcile himself to a loveless marriage and hobbled political career, Remington escapes with his mistress to the Continent. Consumed by selfish interest, he realizes too late that he has exchanged a noble endeavor to remake the "English will" for "a mere shrivelled remnant of life" (374, 377). Readers of the *Comet* will discern a familiar pattern: once again, a Wells hero is presented as the victim of his own ineluctable passions, while the fundamental elusiveness of power in a modern society is, to that extent, obscured. Remington's abandoned wife protests, "You are not really a *civilized* man at all" (374). One is tempted to observe that the Wells hero resists being civilized all the more ardently for knowing that he has always already failed to be fully liberalized and empowered.

The Machine Stops?

The Central Committee announced [new] developments . . . but they were no more the cause of them than were the kings of the imperialistic period the cause of the war. Rather did they yield to some invincible pressure, which came no one knew whither, and which, when gratified was succeeded by some new pressure equally invincible. To such a state of affairs it is convenient to give the name of progress. No one confessed the Machine was out of hand. Year by year it was served with increased efficiency and decreased intelligence. The better a man knew his own duties upon it, the less he understood the duties of his neighbour, and in all the world there was no one who understood the monster as a whole. Those master brains had perished.

—E. M. FORSTER "THE MACHINE STOPS"

One of the characteristic qualities of the Wellsian split between sexual nature and socialist utopia is, therefore, a disavowal of the potentially progressive aspects of "personal life." In previous chapters I have discussed the importance of the personal stress within Victorian culture. By construing charitable and other voluntary social relations as extensions of family intimacy, such discourses helped to persuade contemporaries that they had escaped the depersonalizing rationality of modern life. Intersubjectivity—the liberal ideal of mutual recognition between moral actors—was the utopian aim of the imagined bridge between domestic and civic life. The same rhetoric of the personal pervaded the late-Victorian and Edwardian movement to organize charity, underpinning the unique character-building relation between the trained volunteer and her "case."

By contrast, Wells's beliefs about male sexuality, including his Huxleyan views on man's animal nature, required a radical distancing from the personal. Although Wells endowed interpersonal relations with an aura of authenticity and emotional intensity, what they entirely lacked was utopian potential. For the COS the infinite extendibility of family intimacy made collective purpose tenable. For Wells, by contrast, personal life was inimical to collective ends: the former so dominated by selfish sexual instinct as to undermine the disinterested reason on which the latter depended. Hence, far from being a microcosm of collectivist utopia, the family was, for Wells, a stumbling block to progress. To overcome the downward pull of sexuality, he argued, the intimate domestic sphere must be succeeded by collective living arrangements that were more rational, egalitarian, efficient, and (thus) liberatory, but also—as a consequence— less personal. In effect Wells anticipated a Freudian view of civilization and its discontents, to be combated by a rationalization of eros. "Utopia," whenever it might happen, would require a rigorous sublimation of libidinal urges. Wells thus aimed to hasten that end when he recommended a deliberate sacrifice of intimacy in the interests of community progress.

Here, I suggest, is what E. M. Forster discerned in Wells's vision when, in 1909, he wrote "The Machine Stops," an anti-utopian story praised for having turned Fabian prophesies "inside out."[20] Isolated in private cells that are networked through a central apparatus, Forster's humanity has come to depend slavishly on mechanical pastorship. The story's uncanny anticipation of the Internet cannot but fascinate turn-of-the-millenium readers; but, for the same reason, it also says much about Forster's relation to Wells almost a century ago. According to Forster's biographer, "The Machine Stops" was written with *In the Days of the Comet* specifically in mind (Furnbank 162 n. 1; cf. Beauman 214; Caporaletti). The author of what is arguably English literature's most imperative plea for intersubjectivity—"Only connect . . . "—undoubtedly found much to disparage in the *Comet*'s attempt to rationalize personal life.[21] That said, it seems likely that Forster's tale of technotopia gone awry also responded to Wells's Fabianesque *Utopia*.

In fact, reducing the "personal element" was precisely the purpose of Forster's Machine, built long ago to liberate humanity by eliminating physical labor and minimizing "vulgar" contact (32). Generations later human society has become utterly dependent and thoroughly atomized. Describing this world, Kuno, a lone rebel, evokes a mechanistic simulacrum: "it is we who are dying" and "the only thing that really lives is the Machine" (23). Forster's dystopia is rigidly impersonal. Communication, which is mediated almost entirely through the Machine, consists chiefly in the circulation of information, the delivery of recycled lectures, and the exchange of vapid "ideas." The Machine transmits visual images, but not "*nuances* of expression" (5). Typical citizens, such as Kuno's biological mother, Vashti (who has hardly seen her son since birth), are terrified by direct experience. The same is true of fresh intellectual experience. What began as an elitist privileging of mental life has culminated in a conformist fetishization of ossified "ideas."

Indeed, the Machine foments an insidious postmodernist epistemology in which the emptiness of the signifier is loudly proclaimed. "Beware of first-hand ideas!" warns a typical lecturer: "First-hand ideas do not really exist. They are but the physical impressions produced by love and fear, and on this gross foundation who could erect a philosophy?" (27). In thus ironizing the Machine's attempt to disavow bodily sensation, Forster goes to the heart of what is troubling in a quasi-Idealist stance like Wells's: one that, in the interests of a metaphysics of corporate mind and will, would submit human flesh and human passions to the superior rationality of machinery. Yet, in invoking "physical impressions," Forster by no means seeks to instate the philosophical materialism of Bentham or the Fabians. What Forster has in mind, rather, is a humanist materialism predicated on a transcendent relation between the sentient body and the human heart. In "robbing us of the sense of space and . . . touch," says Kuno, the Machine "has blurred every human relation." The human telos, both individual and collective, has been supplanted by technological progress: "the Machine proceeds—but not to our goal" (23).

In *A Modern Utopia* Wells depicted a quasi-panoptical system of surveillance achieved through centralized record keeping. To ensure a "world of responsible citizens," he reasoned, society must "devise some scheme by which every person in the world can be promptly and certainly recognised." Yet Forster's tale does not dwell on the threat of what Wells called "organised clairvoyance" (162–63, 165). Although the Machine is equipped with Big Brother–like capabilities—capturing Kuno, for example, when he attempts to escape—Forster's point is neither that citizens' liberties are undermined by covert surveillance, nor that they have interiorized this disciplinary function. Rather, Forster's message is closer in spirit to J. S. Mill's warning against the dangers of paternalistic legislation: "what is done for the people benefits them only when it assists them in what they do for themselves" (qtd. in MacDonagh 68; cf. *On Liberty* 104). Over the course of the tale the deleterious impact of dependence is dramatized as the Machine evolves from a pervasive technological crutch into a fetishized object of worship: "The Machine . . . feeds us and clothes us and houses us; through it we speak to one another, through it we see one another, in it we have our being. . . . [T]he Machine is omnipotent, eternal; blessed is the Machine" (28–29).

Written by an author who located himself at "the fag-end of Victorian liberalism" (qtd. in Furnbank 2), "The Machine Stops" goes far toward establishing the anti-utopian mind-set concisely expressed in the epigraph to *Brave New World*: "Perhaps a new age is beginning, an age in which the intellectuals and the cultivated class will dream of avoiding utopia and of returning to a society that is non-utopian, less 'perfect' but more free" (Nicholas Berdyaev, qtd. in Huxley). In striving for mastery over nature, humankind, "the flower of all flesh," has strangled itself in garments of its own weaving. The alternative to the Machine's antihumanist technological advance—its cultivation of fleshless pseudointellect—is a visceral return to "muscles and the nerves." At the end of the story the Machine breaks down, destroying the entire civilization. Forster concludes with a vision of apocalypse redeemed by intersubjective possibility: "I am dying," Kuno tells his mother as their bodies merge through kisses, blood, and tears, "but we touch, we talk, not through the Machine" (36). Articulating a powerful humanist mandate, Forster in this way calls for an end to the imaginative split between real and ideal.

To read Wells from Forster's point of view is thus to repudiate an insidious fore-closure on "the personal element," and a dangerous privileging of materialistic and technological progress in the interests of efficiency. But to do so is also to overlook the difference between Wells and the Fabians while obscuring the evidence of Wells's profound attachment to liberal ideals much like Forster's own. Forster had been inspired by the liberal philosophy of C. F. G. Masterman, a writer and radical member of Parliament. But Masterman's portrait of a society without "evident system, or mutual dependence, or effort towards an organic whole" might easily have been drawn by Wells (qtd. in Beauman 219). Of course, Forster's repugnance to scientific progress bordered on technophobia, while Wells, a lifelong science buff, tended toward the other extreme. That said, Forster's fear that a "soul" such as his own would be "crushed out" by technological advance resonates with Wells's ambivalence toward the comet (qtd. in Beauman 214).

Wells and Forster are most alike in their common apprehension of diminished individuality and diffused modern power. In the *Comet* an "aimless energy" propels everything from newspapers to the monstrous waste of capitalist competition, and imperialistic war. This unlocatable power is analogous to the "invincible pressure, which came no one knew whither"—the power that drives the Machine towards self-destructive "progress" (29). This crucial passage (quoted at length in the earlier epigraph) makes clear that Forster envisioned the Machine as the technological facilitator of indirect social relations, not a directive master agency. As a technophobe, Forster readily understood the diminished individual as a product of specialization: "The better a man knew his own duties . . . the less he understood the duties of his neighbour." As a technophile, Wells was more likely to extol the liberatory potential of scientific advance. But, in describing the world around them, both writers agreed that "there was no one who understood the monster as a whole." Like Mill before them, both Wells and Forster knew that to apprehend modern civilization was to recognize that the "master brains had perished."

New Liberalism

Nothing would be more fatal than for the Government of States to get in the hands of experts. Expert knowledge is limited knowledge: and the unlimited ignorance of the plain man who knows where it hurts is a safer guide than any vigorous direction of a specialized character.

— WINSTON CHURCHILL TO H.G. WELLS

If I had to sum up the immediate future of democratic politics in a single word I should say "Insurance." That is the future.

—WINSTON CHURCHILL, "THE BUDGET AND

NATIONAL INSURANCE"

"There was no common idea at all" (*Comet* 673). So laments the hero of Wells's *Comet* in a statement as pertinent to the literature of this era, as to divisions within the 1905–9 Royal Commission on the New Poor Law. While the COS saw character building as the common aim around which to mobilize an army of trained volunteers, the Fabians insisted that only technocrats were competent to promote national efficiency. Late-Victorian and Edwardian literature recoiled from both pastoral projects, without successfully imagining a compromise. As liberal humanists, the writers of the period hallowed the self-originating force of character, cherished personal intimacy, aspired to cultivating individuality, and dreamed of intersubjective utopia. As realists and beneficiaries of socialist critique, they recognized that these humanist possibilities could not be isolated from underlying material conditions. The disjunctive tensions of their writings thus characterize the era's dueling worldviews.

Here, then, in the widening gulf between unrealizable moral ideal and ominous material reality was a mandate for the invention and mass production of a new turn-of-the-century tradition: the revamped liberalism of Winston Churchill and David Lloyd George.[22] Churchill's Edwardian speeches were a rhetorical triumph, playing off Fabian and COS antitheses to evoke buoyant New Liberal syntheses. Speaking in 1906, Churchill married liberalism to socialism, vowing simultaneously to preserve the "vigour of competition," and "to mitigate the consequences of failure" (82). Civilization, he argued in Bosanquet's evolutionary vein, depends on "competitive selection." But, he insisted, that is no reason to object to the Liberal Party's provision of (politically popular) old-age pensions. Such measures would not interfere with self-reliance but would merely "strap a lifebelt around" the laborer, the "buoyancy" of which, "aiding his own strenuous exertions, ought to enable him to reach the shore" (208, 210).

Old-age pensions and school meals were the means by which New Liberal politicians proposed "to spread a net over the abyss" without hazard to Britain's mythic entrepreneurial spirit (82–83). Nevertheless, the centerpiece of what was "new" in this reconstructed liberalism was the (German-originated) notion of national insurance: a social security measure rhetorically amplified to suggest a quasi-collectivist foundation for national progress. The landmark National Insurance Act of 1911 was not a compromise between the two rival Poor Law reports, but a maneuver, in the words of one contemporary, to "render . . . both unnecessary" (John Burns, qtd. in Fraser 163; cf. Searle 252–53). Offering guaranteed unemployment benefit in exchange for workers' compulsory contributions, the act was not, as it might seem, a "half-way house to socialism," but, rather, a bulwark for private property. By providing nonstigmatic support for the unemployed, the act established a minimal basis for national efficiency.[23] It thus appeared to obviate Fabianism's pastoral state and even radical socialist demands for the collectivization of wealth. Yet, for the very same reason, the act "cut the ground" from beneath the COS's call for stiffened deterrence and rigorous self-reliance. Indeed, both Lloyd George and Churchill argued that the notion of "undeserving poor" was irrelevant to the premise of "universal entitlement earned by contributions." Churchill in particular declared himself unwilling to mix up "moralities and mathematics"—a point to which I will return (qtd. in Fraser 162, 172; cf. Searle 253).[24]

Historians sometimes attribute the Liberals' preference for National Insurance to Lloyd George's opportunism and political savvy (Perkin, *Rise* 208; Fraser 162–63, 173–75; Searle 249). Be that as it may, the conflicts I have described were the underlying context for that calculated move. The politics of the day pitted individual liberty against social equality, self-help against national efficiency. Yet, as Alfred Marshall's revised political economy suggests, many leading authorities saw formal collectivism of some kind as the only viable means to countering individual powerlessness in a mass capitalist society. Edwardian policy makers were thus charged simultaneously with promoting prosperity and preserving character when, in fact, the integrity of the latter had long been questionable. Precisely because they proposed a cure for something ailing, both of the commission's reports betrayed the vulnerable condition of the Victorian era's most hallowed myth.

By contrast, New Liberal rhetoric might pay lip service to character without constituting it as a direct object of state action. Rather than officious pastorship in any form, New Liberalism offered a comparatively unobtrusive link between the individual and the state—much like the early-Victorian ideal of aloof, disinterested government. Indeed, Churchill might have said "Whig" when, in 1909, while campaigning on an insurance platform, he defined a Liberal as "a man who . . . stand[s] as a restraining force against . . . extravagant policy" (303). In a 1902 letter to Wells, Churchill proclaimed his old-fashioned allegiance to the administrative capabilities of the "plain man," insisting that "nothing would be more fatal" than to entrust the state to the "limited knowledge" of experts (qtd. in Perkin, *Rise* 169). If National Insurance lacked the pastoral embrace of Fabian technocracy or COS casework, it did not pry, visibly coerce, or moralize. Not the dawn of a new philosophy, but a restrained approach to the play of contrary extravagances was the significance of the measure (Harris, "Society" 69–70).

"A man of his day" like Gissing's Jasper Milvain, Lloyd George may well have seized upon the New Liberal agenda at least partly for political gain. In so doing, he penetrated the logic of liberalism as elucidated by the later essays of Michel Foucault. In opting for National Insurance's balanced check between voluntarism and compulsion, Lloyd George recognized that, "if one governed too much, one did not govern at all" ("Space" 242). Like Foucault's revised model of power, New Liberalism encouraged social welfare comparatively indirectly: neither as tutelary state nor as personal benefactor but as a mode of action upon the action of others.

Campaigning in 1908, Winston Churchill argued that "Socialism assails the maximum preeminence of the individual," whereas New Liberalism "seeks to build up the minimum standard of the masses" (qtd. in Fraser 163). In the slippage between the individual preeminence that socialism putatively destroys, and the standardized mass that liberalism explicitly promotes, John Stuart Mill's 1836 analysis of modernity—in which power passes from individuals to masses—becomes the policy of Edwardian government. The turn-of-the-century rhetoric of insurance was, in this respect, fundamentally unlike the early- and mid-Victorian rhetoric of self-generating character.[25] Nevertheless, in distinguishing between morality (the subject of personal relations in civil society) and mathematics (the properly impersonal object of state initiative), Churchill created the basis for a new liberal mythology without necessarily dismantling the old: "The wonderful century which followed the . . . downfall of the Napoleonic domination, which secured to this small island so long and so resplendent a reign, has come to an end. We have arrived at a new time. Let us realise it. And with that new time strange methods, huge forces, larger combinations—a Titanic world— have sprung up around us. The foundations of our power are changing. . . . We must go forward. . . . We will go forward into a way of life more earnestly viewed, more scientifically organised, more consciously national than any we have known" (317). The progressive "way of life" to which Churchill pointed was predicated on insurance: "Insurance against dangers from abroad, Insurance against dangers scarcely less grave and much more near" (309). By thus taking full advantage of the word's rhetorical force, Churchill invented a foundation to replace, at least for a time, the flagging symbolic power of character in a world of "combined forces." Insurance could provide the absent "common idea" decried by Wells and others. An invented tradition in an age of mass politics, insurance was conspicuously national and morally neutral. In this form it promised to protect workers against fatalities beyond their control without impinging on liberties that were the hallowed birthright of every Briton.[26]

Nevertheless, if Churchill's "Titanic world" seems to anticipate a more ambitious "organisation" than that afforded by a modest unemployment benefit, that is probably because he privately recognized that a "tremendous policy in Social Organisation" might eventually be built under the New Liberal banner (qtd. in Fraser 173). Lloyd George's pre-1914 measures were but the rudiments of an efficiency state that, prior to the war, cautious and self-reliant Britons remained reluctant to endorse. Although the New Liberal agenda consigned the Poor Law to gradual desuetude, insurance did not, as we have seen, even profess to provide intrusive pastorship. At "no time prior to the Second World War," writes George Behlmer, "did English social casework offer anything resembling a coherent 'programme'" for working-class discipline ("Character Building" 18–19). Britain's eventual readiness to expand the purview of the state—in essence, the close of a liberal era based on the putative self-reliance of individuals—did not, by and large, develop until after the debacle of another world war. The welfare state that eventually emerged was a triumph of social policy over socialism.

Although a full-scale account of the circumstances surrounding the welfare state is well beyond the scope of this study, there are at least two insights that analysis of Victorian and Edwardian governance may contribute to that end. The first was the subject of chapter 4: that particular aura of classed gentility which mid-Victorian civil service reformers, novelists such as Anthony Trollope, and essayists such as Matthew Arnold brought to the idea of disinterested government by well-bred men. As Winston Churchill's entrenched distrust of "experts" testifies, New Liberalism was neither ready nor willing to transfer the pastoral mantle from highborn gentlemen to déclassé technocrats.

The second insight concerns the welfare state's unquestionable debts to the philanthropic visiting practice that originated with Thomas Chalmers, and reached a head in the Charity Organization Society. Clearly, the charitable casework of women such as Helen Dendy and Beatrice Webb was crucial in breaking down resistance to the professionalization, if not necessarily to the state bureaucratization, of social work. The dramatic twentieth-century "rise" of professional society thus entailed men's appropriation of women's long-evolving pastoral authority. Women's "feminine" claims on voluntary social work lost out to men's "masculine" claims on well-paid, high-status employment. Nonetheless, it seems clear that the high profile of women such as Octavia Hill, Helen Dendy, and Beatrice Webb helped to facilitate a solution to the problem of dueling worldviews.[27] Their quasi-feminine, quasi-professional authority enabled the momentous transition from a moral pastorship, predicated on the symbolic capital of the personal, to a modern pastorship predicated on the subtly gendered, well-bred, and therefore suitably "English" symbolic capital of the public service professional.

Epilogue: Social Security

> The term, "local self-government," signifying as it does the direct indi-
> vidual knowledge of the local affairs of the local unit of administration
> and the participation of the ratepayer in the expenditure of his own
> money, is in the majority of cases a mischievous fallacy. As the demands of
> attention to his own personal or private affairs increase, the citizen's
> . power of attention to the public affairs of increasing magnitude dimin-
> ishes, and he is obliged to let his local affairs go as they may to persons of
> whose fitness he has no knowledge, and with whom he has only an infini-
> tesimal power of interfering.
> — EDWIN CHADWICK, *On the Evils of Disunity in
> Central and Local Administration*

> The aim of optimal social security combined with maximum independ-
> ence is clear enough. As to attaining it . . .
> —MICHEL FOUCAULT, "SOCIAL SECURITY"

"It is but a small portion of the public business of a country," wrote John Stuart
Mill in 1861, "which can be well done, or safely attempted, by the central
authorities." While Mill had long before discerned that modern civilization
diminished the power of individuals, he held nevertheless that local self-
government and civic participation were crucial countermeasures. To "nourish"
public spirit and diffuse intelligence, citizens not only must vote but must also
take part in local affairs—acting, thinking, and speaking for the community interest (*Representative* 286). Three decades later Mill's directive became a central
tenet of British Idealism. Building citizen character, according to Bernard
Bosanquet, required locating "some plan or value in the circumstances that press
upon us, in relation to which we can assert ourselves." Not passive laissez faire
but active commitment to a common purpose was the route to reclaiming the
individual from the "modern wilderness of interests" ("Duties" 5–6).

In a contemporaneous Fabian essay Sidney Webb envisioned a rather different means of resolving the problem of individual powerlessness: "By himself the typical Londoner is a frail and sickly unit, cradled in the gutter, housed in a slum, slaving in a sweater's den, and dying in the workhouse infirmary. Collectively he is a member of the greatest and most magnificent city which the world has known, commanding all the latest resources of civilization, and disposing of almost boundless wealth" (*London* 207). Transforming the sweated, pauperized laborer into the prosperous citizen of a modern utopia, Webb's rhetorical sleight of hand elided the matter of means. By what tremendous agency was a world of frail and sickly units metamorphosed into the beneficiaries of collective wealth? When H. G. Wells attempted to answer that question, he produced two forbidding replies: the "clairvoyant" state of *A Modern Utopia*, and the "suffocating" calm of the Great Change. In yet another variation on the theme Forster imagined an elaborate pastoral and communications network and called it the Machine. In a 1983 interview Michel Foucault described its late-twentieth-century incarnation—the modern welfare state—in terms of "perverse effects." For Foucault, as for Forster, the same bureaucratic mechanisms that aim to safeguard individual welfare also foster "increasing rigidity" and "a growth of dependence" ("Social" 160).

In one of the few Fabianesque images to appear in the *Comet*, Wells describes the "gigantic consolidations and gigantic economies" effected in the wake of atmospheric change. "One was a Titan in that Etna," Wells exults (696), in a fleeting affirmation of collectivization's capacity to empower individuals. But elsewhere the *Comet*'s utopia is rife with contradiction. The transformed humanity of Wells's brave new world gleefully burn the "deeds, documents, debts [and] vindictive records" of a destructive materialistic age (700). Yet Leadford becomes a professional secretary and statistician—one of those experts, perhaps, whose "limited knowledge" Winston Churchill contrasted to the "plain man who knows where it hurts" (qtd. in Perkin, *Rise* 169).

At the close of the *Comet* an unnamed narrator, whose discovery of Leadford's manuscript frames the tale, recoils from what he has read. As usual, sex is the ostensible culprit, with the narrator offended by Leadford's extramarital affair with Nettie. Once again, Wells's problematic overtures toward sexual liberation serve as a decoy for more fundamental objections to the Great Change. "In a manner," the narrator explains, the comet "had dehumanised the world, had robbed it of its spites, its intense jealousies, its inconsistencies, its humour" (708). Seen from this view, the comet produces a total bureaucratizing effect that seventy years of British poor law administration had been unable to impose. Like modern legal rationality, the comet subdues "every purely personal, especially irrational and incalculable, feeling" (Weber, *Law* 351). Ironically, then, Wells's socialist confraternity is born of the same formalized impersonality that Weber had claimed for the service of capitalism.

A 1982 study of twentieth-century Britain suggests that, to some degree, both the Fabians' and the Charity Organization Society's goals materialized. Alongside the massive state expansion of the post–World War II era, Britain also experienced an "unprecedented" proliferation of pluralistic voluntary organizations. The author concludes that both the state and the individual had, paradoxically, become less powerful than they had been under the restricted centralization and limited democracy of mid-Victorian liberalism (Beer; Harris, "Society" 63). Thus, Mill's 1836 prognosis holds for the later developments of an advanced liberal society: power passes from the relatively autonomous individual to diffused social practices that, both inside and out of the state, influence a dependent and atomized mass. A similar eventuality was anticipated by Edwin Chadwick, who, decades after having been forced out of public service, proclaimed his old nemesis, "local self-government," to be "a mischievous fallacy." In a world increasingly reliant on specialized knowledge and bureaucratic management, Chadwick believed, citizens are practically obliged to abdicate their affairs to strangers with whom they have "only an infinitesimal power of interfering" (qtd. in Hanham 383). The choice Chadwick presented was less between local and centralized government, or voluntary and state action, than between good experts and bad.

In such a society liberty can never be a passive inheritance. "The liberty of men is never assured by the institutions and laws that are intended to guarantee them . . . 'liberty' is what must be *exercised*" ("Space" 245). This exhortation to the individual's latent participatory power was integral to Mill's tenuous vision of human progress. In the preceding chapter I have demonstrated its far-reaching impact on a range of late-Victorian and Edwardian moderns. Caught in the clash between dueling worldviews, the men and women of this era struggled to retain their Millite commitment to liberty's positive "exercise" even as they helped to build Machines to serve human needs in a modern society. While the quotation thus encapsulates the most utopian of ends in an age less reticent toward utopias than our own, it was not written by Mill, but by Michel Foucault.[1] For those who study the past, Foucault's late works present a way of rethinking utopian possibility along with an implicit historiographic mandate. To leave behind the disciplinary monolith in favor of liberalism's tenacious paradoxes is, at the very least, to return to the problem of pastorship as the Victorians saw it.

And perhaps it is also more than that. When Charles Mowat wrote his history of the Charity Organization Society in 1961, he characterized the belief in "individual responsibility" as "an outdated idea" (xi). Similarly, in his 1967 introduction to *A Modern Utopia* Mark Hillegas claimed that Wells's quasi-dystopian statism "represent[ed] . . . the inevitable forward movement of our culture" (xviii). Yet within twenty years of these pronouncements a major sea change occurred. The year 1989 saw scholars ceasing to write of liberalism "in terms of crisis or collapse," and beginning to write "in terms of . . . tensions and contradictions—in short, the language used to describe the workings of a hegemonic movement or ideology" (Soper and Schmidt-Nowara 88). Francis Fukuyama's landmark essay set the stage for this shift, proclaiming that the post–Cold War triumph of liberalism had marked the "End of History." But, even earlier, one found Margaret Thatcher invoking "Victorian values" (qtd. in Himmelfarb, *De-Moralization* 3), while Ronald Reagan extolled free trade, in Gladstonean terms, as the foundation of "human progress and peace among nations" (qtd. in D. Gordon). Such echoes of Victorian-era liberalism have intensified, culminating in welfare reforms harking back to the days of Chalmers and Chadwick, the privatization of public services, deregulation, and "charitable choice" initiatives evoking the legacy of the COS and its ilk (see Willis).

Yet, in likening neoliberalism to its Victorian precursors, I do not mean to suggest a simple turning back of the clock. The question of pastorship is no longer reducible, as it once seemed to be, to "the dream or nightmare" of statism (N. Rose 38). Edwardians such as H. G. Wells were poised between the individualized morality of the nineteenth century, and the socialized needs of the welfare state. Today, by contrast, the welfare state has itself become the object of attack (e.g., Himmelfarb, *Poverty* 381–89; *De-Moralization* 221–57).[2] What Nikolas Rose calls "advanced liberal rule" has thus sought "to degovernmentalize the State and to de-statize practices of government," relocating the pastoral mission to a market "governed by the rationalities of competition, accountability and consumer demand" (41). This marketized governmentality asks us to imagine Forster's Machine as a commercial invention. The subject of neoliberal governance is, like the inhabitant of one of Forster's cells, a consumer-individual who maximizes "quality of life through acts of choice." Hence, the intensive pastorship imagined by the Fabians and their COS rivals has given way to "the private counsellor, the self-help manual," and the virtual or telephone helpline (N. Rose 57, 58). Pastorship, in other words, remains as vexing a question for today's progressives as it was for their Victorian forebears. Critics on the Left have offered powerful critiques of social control, but have yet to imagine alternatives to the market's allegedly liberating approach to producing responsible citizens.

Significantly, the influential liberal theory of the late John Rawls evades the issue of pastorship entirely. For Mill, as for Wells, the foundation of a liberal society was a citizenry capable of identifying the public good with individual interest. For Rawls, by contrast, notions of the good are deliberately cast as pluralized, private pursuits. Whereas Mill had emphasized liberty, identifying it with the fundamentally pastoral aim of promoting individual development and civic participation, Rawls emphasizes justice, and defines it in terms of formal guarantees on "basic rights" and "political liberties" (5). In effect, Rawls assumes that pastorship is a fait accompli: that individuals already possess the "intellectual and moral capacities proper to" citizenship; that men and women "are grown up before they have been born" (Bridges 6; Benhabib 157). In so doing, Rawls distances the liberal project from many root concerns. He neither queries the nature of human freedom, nor negotiates the tensions between positive and negative liberty, nor addresses the question of whether illiberal conceptions of the good may properly constitute a liberal society.[3] Rawls thus advocates equality (as a procedural enterprise), yet evokes a society as atomized and, potentially, as divisive as Wells's dysfunctional pre-comet world.

Yet, if Rawls calls for equality without respect to the pastoral aim of character building, Francis Fukuyama may be seen to call for character building without equality. Fukuyama, that is, declares that liberal democracy is the "end of history," yet further insists that it produces an effete society of Nietzschean "last men," or "men without chests" (300). Hence, Fukuyama's ultimate purpose in privileging liberalism is to subject it to right-wing critique. Equal rights, he argues, may satisfy human needs sufficiently to mark the end of history; but liberal democracies fail to gratify still deeper urges for human greatness.

Significantly, Fukuyama's (superficially Hegelian) notion of liberalism is founded on Rawlsian rather than Millite premises. In Mill's thought normative conceptions of the good appear frequently, as when Mill asserts—to take one memorable example—that it is better to be "Socrates dissatisfied" than a satisfied fool or pig ("Utilitarianism" 281). By contrast, the society Fukuyama evokes recognizes the equal legitimacy of "all lifestyles and values," while refusing to distinguish between "better and worse, good and bad" (305, 306). Hence, as Fukuyama sees it, the goal of the political Left is to forward processes of equalization which have already gone too far. To make this argument, Fukuyama must minimize the importance of socioeconomic inequalities: the very inequalities that were dramatically increasing when his thesis first appeared, and have continued to rise since that time. By thus setting aside the effects of material disadvantage (as Rawls would not), Fukuyama relegates the post-1989 Left to the risible goal of neutralizing differences of talent, beauty, and physique.

Nevertheless, it is important to note that what Fukuyama thus casts as a conservative Nietzschean critique of liberalism is, at bottom, the same diminished individuality that troubled Mill. "It is not an accident that people in democratic societies are preoccupied with material gain," Fukuyama writes (305). Human beings, he adds, "will want to be citizens rather than *bourgeois*" (314), implying that liberalism—which is to say, the atomized procedural liberalism that he himself has defined as the end of history—works to repress the development of *homo civicus*. As described by Fukuyama, liberalism is thus antithetical to character building, not only because of materialism, but also because effete liberal tendencies such as "compassion and equality" breed "potentially debilitating spiritual effects" (313). Indeed, according to this prescription, citizenship in a liberal society must be entrusted to society's least liberal tendencies: the *über*-building effects of capitalist competition, and the antiegalitarianism and traditional communitarianism valued by conservatives.

Ironically, Fukuyama's conservative critique of liberalism might constitute the basis of a Left-liberal and Millite critique of liberal democracy as theorized by Rawls. What Rawls's procedural liberalism lacks, according to Charles Taylor, is precisely a way of accounting for the cohesiveness necessary to a functioning democracy ("Cross Purposes"). The autonomous self on whom Rawls predicates his theory is, writes Seyla Benhabib, "disembedded and disembodied" (157). Proceduralists ignore the "ontological" question of how republics work to foster affective bonds between anonymous members of the imagined community (Taylor, "Liberal Politics" 276). For Mill this crucial community-building effect, including the social embeddedness of developing selves, was built into the pastoral function itself. To "cultivate and call forth" individuality, he believed, was simultaneously to "strengthen the tie which binds every individual to the race" (*Liberty* 109). Embracing atomist assumptions that Mill fought hard to contest, proceduralist liberals abandon the character-building and community concerns that ignited Victorian literature. Mill's latter-day heirs neglect that aspect of his thought which recognizes the social situation of human agents, and, simultaneously, prizes liberty and individuality "very highly" (Taylor, "Cross-Purposes" 185). In so doing, they enable conservatives such as Fukuyama to dismiss the pastoral credentials of the Left.

Foucault's discernment of these political challenges, I believe, catalyzed the revision of his own Nietzschean project. Whereas the genealogical analysis of power was developed in response to Marxist dilemmas, the later essays offer a fitting rejoinder to the ever more grandiose claims of free-market neoliberals. As a genealogist, Foucault saw that the socialist dream of utopian transformation committed the Left to completing a bourgeois social project not unlike Bentham's—a project that "in its totalising ambitions of exhaustive control, spells death to the relatively plural forms of popular democratic social organization . . . which socialists in fact want to bring about" (Minson 222). Foucault thus speaks as both liberal and radical when he writes that liberation "can only come from attacking . . . the very roots" of the prevailing political rationality, especially its totalizing and normalizing effects ("Politics" 85). What is, or should be, different about socialism is not the *form* of governance it offers, but the *object* (Minson 223). Hence, the radicalization and liberalization of political rationality must involve, first and foremost, new ways of thinking about pastorship—which is to say, ways of promoting new kinds of subjectivities (Foucault, "Subject" 216). To move beyond raison d'état and beyond the new free-market orthodoxy, pastorship must involve ways of strengthening individuals without, in so doing, engineering their conformity.

Pastorship also comes to the fore in Amartya Sen's influential writings on globalization. Sen has argued against Rawls and others that what is crucial to global development is not the proliferation of commodities themselves, but, rather, the consequences that commodities may or may not generate: "the substantive freedoms," and the "capabilities . . . to choose a life one has reason to value" (74). Here is a line of politico-economic thinking which resonates with the concerns of Mill and Foucault. With their powerful return to pastoral questions, Foucault's late essays thus mark a shift from an analytics of exhaustive control to an inquiry into liberty's present-day foundations. Victorian literature's intense reflections on character and governance in a liberal society cannot but provide a valuable resource for this most timely critical enterprise; as well as the opportunity to imagine the history of a different kind of present.

Notes

Preface

1. For all its longevity the *new historicism* remains ambiguous, a term that, as Gallagher and Greenblatt attest, "has been applied to an extraordinary assortment of critical practices" (2).

2. In his conservative critiques of today's right-wing dogmas, Gray uses the term *paleoliberalism* to describe the recent rise of "market fundamentalism" (see *Beyond* and *Enlightenment's*, chap. 7). For a left critique of a related phenomenon, "market populism," see Frank.

3. For a concise (if openly partisan) account of British liberalism, see Bradley, who distinguishes between the negative libertarianism of the first half of the nineteenth century, and the later positive effort to liberate the downtrodden from "poverty, illness, bad housing, and inadequate education" (26). This shift corresponds to what political theorists typically describe as the distinction between *classical liberalism*, with its focus on emancipating individual self-interest, and *modern liberalism*, with its counter-investment in developing citizenship and community.

4. An exception to the narrowing trend is Warner's trenchant response to Frow, which argues that the critique of neoliberalism would be more powerful were Frow to "lay claim to those [other] parts of liberal thought" which can be seen to motivate Frow's own political goals (431–32).

5. On the continuing importance of the civic republican tradition in the nineteenth century, see Pocock, *Virtue*; and *Machiavellian*; as well as Burrow. Kaufmann's Pocock-influenced account of classical liberalism and the novel in the late eighteenth and early nineteenth centuries focuses on the tensions between propertarian rights and distributive justice. Dowling, by way of explaining the eventual emergence of a homosexual counterdiscourse, concentrates on the Hellenistic liberalism that, through mid-Victorian Oxford, modified what had been a martial civic republican ideal along classical and German-Romantic lines. On the modern liberalism of the post–French Revolutionary era, see also Skorupski, "Introduction"; Kahan; Stafford; and Gibbins; and, on its eventual efflorescence in British Idealism, den Otter. On religion's influence, see Hilton; Burrow; Collini, *Public*; Taylor, *Sources*; and R. K. Webb, "Emergence."

6. Bentham's thought is also artificially simplified by this perspective: for Bentham

paradoxically assumed a natural harmony of interests while calling for tutelage to maximize happiness (see, e.g., Conway, esp. 75).

7. In restricting my view of the Victorian state to centralized bureaucratic institutions and the surrounding debates, my approach differs markedly from that of Lloyd and Thomas. In *Culture and the State* (1998) Lloyd and Thomas follow a selective reading of Gramsci, arguing that the allegedly private "institutions of civil society . . . are actually part of" a unified and hegemonic "state formation" (21). At the same time, they insist that Matthew Arnold's philosophy of governance, with its embrace of Continental statism, was dominant throughout the nineteenth century—an assertion that, as my own work on civil service reform especially suggests, is highly debatable (see chap. 4). Hence, while *Culture and the State* contains many important insights, it tends to ignore what is of central importance to the account of Victorian governance offered in this book: that is, the intense privileging of "self-governing" activities; the reflexive recoil from statist bureaucracy; and, as a result, the "pastoral" dilemmas that faced Victorian Britain and, indeed, continue to face any self-consciously liberal society.

8. See also Nunokawa, who has argued that our historical understanding of the impact of embourgeoisement "may owe its largest debt . . . to the Victorian novel and its narrative heirs; for here, the diffuse, diffusive, subject of commodification comes home" (4). Childers has granted a special "constitutive status" to novels, arguing that novelistic discourse gained primacy over reports and treatises, "subsuming" them and "reshaping" the epistemological and ontological boundaries of, for example, parliamentary politics (*Novel* 4, 47, 40). I have not followed Childers in tracing a competition between literary and nonliterary discourses.

9. Unfortunately, I have been unable to devote space to the interesting question of where and how formal differences between various novelists illuminate the relation between literature and governance.

ONE: Beyond the Panopticon

1. The term *genealogy* refers primarily to *Discipline and Punish*, the first volume of *The History of Sexuality*, and related essays such as "Nietzsche, Genealogy, History."

2. Patterson has argued that genealogy's model of "dominance and subordination" "drain[s] the heterogeneity and conflict out of culture, and with them the possibility of change" (261). For Eagleton the positing of a uniform, omnipresent "power," like the accompanying shift from "ideology" to "discourse," erases meaningful difference (7–8). According to Walzer, Foucault's relativist and contingent conceptions of truth and knowledge permit "no independent standpoint, no possibility for the development of critical principals" (64). There is, of course, a vast critical literature devoted to Foucault's works. In addition to those I have already cited, I have also benefited especially from Habermas, *Philosophical*; Hoy, "Introduction"; and Said, "Foucault."

3. Rather than acknowledge culture, either as the site of ideological contest or as the medium of everyday life, Foucault asks us to consider power relations as they are first articulated in institutional structures, then gradually disseminated through intangible net-

works and, ultimately, inscribed in subjectivities. From the genealogical perspective "culture" is an essentialist category, much like the Marxist's "ideology" or the Romantic's "self."

4. According to Pat Thane, the eighteenth-century state "had the will and the capacity to influence the lives of citizens" but "did so by methods markedly less visible than those of its European counterparts." Britain's "amateur administration," drawn from the local gentry and magistracy, "evaded the resentment aroused" by French officials and their "more openly severe legal powers" (5, 4). See also Brewer.

5. On the importance of civic republicanism, see Pocock, *Machiavellian;* and *Virtue.* Paraphrasing the former, Collini defines *civic republicanism* as a "commitment to fostering the moral qualities appropriate to a citizen in a free state" (*Public* 95). On the Norman Yoke, see Christopher Hill. Throughout this study I generally use *British* rather than *English* to denote the national identity of Victorians, except where I am citing other authors. There are, of course, potentially significant differences between the two. On the nineteenth-century consolidation of "Britishness," see Colley. On the ubiquitous contrast between free Britons and tyrannized Continentals, see Colley; and Goodlad, "Middle Class."

6. Yet another important interpretation, Lubenow's "incrementalist" approach, explains Victorian administrative history as a slowly evolving compromise between social pressures demanding centralized interference, and long-standing traditions of local self-government. For a useful summary of the debate, see Fraser 111–17. Poovey has argued that the historians' debate relies upon a specious distinction between charisma and historical process (*Making* 98–114). For a different view, see Goodlad, "England's."

7. According to McCandless, supervision under the Metropolitan Lunacy Commission was largely "a sham" ("Dangerous" 90); according to Bartrip, mining inspectors throughout the century testified to the "monstrous impossibility" of their visiting every workplace (79). For comparable observations on prisons, see DeLacy and Henriques "Separate."

8. On Tocqueville's contrast between France's reliance on "la tutelle" and Britain's "free moeurs," see Siedentop 164–71; Marx's belief that Britain lacked a "ready-made state machinery" was noted by Lenin 33–34; G. M. Young argued that the English bourgeoisie imitated the institutions of the upper classes (75); Gramsci, articulating the crucial give-and-take of Victorian Britain's constitutional consensus, pointed out that Britain's middle classes gained economic supremacy, yet left "the old land-owning class [to] preserve its position of virtual monopoly" (18); Weber's works are peppered with illuminating references to Britain's exceptional status, some of which I cite below; I also cite Taylor's and Foucault's remarks below.

9. On the *Constitutional Code*, see Hume, "Jeremy Bentham" 365–70; and *Bentham* 5–6. On the importance of public opinion, see Blake 3–4.

10. On genealogy's nonsubstantive approach to analyzing power, a Nietzschean innovation, see Schrift 187–88.

11. See Althusser, esp. 162–74; and, for a helpful critique, Eagleton 136–56.

12. My ideas on governmentality are based primarily on "The Subject and Power," "Governmentality," "Space, Knowledge, and Power," "Social Security," and "Politics and Reason."

13. As Foucault eventually acknowledged, genealogical analysis tends to emphasize objectifying domination at the expense of subject-making processes. In the absence of the latter, human subjectivity is reduced to the application of power on docile bodies: "The soul is the effect and instrument of a political anatomy; the soul is the prison of the body" (*Discipline* 30). In his later works Foucault stressed the importance of subjectivizing processes, or "the way a human being turns him—or herself—into a subject" ("Subject" 208; cf. 212).

14. I allude to early-Victorian reforms such as the 1834 New Poor Law, the introduction of the Metropolitan Police in 1828, and the Police Act of 1839. On the uneven implementation of police reforms, see Emsley, especially 41–61.

15. Marx and Engels critiqued the illusory freedom of laissez faire in the *Manifesto*, describing bourgeois freedom as, in effect, the freedom of capital rather than people (485–86). In his trenchant post-Marxist reply to present-day libertarians, Cohen argues that the state's protection of property, so far from negative, constitutes a positive curb on the freedom of nonproprietors (56–57).

16. On the use of blasphemy law to repress political dissidence, see Marsh 78–126. Another crucial aspect of state force was, of course, its colonial deployment. As Radhakamal Mukerjee has observed, "It is striking that English . . . statesmen became adherents of the doctrine of free trade," when the advancement of British industry had depended on colonial force abroad and tariffs at home (qtd. in Chomsky 362–63). On the de-industrialization of India under British rule, see Moore, "India."

17. Although not explicitly committed to Foucault's work on governmentality, Poovey's introductory analysis in *Making the Social Body* seems to provide a view of nineteenth-century developments as structured by this kind of abstraction (see 1–24).

18. "The English," Foucault explains, "did not develop a comparable ['police'] system, mainly because of the parliamentary tradition on one hand, and the tradition of local, communal autonomy on the other, not to mention the religious system" ("Space" 241; cf. *Discipline* 213).

19. Foucault argues that the "word *rationalization* is dangerous. What we have to do is analyze specific rationalities rather than always invoking the progress of rationalization in general" ("Subject" 210).

20. Following Roland Barthes and Pierre Bourdieu, I view such myths as powerful representational devices through which worldviews were naturalized, authorized, and sustained (see Barthes; Bourdieu 163–70).

21. Raymond Williams has described Mill's attempt to synthesize Bentham's and Coleridge's legacies as "a prologue to a very large part of the subsequent history of English thinking" (*Culture* 49).

22. In this way Weber's emphasis on *what* may be contrasted to Foucault's genealogical emphasis on *how*. For comparisons between Weber and Foucault, see Dandeker 23, 27; Rabinow, "Introduction" 267; and Colin Gordon, who argues that "Weber is as innocent as Foucault of the so-called Weberianism that adopts a uniform, monolithic conception of historical phenomena of rationalization" ("Soul" 293–94).

23. See also Burrow, who describes character as the more democratic nineteenth-

century successor to the civic virtue idealized by the eighteenth-century ruling classes (89); Hadley, who sees *character* as "Victorian liberalism's chief creation," a concept that, paradoxically, "relies on and effaces its origins in property" and the attendant class system (14); and Glover, for whom Victorian character was a "function of human willpower, a disciplined effort called into play by the idiosyncracies of the self and the vagaries of one's situation" (60).

24. For a critique of liberalism's constitutive inability to deliver on the emancipatory pretensions of liberal imperialism, see Mehta.

25. I do not suggest that social scientific knowledge and the symbolic power of class were mutually exclusive. Clearly, social science could and often did provide evidence to justify the truth claims of class and other differences. My point is simply that the mid-Victorian gentleman's upper-class character could be successfully constructed without such aid.

26. A crucial exception was Mill's readiness to accept native "childishness" as a justification for empire. For a thoroughgoing critique, see Mehta.

27. Here Mill articulates a modern phenomenon that had already been lamented by Carlyle in "Signs of the Times" (1829): "No individual now hopes to accomplish the poorest enterprise single-handed and without mechanical aids. . . . In these days . . . to live, signifies to unite with a party, or to make one" (467). Carlyle's consequent quest for "heroes" represented a more romantic and less democratic version of Mill's call for character-building individuality.

28. Marx and Mill shared compatible commitments to liberating and developing individuality, but differed markedly as to means. In the *Manifesto* Marx and Engels argued that bourgeois society endows capital with independence and individuality while depriving this cherished autonomy to "living person[s]" (485). In *The German Ideology* communism is described as a mode of organization which will liberate "individuality" from "the domination of material conditions" (464). As Duncan has argued, socialists are often "deeply attached to liberal values," and may "claim to be implementing or completing liberal principles" by seeking to abrogate the liberal institutions that thwart them (296).

29. For a reading in which Mill's likeness to Arnold is more forcefully argued—overstated in my view—see Lloyd and Thomas, especially 120–26.

30. In *The New Zealander* Trollope decried the enervating effects of newspapers ("It is almost as much out of the question for an Englishman to think deeply as for a Chinese woman to walk alone"), and criticized modern dependence in much the same terms as Mill ("Why should a man walk or think, if such labour can be saved him by skilfully devised arrangements of civilization?" [181, 45–46]).

31. See also Richards, who stresses that "the commodity spectacle first synthesized in 1851" with the Great Exhibition (5).

T W O : Making the Working Man Like Me

1. The Royal Commission recommended two basic workhouse structures—one cruciform, one octagonal—both of which were designed to facilitate deterrent principles and

neither of which incorporated the surveillance features of Bentham's Panopticon. On workhouse architecture, see Karel Williams.

2. Peter Mandler has shown that "all the crucial elements of the New Poor Law" were current among the rural gentry before 1820. Chadwick's main contribution to the drafting of the act—and its most controversial feature—was the creation of a centralized commission to help implement these principles nationwide ("Making," esp. 146; "Tories"). On Christian political economy, see Hilton, especially chapter 2.

3. Seleski is citing an 1814–15 report on mendicity in London (20). She demonstrates that by creating a multifarious urban population of foreign-born poor, Irish and other colonial immigration after 1790 further amplified the inadequacies of the Old Poor Law.

4. As we shall see in chapter 4, a similar logic, predicated on the Anglicization of colonial subjects, underwrote the "liberal" colonialism of the British in India.

5. Early nineteenth-century figures such as Chalmers and Kay tended to present pastoral work as a chiefly male endeavor. Yet, as Summers has shown, women's increasing philanthropic activity helped to mask the potentially glaring contradiction between alleged spiritual equality and entrenched socioeconomic difference (43). Clearly, the rhetoric of the personal enabled male philanthropists to harness middle-class women's domestic authority by invoking familial metaphors in which bourgeois society's separate spheres and competitive relations were symbolically bridged.

6. Like Chalmers's plan, municipal socialism was a middle-class attempt to ensure social harmony by providing beneficial services on a voluntary basis (see McCaffrey).

7. On Chalmers's 1817 proposal, see Brown 117–19. Peel considered but did not adopt a bill based on Chalmers's principles (152–53). Opposition came from conservatives who feared upsetting the existing social formation, from Dissenters who disliked the plan's relation to the established church, and (at the same time) from the church itself, which was not eager to assume responsibility for poor relief.

8. That said, the scope of centralization for Chalmers remained limited to towns and parishes; Chalmers, an ardent localist, would not have ceded administrative power to London-based officials.

9. According to Gallagher, reformers of the period were "torn" between conflicting impulses "to assert their belief in human free will," and "to illustrate the helplessness of individuals caught in the industrial system" (*Industrial* 28). Anderson builds on this tension, showing how "the category of character," which signified the potential for autonomous will, became an "object of struggle" in nineteenth-century thought (*Tainted* 29–30).

10. That is so whether or not one is ready to conclude with Poovey (and I am not) that the historical interdependence between Chalmers's charisma, and the organization he contrived to disseminate it, justifies "dissolving" Max Weber's (or, for that matter, any other considered) distinction between bureaucracy and charisma.

11. Significantly, however, Gaskell's representation of the Christian and civic community stops short of advocating an intensely formalized visiting relationship such as Chalmers's or Tuckerman's—even though middle-class women in the 1850s were increasingly prominent in these activities. As Deirdre D'Albertis has argued, Gaskell shied

away from organized female philanthropy because she feared corrupting "the selfless qualities associated with domestic womanhood" (49). Gaskell's chariness thus represents a reluctance to bureaucratize personal bonds, with pristine femininity operating (as it does in *Bleak House*) as the ultimate bulwark against depersonalized social relations.

12. According to Selleck, not only the prefatory letter, but also the revised text of the second edition of *Manchester* had been greatly influenced by Chalmers's marginal notes on the first edition (77–78).

13. One must bear in mind, however, that a great many of the "police regulations" proposed by Kay, and later Chadwick, affected property-owning landlords as well as working-class inhabitants. For example, "Landlords should be compelled . . . to provide sufficient means of drainage, and each to pave his respective area of the street. Each habitation should be provided with a due receptacle for every kind of refuse, and the owner should be obliged to whitewash the house, at least once every year. Inspectors of the state of houses should be appointed: and the repair of all those, reported to be in a state inconsistent with the health of the inhabitants, should be enforced at the expense of the landlords" (106). That is why it is crucial to recognize, as I emphasize in chapter 3, that the sanitary debates concerned irreconcilable political, ideological, and economic differences *within* Britain's governing classes.

14. As Laqueur has demonstrated, the potential for this split ran deep, manifesting itself in recurrent linkages between documentation and personal affect: in the eighteenth century detailed accounts of working-class suffering, including Kay-like investigations, disseminated precisely the "humanitarian" sentiments to which Chalmers appealed ("Bodies").

15. Ironically, in spite of his high civic profile, Kay failed to support himself as a Manchester physician. Had he succeeded, he would have been unlikely to seek an administrative appointment (Selleck 100–102).

16. As Selleck suggests, Kay's enthusiasm can, perhaps, be explained in biographical terms; for Kay's own class identity had been battered by the failure of his medical career.

17. Poulett Thomson, one of Kay's Manchester allies, encouraged voluntary statistical societies on precisely these grounds (qtd. in Selleck 97).

18. Here I differ with Logan, who has seen the excessive determinism and objectivist stance of Chadwick's sanitary *Report* in unequivocal terms, as a source of middle-class empowerment. In my view Chadwick's objectivism could not but be a double-edged sword, since it threatened the character-building reciprocity on which middle-class authority was predicated. The "readerly surveillance" (165) encouraged by Chadwick's *Report* might complement, but could not entirely replace, the self-affirming qualities attributed to the latter relation. Thus, Chadwick's deterministic assumptions and technocratic pastoral approach triggered the midcentury backlash I describe in the next chapter.

19. In the early stages of her career, however, Martineau devoted little energy to pastoral work. She may have sought to enhance her authorial credentials by identifying herself wholly with "masculine" letters (cf. Peterson, esp. 178). In an 1832 letter Martineau delegated pastoral concerns to her clergyman brother James, devoting herself to the social scientific task of "analyzing" the poor (*Selected* 38).

20. As we shall see in chapter 6, that was the rationale of the influential Charity Organization Society (1869–1913), whose members saw their own organized efforts as a superior alternative to state welfare.

21. In practice, however, very few early-Victorian unions were able to provide separate and less deterrent accommodation for the non-able in the manner recommended by the Royal Commission, and supported by Martineau's tale. As a result, the impact of deterrence was overwhelmingly experienced by those least able to respond by choosing independent labor over the "less eligible" workhouse (Wood 113–14).

22. Bodenheimer describes the Maylie world as a Wordsworthian evocation of an "idealized eighteenth-century village order" (119).

23. *Twist* was influenced by the *Times'* contemporaneous campaign to expose the New Poor Law as "most difficult to reconcile with Christianity or civilization" (qtd. in Walder 518); cf. Marcus, *Dickens* 73; and Colby 115.

24. See also Kettle, who notes Dickens's retreat from an unsparing examination of working-class misery to a classist battle between good and evil (123–38); and, for a different approach to the split, Petterson.

25. This ambiguity was sufficient to persuade Chadwick (mistakenly) to regard Dickens as a potential supporter (see Flinn 56–57). Dickens colorfully describes the workhouse test as "the rule, that all poor people should have the alternative . . . of being starved by a gradual process in the house, or by a quick one out of it." Less eligibility is epitomized in this way: "The relief was inseparable from the workhouse and the gruel; and that frightened people. . . . [T]he number of workhouse inmates got thin as well as the paupers; and the board were in ecstasies" (26).

26. On Fagin's unsuccessful plan to educate Oliver through "criminal reading," see Brantlinger, "Oliver," especially 61–62.

27. In *Little Dorrit* the Plornishes struggle to maintain cheerful domesticity while forced to send their father to the workhouse. In chapter 5 I describe *Our Mutual Friend's* depiction of Betty Higden, an aged laborer who would rather die than compromise her economic dependence.

28. A telling example of Oliver's innate middle-class identification is his initial response to the Dodger. Oliver assumes that the latter's relation to a "'spectable old gentleman" (i.e., Fagin) either is or ought to be the kind of reciprocal pastoral bond that *he* later cultivates with Brownlow. When Oliver concludes that "the moral precepts of [this] benefactor had . . . been thrown away," he resolves "to cultivate the good opinion" of the Dodger's benefactor, and to "decline the honour of [the Dodger's] farther acquaintance" (63–64).

29. Bodenheimer's description of a romantic "natural history of character," predicated on a combination of "nature, inheritance, and spirit," is largely compatible with what I have called Dickens's essentialized and fairy-tale rendering of middle-class character (119–20). On the other hand, my reading would stress the extent to which Oliver's innate qualities preempt romantic *Bildung*. As Baldridge notes, "Dickens is under no illusion that he is writing a traditional *Bildungsroman* in which the forging of his protagonist's personality will be experienced by readers as a process of becoming" (85).

30. More insistently even than J. S. Mill, Martineau imagined individual character as largely self-determined. But, in addressing the character of the nation as a whole, she insisted on the influence of "custom," "climate," "productions," *and* "genealogy" (*Society* 1:33). For John Austin, a friend of Mill's, national character was "imputable to race, or to a long and steady action of outward influences" (226). And for Walter Bagehot the origins both of national and individual character remained "one of the most secret of marvelous mysteries" (*Collected* 4:49).

31. Yet another example is Uriah Heep, whose infamous pretense to "'umbleness" was acquired "at a foundation school for boys" (Dickens, *David Copperfield* 530–31).

32. Dickens spares the recently instituted Metropolitan police (whom he later commended in *Bleak House*) by making the incompetent Blathers and Duff members of the outdated Bow Street Runners. The latter were an informal London patrol that operated on an entrepreneurial basis, claiming statutory rewards for bringing offenders to justice (Emsley 19). As Brantlinger notes, "the Bow Street runners" are "doubly outsmarted": "both the criminals and the respectable bourgeoisie foil" them ("Oliver" 66).

33. This is the title of the original serial publication, which began in December 1842. The three-volume edition of 1843 (from which my citations are drawn) was entitled *Jessie Phillips: A Tale of the Present Day.*

34. Thompson is particularly keen to stress the extent to which working self-discipline evolved independently of middle-class efforts so that the standards of respectability developed and enforced within working-class communities were distinct from (although undeniably influenced by) ruling-class notions. Thus, as Thompson sees it, every group within Victorian society "operated its own social controls, often devised in reaction to behaviour patterns which law and authority sought to impose." Respectability was, consequently, "internalized and diversified"—unlike "the cohesive force which its middle-class and evangelical proponents had imagined" (360).

35. Trollope's novel thus supports Mandler's claims that liberal Tories had espoused a Christianized view of the value of deterrent poor laws, but without endorsing the centralized administrative apparatus that was later added by Chadwick, and without necessarily wishing to eliminate a personalized character test to distinguish between deserving and undeserving applicants for relief ("Making"). Recall that even Martineau's solidly pro–New Poor Law tale featured local control, free of centralized interference.

36. For a supportive reading of the disappearance of the *Pamela* plot in Victorian fiction, a sign of increasing social conservatism, see Langland, *Nobody's* 1–2 and 210–11.

37. Deepbrook's workhouse is neither a likely institutional mechanism for the generalization of panopticism, nor—like the majority of post–New Poor Law workhouses—a model of the commission's recommendations. It is, rather, a chaotic and "liminal" institution, much like the "old-style prisons" described in Bender (26–35). That said, Trollope does reproduce some of the most notorious features of the post-1834 model: walled isolation from the oustide world, and a "painful initiatory process" including a haircut and uniform (2:190–92).

38. Dickens also appeals to gendered forms of knowledge. When Mr. Brownlow is influenced by Grimwig's skepticism regarding Oliver's character, Mrs. Bedwin, who

nursed Oliver through his illness, retorts, "I never will believe it, sir" (124). Both Rose and Mrs. Maylie immediately determine Oliver's goodness through his appearance (197).

39. Moreover, numerous efforts were made to placate popular antagonism, including the scapegoating of key officials, the removal of Chadwick, the dissolution of the original commission, and the issuing of revised central orders.

40. See also Thompson, "Social Control," especially 189–208; and, for an example of the "social control" thesis, see Donajgrodzki, "'Social Police.'" Lloyd and Thomas support Thompson's conclusion: the "'respectability' of the working class," they argue, "was seen by themselves in relation to their own longstanding moral self-reliance not as an aping of middle-class values" (111).

THREE: Is There a Pastor in the *House?*

1. In an important chapter in *Dombey and Son* (1846) Dombey's corrupt nature is linked to "moral pestilence" and "contagion" among the poor" (737–38). In an 1851 article in *Household Words* Dickens described the stonewalling of sanitary reform by systematic "Red Tape." The article establishes a clear connection between *Bleak House*'s sanitary plot and *Little Dorrit*'s Circumlocution Office—and one that predates the Crimean debacle with which the later novel is typically associated ("Red Tape" 481–83; see also Philpotts).

2. Carlyle's tale of the contagious Irish widow appears in the "Gospel of Mammonism," in book 3 of *Past and Present* (1843).

3. In *Our Mutual Friend* Podsnap dismisses an appeal on behalf of the starving poor with a refusal to consent to un-English "Centralization" (187).

4. Compare to *Bleak House:* "England has been in a dreadful state for some weeks. Lord Coodle would go out, Sir Thomas Doodle wouldn't come in, and there being nobody in Great Britain (to speak of) except Coodle and Doodle, there has been no Government" (619). On the "tepid" coalition that eventually emerged," see Briggs, *Victorian* 68; and Clark, *Making* 209.

5. The *Times'* radical-sounding rhetoric should not, however, be mistaken for a predisposition to favor Chadwick. On the contrary, the *Times* had persistently opposed the New Poor Law and was eventually to side with London radicals (and others) against the Public Health Act. According to Lubenow, fear of patronage and jobbery was the most persistent ground of opposition to reform (85–88).

6. Brundage's political biography of Chadwick is subtitled *England's "Prussian Minister,"* following a contemporary description by Lord John Russell. According to his first biographer, "As an administrator [Chadwick] might typify Prussia: in England he is unique" (Finer 475). Mandler has argued that Chadwick's still-inflated reputation among modern historians stems from Finer's authoritative biography, "which, by drawing so heavily on Chadwick's private papers," inevitably partook of his self-promoting "megalomania" ("Tories" 82 n. 4).

7. Logan argues more loosely that the sanitary *Report* sparked a surveillant reading culture: middle-class Britons were exhorted to "symbolically cure" working-class mal-

adies by engaging in a new and voyeuristic "readerly surveillance" (164–65). Poovey argues persuasively that the *Report* naturalized middle-class domesticity while impeding the political consolidation of the laboring classes, whose moral failings it documented (117).

8. Describing the same passage, Childers calls this deterministic logic, a "controlling assumption of the *Report*" ("Observation" 411).

9. Chadwick's reduction of morality from a subject-making antecedent to an environmental effect does not, however, imply a diminished interest in morality. As Marcus has noted, the human waste and other refuse that Chadwick's *Report* so relentlessly exposed was "wealth's symbolic negative counterpart," and a "virtual objectification" of the working-class social condition (*Engels* 185).

10. The notion of the heroic era in the early-Victorian state originated in the work of Clark, "Statesmen"; see also R. Johnson, "Administrators" 114 n. 6; and Fraser 61–62 and 82–84.

11. Moreover, like Bentham before him, Chadwick was as ready to introduce his revolutionary ideas through private enterprise as he was to implement them legislatively. For a fascinating account of his failed attempt in 1844–46 to launch the Sanitary Idea through the "British, Colonial and Foreign Drainage, Water Supply, and Towns Improvement Company" (a period during which he privately lobbied *against* public health legislation), see Brundage 101–12.

12. Miller specifies numerous ways in which the nineteenth-century novel dovetails with the modern regime of *Discipline and Punish*. Novels represent the shift from "corporal and spectacular punishment to a hidden and devious discipline"; they "assume a fully panoptic view of the world." Novels further enact a narrative form of disciplinary technology wherein resistance to novelistic control functions as "a technique for achieving it" (21–27). LaCapra has argued that Miller's reading of *Bleak House* "limit[s] a text to the uncritical harmonization of inconsistencies" (117); cf. A. Anderson, *Tainted* 201–2. Danahay's reading of *Bleak House* is supportive of Miller's precedent. Robbins argues that *Bleak House* anticipates Foucault's theoretical position, offering a critique of institutional modernity which, like Foucault's, is "wary" of certain humanistic values. For Robbins, Miller's reading is persuasive but "leaves undone the job of instructing those who, when analysis is finished, must decide to act from positions within the system" ("Telescopic" 220).

13. Esther herself commends the uniformed police, who conduct themselves "with the greatest despatch, and without the waste of a moment" (826). By contrast, Allan Woodcourt declares that he does not "take kindly" to the New Poor Law's "system" on account of which he is "evaded and shirked, and handed about from post to pillar" (694). See also Liz's experience attempting to admit Jo to a public hospital (487). Dickens's commendation of the Metropolitan Police may have been tied to the popularity they enjoyed after their oversight of the Great Exhibition (see Emsley 40, including n. 1, and 59).

14. Bucket first arrives on the scene in what we might call a closed-door mystery, but one that (unlike Conan Doyle's in *Sign of Four*) is never explained (361). In a classical example of deduction Bucket concludes that Jenny's husband is concealing Lady Dedlock's watch (836). Bucket plays a version of good cop / bad cop with Hortense, comparing himself to the "rougher ones outside" as he interrogates her (793). Like Auguste Dupin, Sher-

lock Holmes and, later, Hercule Poirot, Bucket plays to his audience, publicly predicting his ability to solve his "beautiful case" in just a few hours (775). Like television's Lieutenant Columbo, Bucket has a wife about whom we hear much but whom we never see.

15. This promiscuous mingling between "Tom's slime" and the very highest orders of society thus subverts what Stallybrass and White have described as the nineteenth century's obsessive distinctions between "high" bourgeois culture and its "low" working-class counterpart (125–48). See also Nord, who argues that "the litigious, labyrinthine, fog-ridden London of *Bleak House* connect[s] the high and low through analogy, metaphor, and outright contagion" (*Walking* 84; cf. 97–98).

16. According to Emsley, early-Victorian town councils (usually composed of the most powerful ratepayers) "considered the police to be their servants who could be used at their discretion, and not simply for the prevention of crime." Local leaders, eager to squeeze maximum service out of minimum police expenditure, also foisted cumbersome sanitary duties on their newly engaged police forces (41–42). For a fictional example of the local police's accepting a high fee in exchange for preferential treatment, see Charles Reade's *Hard Cash* (1863), chap. 27, 116.

17. On increasing police repression between 1750 and 1850, see Gatrell, especially 243–68.

18. Chadwick's proposals were undermined by a weak Whig ministry. Once again, Chadwick was personally demonized in the press, in which he was accused of trying to "enforce his rule through . . . centralized police forces," and to imprison the Queen in a workhouse (qtd. in Finer 175–76).

19. Sir James Graham, the Tory home secretary, disliked administration by "philosophers and wise men" and for years had "wished heartily 'to get rid of'" Kay-Shuttleworth; while Jowett, the Oxford don and university reformer whose impact on civil service reform I discuss in chapter 4, likened him to "the two barbarians Hengist and Horsa" (qtd. in R. Johnson, "Administrators" 124–25, 130).

20. See Levine's description of *Little Dorrit* as a novel in which strong will becomes "ineffectual" and energy "dissipates" with Doyce as the would-be antithesis (9, 5).

21. Here I am distinguishing between Chancery's institutional archaism, and the comparatively modern forms of agency which may profit from it.

22. In the early nineteenth century *bureaucracy* remained a foreign (French) word, and references to the term "invariably included a self-congratulatory rider on how different things were in England" (Albrow 21). Writing in 1850, Carlyle described bureaucracy as a "continental nuisance," with no future in England (*Latter-Day* 173).

23. On the domestic woman's perceived apoliticism, see Armstrong, especially 3–27. Nord describes Esther's embodiment of "Right Woman" as "a model for the salvation of society" (*Walking* 85).

24. Because my emphasis is philanthropy within Britain, I focus on Pardiggle rather than Jellyby. For a nuanced reading of the latter, see Robbins "Telescopic."

25. Prochaska notes that in 1893 an estimated twenty thousand women worked as full-time paid officials in charities, excluding nurses, "making it one of the leading female

professions" (385). Octavia Hill has been called "the grandmother of modern social work" (Young and Ashton 115).

26. In *Little Dorrit* Dickens detailed the depersonalization of Nandy, an aged pauper, forced to wear workhouse garments "that [were] never made for him, nor for any individual mortal" (354). On Dickens's personal involvement in Urania Cottage, a rehabilitative asylum for prostitutes, see A. Anderson, *Tainted* 73–79.

27. For example, Noah Claypole in *Oliver Twist*, Rob in *Dombey and Son*, and Uriah Heep in *David Copperfield*, whose relation to charity schools I discussed in chapter 2.

28. Bagehot's remarks were referred to earlier. Eliot's pseudonymous comments on Dickens, published in her famous *Westminster Review* article, "The Natural History" (264), are discussed in Rotkin. Trollope's satire of Dickens as Mr. Popular Sentiment appeared in chapter 15 of *The Warden* (1855); see also *Autobiography* 160.

29. Parry goes so far as to argue that the General Board was "the least significant" of the Public Health Act's provisions. Far more important was the act's success in rationalizing and strengthening local government—the key strategy of the early-Victorian Whig social agenda. By encouraging municipal improvements, the act "marked the key stage in the development of the distrusted municipal corporation into the proud Victorian civic authority" (204–5).

30. Hill's contemporary biographer is at pains to assure us that Hill "believed in personal and sympathetic intercourse with the poor, as far more important than any organisation," and "preferred small local efforts to great centralised schemes" (Maurice 257).

31. The Charity Organization Society's six members on the 1905–9 Royal Commission included Octavia Hill and Helen Bosanquet. Beatrice Webb, who began her career as a COS visitor, was the most prominent Fabian member of the Royal Commission.

F O U R : An Officer and a Gentleman

1. See Briggs, *Victorian* 61; and O. Anderson, *Liberal*, especially 29–94; "Administrative"; and "Janus."

2. Gowan's dissent from this view, to which I am indebted, is situated especially in contrast to the work of MacDonagh, "Nineteenth-Century"; and Hart.

3. Coleridge urged the propertied classes to support an established class of enlightened pastors, or "clerisy," to counter the divisive effects of capitalism. As Gallagher emphasizes, Coleridge's state was neither a social institution nor a mere empirical government but an eternal "Idea that finds its expression in particular governments and social groups," especially the landed aristocracy (*Industrial* 193). Lloyd and Thomas's understanding of Coleridge's contribution to the Victorian state, which is premised on a much broader concept of the state than I find helpful, should be contrasted to the argument in this chapter.

4. The term *civil service* itself originated in India, where it was used to differentiate those in administration from their counterparts in the military. Trollope and other contemporaries often used *public service* as an alternative.

5. According to A. D. Webb, Trevelyan was an unswerving zealot who, like Chadwick, leaked confidential information to newspapers, testified before Parliaments, exploited personal contacts, and manipulated administrative procedures.

6. Here and throughout this chapter I adopt Stokes's terminology, using *liberal* especially to describe the antistatist and voluntarist governing philosophy favored by Trevelyan and Macaulay in India, in contrast to the centralized intervention favored by Benthamite rivals such as James Mill.

7. Whereas in India Trevelyan's devotion to "the moral and intellectual regeneration" of colonial subjects had taken the form of an educational mission (qtd. in Hernan 19), in Ireland Trevelyan held that undue government interference was to blame for the social crisis. This seeming inconsistency is explained by the English readiness to charge Irish landowners with social obligations from which their Oriental counterparts were exempt. Trevelyan thus believed himself justified in applying a negative policy that, like the New Poor Law, would stimulate individual and local self-reliance.

8. On gentility's unstable definition, see Burn (253–67); and, more recently, Adams, who describes the "dandaical" theatricality upon which genteel masculinity ambivalently depends.

9. "In England," Scoones lamented, "an appointment in the Civil Service . . . confers neither status nor consideration. . . . Here the Civil Servant is looked upon rather in the light of an outgrowth, to be tolerated because it cannot be shaken off" (349). Scoones's remarks thus attest to the lasting power of *Little Dorrit's* midcentury satire on civil servant "Barnacles."

10. Compton's remark is more striking for having been made with regard to the Indian Civil Service, which was both more interventionist and more well respected than its English counterpart.

11. Marion is citing Kendrick's unpublished paper for the American Political Science Association.

12. Cf. Frederic Harrison's 1895 comparison: "For the ordinary incidents of life amongst well-bred and well-to-do-men and women of the world, the form of Trollope's tales is almost as well adapted as [Austen's]" (qtd. by N. Thompson 166).

13. Trollope's manuscript was rejected for publication in April 1855, after which time he substantially revised it. Although Trollope used some of the material in various novels, including *The Three Clerks*, the bulk of *The New Zealander* remained unpublished until 1972. The title of the work is drawn from Macaulay's "Prophecy" (1840), predicting that a visiting New Zealander will someday sketch the ruins of a decayed England.

14. Trollope consistently held that *detur digno*, which translated into limited competition among those nominated for a position, was an appropriate means to improving civil service recruitment and promotion. *Detur digniori*, on the other hand, favored by the Northcote- Trevelyan *Report*, was, he held, "a fearful law for such a profession as the Civil Service" (62). Trollope revisited this theme in his 1865 essay in the *Fortnightly Review* (see 617–18 and 629) and his 1861 *Cornhill* essay, "The Civil Service as a Profession." Passing over the long-serving Brown to favor the young whippersnapper Green is, he argues, injurious to both ("Profession," 224–25). Hence, in *The Three Clerks* office-wide compe-

tition, a small instance of the open competition the *Report* sought to implement on a nationwide scale, is critiqued on two grounds: first, because it results in passing over the long-serving worthy; second, because, the *most* worthy man (Harry Norman) is not in fact identified by an examination. See also *Autobiography* 29–31.

15. In the Oxford edition this chapter, which was excised from later editions of *The Three Clerks*, is published as appendix A.

16. As Bareham points out, "Excelsior" is an echo from Longfellow's poem on self-destructive aspiration (77); cf. *Clerks* 131.

17. On Arnold's professional polemic, see Goodlad, "'Middle Class.'"

18. Trollope's persistent critique of the popular press had begun with *The Warden;* see also Hall, "Introduction" xxii–xxiii.

19. On Smiles's debts to George Lillie Craik's popular 1830–31 essay "Knowledge Pursued under Difficulties," see "Samuel Smiles" in *Dictionary of National Biography.* On problems publishing *Self-Help,* see O. Anderson, *Liberal* 109. According to Briggs, twenty thousand copies of *Self-Help* sold in the first year and over a quarter of a million by 1905—sales that "far exceeded those of the great nineteenth-century novels" (*Victorian* 118).

20. This aspect of Trollope's novel bears comparison to the thesis of Wiener's work on the decline of industrial spirit during this period.

21. "The absolute frankness of *An Autobiography* is most characteristic of Mr. Trollope: and so is its unequalled—manliness we were going to say;—but we mean something both more and less than manliness, covering more than the daring of manliness and something less than the quietness or equanimity which we are accustomed to include in that term, so we may call it, its unequalled masculineness" (Richard Holt Hutton, qtd. in N. Thompson 157).

22. The Scott analogy is also apt insofar as the Norman-Saxon antithesis of *Ivanhoe* (1819) anticipates the Norman-Tudor structure of *The Three Clerks.* As Lukács has demonstrated, Scott's novels narrate England's historical development as a process of Hegelian synthesis: the location of a "glorious 'middle way'" between "warring extremes" (32).

23. Nardin aligns Trollope's moral philosophy with the writings of Cicero (4), whose stoic idea of binding morality is compatible with the ends of a Coleridgean clerisy.

24. Yet Trollope remains as averse as ever to the "vogue" for competitive examinations—a system that excludes "the best gentlemen" while giving "the Devil . . . the pick of the flock" (*Chronicle* 142).

FIVE: A Riddle without an Answer

1. The prescriptive view of character implied the theoretical perfectibility of all human beings.

2. I emphasize schoolmasters, since the tensions that I describe here were focused almost exclusively on working-class males. Although Kay-Shuttleworth likened the pedagogical bond to the maternal, he made clear that male teachers were preferred to female because women's inferior strength forced them to adopt tyrannical measures (*Training* 25–26). Dickens, for his part, was more anxious about the effects of training on men than

women. Miss Peecher, Headstone's female counterpart, is relatively unscathed: "Small, shining, neat methodical, and buxom was Miss Peecher; cherry-cheeked and tuneful of voice" (268).

3. Beiderwell discusses these divisions in stylistic terms, arguing that "*Our Mutual Friend* is both a multi-plotted novel and a multi-styled novel" (234). According to J. Hillis Miller, the novel constructs a cluster of "impenetrable milieus" that "exist side by side, but do not organize themselves into a larger whole" (*Charles* 316). Farrell's thought-provoking "dialogical" reading qualifies the emphasis on division, but does not, to my mind, neutralize the arguments I have so far cited. My reading pays special attention to the split between the sentimental Harmon/Bella marriage plot, and the comparatively re-alist Headstone/Wrayburn rivalry plot. Yet another relatively discrete aspect of the novel is the satire on the Veneerings.

4. Robbins's reading of the upward mobility narrative in *Great Expectations* illuminates Dickens's vexed striving after a suitable character-building agency. Upward mobility, Rob-bins writes, "does not happen to you without some endorsement, sponsorship, [or] sup-port" ("Benefactor" 181). Dickens is not so much "walling off" domestic space as he is anticipating an "as yet unrealized, impersonal agency" that eventually materialized in the welfare state (187–88).

5. Fulweiler likens the mounds to a Victorian fossil record in which, as in paleontol-ogy, "the secret of inheritance" is at stake (61–62). In her seminal reading of homoso-ciality in *Our Mutual Friend* Sedgwick reviews various critical responses to the mounds, concluding that critics' attention to excremental themes betrays their repression of themes of anality (164).

6. Dickens explicitly links the symbolism of the mounds to his poor law critique: their "slow" dismantling is explicitly tied to the "dust-shovelling" of legislators whose "moun-tain of pretentious failure" threatens to "bury us alive" (565).

7. See Wood 99; Crowther, *Workhouse* 72; and M. Rose 67. See also Dickens's 1850 essay "A Walk in the Workhouse," in which he remarks that "the dragon Pauperism" was, on the whole, "in a very weak and impotent condition; toothless, fangless, drawing his breath heavily enough, and hardly worth chaining up" (537–38). In "Wapping Work-house" (1860), Dickens describes "a bright-eyed old soul" much like Betty Higden, crit-icizing a system that has failed to relieve her humanely (26).

8. Dickens's source for Betty may have been Henry Mayhew's report of a destitute old woman who preferred to "die in the street" rather than enter the "great house," or it may have been Charles Reade's 1863 novel, *Very Hard Cash*, in which another aged Betty's "horror of the workhouse" is so great that she resolves to "go out on the common, and die there" (see *Our Mutual Friend*, chap. 16, n. 1, 901–2). In "Of Kings' Treasuries" (1864) Ruskin cites a recent newspaper account of an impoverished bootmaker who died of star-vation rather than enter the workhouse (37). In Dickens's "Podsnappery" chapter a din-ner guest affronts his host with an "ill-timed" allusion to the starvation of "some half-dozen people [who] had lately died in the streets" (187).

9. On the resistance to working-class education, see Sutherland, "Education" 129; and (in light of *Oliver Twist*) Brantlinger, "Oliver," especially 65–70. Brougham, the lib-

eral-minded founder of the Society for the Diffusion of Useful Knowledge, favored an indirect approach. Governments must decline to "meddle," and philanthropists ought to assist, but without impeding working-class self-help (1, 11–12). By far the most tenacious obstruction to state education was religious rivalry. Dissenters and Roman Catholics resisted the idea that Anglicans had a special right to the state's patronage. But, since few were attracted to secular alternatives, proponents of state-supported education were trapped in a sectarian deadlock, the effects of which lasted for many decades.

10. In 1869 fewer than 10 percent of children were enrolled in school, and the majority of those who had attended were unable to write a letter or add up a bill. For these and other statistics, see Fraser 85.

11. On Kay-Shuttleworth and education, see the articles by R. Johnson and Paz, as well as Selleck's and Smith's biographies. Working-class education is also discussed in Paz, *Politics;* Fraser 78–98; Sutherland, "Education"; and Digby and Searby. For a discussion of early-Victorian educational reforms which stresses working-class resistance to middle-class agenda, see Lloyd and Thomas, chap. 3, esp. 103–5.

12. This quotation from Fletcher, a school inspector influenced by Kay-Shuttleworth's philosophy, is cited in R. Johnson, "Education Policy" 112.

13. As Amanda Anderson has shown, Kay-Shuttleworth urged Dickens to adopt this kind of personalized "moral" approach to reform, in lieu of the hedonistic marking system that the latter had installed at Urania Cottage, a home for fallen women (77–78).

14. Building on Johnson's work, as well as their own research into educational discourse, Lloyd and Thomas also emphasize the intrication of intersubjective ideals and middle-class interests. In their concise formulation the "illusion of democratic pedagogy" is constituted precisely when the "appearance of autonomy" on the part of a subordinate learner is "preserved by the shared performance of a mutual project" (129).

15. For an example of a critique of Continental schools, see Laing, especially 496. On the popularity of singing in Victorian schools, see Rainbow.

16. For example, Kay-Shuttleworth extensively describes the importance of building students' independent critical faculties (*Training* 27–28); yet, at the same time, he describes the gallery as an architectural means by which to keep children "under the eye of their teacher, . . . enabling him more readily to inspect and control them by arousing their attention, and bringing the sympathies of the body to act" (28). Here is a call, then, not only for panopticism, but also for the disciplinary incitement that Poovey has described in relation to Chalmers's activities (*Making* 99–106).

17. Of course, the history of popular education in Scotland, renowned for the quality of its schools and teachers throughout this period, is distinct from that of England.

18. R. Johnson elaborates on one inspector's objection to a training college where sympathetic equality between teachers and working-class parents was stressed. The inspector feared that such an approach would separate the teacher from the class above him: "that class in which all his better and higher impulses will find their chief stay and support" (qtd. in "Educational" 115).

19. Behind this ideological shift was, as we saw in the last two chapters, a struggle between middle-class experts like Kay-Shuttleworth and Edwin Chadwick, and the tradi-

tional upper-class elite. The Education department was one of the earliest battlegrounds, with Kay-Shuttleworth's 1849 resignation signaling the winding down of a reform era first spurred by middle-class enfranchisement in 1832 (see R. Johnson, "Administrators").

20. Under the 1862 code government grants were awarded on the basis of students' attendance and performance on basic examinations. The key figures involved in these reforms, such as Robert Lowe, were adamantly opposed to expanding the franchise. Unsurprisingly, the unanticipated passage of a far-reaching Reform Act in 1867 precipitated renewed interest in broadening popular education. Gladstone, who supported reform, argued that the qualified voter must exhibit "self command [and] self control" but also "respect for order, patience under suffering, confidence in the law, [and] regard for superiors" (qtd. in Parry 209). His description contrasts with that of a public school gentleman (able to control himself and govern others), and resembles the early-Victorian construction in which workers both were and were not autonomous. For a reading of education in *Our Mutual Friend* stressing the importance of examination and "payment by results," see Shuman.

21. Dickens reiterates the point when Headstone, disguised for murder, at last appears in clothes that express—rather than affect to make—the man. When Headstone assumes the garb of bargeman Rogue Riderhood, the narrator observes, "whereas, in his own schoolmaster clothes, he usually looked as if they were the clothes of some other man, he now looked, in the clothes of some other man or men, as if they were his own" (697).

22. Cf. Farrell, who describes the "entrepreneurial indolence" of the two partners (767).

23. Dickens's readiness to have Eugene assert Lizzie's worth, however inconsistent with the latter's actions, contrasts with Trollope's insistence that Charlie Tudor's marriage to barmaid Norah Geraghty would entail his moral ruin. Like Bradley, Norah is represented in terms of her physical habitus: her dirty fingernails and cheap-smelling pomatum (see chap. 4).

24. In an otherwise superb analysis Collins mistakenly insists that Wrayburn is "innocent of any evil intent" toward Lizzie (165). To my mind there is no evidence to justify this conclusion. Although Wrayburn tells Lightwood early on that he has "no design whatever" toward Lizzie, Lightwood is not satisfied by his denial, and neither should we be. When the chivalrous Riah urges Wrayburn to leave Lizzie alone, the latter resists, exulting in his "power over her" (464–65). When Lizzie confides her fears to Bella regarding "a gentleman far above me and my way of life," Bella responds by clasping her friend in a "living girdle," creating a kind of human chastity belt. These passages, in addition to the crucial scene just considered, make it clear that Wrayburn's intention to seduce Lizzie is, if not inevitable, then quite probable. Indeed, after the assault the penitent Wrayburn avers that he has "wronged [Lizzie] enough in fact" and "still more in intention" (808).

25. Charlie's selfishness is directly tied to the reprehensible effects of the Ragged School, where he learns "that you were to do good, not because it *was* good, but because you were to make a good thing of it." Here, as in "The Short-Timers," Dickens expresses particular disdain toward those boys singled out to assist with teaching, including the "exceptionally sharp" Charlie (264–65).

26. Langland describes the marriage as "a notable exception" to the "nonnarratability" of marriages "between a working-class woman and a higher-class man," a trend tied to the increasing importance of the wife's ability to "perform the ideological work of managing the class question" ("Nobody's" 290–91).

27. Here I agree with Jaffe's observation that the novel is "obsessively concerned with insides and outside," but disagree that this obsession results in leading "the reader to believe in distinctions between deceitful surface and underlying truth" (95). Rather, in focusing on insides and outsides, Dickens prompts readers to desire a stable correspondence between what they can and cannot validate through sense perception: between material and moral criteria. On the whole, surfaces—from Bradley's dysfunctional body to the Veneerings surface-without-depth—serve as remarkably reliable indicators of what readers ought to condone. Boffin's ruse (one of Jaffe's emphases) is an important exception. In my reading the most relevant exception is Eugene Wrayburn's public school surface, which, as I have argued, is valued—up to a point—for its special symbolic power.

28. In *For a Critique of the Political Economy of the Sign* and *The Mirror of Production* Jean Baudrillard questions Marx's distinction between the arbitrariness of exchange-value and the solidity of use-value. In a capitalist economy, he argues, all value, including that which determines questions of usefulness and productivity, is structured by representation. Mill's "Civilization" anticipates a postmodernist epistemology of this kind, as do the aspects of Dickens's satire I now describe. Indeed, Dickens heightens the proto-Baudrillardian qualities of his social critique by representing Veneering society as reflected by a "great looking-glass" (52), a technique that, as Beiderwell notes, emphasizes the Veneerings' one-dimensional insubstantiality (239). Gallagher has argued that the novel exhibits a "curiously death-centered bioeconomics" wherein humane critics of political economy such as Dickens imagine "the commodity, the bearer of value, as freighted with mortality, as a sign of spent vitality, in order to demand all the more strenuously that it have a vitality replenishing potential" ("Bioeconomics" 53). In another post-Marxist reading Poovey links *Our Mutual Friend* to the midcentury passage of limited liability legislation, arguing that the novel privileges metaphorical rather than literal understandings of the value of money.

SIX: Dueling Pastors, Dueling Worldviews

1. Collini describes Idealism as the dominant philosophy of late-Victorian and Edwardian Britain, a philosophy characterized by thoroughgoing rejection of empiricism in favor of Kantian and Hegelian metaphysics ("Sociology" 4; cf. den Otter 1).

2. Dendy was the maiden name of the future Mrs. Bosanquet. Although Dendy's lecture was written in 1893, it precisely anticipates the methods prescribed by the Majority Report. No less than six of the commission's nineteen members were prominent COS members, including C. S. Loch, Octavia Hill, and Helen Bosanquet. Both Sidney Webb and Bernard Bosanquet published supportive arguments for and were acknowledged exponents of the Minority and Majority Reports, respectively. Nevertheless, neither of the husbands was a formal member of the Royal Commission. Charles Booth, whose influential social investigations I discuss later, was also a member of the commission.

3. The Fabians, by contrast, perfectly illustrate the professional ideal at work, as Perkin himself argues (*Rise* 125).

4. In the 1920s, while credentialed sociologists proliferated in Continental and North American universities, L. T. Hobhouse, a respected but out-of-date figure, was Britain's only professor of sociology (Collini, *Liberalism* 248–49).

5. Another and prior positivist influence in sociology was Auguste Comte, the Frenchman who had invented the term. Spencer's and Comte's theories shared much in common but differed dramatically on the role of the state (see den Otter 124–27).

6. Raymond Williams has tied Fabianism to Mill's "spirit," describing it as "utilitarianism refined by experience of a new situation in history" (*Culture* 181). Yet in certain respects Mill's spirit resides more comfortably with the Idealists than with the Fabians, who, as Williams himself shows, lapsed into mechanistic thinking that Mill had been at pains to repudiate.

7. Bosanquet was strongly influenced by the Kantian notion that "will, and not force, is the only legitimate basis" of a state, and by Hegel's view of *Sittlichkeit*, a moral community within civil society, including special emphasis on the family (den Otter 23, 30).

8. This was ultimately a self-defeating strategy: as Perkin explains, scientific charity eventually led, "despite [the COS's] dislike of state intervention, to the development of the professional, and eventually state-employed, social worker" (*Rise* 124).

9. The tendency to equate *collectivism* with *socialism* was not unique to the Fabians (see Collini, *Liberalism* 17).

10. The report proposed that authorities not only treat but also actively "search out" and prevent cases of "incipient destitution" *before* they arise. The Webbs thus called for the "systematic prevention and cure" of chronic alcoholism, and the establishment of "detention colonies" for the treatment of the irremediably unemployable (S. and B. Webb 306–7).

11. Of course, this split is immanent in the realist genre itself, which, as Brantlinger has argued, betrays its own bourgeois origins, by "announc[ing] its inability to do anything other than mimic the real." For Brantlinger what is distinctive about the late-Victorian period is the erosion of realism "into the forms of mass culture" (*Fictions* 144, 143).

12. Williams argues that the naive socialist ardor of Gissing's early novels was based on a "negative identification" between the author's bourgeois rebelliousness and the marginalized position of the poor. As the working classes fell short of Gissing's narcissistic ideal, he first expressed disdain and finally disillusionment (*Culture* 176–79). Yet, as Gissing's autobiographical novels make clear, the author persistently saw his own material position in terms analogous to that of his working-class characters. In *The Private Papers of Henry Ryecroft* the Gissing-like narrator looks back on his career in letters and asks, "Could the position of any toiling man be more precarious than mine? . . . I marvel at the recollection that for a good score of years this pen and a scrap of paper . . . held at bay all those hostile forces of the world" (22).

13. Two important exceptions are the invisible effects of the New Poor Law, which I describe later, and the subtle appeal of jingoism, which Gissing illustrates in the famous chapter "Io Saturnalia" (107).

14. Wells's 1906 address to the Fabians, "Socialism and the Middle Classes," was published as *Socialism and the Family* in 1908.

15. Morris's utopian romance *News from Nowhere* (1890), and Wilde's essay "The Soul of Man under Socialism" (1891) both envision socialism as a foundation for aesthetic self-realization. Wells, however, was also optimistic toward technological progress. In his Fabian address he regretted the extent to which socialism "has got mixed up with Return-to-Nature ideas, with proposals for living in . . . purely hand-made houses" ("Socialism" 26)—in other words, precisely the kind of utopianism which Morris promoted in *Nowhere*.

16. As in Dickens, the naming of the rivals in itself symbolizes the advantages of wealth and breeding: while Headstone/Leadford convey a sense of stultifying materiality, Wrayburn/Verrall suggest intangible ideals such as light and truth.

17. Indeed, Spencer is an important figure in pinpointing the difference between Fabian and Wellsian worldviews. By holding with Spencer that progress is "the grand and irresistible law of human existence" (*Proper* 24), the Webbs enjoyed a certitude that Wells, a disciple of Huxley rather than Spencer, refused. Yet, by envisioning the tutelary state as the means by which to hasten inevitable progress, the Webbs dismissed Spencer's laissez-faire principles without Wells's reluctance. T. H. Huxley, the author of *Evolution and Ethics* (1895), argued that biological evolution did not, as Spencer had believed, provide a guide for society, since the struggle for existence was ethically deficient. Thus, for Huxley "the ethical progress of society depends not on imitating the cosmic process, . . . but in combating it" (qtd. in den Otter 88). Wells revisited the theme of the libertarian utopia in *Men Like Gods* (1923), in which he depicted a society free of authoritarian institutions, including parliament, private enterprise, police, and prisons.

18. Interestingly, the upper classes of the *Comet* have co-opted Leadford's hallowed socialist beliefs. In what is perhaps the pinnacle of his Wrayburnian self-possession, Verrall tells Leadford, "We're all socialists nowadays." Another defender of the status quo tells Leadford: "*I'm* a socialist too. Who isn't? But that doesn't lead me to class hatred" (587, 622).

19. On the newspaper's role in the modern nation as "imagined community," see B. Anderson, especially chapter 1.

20. Hillegas is paraphrasing the 1928 remarks of G. Lowes Dickinson, who described Forster's story as the "first-full scale emergence of the twentieth-century anti-utopia" (4).

21. See the famous epigraph to *Howards End*.

22. On the notion of the "mass-generation of traditions" in Europe between 1870 and 1914, see Hobsbawm, who defines them as "new devices to ensure or express social cohesion and identity and to structure social relations" ("Mass-Producing" 263).

23. Paul Thompson emphasizes that nationalized insurance "helped those best able to help themselves" while leaving many dependent on poor relief (220). The working-class politician Keir Hardie described the measure as a refusal to "uproot the cause of poverty," and, instead, a way to give workers "a porous plaster to cover the disease that poverty causes." The Webbs objected that "it's criminal to take poor people's money and use it to insure them, if you take it you should give it to the Public Health Authority to prevent their being ill again" (qtd. in Fraser 164, 168). Cf. Collini, who argues that "it

was . . . the peculiar achievement of New Liberalism" to undermine socialism's "intricate blend of moral and economic arguments from within" (*Liberalism* 26).

24. Churchill's insistence that insurance be operated on "actuarial" rather than moral principles was not entirely antithetical to COS doctrine, since it was based on the COS-like premise that workers *earned* entitlements through contributions (the compulsory rather than voluntary nature of which the COS, of course, rejected). In the end Churchill was overruled and a compromise made: workers dismissed for misconduct were deprived of benefit but on actuarial rather than moral grounds (see Fraser 162, 172).

25. That is not, however, to suggest that either the language of character or the Smile-sean myth entirely disappeared, only that the particular exigencies of the pre-War period required a different rhetorical ground. As I have elsewhere noted, contrasts between British and Continental character are a regular feature of the United Kingdom's con-temporary Euro-politics, and, as recently as 1996, Smiles's *Self-Help* was lauded in the *Observer* as a "lodestar" for the twenty-first century (see "Middle Class" 168).

26. Hobsbawm implies that mass-produced traditions in and of themselves supplied the "social cement" of mass societies, legitimating the social bonds and ties of authority which liberalism failed to provide (268–69). The New Liberal insurance platform can be understood both as a tradition in Hobsbawm's sense as well as a specific social policy that, in effect, mandated working-class thrift.

27. Summers emphasizes that many of the earliest welfare state provisions of the twentieth century relied on the continuing existence of a largely female volunteer work-force (33). On the link between feminine domesticity and professionalism, see also Nord, *Apprenticeship*, especially 119–36; and Langland, *Nobody's Angels*.

Epilogue

1. See also Foucault's later remarks, in which active citizenship becomes part of an "aesthetics of existence." "We can," Foucault insists, "demand of those who govern us a certain truth as to their ultimate aims. . . . [T]his is the *parrhesia* (free speech) of the gov-erned, who can and must question those who govern them . . . by virtue of being citizens" (51).

2. For two recent discussions of the Victorian context for these neoconservative at-tacks, see Hadley and Joyce; on comparable Thatcherite discourse, see Wolfreys, espe-cially 152.

3. On the latter contrast between Rawls's liberalism and Mill's, see Ryan 519–28. Rawls himself distinguishes between Mill's thought—which might lead to educational "requirements designed to foster the values of autonomy and individuality"—and his own concept of political liberalism, which "has a different aim and requires far less" (199). See also Appiah, who argues that the multiple conceptions of the good which Rawlsian theory intends to allow "will depend on what goes on in education. Teach all children only that they must accept a politics in which other people's conceptions of the good are not rid-den over and we risk a situation in which there are substantive conceptions of the good incompatible with liberal principle or, at least, with each other" (158).

Works Cited

Adams, James Eli. *Dandies and Desert Saints: Styles of Victorian Masculinity.* Ithaca: Cornell University Press, 1995.

Albrow, Martin. *Bureaucracy.* New York: Praeger, 1970.

Althusser, Louis. "Ideology and Ideological State Apparatuses (Notes towards an Investigation)." *Lenin and Philosophy and Other Essays.* Trans. Ben Brewster. London: New Left Books, 1977. 127–86.

Anderson, Amanda. *Tainted Souls and Painted Faces: The Rhetoric of Fallenness in Victorian Culture.* Ithaca: Cornell University Press, 1993.

———. "The Temptations of Aggrandized Agency: Feminist Histories and the Horizon of Modernity." *Victorian Studies* 43.1 (Fall 2000): 43–63.

Anderson, Benedict. *Imagined Communities: Reflections on the Origin and Spread of Nationalism.* 1983. Rev. ed. London: Verso, 1992.

Anderson, Linda R. *Bennett, Wells, and Conrad: Narrative in Transition.* New York: St. Martin's, 1988.

Anderson, Olive. "The Administrative Reform Association, 1855–1857." In *Pressure from Without in Early Victorian England.* Ed. Patricia Hollis. London: Edward Arnold, 1974. 262–87.

———. "The Janus Face of Mid-Nineteenth-Century English Radicalism: The Administrative Reform Association of 1855." *Victorian Studies* 8.3 (1965): 232–42.

———. *A Liberal State at War: English Politics and Economics during the Crimean War.* London: Macmillan, 1967.

Appiah, K. Anthony. "Identity, Authenticity, Survival: Multicultural Societies and Social Reproduction." In *Multiculturalism: Examining the Politics of Recognition.* Ed. Amy Gutmann. Princeton: Princeton University Press, 1994. 149–63.

Arac, Jonathan. *Commissioned Spirits: The Shaping of Social Motion in Dickens, Carlyle, Melville, and Hawthorne.* New York: Columbia University Press, 1989.

Arata, Stephen. *Fictions of Loss in the Victorian Fin de Siècle.* Cambridge: Cambridge University Press, 1996.

Armstrong, Nancy. *Desire and Domestic Fiction: A Political History of the Novel.* Oxford: Oxford University Press, 1987.

Arnold, Matthew. *Culture and Anarchy and Other Writings.* Ed. Stefan Collini. Cambridge: Cambridge University Press, 1993.

———. "Democracy." *Culture and Anarchy* 1–25.

————. "The Function of Criticism in Our Time." *Culture and Anarchy* 26–52.

Bagehot, Walter. "Charles Dickens." *Collected Works* 2:76–107.

————. *Collected Works of Walter Bagehot*. Ed. Norman St. John–Stevas. 15 vols. London: The Economist, 1965–66.

————. *The English Constitution*. Ed. and intro. R. H. S. Crossman. Ithaca: Cornell University Press, 1963.

Bailey, Victor, ed. *Policing and Punishing in Nineteenth-Century Britain*. London: Croom Helm, 1981.

Baldridge, Cates. "The Instabilities of Inheritance in *Oliver Twist*." *Studies in the Novel*. 25.2 (Summer 1993): 184–95.

Bareham, Tony. "Patterns of Excellence: Theme and Structure in *The Three Clerks*." In *Anthony Trollope*. Ed. Tony Bareham. London: Vision Press, 1980. 54–80.

Barry, Andrew, Thomas Osborne, and Nikolas Rose, eds. *Foucault and Political Reason: Liberalism, Neo-Liberalism and Rationalities of Government*. Chicago: University of Chicago Press, 1996.

————. "Introduction." In Barry et al. 1–17.

Barthes, Roland. *Mythologies*. 1957. Trans. Annette Lavers. New York: Hill and Wang, 1972.

Bartrip, P. W. J. "State Intervention in Mid-Nineteenth Century Britain: Fact or Fiction." *Journal of British Studies* 23 (Fall 1983): 63–83.

Beauchamp, Gorman. "Technology in the Dystopian Novel." *Modern Fiction Studies*. 32.1 (Spring 1986): 53–63.

Beauman, Nicola. *Morgan: A Biography of E. M. Forster*. London: Hodder and Stoughton, 1993.

Beer, Samuel H. *Britain against Itself*. London: Faber, 1982.

Behlmer, George K. "Character Building and the English Family: Continuities in Social Casework, c. 1870–1930." In Behlmer and Leventhal 58–74.

————. *Friends of the Family: The English Home and Its Guardians, 1850–1940*. Stanford: Stanford University Press, 1998.

Behlmer, George K., and Fred Leventhal, eds. *Singular Continuities: Tradition, Nostalgia and Identity in Modern British Culture*. Stanford: Stanford University Press, 2000.

Beiderwell, Bruce. "The Coherence of *Our Mutual Friend*." *Journal of Narrative Technique* 15.3 (Fall 1985): 234–43.

Bell, E. Moberly. *Octavia Hill*. London: Constable, 1942.

Bellamy, Richard. "Introduction." In Bellamy 1–14.

————. "T. H. Green and the Morality of Victorian Liberalism." In Bellamy 131–51.

————, ed. *Victorian Liberalism: Nineteenth-Century Political Thought and Practice*. London: Routledge, 1990.

Bender, John. *Imagining the Penitentiary: Fiction and the Architecture of Mind in Eighteenth-Century England*. Chicago: University of Chicago Press, 1986.

Benhabib, Seyla. *Situating the Self: Gender, Community and Postmodernism in Contemporary Ethics*. New York: Routledge, 1992.

Bennett, Arnold. *Clayhanger*. 1910. Harmondsworth: Penguin, 1985.

Bentham, Jeremy. *Pauper Management Improved: Particularly by Means of an Application of the Panopticon Principle of Construction*. 1797. 2d ed. London, 1812.

———. *Works*. Ed. John Bowring. Vol. 8. Edinburgh: Tait, 1843.

Best, Geoffrey. *Mid-Victorian Britain, 1851–75*. 3d ed. London: Fontana, 1985.

Birdwood, G. C. M. *On Competition and the Indian Civil Service*. London: 1872.

Blake, Kathleen. "*Bleak House*, Political Economy, Victorian Studies." *Victorian Literature and Culture* 25.1 (1997): 1–21.

Bodenheimer, Rosemarie. *The Politics of Story in Victorian Social Fiction*. Ithaca: Cornell University Press, 1988.

Bosanquet, Bernard, ed. *Aspects of the Social Problem*. 1895. Reprint. New York: Kraus, 1968.

———. "Character in Its Bearing on Social Causation." In Bosanquet, *Aspects* 103–17.

———. "The Duties of Citizenship, I and II." In Bosanquet, *Aspects* 3–27.

———. *Philosophical Theory of the State*. 1899. 4th ed. London: Macmillan, 1923.

———. "Socialism and Natural Selection." In Bosanquet, *Aspects* 289–307.

Bourdieu, Pierre. *Language and Symbolic Power*. Trans. Gino Raymond and Matthew Adamson. Ed. John B. Thompson. Cambridge: Harvard University Press, 1991.

Boyd, Nancy. *Josephine Butler, Octavia Hill, Florence Nightingale: Three Victorian Women Who Changed Their World*. London: Macmillan, 1982.

Braddon, Mary Elizabeth. *Aurora Floyd*. 1862–63. Ed. Richard Nemesvari and Lisa Surridge. Toronto: Broadview, 1998.

Bradley, Ian. *The Strange Rebirth of Liberal Britain*. London: Chatto and Windus, 1985.

Brantlinger, Patrick. *Fictions of State: Culture and Credit in Britain, 1694–1994*. Ithaca: Cornell University Press, 1996.

———. "How Oliver Twist Learned to Read, and What He Read." In *Culture and Education in Victorian England*. Ed. Patrick Scott and Pauline Fletcher. Lewisburg, Va.: Bucknell University Press, 1990. 59–82.

———. *Rule of Darkness: British Literature and Imperialism, 1830–1914*. Ithaca: Cornell University Press, 1988.

———. *The Spirit of Reform: British Literature and Politics, 1832–1867*. Cambridge: Harvard University Press, 1977.

Brewer, John. *Sinews of Power: War, Money and the English State, 1688–1783*. Cambridge: Harvard University Press, 1990.

Bridges, Thomas. "Rawlsian Reasonableness and the Creation of Citizens." <http://www.civsoc.com/review1b.html>.

Briggs, Asa. *The Age of Improvement, 1783–1867*. London: Longman, 1979.

———. *Victorian People: A Reassessment of Persons and Themes, 1851–1867*. 3d ed. Chicago: University of Chicago Press, 1972.

Brougham, [Lord] Henry. *Practical Observations upon the Education of the People*. 9th ed. London, 1825.

Brown, Stewart T. *Thomas Chalmers and the Godly Commonwealth in Scotland*. Oxford: Oxford University Press, 1982.

Brown, Wendy. *States of Injury: Power and Freedom in Late Modernity*. Princeton: Princeton University Press, 1995.

Brundage, Anthony. *England's "Prussian Minister": Edwin Chadwick and the Politics of Government Growth, 1832–1854.* University Park: Penn State University Press, 1988.

Burchell, Graham, Colin Gordon, and Peter Miller, eds. *The Foucault Effect: Studies in Governmentality.* Chicago: University of Chicago Press, 1991.

Burn, W. L. *The Age of Equipoise: A Study of the Mid-Victorian Generation.* New York: Norton, 1964.

Burrow, J. W. *Whigs and Liberals: Continuity and Change in English Political Thought.* Oxford: Clarendon Press, 1988.

Butt, John, and Kathleen Tillotson. *Dickens at Work.* London: Methuen, 1957.

Cannadine, David. *The Decline and Fall of the British Aristocracy.* New Haven: Yale University Press, 1990.

Caporaletti, Silvana. "Science as Nightmare: 'The Machine Stops' by E. M. Forster." *Utopian Studies* 8.2 (1997): 32–47.

Carlyle, Thomas. *Carlyle's Works: Centennial Memorial Edition.* 26 vols. Boston: Dana Estes and Co., n.d.

———. *Latter-Day Pamphlets.* 1850. *Works* 20:261–455.

———. *Past and Present.* 1843. New York: New York University Press, 1965.

———. "Signs of the Time." 1829. In Carlyle, *Works* 15:462–87.

Carson, Penelope. "Golden Casket or Pebbles and Trash? J. S. Mill and the Anglicist/Orientalist Controversy." In *J. S. Mill's Encounter with India.* Ed. Martin I. Moir, Douglas M. Peers, and Lynn Zastoupil. Toronto: University of Toronto Press, 1999. 149–72.

Chadwick, Edwin. "The New Poor Law." *Edinburgh Review* 63 (1836): 487–573.

———. *Report on the Sanitary Condition of the Labouring Population of Great Britain.* 1842. Ed. M. W. Flinn. Edinburgh: Edinburgh University Press, 1964.

Chalmers, Thomas. *The Christian and Civic Economy of Large Towns.* 3 vols. Glasgow, 1821–26.

Chapman, Richard, and J. R. Greenaway. *The Dynamics of Administrative Reform.* London: Croom Helm, 1980.

Chatterjee, Partha. *The Nation and Its Fragments: Colonial and Postcolonial Histories.* Princeton: Princeton University Press, 1993.

Childers, Joseph W. *Novel Possibilities: Fiction and the Formation of Early Victorian Culture.* Philadelphia: University of Pennsylvania Press, 1995.

———. "Observation and Representation: Mr. Chadwick Writes the Poor." *Victorian Studies* 37.3 (1994): 405–31.

Christensen, Jerome. *Romanticism at the End of History.* Baltimore: Johns Hopkins University Press, 2000.

Churchill, Winston Spencer. *Liberalism and the Social Problem.* 2d ed. New York: Haskell House, 1973.

Clark, G. Kitson. *An Expanding Society: Britain, 1830–1900.* Cambridge: Cambridge University Press, 1967.

———. *The Making of Victorian England.* New York: Atheneum, 1967.

———. "'Statesmen in Disguise': Reflections on the Neutrality of the Civil Service." *Historical Journal* 2.1 (1959): 19–39.

Cockshut, A. O. J. *The Imagination of Charles Dickens.* London: Collins, 1961.

Cohen, G. A. *Self-Ownership, Freedom, and Equality.* Cambridge: Cambridge University Press, 1995.

Cohn, Bernard S. "Representing Authority in Victorian India." In Hobsbawm and Ranger 165–209.

Colby, Robert A. "Oliver's Progeny: Some Unfortunate Foundlings." *Dickens Quarterly* 4.2 (June 1987): 109–21.

Colley, Linda. *Britons: Forging the Nation, 1707–1837.* New Haven: Yale University Press, 1992.

Collini, Stefan. *Liberalism and Sociology: L. T. Hobhouse and English Political Argument, 1880–1914.* London: Cambridge University Press, 1979.

———. *Public Moralists: Political Thought and Intellectual Life in Britain, 1850–1930.* Oxford: Clarendon, 1991.

———. "Sociology and Idealism in Britain, 1880–1920." *Archives Europeenes Sociologie* 19 (1978): 3–50.

Collins, Philip. *Dickens and Education.* London: Macmillan, 1963.

"Common Sense of the Civil Service Question." 25 March 1854. *The Spectator* 322.

Compton, J. M. "Open Competition and the Indian Civil Service, 1854–1876." *English Historical Review.* 83 (1968): 265–84.

Conway, Stephen. "Bentham and the Nineteenth-Century Revolution in Government." In Bellamy 71–90.

Cotsell, Michael. "Politics and Peeling Frescoes: Layard of Nineveh and *Little Dorrit.*" *Dickens Studies Annual* 15 (1986): 181–200.

Crossman, R. H. S. "Introduction." In Bagehot, *English Constitution* 1–57.

Crowther, M. A. *Church Embattled: Religious Controversy in Mid-Victorian England.* Devon, U.K.: David and Charles, 1970.

———. *The Workhouse System, 1834–1929: The History of an English Social Institution.* Athens: University of Georgia Press, 1982.

D'Albertis, Deirdre. *Dissembling Fictions: Elizabeth Gaskell and the Victorian Social Text.* New York: St. Martin's, 1997.

Danahay, Martin A. "Housekeeping and Hegemony in *Bleak House.*" *Studies in the Novel.* 23 (1991): 416–31.

Dandeker, Christopher. *Surveillance, Power and Modernity: Bureaucracy and Discipline from 1700 to the Present Day.* Cambridge: Polity, 1990.

David, Deirdre. *Intellectual Women and Victorian Patriarchy: Harriet Martineau, Elizabeth Barrett Browning, George Eliot.* Ithaca: Cornell University Press, 1987.

———. *Rule Britannia: Women, Empire and Victorian Writing.* Ithaca: Cornell University Press, 1995.

DeLacy, Margaret E. "Grinding Men Good? Lancashire's Prisons at Mid-Century." In Bailey 182–216.

Dellamora, Richard. *Masculine Desire: The Sexual Politics of Victorian Aestheticism.* Chapel Hill: University of North Carolina Press, 1990.

Dendy, Helen. "Meaning and Methods of True Charity." In Bosanquet, *Aspects* 167–79.

Den Otter, Sandra. *British Idealism and Social Explanation: A Study in Late-Victorian Thought*. Oxford: Clarendon Press, 1996.

Dickens, Charles. *Bleak House*. 1852–53. Ed. Norman Page. Harmondsworth: Penguin, 1985.

———. *David Copperfield*. 1849–50. Ed. Jeremy Tambling. Harmondsworth: Penguin, 1996.

———. *Dombey and Son*. 1846–48. Ed. Peter Fairclough. Harmondsworth: Penguin, 1985.

———. *Great Expectations*. 1860–61. Ed. Janice Carlisle. Boston: Bedford, 1996.

———. *Hard Times: For These Times*. 1854. Ed. Graham Law. Peterborough, U.K.: Broadview, 1996.

———. *Little Dorrit*. 1855–57. Ed. Stephen Wall and Hellen Small. Harmondsworth: Penguin, 1998.

———. *Oliver Twist*. 1837. Ed. Fred Kaplan. New York: Norton, 1993.

———. *Our Mutual Friend*. 1864–65. Ed. Stephen Gill. Harmondsworth: Penguin, 1971.

———. "Red Tape." *Household Words* (15 Feb. 1851): 481–84.

———. "The Short-Timers." *The Uncommercial Traveller*. Vol. 11: *Complete Works of Charles Dickens*. New York: De Fau, 1904. 308–19.

———. *Sketches by Boz*. 1836–37. Oxford: Oxford University Press, 1987.

———. *The Speeches of Charles Dickens*. Ed. K. J. Fielding. Atlantic Highlands, N.J.: Harvester, 1988.

———. "A Walk in a Workhouse." In *Uncommercial Traveller* 537–43.

———. *The Uncommercial Traveller* and *Reprinted Pieces*. *The Oxford Illustrated Dickens*. Oxford: Oxford University Press, 1987.

———. "Wapping Workhouse." In *Uncommercial Traveller* 18–28.

Dictionary of National Biography. 2d supp. Vol. 3. Ed. Sir Sidney Lee. New York: Macmillan, 1912.

The Dictionary of Phrase and Fable. Ed. E. Cobham Brewer. First hypertext ed. from the 1894 ed. < http://www.bartleby.com/81/>.

Digby, Anne. *Pauper Palaces*. London: Routledge, 1978.

———. *The Poor Law in Nineteenth-Century England and Wales*. London: Historical Association, 1989.

Digby, Anne, and Peter Searby. *Children, School, and Society in Nineteenth-Century England*. London: Macmillan, 1981.

Donajgrodzki, A. P., ed. *Social Control in Nineteenth-Century Britain*. London: Croom Helm, 1977.

———. "'Social Police' and the Bureaucratic Elite: A Vision of Order in the Age of Reform." In Donajgrodzki, *Social Control* 51–76.

"Dr. Thomas Chalmers." *Encyclopedia Britannica*. Vol. 5. New York: Werner, 1902. 374–78.

Dowling, Linda. *Hellenism and Homosexuality in Victorian Oxford*. Ithaca: Cornell University Press, 1994.

Duncan, Graeme. *Marx and Mill: Two Views of Social Conflict and Social Harmony*. Cambridge: Cambridge University Press, 1973.

Eagleton, Terry. *Ideology: An Introduction.* London: Verso, 1991.

Eliot, George. "The Natural History of German Life." In *George Eliot: Selected Critical Writings.* Ed. Rosemary Ashton. Oxford: Oxford University Press, 2000. 260–95.

Ellis, Mrs. [Sara]. *The Mothers of England: Their Influence and Responsibility.* New York: Appleton, 1844.

Emsley, Clive. *The English Police: A Political and Social History.* New York: St. Martin's, 1991.

"Encroaching Bureaucracy." *Quarterly Review* 221 (July-Oct 1914): 51–75.

Farrell, John P. "The Partners' Tale: Dickens and *Our Mutual Friend.*" *ELH* 66.3 (Fall 1999): 759–99.

Finer, S. E. *The Life and Times of Edwin Chadwick.* London: Methuen, 1952.

Flinn, M. W. "Introduction." In Chadwick, *Report* 1–73.

Fontana, Bianca. "Whigs and Liberals: The *Edinburgh Review* and the 'Liberal Movement' in Nineteenth-Century Britain." In Bellamy 42–57.

Forster, E. M. *Howards End.* 1910. Ed. David Lodge. Harmondsworth: Penguin, 2000.

———. "The Machine Stops." 1909. *The Eternal Moment and Other Stories.* San Diego: Harvest, 1956. 3–37.

Foucault, Michel. "An Aesthetics of Existence." In Foucault, *Politics* 47–53.

———. *Discipline and Punish: The Birth of the Prison.* Trans. Alan Sheridan. New York: Vintage, 1977.

———. "Governmentality." In Burchell et al. 87–104.

———. *The History of Sexuality,* vol. 1. Trans. Robert Hurley. New York: Vintage, 1990.

———. "Nietzsche, Genealogy, History." In Rabinow 76–100.

———. *Politics, Philosophy, Culture: Interviews and Other Writings, 1977–1984.* Ed. Lawrence D. Kritzman. Trans. Alan Sheridan et al. New York: Routledge, 1988.

———. "Politics and Reason." In *Politics, Philosophy, Culture* 57–85.

———. "Social Security." In *Politics, Philosophy, Culture* 159–77.

———. "Space, Knowledge, and Power." In Rabinow 239–56.

———. "The Subject and Power." In *Michel Foucault: Beyond Structuralism and Hermeneutics.* Ed. Herbert L. Dreyfus and Paul Rabinow. Chicago: University of Chicago Press, 1983. 208–26.

———. "What Is Enlightenment?" In Rabinow 32–50.

Frank, Thomas. *One Market under God: Extreme Capitalism, Market Populism, and the End of Economic Democracy.* New York: Doubleday, 2000.

Fraser, Derek. *The Evolution of the British Welfare State.* 2d ed. London: Macmillan, 1984

Freeden, Michael. "The New Liberalism and Its Aftermath." In Bellamy 175–92.

Freedgood, Elaine. "Banishing Panic: Harriet Martineau and the Popularization of Political Economy." *Victorian Studies* 39.1 (Fall 1995): 33–53.

Frow, John. "Cultural Studies and the Neoliberal Imagination." *Yale Journal of Criticism* 12.2 (1999): 423–30.

Fukuyama, Francis. *The End of History and the Last Man.* New York: Avon, 1992.

Fulweiler, Howard W. "'A Dismal Swamp': Darwin, Design, and Evolution in *Our Mutual Friend.*" *Nineteenth-Century Literature* 49.1 (June 1994): 50–74.

Furbank, P. N. *E. M. Forster: A Life.* London: Secker and Warburg, 1977.

Regenia. *Idylls of the Marketplace : Oscar Wilde and the Victorian Public.* Stanford: ⟩rd University Press, 1986.

———. *Subjectivities: A History of Self-Representation in Britain, 1832–1920.* New York: Oxford University Press, 1991.

Gallagher, Catherine. *The Industrial Reformation of English Fiction: Social Discourse and Narrative Form, 1832–1867.* Chicago: University of Chicago Press, 1985.

———. "The Bioeconomics of *Our Mutual Friend.*" In *Subject to History: Ideology, Class, Gender.* Ed. David Simpson. Ithaca: Cornell University Press, 1991. 47–64.

———. "Marxism and the New Historicism." In *The New Historicism.* Ed. Harold Veeser. New York: Routledge, 1989. 37–48.

Gallagher, Catherine, and Stephen Greenblatt. *Practicing New Historicism.* Chicago: University of Chicago Press, 2000.

Gaskell, Elizabeth. *North and South.* 1854–55. Ed. Patricia Ingham. Harmondsworth: Penguin, 1995.

Gatrell, V. A. C. "Crime, Authority and the Policeman-State." In F. M. L. Thompson, *Cambridge Social History* 243–310.

Gibbins, John. "J. S. Mill, Liberalism, and Progress." In Bellamy 91–109.

Gilmour, Robin. *The Idea of the Gentleman in the Victorian Novel.* London: George Allen, 1981.

———. "Introduction." In Trollope, *Barchester Towers* xv–xxxi.

Gissing, George. *The Immortal Dickens.* London 1925.

———. *The Nether World.* 1889. Ed. Stephen Gill. Oxford: Oxford University Press, 1992.

———. *New Grub Street.* 1891. Ed. Bernard Bergonzi. Harmondsworth: Penguin, 1983.

———. *The Private Papers of George Ryecroft.* 1903. Ed. Mark Storey. Oxford: Oxford University Press, 1987.

Glendenning, Victoria. *Anthony Trollope.* New York: Knopf, 1993.

Glover, David. *Vampires, Mummies, and Liberals: Bram Stoker and the Politics of Popular Fiction.* Durham: Duke University Press, 1996.

Goode, John. "George Gissing's *The Nether World.*" In *Tradition and Tolerance in Nineteenth-Century Fiction.* Ed. David Howard, John Lucas, and John Goode. New York: Barnes and Noble, 1967. 27–42.

Goodlad, Lauren M. E. "'A Middle Class Cut into Two': Historiography and Victorian National Character." *ELH* 67 (Spring 2000): 143–78.

———. "England's 'Glorious "Middle Way"': Self-Disciplinary Self-Making and Jane Austen's *Sense and Sensibility.*" *Genre* 33 (Spring 2000): 51–81.

Gordon, Colin. "Governmental Rationality: An Introduction." In Burchell et al. 1–51.

———. "The Soul of the Citizen: Max Weber and Michel Foucault on Rationality and Government." In *Max Weber, Rationality and Modernity.* Ed. Scott Lash and Sam Whimster. London: Allen and Unwin, 1987. 293–316.

Gordon, David M. "Do We Need to Be No. 1?" *Atlantic Monthly* (Apr. 1986) <online archive: http://www.theatlantic.com/politics/foreign/gordon.htm>.

Gowan, Peter. "The Origins of the Administrative Elite." *New Left Review* 162 (1987): 4–34.

Gramsci, Antonio. *Selections from the Prison Notebooks*. Ed. and trans. Quintin Hoare and Geoffrey Nowell Smith. New York: International, 1971.

Gray, John. *Beyond the New Right: Markets, Government and the Common Environment*. London: Routledge, 1993.

———. *Enlightenment's Wake: Politics and Culture at the Close of the Modern Age*. London: Routledge, 1995.

Greaves. H. R. G. *The Civil Service in the Changing State*. London: Harrap, 1947.

Gunn, Simon. "The Ministry, the Middle Class and the 'Civilizing Mission' in Manchester, 1850–80." *Social History* 21.1 (Jan. 1996): 22–36.

Habermas, Jürgen. *The Philosophical Discourse of Modernity* Trans. Frederick G. Lawrence. Cambridge: MIT Press, 1987.

———. *The Structural Transformation of the Public Sphere: An Inquiry into a Category of Bourgeois Society*. Trans. Thomas Burger. Cambridge: MIT Press, 1989.

Hadley, Elaine. "The Past Is a Foreign Country: The Neo-Conservative Romance with Victorian Liberalism." *Yale Journal of Criticism* 10.1 (1997): 7–38.

Hall, N. John. "Introduction." In Trollope, *The New Zealander* xi–xlv.

Halperin, John. *Trollope and Politics: A Study of the Pallisers and Others*. New York: Barnes and Noble, 1977.

Hanham, H. J. *The Nineteenth Century Constitution, 1815–1914: Documents and Commentary*. Cambridge: Cambridge University Press, 1969.

Harootunian, H. D. "Foucault, Genealogy, History: The Pursuit of Otherness." In *After Foucault: Humanistic Knowledge, Postmodern Challenges*. Ed. Jonathan Arac. New Brunswick: Rutgers University Press, 1988. 110–37.

Harris, Jose. *Private Lives, Public Spirit: Britain, 1870–1914*. Harmondsworth: Penguin, 1993.

———. "Society and the State in Twentieth-Century Britain." In F. M. L. Thompson, *Cambridge Social History* 63–118.

Hart, Jennifer. "Nineteenth-Century Social Reform: A Tory Interpretation of History." *Past and Present* 31 (1965): 39–61.

Heineman, Helen. *Mrs. Trollope: The Triumphant Feminine in the Nineteenth Century*. Athens: Ohio University Press, 1982.

Hellegas, Mark R. *The Future as Nightmare: H. G. Wells and the Anti-Utopians*. New York: Oxford University Press, 1967.

Henriques, Ursula. "How Cruel Was the Victorian Poor Law?" *Historical Journal* 11 (1968): 365–73.

———. "The Separate System of Prison Discipline." *Past and Present* 54 (1972): 61–93.

Hernon, Joseph M., Jr. "A Victorian Cromwell: Sir Charles Trevelyan, the Famine and the Age of Improvement." *Eire-Ireland* 22.3 (1987): 15–29.

Hickox, M. S. "The Problem of Early English Sociology." *Sociological Review* 32.1 (Feb. 1984): 1–17.

Hill, Christopher. *Puritanism and Revolution: Studies in Interpretation of the English Revolution in the Seventeenth Century*. London: Secker and Warburg, 1958.

Hilton, Boyd. *The Age of Atonement: The Influence of Evangelicalism on Social and Economic Thought, 1795–1865*. Oxford: Clarendon Press, 1988.

Himmelfarb, Gertrude. *The De-Moralization of Society: From Victorian Virtues to Modern Values.* New York: Vintage, 1994.

———. "The Haunted House of Jeremy Bentham." *Victorian Minds: A Study of Intellectuals in Crisis and of Ideologies in Transition.* New York: Harper, 1952. 32–75.

———. *Poverty and Compassion: The Moral Imagination of the Late Victorians.* New York: Knopf, 1991.

———. *The Idea of Poverty: England in the Early Industrial Age.* New York: Knopf, 1984.

Hobsbawm, E. J. *Industry and Empire.* 1968. Harmondsworth: Penguin, 1969.

———. "Mass-Producing Traditions: Europe, 1870–1914." In Hobsbawm and Ranger 263–307.

Hobsbawm, Eric, and Terence Ranger. *The Invention of Tradition.* Cambridge: Cambridge University Press, 1983.

House, Humphrey. *The Dickens World.* London: Oxford University Press, 1942.

Hoy, David Couzens, ed. *Foucault: A Critical Reader.* Oxford: Blackwell, 1986.

———. "Introduction." In Hoy 1–25.

Hughes, Edward. "Sir Charles Trevelyan and Civil Service Reform, 1853–5." Pt. 1. *English Historical Review* 64 (Jan. 1949): 53–88.

Hume, L. J. *Bentham and Bureaucracy.* Cambridge: Cambridge University Press, 1981.

———. "Jeremy Bentham and the Nineteenth-Century Revolution in Government." *Historical Journal* 10.4 (1967): 361–75.

Huntington, John, ed. *Critical Essays on H. G. Wells.* Boston: G. K. Hall, 1991.

Huxley, Aldous. *Brave New World.* 1932. New York: Vintage, 1998.

Jaffe, Audrey. "Omniscience in *Our Mutual Friend:* On Taking the Reader by Surprise." *Journal of Narrative Technique* 17.1 (Winter 1987): 91–101.

James, Henry. "*Our Mutual Friend.*" *Nation,* 21 December 1865, 786–87.

JanMohamed, Abdul. "The Economy of Manichean Allegory: The Function of Racial Difference in Colonialist Literature." In *"Race," Writing, and Difference.* Ed. Henry Louis Gates Jr. Chicago: University of Chicago Press, 1986. 78–106.

Johnson, Edgar. *Charles Dickens: His Tragedy and Triumph.* 2 vols. New York: Simon and Schuster, 1952.

Johnson, Richard. "Administrators in Education before 1870: Patronage, Social Position and Role." In *Studies in the Growth of Nineteenth-Century Government.* Ed. Gillian Sutherland. Totowa, N.J.: Rowman and Littlefield, 1972. 110–38.

———. "Educating the Educators: 'Experts' and the State 1833–9." In Donajgrodzki, *Social Control* 77–107.

———. "Educational Policy and Social Control in Early Victorian England." *Past and Present* 49 (1970): 96–119.

Jones, David. *Crime, Protest, Community and Police in Nineteenth-Century Britain.* London: Routledge, 1982.

Joyce, Simon. "Victorian Continuities: Early British Sociology and the Welfare of the State." In *Disciplinarity at the Fin de Siècle.* Ed. Amanda Anderson and Joseph Valente. Princeton: Princeton University Press. 261–80.

Kahan, Alan S. *Aristocratic Liberalism: The Social and Political Thought of Jacob Burckhardt, John Stuart Mill, and Alexis de Tocqueville.* Oxford: Oxford University Press, 1992.

Kaufmann, David. *The Business of Common Life: Novels and Classical Economics between Revolution and Reform.* Baltimore: Johns Hopkins University Press, 1995.

Kay, James Phillips. *The Moral and Physical Condition of the Working Classes Employed in the Cotton Manufacture in Manchester.* 2d ed. 1832. Reprint. New York: Kelley, 1970.

———. "On the Punishment of Pauper Children in Workhouses." 1841. Reprinted as "College of St. Mark and St. John: Occasional Papers No. 1." The Library, 1961.

Kay-Shuttleworth, Sir James. *The Training of Pauper Children: A Report Published by the Poor Law Commissioners in Their Fourth Report.* London, 1839.

Keating, Peter. *The Working Classes in Victorian Fiction.* New York: Barnes and Noble, 1971.

Kettle, Arnold. *An Introduction to the English Novel.* Vol. 1. London: Hutchinson, 1951.

Kidd, Alan J. "Philanthropy and the 'Social History Paradigm.'" *Social History* 21.2 (May 1996): 180–92.

Korg, Jacob. *George Gissing: A Critical Biography.* Seattle: University of Washington Press, 1963.

LaCapra, Dominick. "Ideology and Critique in Dickens's *Bleak House.*" *Representations* 6 (Spring 1984): 116–23.

Laing, Samuel. *Notes of a Traveller, on the Social and Political State of France, Prussia, Switzerland, Italy, and Other Parts of Europe during the Present Century.* London: 1842.

Lane, Christopher. *The Burdens of Intimacy: Psychoanalysis and Victorian Masculinity.* Chicago: University of Chicago Press, 1999.

Langland, Elizabeth. *Nobody's Angels: Middle-Class Women and Domestic Ideology in Victorian Culture.* Ithaca: Cornell University Press, 1995.

———. "Nobody's Angels: Domestic Ideology and Middle-Class Women in the Victorian Novel." *PMLA* 107.2 (Mar. 1992): 290–304.

Laqueur, Thomas. "Bodies, Death, and Pauper Funerals." *Representations* 1.1 (Feb. 1983): 109–31.

———. "Bodies, Details, and the Humanitarian Narrative." In *The New Cultural History.* Ed. Lynn Hunt. Berkeley: University of California Press, 1989. 176–204.

———. "Orgasm, Generation and the Politics of Reproduction." In *The Making of the Modern Body.* Ed. Catherine Gallagher and Thomas Laqueur. Berkeley: University of California Press, 1987. 1–41.

———. "Sexual Desire and the Market Economy during the Industrial Revolution." In *Discourses of Sexuality: From Aristotle to AIDS.* Ed. Donna C. Stanton. Ann Arbor: University of Michigan Press, 1992. 185–215.

Ledger, Sally, and Scott McCracken. *Culture and Politics at the* Fin de Siècle. Cambridge: Cambridge University Press, 1987.

Lenin, V. I. *State and Revolution.* 1918. New York: International Publishers, 1943.

Levine, George. "*Little Dorrit* and Three Kinds of Science." In *Dickens and Other Victorians: Essays in Honor of Phillip Collins.* Ed. Joanne Shattock. New York: St. Martin's, 1988. 3–24.

Lewis, R. A. *Edwin Chadwick and the Public Health Movement, 1832–1854*. London: Longman, 1952.

Lloyd, David, and Paul Thomas. *Culture and the State*. New York: Routledge, 1998.

Loch, C. S. "Some Controverted Points in the Administration of Poor Relief." In Bosanquet, *Aspects* 227–67.

———. "Pauperism and Old-Age Pensions." In Bosanquet, *Aspects* 126–66.

Logan, Peter. *Nerves and Narratives: A Cultural History of Hysteria in Nineteenth-Century British Prose*. Berkeley: University of California Press, 1997.

Longmate, Norman. *The Workhouse*. New York: St. Martin's, 1974.

Lubenow, William C. *The Politics of Government Growth: Early Victorian Attitudes toward State Intervention, 1833–1848*. Devon, U. K.: David and Charles, 1971.

Lukács, Georg. *The Historical Novel*. Trans. Hannah and Stanley Mitchell. Lincoln: University of Nebraska Press, 1983.

Macaulay, Thomas Babington. *Macaulay, Prose and Poetry*. Ed. G. M. Young. Cambridge: Harvard University Press, 1967.

———. "Government in India." 1833. In Macaulay 688–718.

———. "Minute of the 2nd of February, 1835: Indian Education." In Macaulay 719–30.

———. "On Mitford's History of Greece." 1824. *Essays: Critical and Miscellaneous*. New York, 1869. 424–32.

MacDonagh, Oliver. *Early Victorian Government, 1830–1870*. London: Weidenfeld and Nicolson, 1977.

———. "The Nineteenth-Century Revolution in Government." *Historical Journal* 1 (1958): 52–67.

Mandler, Peter. "The Making of the New Poor Law *Redivivus*." *Past and Present* 117 (Nov. 1987): 131–57.

———. "Tories and Paupers: Christian Political Economy and the Making of the New Poor Law." *Historical Journal* 33.1 (1990): 81–103.

Marcus, Steven. *Engels, Manchester, and the Working Class*. 1974. New York: Norton, 1985.

———. *Dickens: From Pickwick to Dombey*. 1965. New York: Norton, 1985.

Marion, David E. "The British Civil Service: A Political Excavation and Review." *Administration and Society* 24.4 (Feb. 1993): 470–86.

Marsh, Joss. *Word Crimes: Blasphemy, Culture, and Literature in Nineteenth-Century England*. Chicago: University of Chicago Press, 1998.

Martineau, Harriet. "The Hamlets." 1833. *Poor Laws and Paupers Illustrated*. Boston, 1836.

———. *Harriet Martineau: Selected Letters*. Ed. Valerie Sanders. Oxford: Clarendon Press, 1990.

———. *Household Education*. 1848. Reprint. Philadelphia, 1849.

———. *Society in America*. 2 vols. London, 1837.

Marx, Karl. *Capital*. Vol. 1. Ed. Friedrich Engels. New York: International, 1967.

Marx, Karl, and Friedrich Engels. *The German Ideology*. 1845–46. Amherst, N.Y.: Prometheus, 1998.

———. *Manifesto of the Communist Party*. 1848. *The Marx-Engels Reader*. 2d ed. Ed. Robert C. Tucker. New York: Norton, 1978. 469–500.

Mason, D. M. "Matthew Arnold and Elementary Education: A Reconsideration." *History of Education* 12.3 (1983): 177–89.

Maurice, C. Edmund, ed. *Life of Octavia Hill as Told in Her Letters.* London: Macmillan, 1914.

McCaffrey, John F. "Thomas Chalmers and Social Change." *Scottish Historical Review* 60.1.169 (Apr. 1981): 32–60.

McCalman, Iain. "New Jerusalems: Prophecy, Dissent and Radical Culture in England, 1786–1830." In *Enlightenment and Religion: Rational Dissent in Eighteenth-Century Britain.* Ed. Knud Haakanssen. Cambridge: Cambridge University Press, 1996. 312–35.

McCandless, Peter. "Dangerous to Themselves and Others: The Victorian Debate over the Prevention of Wrongful Confinement." *Journal of British Studies* 23 (Fall 1983): 84–104.

———. "Liberty and Lunacy: The Victorians and Wrongful Confinement." *Journal of Social History* 11 (1978): 366–86.

Mehta, Uday Singh. *Liberalism and Empire: A Study in Nineteenth-Century British Liberal Thought.* Chicago: University of Chicago Press, 1999.

Miguel-Alfonso, Ricardo, and Silvia Caporale-Bizzini, eds. *Reconstructing Foucault: Essays in the Wake of the 80s.* Amsterdam: Rodopi, 1994.

Mill, John Stuart. "Armand Carrel, His Life and Character." *Westminster Review* 28.6 (Oct. 1837): 33–58.

———. *Autobiography.* 1873. Ed. Jack Stillinger. Boston: Riverside, 1969.

———. "Bentham." In Mill and Bentham 132–76.

———. "Civilization." In *Collected Works* 18:119–47.

———. "Coleridge." In Mill and Bentham 177–227.

———. 1963–91. *The Collected Works of John Stuart Mill.* Ed. John M. Robson. 33 vols. Toronto: University of Toronto Press.

———. *Considerations on Representative Government.* 1861. Amherst, N.Y.: Prometheus, 1991.

———. *On Liberty.* 1859. Ed. Edward Alexander. Toronto: Broadview, 1999.

———. "The Proposed Irish Poor Law." *Collected Works* 24:1069–73.

———. *A System of Logic. Collected Works* 8. 1974.

———. *Utilitarianism.* 1861. Mill and Bentham. 272–338.

Mill, John Stuart, and Jeremy Bentham. *Utilitarianism and Other Essays.* Ed. Alan Ryan. Harmondsworth: Penguin, 1987.

Miller, Andrew. *Novels behind Glass: Commodity Culture and Victorian Narrative.* Cambridge: Cambridge University Press, 1995.

Miller, D. A. *The Novel and the Police.* Berkeley: University of California Press, 1988.

Miller, J. Hillis. *Charles Dickens: The World of His Novels.* Cambridge: Harvard University Press, 1958.

———. *The Form of Victorian Fiction; Thackeray, Dickens, Trollope, George Eliot, Meredith, and Hardy.* Notre Dame: University of Notre Dame Press, 1968.

Minson, Jeffrey. *Genealogies of Morals.* London: Macmillan, 1985.

Moore, R. J. "The Abolition of Patronage in the Indian Civil Service and the Closure of Haileybury College." *Historical Journal* 7.2 (1964): 246–57.

———. "India and the British Empire." In *British Imperialism in the Nineteenth Century.* Ed. C. C. Eldridge. New York: St. Martin's, 1984. 65–84.

Mowat, Charles Loch. *The Charity Organization Society, 1869–1913: Its Ideas and Work.* London: Methuen, 1961.

Mueller, Hans-Eberhard. *Bureaucracy, Education, and Monopoly: Civil Service Reforms in Prussia and England.* Berkeley: University of California Press, 1984.

Nardin, Jane. *Trollope and Victorian Moral Philosophy.* Athens: Ohio University Press, 1996.

Nicholson, Peter. "The Reception and Early Reputation of Mill's Political Thought." In Skorupski 464–96.

Nord, Deborah Epstein. *The Apprenticeship of Beatrice Webb.* Amherst: University of Massachusetts Press, 1985.

———. *Walking the Victorian Streets: Women, Representation, and the City.* Ithaca: Cornell University Press, 1995.

Norris, Christopher. "'What Is Enlightenment?' Kant according to Foucault." In Miguel-Alfonso and Caporale-Bizzini 53–138.

Nunokawa, Jeff. *The Afterlife of Property: Domestic Security and the Victorian Novel.* Princeton: Princeton University Press, 1994.

Page, H. M. "'A More Seditious Book than *Das Kapital*': Shaw on *Little Dorrit*." 20 (1977): 171–77.

Parris, Henry. *Constitutional Bureaucracy.* London: Allen and Unwin, 1969.

Parry, Jonathan. *The Rise and Fall of Liberal Government in Victorian Britain.* New Haven: Yale University Press, 1993.

Parry-Jones, William Ll. "The Model of the Geel Lunatic Colony and Its Influence on the Nineteenth-Century Asylum System in Britain." In Scull 200–216.

Patterson, Lee. "Literary History." *Critical Terms for Literary Study.* 2d ed. Ed. Frank Lentricchia and Thomas McLaughlin. Chicago: University of Chicago Press, 1995. 250–62.

Paz, D. G. "The Limits of Bureaucratic Autonomy." *Historian* 49.2 (Feb. 1987): 167–83.

———. *The Politics of Working-Class Education in Britain, 1830–50.* Manchester: Manchester University Press, 1980.

———. "Sir James Kay-Shuttleworth: The Man behind the Myth." *History of Education* 14.3 (1985): 185–98.

———. "Working-Class Education and the State, 1839–1849: The Sources of Government Policy." *Journal of British Studies* 16.1 (1976): 129–52.

Peel, J. D. Y., ed. *Herbert Spencer on Social Evolution.* Chicago: University of Chicago Press, 1972.

Pence, James W., Jr. "Invention Gone Awry: The London 'Times' and Civil Service Reform in 1854." *Western Speech* 33.3 (Summer 1969): 199–204.

Perkin, Harold. *Origins of Modern English Society.* London: Ark, 1969.

———. *The Rise of Professional Society: England since 1880.* London: Routledge, 1989.

Peterson, Linda H. "Harriet Martineau: Masculine Discourse, Female Sage." In *Victorian Sages and Culural Discourse: Renegotiating Gender and Power.* Ed. Thaïs E. Morgan. New Brunswick: Rutgers University Press, 1990. 171–86.

Petterson, Torsten. "Two Incongruities in *Oliver Twist*." *Orbis Literarum* 45 (1990): 341–50.

Philpotts, Trey. "Trevelyan, Treasury, and Circumlocution." *Dickens Studies Annual* 22 (1993): 283–301.

Pillew, Jill. *The Home Office, 1848–1914: From Clerks to Bureaucrats.* London: Heinemann, 1982.

Pocock, J. G. A. *The Machiavellian Moment: Florentine Political Thought and the Atlantic Republican Tradition.* Princeton, N.J.: Princeton University Press, 1975.

———. *Virtue, Commerce, and History.* Cambridge: Cambridge University Press, 1985.

Poovey, Mary. *Making a Social Body: British Cultural Formation, 1830–1864.* Chicago: University of Chicago Press, 1995.

———. *Uneven Developments: The Ideological Work of Gender in Mid-Victorian England.* Chicago: University of Chicago Press, 1988.

Prochaska, F. K. "Philanthropy." In F. M. L. Thompson, *Cambridge Social History* 357–94.

Pugin, A. W. N. *Contrasts; or, A Parallel between the Noble Edifices of the Fourteenth and Fifteenth Centuries, and Similar Buildings of the Present Day. . . .1836.* Reprint of 2d ed. 1841. New York: Humanities Press, 1969.

Rabinow, Paul, ed. *The Foucault Reader.* Trans. Christian Hubert. New York: Pantheon, 1984.

———. "Introduction." In Rabinow 3–29.

Rainbow, Bernarr. "The Rise of Popular Music Education in Nineteenth-Century England." *Victorian Studies* 30.1 (Fall 1986): 25–49.

Rawls, John. *Political Liberalism.* New York: Columbia University Press, 1993.

Reade, Charles. *Hard Cash: A Matter-of-Fact Romance.* 1863. Reprint. New York, 1871.

Rhodes, A. W. "Wilting in Limbo: Anthony Trollope and the Nineteenth Century Civil Service." *Public Administration* 51.2 (1973): 207–19.

Richards, Thomas. *The Commodity Culture of Victorian England: Advertising and Spectacle, 1851–1914.* Stanford: Stanford University Press, 1990.

Robbins, Bruce. "How to Be a Benefactor without Any Money: The Chill of Welfare in *Great Expectations.*" In *Knowing the Past: Victorian Literature and Culture.* Ed. Suzy Anger. Ithaca: Cornell University Press, 2001.

———. "Telescopic Philanthropy: Professionalism and Responsibility in *Bleak House.*" In *Nation and Narration.* Ed. Homi K. Bhabha. London: Routledge, 1990. 213–30.

Roberts, David. "Jeremy Bentham and the Victorian Administrative State." In *Jeremy Bentham: Ten Critical Essays.* Ed. Bhijhu Parekh. London: Frank Cass, 1974. 187–201.

———. *Paternalism in Early Victorian England.* New Brunswick: Rutgers University Press, 1979.

———. *Victorian Origins of the Modern Welfare State.* New Haven: Yale University Press, 1960.

Rose, Michael. "The Disappearing Pauper: Victorian Attitudes to the Relief of the Poor." In Sigsworth 56–72.

Rose, Nikolas. "Governing 'Advanced' Liberal Democracies." In Barry et al. 37–64.

Rothblatt, Sheldon. *The Revolutions of the Dons: Cambridge and Society in Victorian England.* New York: Basic, 1968.

Rotkin, Charlotte. "The *Athenaeium* Reviews *Little Dorrit.*" *Victorian Periodicals Review* 23.1 (Spring 1990): 25–28.

Rubinstein, W. D. "The End of 'Old Corruption' in Britain, 1780–1860." *Past and Present* 101 (Nov. 1983): 55–86.

Ruskin, John. "Of Kings' Treasuries." 1864. *Sesame and Lilies.* London: J. M. Dent, 1944. 1–47.

———. *Unto This Last.* 1860. Ed. Clive Wilmer. Harmondsworth: Penguin, 1986.

Ryan, Alan. "Mill in a Liberal Landscape." In Skorupski 497–540.

Said, Edward W. "Foucault and the Imagination of Power." In Hoy 149–55.

———. *Orientalism.* New York: Vintage, 1978.

"Samuel Smiles." *Dictionary of National Biography.* 2d supp. 1912 ed.

Schrift, Alan D. "Reconfiguring the Subject: Foucault's Analytics of Power." In Miguel-Alfonso and Caporale-Bizzini 185–99.

Schroeder, Ralph. "'Personality' and 'Inner Distance': The Conception of the Individual in Max Weber's Sociology." *History of the Human Sciences* 4.1 (1990): 61–78.

Schultz, Harold J. *History of England.* 3d ed. New York: Barnes and Noble, 1980.

Schwarzbach, F. S. *Dickens and the City.* London: Athlone Press, 1979.

———. "Terra Incognita—An Image of the City in English Literature, 1820–1855." *Prose Studies* 5.1 (May 1982): 61–85.

Scoones, W. Baptiste. "The Civil Service in England." *Macmillan's Magazine* 31 (Nov. 1874–Apr. 1875): 347–56.

Scull, Andrew, ed. *Madhouses, Mad-Doctors, and Madmen: The Social History of Psychiatry in the Victorian Era.* Philadelphia: University of Pennsylvania Press, 1981.

Searle, Geoffrey. *The Quest for National Efficiency.* Oxford: Oxford University Press, 1971.

Sedgwick, Eve Kosofsky. *Between Men: English Literature and Male Homosocial Desire.* New York: Columbia University Press, 1985.

Seleski, Patty. "Identity, Immigration, and the State: Irish Immigrants and English Settlement in London, 1790–1840." In Behlmer and Leventhal 11–27.

Selleck, R. J. W. *James Kay-Shuttleworth: Journey of an Outsider.* Essex: Woburn Press, 1994.

Sen, Amartya. *Development as Freedom.* New York: Anchor, 1999.

Sharpe, Jenny. *Allegories of Empire: The Figure of Woman in the Colonial Text.* Minneapolis: University of Minnesota Press, 1993.

Shattock, Joanne. "Travel Writing, Victorian and Modern: A Review of Recent Research." *Prose Studies* 5.1 (May 1982): 151–64.

Shuman, Cathy. "Invigilating *Our Mutual Friend:* Gender and the Legitimation of Professional Authority." *Novel* 28.2 (Winter 1995): 154–72.

Shuttleworth, Lord. "A Son's Reminiscences." In F. Smith 326–46.

Shuttleworth, Sally. "Female Circulation: Medical Discourse and Popular Advertising in the Mid-Victorian Era." In *Body/Politics.* Ed. Mary Jacobus, Evelyn Fox Keller, and Sally Shuttleworth. New York: Routledge, 1990. 47–68.

Siedentop, Larry. "Two Liberal Traditions." In *The Idea of Freedom: Essays in Honour of Isaiah Berlin.* Ed. Alan Ryan. Oxford: Oxford University Press, 1979. 154–72.

Sigsworth, Eric M., ed. *In Search of Victorian Values.* Manchester: Manchester University Press, 1988.

Simey, T. S. "The Contribution of Sidney and Beatrice Webb to Sociology." *British Journal of Sociology* 12.2 (June 1961): 106–23.

Skilton, David. *Anthony Trollope and His Contemporaries: A Study in the Theory and Conventions of Mid-Victorian Fiction.* London: Longman, 1972.

———. "Introduction." In Trollope, *An Autobiography* vii–xx.

Skorupski, John. "Introduction: The Fortunes of Liberal Naturalism." In *The Cambridge Companion to Mill.* Ed. John Skorupski, Cambridge: Cambridge University Press, 1998. 1–34.

Skultans, Vieda. *Madness and Morals: Ideas on Insanity in the Nineteenth Century.* London: Routledge and Kegan Paul, 1975.

Smiles, Samuel. *Character.* 1871. New York: Burt, n.d.

———. *Self-Help: With Illustrations of Character and Conduct.* 1859. Reprint. Boston, 1866.

Smith, Frank. *The Life and Work of Sir James Kay-Shuttleworth.* London: John Murray, 1923.

Smith, Joshua Toulmin. *Local Self-Government and Centralization.* London, 1851.

Soper, Steve, and Christopher Schmidt-Nowara. "The Return of Liberalism: Conference Report I." *Social History* 21.1 (Jan. 1996): 88–92.

Spencer, Herbert. *The Proper Sphere of Government.* 1842. Reprint of a Series of Letters originally published in *The Nonconformist.* London, 1843.

———. *Social Statics.* London, 1851.

Stafford, William. "John Stuart Mill: Critic of Victorian Values?" In Sigsworth 88–101.

Stallybrass, Peter, and Allon White. *The Politics and Poetics of Transgression.* Ithaca: Cornell University Press, 1986.

Stansky, Peter. *Gladstone: A Progress in Politics.* New York: Norton, 1979.

Stasiak, Lauren. "The New Man and the Imperial Gothic: Du Maurier's *Trilby* and Haggard's *She.*" MS. University of Washington, 2002.

Stokes, Eric. *The English Utilitarians and India.* Oxford: Clarendon Press, 1959.

Stone, Marjorie. "Dickens, Bentham, and the Fictions of the Law: A Victorian Controversy and Its Consequences." *Victorian Studies* 29 (Aug. 1985): 125–54.

Storch, Robert D. "The Problem of Working-Class Leisure; Some Roots of Middle-Class Moral Reform in the Industrial North: 1825–50." In Donajgrodzki, *Social Control* 138–62.

Strachey, Lytton. *Eminent Victorians.* 1918. New York: Harcourt, n.d.

Summers, Anne. "A Home from Home—Women's Philanthropic Work in the Nineteenth Century." In *Fit Work for Women.* Ed. Sandra Burman. London: Croom Helm, 1979. 33–63.

Super, R. H. *The Chronicler of Barsetshire: A Life of Anthony Trollope.* Ann Arbor: University of Michigan Press, 1988.

Sutherland, Gillian. "Education." In F. M. L. Thompson, *Cambridge Social History* 119–70.

Taylor, Charles. "Cross-Purposes: The Liberal-Communitarian Debate." In *Philosophical Arguments* 181–203.

———. "Liberal Politics and the Public Sphere." In *Philosophical Arguments* 257–88.

———. *Philosophical Arguments.* Cambridge: Harvard University Press, 1995.

———. *Sources of the Self: The Making of the Modern Identity*. Cambridge: Harvard University Press, 1989.

Thane, Pat. "Government and Society in England and Wales, 1750–1914." In F. M. L. Thompson, *Cambridge Social History* 1–62.

Thompson, F. M. L., ed. *The Cambridge Social History of Britain, 1750–1950*. Vol. 3: *Social Agencies and Institutions*. Cambridge: Cambridge University Press, 1990.

———. *The Rise of Respectable Society*. London: Fontana, 1988.

———. "Social Control in Victorian Britain." *Economic History Review* 34.2 (May 1981): 189–208.

Thompson, Nicola. "Gender and the Literary Reception of Anthony Trollope." *Victorian Literature and Culture* 22 (1994): 151–71.

Thompson, Paul. *The Edwardians: The Remaking of British Society*. 2d ed. London: Routledge, 1992.

Trevelyan, Sir Charles. *On the Education of the People of India* (London 1838). Chap. 4: *The Great Indian Education Debate: Documents Relating to the Orientalist-Anglicist Controversy, 1781–1843*. Ed. Lynn Zastoupil and Martin Moir. Surrey: Curzon, 1999. 281–303.

Trilling, Lionel. *The Liberal Imagination: Essays on Literature and Society*. New York: Doubleday, 1949.

Trollope, Anthony. *An Autobiography*. 1883. Harmondsworth: Penguin, 1996.

———. *Barchester Towers*. 1857. Ed. Robin Gilmour. Harmondsworth: Penguin, 1983.

———. "The Civil Service." *Dublin University Magazine* 46.274 (Oct. 1855): 409–26.

———. "The Civil Service." *Fortnightly Review*, 15 October 1865, 613–40.

———. "The Civil Service as a Profession," *Cornhill Magazine* 3 (Feb. 1861): 214–28.

———. *The Last Chronicle of Barset*. 1857. Ed. Stephen Gill. Oxford: Oxford University Press, 1980.

———. *The New Zealander*. Ed. N. John Hall. London: Trollope Society, 1995.

———. "Public Schools." *Fortnightly Review*, 1 October 1865, 476–87.

———. *The Three Clerks*. 1858. Ed. Graham Handley. Oxford: Oxford University Press, 1989.

———. *The Warden*. 1855. Ed. David Skilton. Oxford: Oxford University Press, 1980.

Trollope, Frances. *Jessie Phillips: A Tale of the Present Day*. 3 vols. London: Colburn, 1843.

Uglow, Jenny. *Elizabeth Gaskell: A Habit of Stories*. New York: Farrar, Straus, Giroux, 1993.

Viswanathan, Gauri. *Masks of Conquest: Literary Study and British Rule in India*. New York: Columbia University Press, 1989.

———. *Outside the Fold: Conversion, Modernity and Belief*. Princeton: Princeton University Press, 1998.

———. "Raymond Williams and British Colonialism." *Yale Journal of Criticism* 4.2 (1991): 47–67.

Wach, Howard M. "Civil Society: Manchester and Boston, 1810–1840." *Social History* 21.3 (Oct. 1996): 281–303.

———. "Unitarian Philanthropy and Cultural Hegemony in Comparative Perspective: Manchester and Boston, 1827–1848." *Journal of Social History* 26.3 (Spring 1993): 539–57.

Wahrman, Dror. *Imagining the Middle Class: The Political Representation of Class in Britain, c. 1780–1840*. Cambridge: Cambridge University Press, 1995.

Walder, Dennis. *Dickens and Religion.* London: Allen and Unwin, 1981.

Walton, John. "The Treatment of Pauper Lunatics in Victorian England: The Case of Lancaster Asylum, 1816–1870." In Scull 166–97.

Walzer, Michael. "The Politics of Michel Foucault." In Hoy 51–68.

Warner, Michael. "Liberalism and the Cultural Studies Imagination: A Comment on John Frow." *Yale Journal of Criticism* 12.2 (1999): 431–33.

Webb, A. D. "Charles Edward Trevelyan in India: A Study of the Channels of Influence Employed by a Covenanted Civil Servant in the Translation of Personal Ideas into Official Policy." *South Asia* 6.2 (1983): 15–33.

Webb, Beatrice. *The Diary of Beatrice Webb.* Ed. Norman and Jeanne MacKenzie. 4 vols. London: Virago, 1983–85.

———. *My Apprenticeship.* 2 vols. London: Longman, 1926.

Webb, R. K. "The Emergence of Rational Dissent." In *Enlightenment and Religion: Rational Dissent in Eighteenth-Century Britain.* Ed. Knud Haakanssen. Cambridge: Cambridge University Press, 1996. 12–41.

———. "The Gaskells as Unitarians." In *Dickens and Other Victorians: Essays in Honor of Philip Collins.* Ed. Joanne Shattock. New York: St. Martin's, 1988. 144–71.

———. *Harriet Martineau: A Radical Victorian.* New York: Columbia University Press, 1960.

Webb, Sidney. "Historic." *Fabian Essays in Socialism.* 1889. Ed. George Bernard Shaw. Boston: Ball, 1911. 26–55.

Webb, Sidney, and Beatrice. *English Poor Law Policy.* London: Longman, 1910.

Weber, Max. *Economy and Society.* 2 vols. Ed. Guenther Roth and Claus Wittich. Multiple Trans. Berkeley: University of California Press, 1978.

———. *From Max Weber: Essays on Sociology.* Ed. and trans. H. H. Gerth and C. Wright Mills. New York: Oxford University Press, 1946.

———. *Max Weber on Law in Economy and Society.* Ed. Max Rheinstein. Trans. Max Rheinstein and Edward Shils. Cambridge: Harvard University Press, 1954.

Weiss, Barbara. "Secret Pockets and Secret Breasts: *Little Dorrit* and the Commercial Scandals of the Fifties." *Dickens Studies Annual* 10 (1982): 67–76.

Wells, H. G. *A Modern Utopia.* 1905. Ed. Mark R. Hillegas. Lincoln: University of Nebraska Press, 1967.

———. *In the Days of the Comet.* 1906. *Seven Novels of H. G. Wells.* London: Heinemann, n.d. 548–709.

———. *The New Machiavelli.* 1911. London: J. M. Dent, 1994.

———. "Socialism and the Middle Classes." 1906. Published as *Socialism and the Family.* London, 1908.

Wiener, Martin J. *English Culture and the Decline of the Industrial Spirit, 1850–1980.* London: Penguin, 1981.

Wilde, Oscar. "The Soul of Man under Socialism." 1891. In *The Artist as Critic: Critical Writings of Oscar Wilde.* Ed. Richard Ellmann. Chicago: University of Chicago Press, 1982. 255–89.

Williams, Karel. *From Pauperism to Poverty.* London: Routledge, 1981.

Williams, Raymond. *Culture and Society, 1780–1950.* 2d ed. New York: Columbia University Press, 1983.

———. *Marxism and Literature.* Oxford: Oxford University Press, 1977.

Willis, Ellen. "Freedom from Religion." *Nation* (online archive), 19 February 2001. <http:// www.thenation.com/doc.mhtml?i=20010219&s=willis&c=1>.

Wilt, Judith. "The Imperial Mouth: Imperialism, the Gothic and Science Fiction." *Journal of Popular Culture* 14.4 (1981): 618–28.

Wolfreys, Julian. *Being English: Narratives, Idioms, and Performances of National Identity from Coleridge to Trollope.* Albany: SUNY Press, 1994.

Wood, Peter. *Poverty and the Workhouse in Victorian Britain.* Pheonix Mill, U.K.: Alan Sutton, 1991.

Young, A. F., and E. T. Ashton. *British Social Work in the Nineteenth Century.* London: Routledge, 1956.

Young, G. M. *Portrait of an Age: Victorian England.* 2d ed. Oxford: Oxford University Press, 1953.

Zlotnick, Susan. *Women, Writing, and the Industrial Revolution.* Baltimore: Johns Hopkins University Press, 1998.

Index

288   *Index*

Booth, Charles, 263n. 2, 196–98, 212
Bosanquet, Bernard, 22, 24, 194, 196,
  200–206, 211, 213, 233, 238, 263n. 2,
  264n. 7
Bosanquet, Helen, 109, 194–95, 200–201,
  206, 211, 216, 236–37, 257n. 31, 263n. 2
Bourdieu, Pierre, 13–14, 16, 248n. 20
Boyd, Nancy, 115
Braddon, Mary Elizabeth, *Aurora Floyd*, 25
Bradley, Ian, 245n. 3
Brantlinger, Patrick, 188, 191, 252n. 26,
  253n. 32, 260n. 9, 264n. 11
Brave New World (Huxley), 231
Brewer, John, 247n. 4
Bridges, Thomas, 242
Briggs, Asa, 72, 91, 112, 135, 138, 144, 146,
  254n. 4, 257n. 1
Brougham, Henry, Lord, 159, 167
Brown, Stewart T., 40, 41, 42, 44–45,
  250n. 7
Brown, Wendy, viii
Browning, Elizabeth Barrett, 152
Brundage, Anthony, 92, 94, 113, 126, 254n.
  6, 255n. 11
Burn, W. L., 131
Burns, John, 234
Burrow, J. W., 245n. 5, 248n. 23
Butt, John, 91, 97, 103

Cannadine, David, 7
Carlyle, Thomas, 20, 59, 79, 136–37, 143,
  207; *Latter-Day Pamphlets*, 256n. 22; *Past
  and Present*, 79, 90, 254n. 2; "Signs of the
  Times," 110, 249n. 27
Carpenter, Mary, 109
centralization, 4, 22, 36, 134, 160, 246n. 7,
  247n. 6; Edwin Chadwick and, 51, 240,
  256n. 18; Thomas Chalmers and, 42,
  250n. 8; Charity Organization Society
  and, 115, 257n. 30; Continental, 92, 106;
  Charles Dickens and, 90, 91, 104, 254n.
  3; in *Jessie Phillips*, 71, 73, 78; John Stuart
  Mill and, 28, 238; New Poor Law and,
  33–34, 42, 50, 56, 82, 83, 253n. 35; relative absence of, in Britain, vii–viii, xii,
  3–6, 12, 106

Chadwick, Edwin, xii, 3–4, 11–12, 33,
  50–51, 56, 102, 110, 112–13, 116, 125–26,
  140, 156, 164, 198, 206, 222, 238, 240–41,
  252n. 25, 254n. 5, 255n. 11, 258n. 5, 261n.
  19; Benthamism and, 33; *Bleak House* and,
  95–96, 98–99, 105–6; centralization and,
  51, 91, 240, 250n. 2; New Poor Law and,
  32, 34, 40–42, 56, 79–80, 82–84, 250n. 2,
  253n. 35, 254n. 39; policing and, 101,
  256n. 18; public persona of, 88, 91–96,
  254n. 6; Sanitary Idea of, 4, 51, 84,
  86–87, 92–93, 95–96, 113, 122, 173, 209,
  255n. 11; sanitary reform and, 25, 89,
  92–93, 129, 194–95, 197, 251nn. 13, 18.
  See also sanitary reform
Chalmers, Thomas, viii, xii, 9, 22, 24, 36,
  39–48, 51, 54–56, 59–60, 64, 67, 83–84,
  106, 116, 126, 168–69, 187, 197–98, 201,
  215, 217, 222, 236, 241, 250nn. 5, 6, 7, 8,
  10, 11, 251n. 14, 261n. 16; *Christian and
  Civic Economy of Large Towns*, 40, 60; influence on Sir James Kay-Shuttleworth,
  48–49, 52, 93, 251n. 12; interest in statistics, 49. *See also* Charity Organization Society; intersubjective ideal; organized
  charity; pastorship
Channing, William Ellery, 47
character, viii, ix–xii, 23–29, 38, 51, 58, 84,
  88, 93, 117, 153, 155, 159–60, 173,
  189–91, 197, 199, 204, 235, 244, 248n. 23,
  250n. 9, 253n. 30; in *Bleak House*, 180–81;
  Bernard Bosanquet and, 200–202, 205;
  Clarendon Commission and, 132–33;
  commodification and, 189–91; descriptive
  notion of, 25–26, 119–20, 124–25, 129–30,
  134–36, 146, 152, 161, 188; Fabian approach to, 207–9; of Indians, 125–27; in
  Jessie Phillips, 71–77; late-Victorian crisis
  of, xiv, 192–93, 211, 233–36, 266n. 25; in
  A Modern Utopia, 224–25; national, in
  England, viii, 4–5, 23, 28, 146, 210–11; in
  The Nether World, 193, 212–13, 216–17;
  New Poor Law and, 56, 69, 83–85, 209;
  in *Oliver Twist*, 61, 63–68, 160–61; in *Our
  Mutual Friend*, 161–62, 166, 174, 178–79,
  181–91; perfectibility of, 45; prescriptive

Idealism, British, 193, 196, 200–201, 205–6, 208, 210–12, 218–19, 230, 238, 245n. 5, 263n. 1, 264n. 6. *See also* Bosanquet, Bernard; Charity Organization Society
imperialism. *See* colonialism
India, education in. *See* anglicization
Indian Mutiny (1857–58), 25, 128, 146, 153, 173
intersubjectivity/intersubjective ideal, 43, 53, 84, 229, 233; Thomas Chalmers and, 40, 44, 46, 49; E. M. Forster and, 230–31; Sir James Kay-Shuttleworth and, 49, 170; middle-class civilizing mission and, 38, 261n. 14; threats to, 50–51, 53, 189. *See also* liberalism
In the Days of the Comet. See Wells, H. G.

Jaffe, Audrey, 263n. 27
Jessie Phillips. See Trollope, Frances
Johnson, Edgar, 90
Johnson, Richard, 102, 169–70, 255n. 10, 261nn. 11, 14, 18, 261n. 19
Jowett, Benjamin, 119, 121–22, 129, 131–33, 135, 145, 154–58, 174, 180–81, 256n. 19; satirized as Mr. Jobbles, 139–40
Joyce, Simon, 266n. 2

Kafka, Franz, 78
Kahan, Alan S., 245n. 5
Kant, Immanuel, 200, 263n. 1, 264n. 7
Kaufmann, David, 245n. 5
Kay, Dr. James Phillips. *See* Kay-Shuttleworth, Sir James
Kay-Shuttleworth, Sir James, vii, x, xii–xiii, 9, 12, 48–52, 56, 64, 67, 93, 99, 104, 110, 112, 114, 125, 155, 250n. 5; career of, 48, 51–52, 72, 93–94, 101–2, 171, 214, 251nn. 15, 16, 256n. 19, 261n. 13; contradictory thought of, 49–50, 53–54; founding of Battersea Training College, 171–72; interest in statistics, 19–20, 49, 251n. 17; *Moral and Physical Condition of the Working Classes . . . in Manchester*, 12, 39–40, 48–53, 93, 164, 251nn. 12, 13, 14; son of (Lord Shuttleworth), 53; *Training of Pauper Children*, 52, 168–70, 261n. 16; working-class education and, 5–6, 45, 52, 155,

161, 168–79, 185, 187, 261nn. 11, 12, 13, 16, 261n. 19. *See also* pastorship
Keith, Arthur Berriedale, 126
Kettle, Arnold, 252n. 24
Kidd, Alan J., 38

Labor Party, 217
LaCapra, Dominick, 255n. 12
Ladies' National Association for the Diffusion of Sanitary Knowledge, 109–10
Laing, Samuel, 6, 261n. 15
Lane, Christopher, 18
Langland, Elizabeth, 253n. 36, 263n. 26
Laqueur, Thomas, 202, 251n. 14
Latter-Day Pamphlets. See Carlyle, Thomas
Levine, George, 256n. 20
Lewis, George Cornewall, 15, 34
Lewis, R. A., 89, 92, 95
liberalism/liberals, vii–viii, 22–23, 25, 27–28, 31, 45, 96, 107, 131, 231; backlash against, late-Victorian, 112, 192–93, 198–200, 204, 206–10; bureaucracy and, 23–24; character and, viii, xi, 24–27, 161, 203, 209, 233, 244; Coleridgean philosophy and, 121–22, 133–34, 180; colonialism and, 125–29, 250n. 4, 258n. 6; constitutional consensus and, xiii, 4, 112, 119–20, 122, 130, 132, 136, 145, 154–55, 173, 192, 209; Charles Dickens and, 112–13, 116; early-Victorian, 146, 161; education and, 167, 169–70, 173–75, 260n. 9; elusive definition of, viii–xii, 21–22, 245nn. 3, 4, 5; E. M. Forster and, 232; Francis Fukuyama and, 241–43; George Gissing and, 212–14; Gladstonean era of, 4, 104; governance and, ix–x, 4–6, 12, 14–16, 18–21, 23–24, 83, 91, 102, 124–25, 129, 133–34, 154–55, 163–64, 224–26, 248n. 18; T. H. Green and, 200; intersubjectivity and, 23, 38, 44, 46, 170; C.F.G. Masterman and, 232; as mentality of rule, 15; mid-Victorian, 4, 102, 104, 112–13, 155, 161, 173–74, 261n. 19; paradoxical features of, viii, 20–21, 23–25, 111–12, 128, 160, 240–41; John Rawls and, 242–44; shifts in, 127–28, 161, 198–99, 241–42; Sir Charles Trevelyan and, 127–28; Anthony